2021

International Building Code®

STUDY
COMPANION

From the publisher of the IBC®

Features:

- 18 study sessions and quizzes
- 720 total questions and answers
- Fully illustrated

A great learning tool for:

- Building inspectors
- Plans examiners
- Building contractors

INTERNATIONAL
CODE COUNCIL®

**2021 International Building Code®
Study Companion:
Based on the 2021 *International
Building Code®***

International Code Council Staff:

Executive Vice President and Director of
Business Development:
  Mark A. Johnson

Senior Vice President, Business and
Product Development
  Hamid Naderi

Vice President and Technical Director,
Products and Services:
  Doug Thornburg

Senior Marketing Specialist:
  Dianna Hallmark

Manager of Product Development:
  Mary Lou Luif

Project Manager:
  Doug Thornburg

Publications Manager:
  Anne F. Kerr

Manager of Publications Production:
  Jen Fitzsimmons

Project Editor:
  Phil Arvia

Production Technician:
  Theresa Dal Bianco

Cover Design:
  Ricky Razo

T026543

TABLE OF CONTENTS

INTRODUCTION

This study companion provides practical learning assignments for independent study of the provisions of the 2021 *International Building Code*® (IBC®). The independent study format affords a method for the student to complete the study program in an unlimited amount of time. Progressing through the workbook, the learner can measure his or her level of knowledge by using the exercises and quizzes provided for each study session.

The workbook is also valuable for instructor-led programs. In jurisdictional training sessions, community college classes, vocational training programs and other structured educational offerings, the study guide and the IBC can be the basis for code instruction.

All study sessions begin with a general learning objective, the specific sections or chapters of the code under consideration and a list of questions summarizing the key points of study. Each session addresses selected topics from the IBC and includes code text, a commentary on the code provisions and illustrations representing the provisions under discussion. Quizzes are provided at the end of each study session. Before beginning the quizzes, the student should thoroughly review the referenced IBC provisions, particularly the key points.

The workbook is structured so that after every question the student has an opportunity to record his or her response and the corresponding code reference. The correct answers are indicated in the back of the workbook in the answer key.

This study companion was initially developed by Douglas W. Thornburg, AIA, C.B.O., for the 2000 *International Building Code* (IBC), and it has been revised to reflect each new edition of the IBC. In this publication, he has updated and revised the material based on the 2021 *International Building Code*. Doug is currently Vice-President and Technical Director, Products and Services for the International Code Council®. In addition to authoring numerous educational texts and resource materials, he instructs seminars nationally on the IBC. Doug has over 40 years of experience in the application and enforcement of building codes.

Questions or comments concerning this workbook are encouraged. Please direct your comments to ICC at studycompanion@iccsafe.org.

About the International Code Council

The International Code Council is a nonprofit association that provides a wide range of building safety solutions including product evaluation, accreditation, certification, codification and training. It develops model codes and standards used worldwide to construct safe, sustainable, affordable and resilient structures. ICC Evaluation Service (ICC-ES) is the industry leader in performing technical evaluations for code compliance, fostering safe and sustainable design and construction.

Washington DC Headquarters:

500 New Jersey Avenue, NW, 6th Floor, Washington, DC 20001

Regional Offices:

Eastern Regional Office (BIR)

Central Regional Office (CH)

Western Regional Office (LA)

Distribution Center (Lenexa, KS)

888-ICC-SAFE (888-422-7233)

www.iccsafe.org

Family of Solutions:

Study Session

1

2021 IBC Chapters 1 and 35
Scope and Administration

OBJECTIVE: To obtain an understanding of the administrative provisions of the *International Building Code®* (IBC®), including the scope and purpose of the code, duties of the building official, issuance of permits, inspection procedures, special inspections, existing buildings and referenced standards.

REFERENCE: Chapters 1 and 35, 2021 *International Building Code*

KEY POINTS:
- What is the purpose and scope of the *International Building Code*?
- What are the limitations for use of the *International Residential Code®* (IRC®)?
- When materials, methods of construction or other requirements are specified differently in separate provisions, which requirement governs?
- When there is a conflict between a general requirement and a specific requirement, which provision is applicable?
- When do the provisions of the appendices apply?
- What is the relationship between the I-Codes and the referenced standards? How are any conflicts between the IBC and referenced standards to be addressed?
- What are the powers and duties of the building official in regard to the application and interpretation of the code? Right of entry?
- Under which conditions may the building official grant modifications to the code?
- How may alternative materials, designs and methods of construction be approved?
- What determinations must be made for the building official to grant modifications to provisions addressing flood hazard areas?
- When is a permit required? What types of work are exempted from permits?
- Is work exempted from a permit required to comply with the provisions of the code?
- What is the process outlined for obtaining a permit?
- Which documents must be submitted as part of the permit application process? What information is required on the construction documents?

KEY POINTS:
(Cont'd)

- Which conditions or circumstances would bring the validity of a permit into question?
- When does a permit expire? What must occur when a permit expires prior to completion of a building?
- For what is a registered design professional responsible? When is such an individual required?
- What submittal documents must be provided with each permit application? Under what conditions are submittal documents not required?
- What information is required on the construction documents? What special requirements apply to fire protection system shop drawings, means of egress layouts and exterior wall envelopes?
- What specific information must be included on a site plan?
- What is the process for the review and approval of construction documents? How are phased approvals to be addressed?
- What is the role of a design professional in responsible charge? When is such an individual to be utilized?
- What is a deferred submittal? What is the process for deferring the submittal of construction documents?
- What is the time limit of a permit for a temporary structure? To what criteria must a temporary structure comply?
- How are permit fees to be established? How is work started prior to permit issuance addressed?
- What types of inspections are specifically required by the code? When are inspections required?
- Are third-party inspection agencies permitted to perform the required inspections?
- Who is responsible for notifying the building official that work is ready for an inspection? Who must provide access for the inspection to take place?
- How shall an inspection be recorded? What if the inspection is failed?
- When is a certificate of occupancy required? For what reasons is revocation permitted?
- When may a temporary certificate of occupancy be issued?
- What is the purpose of a board of appeals? Who shall serve on the board?
- Which limitations are placed upon the authority of the board of appeals?
- When should a stop work order be issued?
- What code publication is applicable to existing buildings?
- What are referenced standards? How are they used in the IBC?

Code Text: *The provisions of the* International Building Code *shall apply to the construction, alteration, relocation, enlargement, replacement, repair, equipment, use and occupancy, location, maintenance, removal and demolition of every building or structure or any appurtenances connected or attached to such buildings or structures.* See the exception for dwellings, townhouses and related accessory structures regulated by the *International Residential Code.*

Discussion and Commentary: The *International Building Code* is intended to regulate the broad spectrum of construction activities associated with buildings and structures. General provisions allow for a comprehensive overview of regulations; however, where more specific circumstances exist, any applicable specific requirements will take precedence.

Fundamental purposes of the provisions of the *International Building Code*:

- Safety of building occupants
- Safety of fire fighters and emergency responders
- Safety and protection of others' property
- Safety and protection of own property

The appendices of the *International Building Code* address a diverse number of issues that may be of value to a jurisdiction in developing a set of construction regulations. It should be noted that the provisions contained in the appendices do not apply unless specifically adopted.

Code Text: *Detached one- and two-family dwellings and multiple single-family dwellings (town-houses) not more than three stories above grade plane in height with a separate means of egress, and their accessory structures not more than three stories above grade plane in height, shall comply with* the IBC *or the International Residential Code.*

Discussion and Commentary: Many residential structures are exempt from the requirements of the *International Building Code* and are regulated instead by a separate and distinct document, the *International Residential Code*. The IRC® contains prescriptive requirements for the construction of detached single-family dwellings, detached duplexes, townhouses and all structures accessory to such buildings. Limited to three stories in height above grade plane with individual egress facilities, these residential buildings are fully regulated by the IRC for building, energy, plumbing, mechanical and electrical provisions.

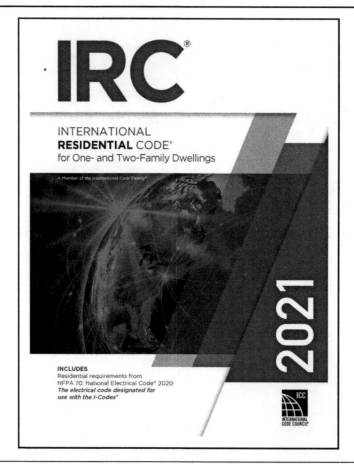

In addition to the general requirements, a townhouse is also limited by definition in the IRC. To fall under the scope of the IRC, each townhouse must be a single unit from the foundation to the roof, with at least two sides open to the exterior.

Code Text: *Provisions in the appendices shall not apply unless specifically adopted.*

Discussion and Commentary: The appendix chapters of the IBC address subjects that have been deemed inappropriate as mandatory portions of the code. Rather, the appendices are optional, with each jurisdiction adopting all, some or none of the appendix chapters, depending on its needs for enforcement in any given area. There are various reasons why certain issues are found in the appendices. Often, the provisions are limited in application or interest. Some appendix chapters are merely extensions of requirements set forth in the body of the code. Others address issues that are often thought of as outside of the scope of a traditional building code. Whatever the reason, the appendix chapters are not applicable unless specifically adopted.

IBC Appendix Chapters

Appendix A	**Employee Qualifications**
Appendix B	**Board of Appeals**
Appendix C	**Group U — Agricultural Buildings**
Appendix D	**Fire Districts**
Appendix E	**Supplementary Accessibility Requirements**
Appendix F	**Rodentproofing**
Appendix G	**Flood-Resistant Construction**
Appendix H	**Signs**
Appendix I	**Patio Covers**
Appendix J	**Grading**
Appendix K	**Administrative Provisions**
Appendix L	**Earthquake Recording Instrumentation**
Appendix M	**Tsunami-Generated Flood Hazard**
Appendix N	**Replicable Buildings**
Appendix O	**Performance-Based Application**

Appendix chapters, where not adopted as a portion of a jurisdiction's building code, may still be of value in application of the code. Provisions in the appendices might provide some degree of assistance in evaluating proposed alternative designs, methods or materials of construction.

Code Text: *The provisions of the* International Existing Building Code *shall apply to matters governing the repair, alteration, change of occupancy, addition to and relocation of existing buildings.*

Discussion and Commentary: The *International Existing Building Code* (IEBC), first published by the International Code Council as the 2003 edition, provides a comprehensive approach to the regulation of existing buildings. Where repairs, alterations, change of occupancy or additions to existing buildings are encountered, such work is solely regulated by the IEBC. The IEBC provides three distinct options for a designer dealing with rehabilitation of existing buildings. They include (1) the Prescriptive Compliance Method in IEBC Chapter 5, (2) the Work Area Compliance Method in IEBC Chapters 6-12, and (3) the Performance Compliance Methods in IEBC Chapter 13.

The IEBC is intended to encourage the use and reuse of existing buildings while adequately protecting public health, safety and welfare. Further founding principles require that the provisions do not unnecessarily increase construction costs; do not restrict the use of new materials, products or methods of construction; and do not give preferential treatment to particular types or classes of materials, products or methods of construction.

Topic: Referenced Codes and Standards	**Category:** Administration
Reference: IBC 102.4	**Subject:** Applicability

Code Text: *The codes and standards referenced in the IBC shall be considered part of the requirements of the IBC to the prescribed extent of each such reference and as further regulated in Sections 102.4.1 and 102.4.2. Where conflicts occur between provisions of the IBC and referenced codes and standards, the provisions of the IBC shall apply. Where the extent of the reference to a referenced code or standard includes subject matter that is within the scope of the IBC or the International Codes listed in Section 101.4, the provisions of the IBC or the International Codes listed in Section 101.4, as applicable, shall take precedence over the provisions in the referenced code or standard..*

Discussion and Commentary: The IBC is, for the most part, a performance-based code, relying on numerous referenced standards to assist the builder and code official in its application. Where standards are referenced in the body of the IBC, the applicable portions of the standard relating to the specific code provision under consideration are considered a part of the code. However, where a referenced standard contains requirements that parallel those in the IBC, the requirements of the IBC take precedence.

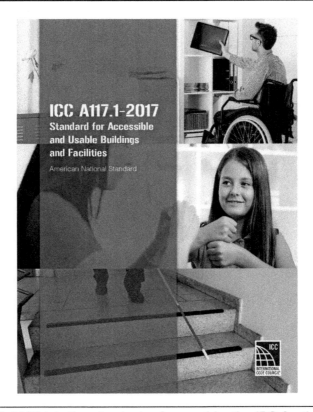

As an example, ICC A117.1 is the standard referenced by the IBC for the technical provisions regulating the design and construction of facilities for accessibility. The A117.1 standard contains provisions for stairway design; however, accessible stairway provisions are also established in Section 1011 of the IBC. For application purposes, the provisions in the IBC take precedence over those in the referenced standard.

Code Text: *The [INSERT NAME OF DEPARTMENT] is hereby created and the official in charge thereof shall be known as the building official. The building official shall be appointed by the chief appointing authority of the jurisdiction. In accordance with the prescribed procedures of this jurisdiction and with the concurrence of the appointing authority, the building official shall have the authority to appoint a deputy building official, other related technical officers, inspectors and other employees. Such employees shall have powers as delegated by the building official.*

Discussion and Commentary: The building official is an appointed officer of the jurisdiction and charged with the administrative responsibilities of the department of building safety. It is not uncommon for the jurisdiction to use a different position title to identify the building official, such as Chief Building Inspector, Superintendent of Central Inspection or Director of Code Enforcement. Regardless of the jurisdictional title, the code recognizes the individual in charge as the building official.

Inspectors, plan reviewers and other technical staff members are typically given some degree of authority to act for the building official in the decision-making process, including the making of appropriate interpretations of various provisions of the code.

Code Text: *The building official is hereby authorized and directed to enforce the provisions of the IBC. The building official shall have the authority to render interpretations of the IBC and to adopt policies and procedures in order to clarify the application of its provisions. Such interpretations, policies and procedures shall be in compliance with the intent and purpose of the IBC. Such policies and procedures shall not have the effect of waiving requirements specifically provided for in the IBC.*

Discussion and Commentary: It is important that the building official be knowledgeable to the point of being able to rule on those issues that are not directly addressed or that are unclear in the code. The basis for such a determination, which often takes some research to discover, is the intent and purpose of the *International Building Code.*

(Jurisdiction)

Department of Building Safety

Photo

_____

Name of individual

_____

Job function

The individual identified on the badge is a duly authorized employee of (the Jurisdiction) and is a designated representative of the Department of Building Safety.

Valid through _____ _____

                Date   **Building Official**

**Sample of Required Identification
Section 104.5**

Although the IBC gives broad authority to the building official in interpreting the code, this authority also comes with great responsibility. The building official must restrict all decisions to the intent and purpose of the code, with the waiving of any requirements being strictly prohibited.

Code Text: *The building official, member of the board of appeals or employee charged with the enforcement of the IBC, while acting for the jurisdiction in good faith and without malice in the discharge of the duties required by the IBC or other pertinent law or ordinance, shall not thereby be civilly or criminally rendered liable personally and is hereby relieved from personal liability for any damage accruing to persons or property as a result of any act or by reason of an act or omission in the discharge of official duties.*

Discussion and Commentary: The protection afforded by the code regarding employee liability is limited to only those acts that occur in good faith. Absolute immunity from all tort liability is not provided where an employee acts maliciously. An employee is not relieved from personal liability where malice can be shown, and it is probable that the jurisdiction will not provide for the employee's defense.

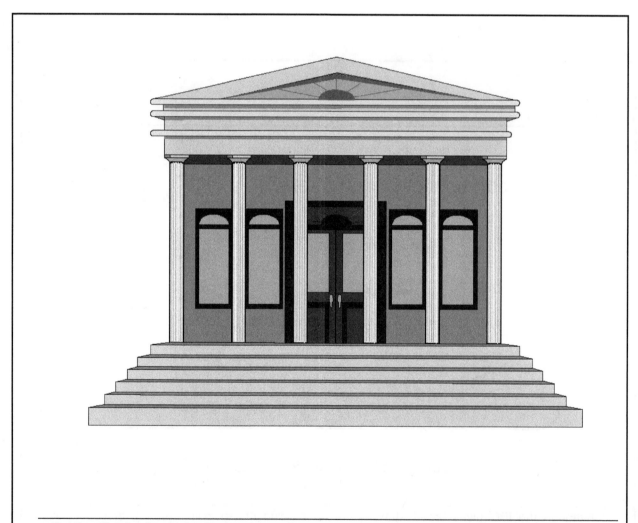

Public officials should familiarize themselves with the laws of their respective states regarding their exposure to tort liability.

Code Text: *The provisions of the IBC are not intended to prevent the installation of any material or to prohibit any design or method of construction not specifically prescribed by the IBC; provided that any such alternative has been approved. An alternative material, design or method of construction shall be approved where the building official finds that the proposed alternative meets all of the following: (1) The alternative material, design or method of construction is satisfactory and complies with the intent of the provisions of the IBC, and (2) provides established equivalency to that prescribed in the IBC.*

Discussion and Commentary: The building official is granted broad authority in the acceptance of alternative materials, designs and methods of construction. Arguably the most important provision of the IBC, the intent is to implement the adoption of new technologies. Furthermore, it gives the code even more of a performance character. The provisions encourage state-of-the-art concepts in construction, design and materials, as long as they meet the performance level intended by the IBC.

Building official may approve alternative materials, design and methods of construction, if

- Proposed alternative is satisfactory
- Proposed alternative complies with intent of code
- Material, method or work is equivalent in:
    - (1) Quality
    - (2) Strength
    - (3) Effectiveness
    - (4) Fire Resistance
    - (5) Durability
    - (6) Safety

Advisable for building official to

- Require sufficient evidence or proof
- Record any action granting approval
- Enter information into the files

Where approval is not granted, the building official is to respond in writing, stating the reasons for the disapproval of the alternative.

The building official should ensure that any necessary substantiating data or other evidence that shows the alternative to be equivalent in performance is submitted. Moreover, where tests are performed, reports of such tests must be retained by the building official.

Topic: Research Reports

Category: Administration

Reference: IBC 104.11.1

Subject: Duties and Powers of Building Official

Code Text: *Supporting data, where necessary to assist in the approval of materials or assemblies not specifically provided for in the IBC, shall consist of valid research reports from approved sources.*

Discussion and Commentary: The most familiar research reports are probably the ICC Evaluation Service Reports maintained by ICC Evaluation Service, Inc. ICC Evaluation Service Reports are developed based upon acceptance criteria and provide evidence that products and systems meet code requirements. These reports are made available to building regulators, contractors, specifiers, architects, engineers and anyone else with an interest in the building industry or construction. The building official can also recognize the evaluation of products, assemblies and systems by other third-party agencies having the necessary credentials.

Although ICC Evaluation Service Reports are generally recognized nationally as valid reports developed by an approved source, the building official is the final authority on the acceptance of any research report for the purpose of accepting an alternate material, method or design.

Code Text: *Any owner or owner's authorized agent who intends to construct, enlarge, alter, repair, move, demolish, or change the occupancy of a building or structure . . . shall first make application to the building official and obtain the required permit.* See thirteen exemptions where a building permit is not required. *Exemptions from permit requirements of the IBC shall not be deemed to grant authorization for any work to be done in any manner in violation of the provisions of the IBC or any other laws or ordinances of this jurisdiction.*

Discussion and Commentary: Except in those few cases specifically listed, such as small accessory structures and finish work, all construction-related work requires a permit and is subject to subsequent inspections.

Work exempt from permit:

- One-story detached accessory buildings where limited to 120 square feet in floor area

- Fences not over 7 feet high

- Oil derricks

- Retaining walls limited to 4 feet in height, unless supporting a surcharge or impounding Class I, II or III-A liquids

- Water tanks supported directly on grade, limited to capacity of 5,000 gallons and a ratio of height to diameter not exceeding 2 to 1

- Sidewalks and driveways limited to 30 inches above grade, not over any basement or story below, and not part of an accessible route

- Painting, papering, carpeting, cabinets, counter tops and similar finish work

- Temporary motion picture, television and theater stage sets and scenery

- Prefabricated swimming pools accessory to a Group R-3 occupancy when capacity is limited to 5,000 gallons, depth limited to 24 inches and installed entirely above ground

- Shade cloth structures used for nursery or agricultural purposes

- Swings and other playground equipment accessory to detached one- and two-family dwellings

- Window awnings supported by an exterior wall in Groups R-3 and U, where the maximum projection is 54 inches

- Movable fixtures, racks, cases, counters and partitions limited to 5 feet 9 inches in height

---

Whether or not a building permit is required by the code, it is intended that all work be done in accordance with the code requirements. The owner is responsible for all construction being done properly and safely.

Code Text: *Submittal documents consisting of construction documents, statement of special inspections, geotechnical report and other data shall be submitted in two or more sets, or in a digital format where allowed by the building official, with each permit application. The construction documents shall be prepared by a registered design professional where required by the statutes of the jurisdiction in which the project is to be constructed.* See the exception for projects where nature of work is such that review of construction documents is unnecessary.

Discussion and Commentary: Submittal documents must be provided to the jurisdiction to allow for full review and approval prior to issuance of any required permits. In addition to plans and specifications, the submittal must include any applicable support documents such as a geotechnical report or a statement of special inspections. State law typically regulates the scope of buildings required to be prepared by a registered design professional; however, in special cases the building official can require preparation by such an individual where state law does not.

Unless a digital submission of construction documents is provided, a minimum of two sets of submittal documents must be provided as part of the permit application. At least one set is to be retained by the building department, with the other set returned to the applicant. Many jurisdictions require that additional sets of such documents be submitted in order to provide sets to various departments that will be reviewing different portions of the submittal.

Code Text: *The building official is authorized to issue a permit for temporary structures and temporary uses. Such permits shall be limited as to time of service, but shall not be permitted for more than 180 days. The building official is authorized to grant extensions for demonstrated cause. The building official is authorized to terminate such permit for a temporary structure or use and to order the temporary structure or use to be discontinued.*

Discussion and Commentary: Structures that are seasonal in nature or have limited service life are regulated in a somewhat different manner than permanent structures. However, the general requirements of the code must still be met in the areas of structural strength, fire safety, means of egress, accessibility, light, ventilation and sanitation. These criteria are essential for measuring the safety of any structure or use, temporary or permanent.

Reference to Section 3103 provides further direction in the regulation of temporary buildings. Specific provisions address the building's location on the lot as well as its means of egress system. A site plan along with other necessary construction documents must be provided at the time of permit application.

Code Text: *A permit shall not be valid until the fees prescribed by law have been paid. Where a permit is required, a fee for each permit shall be paid as required, in accordance with the schedule as established by the applicable governing authority. The applicant for a permit shall provide an estimated permit value at the time of application. Permit valuations shall include total value of the work, including materials and labor, for which a permit is being issued, such as electrical, gas, mechanical, plumbing equipment and other permanent systems.*

Discussion and Commentary: Fees are typically established at a level that will provide enough funds to adequately pay for the costs of operating the various building department functions, including administration, plan review and inspection. It is common that the fee schedule be based on the projected construction cost (valuation) of the work. Although there are several different methods for determining the appropriate valuation, it is important that a realistic and consistent approach be taken so that permit fees are applied fairly and accurately.

Fee schedules are not established by the code. Rather, the local jurisdiction is required to establish the appropriate fees to fund the operation of the building safety department.

Code Text: *Construction or work for which a permit is required shall be subject to inspection by the building official and such construction or work shall remain visible and able to be accessed for inspection purposes until approved. Approval as a result of an inspection shall not be construed to be an approval of a violation of the provisions of the IBC or of other ordinances of the jurisdiction.*

Discussion and Commentary: The inspection function is possibly the most critical activity in the entire code enforcement process. At the varied stages of construction, an inspector often performs the final check of the building for safety-related compliance. If necessary, the building official may require a preliminary inspection of the site, building or structure to gain information that may be of assistance in the issuance of a permit.

Required inspections (where applicable):

- Footing and foundation
- Concrete slab or under-floor
- Lowest floor elevation
- Frame
- Types IV-A, IV-B and IV-C connection protection
- Lath, gypsum board and gypsum-panel product
- Weather-exposed elevated walking surfaces waterproofing
- Fire and smoke resistant penetrations
- Energy efficiency
- Others as required by the building official
- Special inspections
- Final

It may be necessary to have materials removed in order to provide inspection access or observation for a portion of the building. The responsibility rests with the permit applicant to make the work available for inspection, with no expenses to be borne by the jurisdiction.

Code Text: *Work shall not be done beyond the point indicated in each successive inspection without first obtaining the approval of the building official. The building official, upon notification, shall make the requested inspections and shall either indicate the portion of the construction that is satisfactory as completed, or notify the permit holder or his or her agent wherein the same fails to comply with* the IBC. *Any portions that do not comply shall be corrected and such portions shall not be covered or concealed until authorized by the building official.*

Discussion and Commentary: It is important that each successive inspection be approved prior to continuing further work. This practice helps to control the concealment of any work that must be inspected, resulting in the unnecessary removal of materials that might block access.

Any request for inspection is the responsibility of the building permit holders or their duly authorized agent. They must contact the building official when the work is ready for inspection, as well as provide access to that work

Code Text: *A building or structure shall not be used or occupied in whole or in part, and a change of occupancy of a building or structure or portion thereof shall not be made, until the building official has issued a certificate of occupancy therefor as provided herein. Issuance of a certificate of occupancy shall not be construed as an approval of a violation of the provisions of* the IBC *or of other ordinances of the jurisdiction.* See the exception for work exempt from permits.

Discussion and The certificate of occupancy is the tool with which the building official can regulate and
Commentary: control the uses and occupancies of the various buildings and structures within the jurisdiction. The code makes it unlawful to use or occupy a building unless a certificate of occupancy has been issued for that specific use.

Certificate of Occupancy
(Address of Structure)

This (applicable portion of structure) has been inspected for compliance
with the laws and ordinances of (jurisdiction) and is hereby issued a
Certificate of Occupancy

Building permit number _____   Special conditions _____

Applicable edition of code _____   _____

Use and occupancy _____   _____

Type of construction _____   _____

Design occupant load _____

Sprinkler system required _____   Building Official _____

Name and address of owner _____

_____

Sample of Certificate of Occupancy

The building official is permitted to suspend or revoke a certificate of occupancy for any of the following reasons: (1) when the certificate is issued in error, (2) when incorrect information is supplied, or (3) when the building is in violation of the code.

Code Text: Chapter 35 lists the standards that are referenced in various sections of the IBC. The standards are listed herein by the promulgation agency of the standard, the standard identification, the effective date and title, and the section or sections of the IBC that reference the standard. The application of the referenced standards shall be as specified in Section 102.4.

Discussion and Commentary: Limited in their scope, standards define more precisely the general provisions set forth in the code. The *International Building Code* references several hundred different standards, each addressing a specific aspect of building design or construction. In general terms, the standards referenced by the IBC are primarily materials, testing, installation or engineering standards.

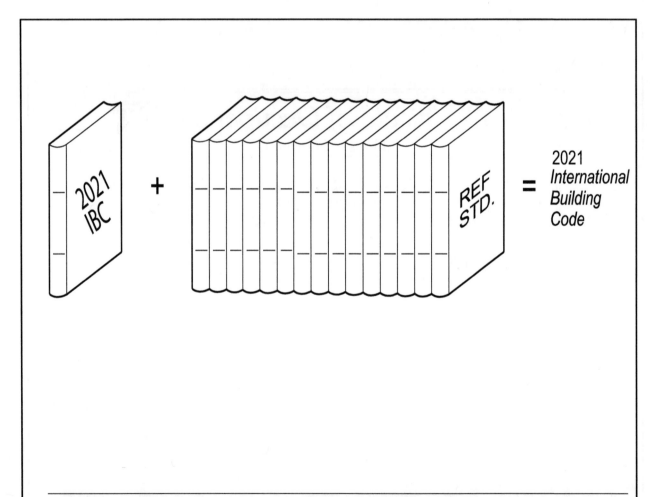

Those codes and standards referenced in the IBC are considered an extension of the code, but only to the degree prescribed by the IBC. Where there is a conflict between the provisions in the IBC and any referenced code or standard, the provisions of the IBC apply.

Quiz

Study Session 1
IBC Chapters 1 and 35

1. The *International Residential Code* is applicable to townhouses a maximum of
   _____ above grade plane in height and provided with separate means of
   egress.

       a. 35 feet   b. 40 feet

       c. three stories   d. four stories

   Reference_____

2. Provisions of the appendix do not apply unless _____.

       a. specified in the code   b. applicable to unique conditions

       c. specifically adopted   d. relevant to fire or life safety

   Reference_____

3. If there is a conflict in the code between a general requirement and a specific requirement, the _____ requirement shall apply.

       a. general   b. specific

       c. least restrictive   d. most restrictive

   Reference_____

4. The _____ is considered by the code as the term to describe the individual
   in charge of the code compliance agency.

       a. building official   b. code official

       c. code administrator   d. chief building inspector

   Reference_____

5. The building official has the authority to _____ the provisions of the code.

    a. ignore   b. waive

    c. violate   d. interpret

Reference_____

6. Used materials may be utilized under which of the following conditions?

    a. They meet the requirements for new materials.

    b. They are limited to 10 percent of the total materials.

    c. Used materials may never be used in new construction.

    d. A representative sampling is tested for compliance.

Reference_____

7. The building official has the authority to grant modifications to the code _____ .

    a. for only those issues not affecting life safety or fire safety

    b. for individual cases where the strict letter of the code is impractical

    c. where the intent and purpose of the code cannot be met

    d. related only to administrative functions

Reference_____

8. In order for an alternative material, design or method of construction to be considered acceptable, it must be equivalent to the code based on all but which of the following criteria?

    a. durability   b. practicality

    c. strength   d. fire resistance

Reference_____

9. Tests performed by _____ may be required by the building official where there is insufficient evidence of code compliance.

    a. the owner   b. the contractor

    c. an approved agency   d. a design professional

Reference_____

10. A permit is not required for the construction of a one-story detached accessory structure used as a storage shed when it has a maximum floor area of _____ square feet.

    a. 100   b. 120

    c. 150   d. 200

    Reference_____

11. Movable fixtures, cases, counters and partitions are exempt from a building permit where they have a maximum height of _____.

    a. 5 feet, 0 inches   b. 5 feet, 6 inches

    c. 5 feet, 9 inches   d. 6 feet, 0 inches

    Reference_____

12. Where a building is constructed in a flood hazard area, documentation of the lowest floor elevation shall be submitted to the building official prior to _____.

    a. any framing work above the lowest floor level

    b. approval of the framing inspection

    c. the final inspection

    d. issuance of the certification of occupancy

    Reference_____

13. The building permit, or a copy of the permit, shall be kept _____ until completion of the project.

    a. at the job site

    b. by the permit applicant

    c. by the contractor

    d. by the design professional in responsible charge

    Reference_____

14. When a building permit is issued, the construction documents shall be approved as _____.

    a. "Approved for Construction"

    b. "Conditional Approval"

    c. "Accepted as Reviewed"

    d. "Reviewed for Code Compliance"

    Reference_____

15. Unless otherwise mandated by state or local laws, one set of approved construction documents shall be retained by the building official for a minimum of _____ from the date of completion of the permitted work.

    a.   90 days   b.   180 days

    c.   1 year   d.   2 years

Reference_____

16. Which one of the following inspections is not specifically identified by the *International Building Code* as a required inspection, where applicable?

    a.   footing inspection

    b.   frame inspection

    c.   soil classification inspection

    d.   weather-exposed balcony waterproofing inspection

Reference_____

17. In addition to their authorized agent, whose duty is it to notify the building official that the work is ready for inspection?

    a.   the permit holder   b.   the owner

    c.   the contractor   d.   the architect

Reference_____

18. The certificate of occupancy shall contain all of the following information except:

    a.   the name of the building owner or owner's authorized agent

    b.   the name of the building official

    c.   the building's type of construction

    d.   the building's allowable height and area

Reference_____

19. A temporary certificate of occupancy is valid for what maximum period of time?

    a.   30 days   b.   60 days

    c.   180 days   d.   a period set by the building official

Reference_____

20. The board of appeals is not authorized to rule on an appeal based on a claim that
_____.

    a.   the provisions of the code do not fully apply

    b.   a code requirement should be waived

    c.   the rules have been incorrectly interpreted

    d.   a better form of construction is provided

Reference_____

21. A one-family dwelling's accessory structure is regulated by the *International Residential Code* provided it is a maximum of _____ story (stories) in height above grade plane.

    a.   one

    b.   two

    c.   three

    d.   four

Reference_____

22. The provisions of _____ shall apply to the repair, alteration, change of occupancy, addition to and relocation of existing buildings.

    a.   *International Building Code Chapter 1*

    b.   *International Building Code Chapter 34*

    c.   *International Existing Building Code*

    d.   *International Property Maintenance Code*

Reference_____

23. Where a conflict occurs between provisions in the *International Building Code* and those in a referenced standard, which provision(s) shall apply?

    a.   *International Building Code*

    b.   referenced standard

    c.   the more restrictive of the *International Building Code* or the referenced standard

    d.   the provision as determined by the building official

Reference_____

24. A permit is not required for the construction of a fence where the fence is a maximum of _____ feet in height.

    a. 5   b. 7

    c. 6   d. 8

Reference_____

25. ASTM C1280 is a referenced standard addressing _____ .

    a. structural concrete   b. light-frame wood construction

    c. structural steel buildings   d. exterior gypsum sheathing application

Reference_____

26. A permit is required for a prefabricated above-ground swimming pool, accessory to a Group R-3 occupancy, that is a minimum of _____ in depth or has a capacity of more than _____.

    a. 18 inches; 4,000 gallons   b. 24 inches; 5,000 gallons

    c. 30 inches; 5,000 gallons   d. 36 inches; 6,000 gallons

Reference_____

27. In Group R-3 and U occupancies, the installation of window awnings is exempt from a permit, provided the awnings each project a maximum of _____ inches from the exterior wall and do not require additional support.

    a. 30   b. 36

    c. 48   d. 54

Reference_____

28. A permit may be suspended or revoked for all of the following reasons, except _____ .

    a. where it is issued in error

    b. on the basis of incomplete information

    c. where issued in violation of a jurisdictional ordinance

    d. where other permits by the contractor have been voided

Reference_____

29. Unless extended by the building official, what is the maximum time period allowed to be granted for a permit issued on a temporary structure?

    a. 90 days

    b. 180 days

    c. 1 year

    d. 2 years

    Reference_____

30. The inspection of gypsum board installation is required where the gypsum board is part of_____.

    a. a shear assembly only

    b. a fire-resistance-rated assembly only

    c. either a fire- or smoke-resistant assembly

    d. either a shear assembly or a fire-resistance-rated assembly

    Reference_____

31. A permit is not required for the installation of a self-contained refrigeration system, provided it contains a maximum of _____ pounds of refrigerant and is actuated by a maximum _____-horsepower motor.

    a. 5, 1

    b. 10, 1

    c. 5, $1^1/_2$

    d. 10, $1^1/_2$

    Reference_____

32. The means of egress layout required as a part of the construction documents for which of the following occupancies must include the number of occupants to be accommodated?

    a. Group F-1

    b. Group I-1

    c. Group R-2

    d. Group R-3

    Reference_____

33. The final permit valuation shall be set by the _____ .

    a. owner

    b. building official

    c. design professional

    d. general contractor

    Reference_____

34. Who is responsible for ensuring that the work is accessible and exposed for inspection purposes?

    a.   owner or owner's authorized agent

    b.   contractor

    c.   permit applicant or their authorized agent

    d.   design professional

Reference _____

35. A stop work order shall be in writing and given to any of the following individuals except the _____.

    a.   owner of the property involved

    b.   owner's agent

    c.   permit holder

    d.   person doing the work

Reference _____

36. Inspection reports shall be retained by the building official for what minimum period of time?

    a.   90 days after issuance of the certificate of occupancy

    b.   180 days after issuance of the certificate of occupancy

    c.   As determined by the building official

    d.   As required for retention of public records

Reference _____

37. The design live loads for floors in an industrial building do not need to be posted where the design live load is a maximum of _____ psf.

    a.   50   b.   80

    c.   100   d.   125

Reference _____

38. Where connection fire-resistance ratings are provided by wood cover, inspection of the cover is required in all mass timber buildings except _____ construction.

    a.   Type IV-A   b.   Type IV-B

    c.   Type IV-C   d.   Type IV-HT

Reference _____

39. The referenced standard dealing with accessible buildings is _____.

    a.   ASME A17.1—CSA 19/CSA B44-19

    b.   DOC PS 1—19

    c.   ICC A117.1—17

    d.   FEMA 4880—2017

Reference _____

40. Where the extent of a reference to a referenced standard includes subject matter that is within the scope of the IBC, the _____ provisions shall apply.

    a.   most restrictive   b.   least restrictive

    c.   IBC   d.   referenced standard

Reference _____

2021 IBC Chapter 3 and Sections 508 and 509
Occupancy Classification and Use

OBJECTIVE: To gain an understanding of how an occupancy is classified based on its intended use and how a building with incidental uses and/or mixed occupancies is addressed.

REFERENCE: Chapter 3 and Sections 508 and 509, 2021 *International Building Code*

KEY POINTS:
- What are the 10 general occupancy groups?
- How is a space that is intended to be occupied at different times for different purposes to be addressed?
- How is an occupancy that is not specifically described to be classified?
- Which types of activities are considered assembly uses? What is their general classification?
- How are small assembly uses classified where accessory to a different occupancy?
- What is the classification for restaurants and cafes? Theaters? Places of religious worship, conference rooms and libraries? Arenas? Grandstands?
- What is the primary use classified as Group B?
- Group E occupancies describe educational uses for individuals of what age group?
- Which types of day care are considered Group E occupancies?
- Manufacturing operations fall into what occupancy group? How do the two divisions of factory-use differ from each other?
- What type of operations or materials cause a use to be considered Group H?
- How does the amount of hazardous materials affect the occupancy classification?
- Which occupancies address physical hazards? Health hazards? Semiconductor fabrication facilities?
- Which characteristics are typical of a Group I occupancy?
- In which institutional occupancies are the occupants considered incapable of self-preservation?

- For which types of institutional uses may the *International Residential Code* be utilized?
- What general type of building is considered a Group M occupancy?
- How are residential occupancies classified?
- What is the key difference between a Group R-1 and Group R-2 occupancy?
- What is a congregate living facility? How should such a facility be classified?
- When is a residential use permitted to be constructed under the provisions of the *International Residential Code*?
- What do storage occupancy classifications have in common with those of manufacturing uses?
- How is a vehicle repair garage classified? An aircraft hangar?
- What is the classification of an enclosed parking garage? An open parking garage?
- What is a utility occupancy? How does its classification differ from that of other occupancies?
- Which three options are available for addressing multiple occupancies within a building?
- What is an accessory occupancy? What benefit is derived from such a designation?
- What is the concept of the nonseparated occupancy provisions? What conditions apply to buildings with nonseparated occupancies?
- What is the basis for separated occupancies? How are the minimum required fire-resistive separations determined?
- How is the fire-resistance rating for an occupancy separation determined? How does the presence of an automatic sprinkler system affect the required rating?
- What is an incidental use? How must such an area be separated from the remainder of the building? When is sprinkler protection required?

Code Text: *Occupancy classification is the formal designation of the primary purpose of the building, structure or portion thereof. Where a structure is proposed for a purpose which is not specifically listed in Section 302.1, such structure shall be classified in the occupancy it most nearly resembles, based on the fire safety and relative hazard.*

Discussion and Commentary: The perils contemplated by the occupancy groupings are divided into two general categories: those related to people and those related to content. People-related hazards include the number and density of the occupants, their age and mobility, and their awareness of surrounding conditions. Content-related hazards include the storage and use of hazardous materials, as well as the presence of large quantities of combustible materials.

Assembly	**Business**
Educational	**Factory**
Hazardous	**Institutional**
Mercantile	**Residential**
Storage	**Utility**

Proper occupancy classification is critical in making appropriate code determinations throughout a project. In the classification process, the building official must use judgment in the determination of the potential hazards of an affected occupancy.

Code Text: *Assembly Group A occupancy includes, among others, the use of a building or structure, or a portion thereof, for the gathering of persons for purposes such as civic, social or religious functions, recreation, food or drink consumption or awaiting transportation. See other classification allowances for assembly buildings and assembly spaces with an occupant load of less than 50, accessory assembly spaces less than 750 square feet in floor area, and those assembly spaces associated with Group E occupancies.*

Discussion and Commentary: The conditions related to a typical Group A occupancy suggest a moderate hazard use. This use often includes sizable numbers of people who are generally mobile and aware of the surrounding conditions. The extremely high occupant density level often present in an assembly occupancy is what distinguishes Group A from other occupancies. Where the occupant load of an assembly building or tenant space does not exceed 50, a Group B classification is typically more appropriate owing to the lesser hazard.

Group A-1

Motion picture theaters
Theaters
Symphony and
    concert halls

Group A-2

Banquet halls
Casino gaming areas
Night clubs
Restaurants
Taverns

Group A-3

Amusement arcades
Art galleries
Bowling alleys
Places of worship
Community halls
Conference rooms
Exhibition halls
Lecture halls
Libraries
Museums
Passenger stations

Group A-4

Arenas
Skating rinks
Swimming pools
Tennis courts

Group A-5

Amusement park
    structures
Bleachers
Grandstands
Stadiums

Unique conditions are represented by the classifications of Groups A-1, A-2, A-4 and A-5. However, the category Group A-3 includes a variety of broad and diverse assembly uses. It is not uncommon to find high combustible loading in Group A-3 occupancies.

Code Text: *Business Group B occupancy includes, among others, the use of a building or structure, or a portion thereof, for office, professional or service-type transactions, including storage of records and accounts.*

Discussion and Commentary: Business occupancies typically have a low to moderate fire load, a moderate density level, and occupants who are usually mobile and have a general awareness of the surrounding conditions. As such, business occupancies are grouped into a classification based upon a relatively moderate fire hazard level. Group B occupancies are not restricted by occupant load, as the number of people in a business use, such as an office, can range from one person to thousands of people.

Group B

Ambulatory care facilities
Animal hospitals, kennels and ponds
Banks
Barber and beauty shops
Car wash
Civil administration
Clinic-outpatient
Educational occupancies above the 12th grade
Food processing ≤ 2,500 sf
Laboratories; testing and research
Motor vehicle showrooms
Post offices
Print shops
Professional services
Radio and television stations
Training and skill development

As is the case for many of the occupancy groups, a review of the building's intended uses is necessary to determine the amount of hazardous materials that may be stored, handled or used. If the amounts exceed a specified quantity, then a Group H classification will be in order.

Code Text: *Educational Group E occupancy includes, among others, the use of a building or structure, or a portion thereof, by six or more persons at any one time for educational purposes through the 12th grade. This group includes buildings and structures or portions thereof occupied by more than five children older than $2^{1}/_{2}$ years of age who receive educational, supervision or personal care services for fewer than 24 hours per day.*

Discussion and Commentary: Educational occupancies include classroom uses for students of high school age and younger. Education facilities limited to use by older students, such as college classrooms, are classified as Group B occupancies; however, a Group A classification should be considered for lecture halls and similar large occupant load spaces.

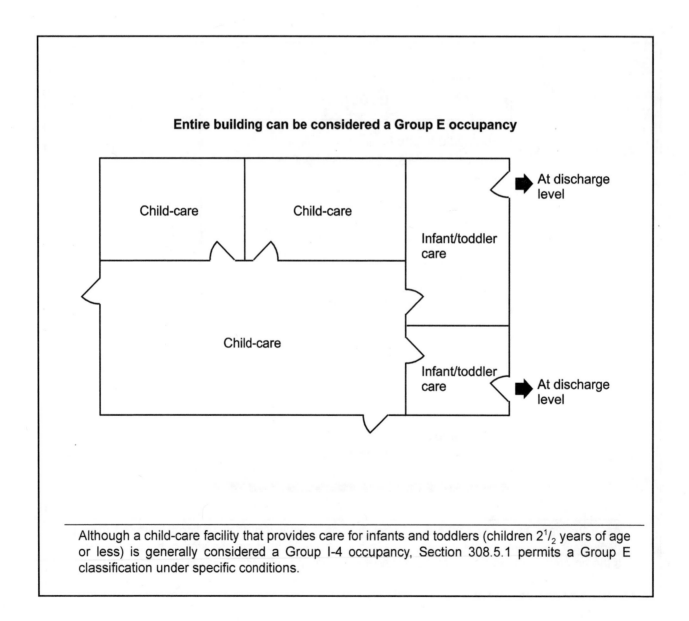

Entire building can be considered a Group E occupancy

Child-care

Child-care

Infant/toddler care

At discharge level

Child-care

Infant/toddler care

At discharge level

Although a child-care facility that provides care for infants and toddlers (children $2^{1}/_{2}$ years of age or less) is generally considered a Group I-4 occupancy, Section 308.5.1 permits a Group E classification under specific conditions.

Code Text: *Factory Industrial Group F occupancy includes, among others, the use of a building or structure, or a portion thereof, for assembling, disassembling, fabricating, finishing, manufacturing, packaging, repair or processing operations that are not classified as a Group H hazardous or Group S storage occupancy.*

Discussion and Commentary: Although the potential hazard and fire severity varies among the many uses categorized as Group F occupancies, the uses still share elements in common. The occupants are adults who are awake and who generally have enough familiarity with the premises to be able to exit the building with reasonable efficiency. The presence of combustible materials in the industrial process causes a classification of Group F-1, which is by far the most common factory use.

Group F-1	Group F-2
Aircraft	Brick and masonry
Appliances	Ceramic products
Automobiles	Foundries
Bakeries	Glass products
Business machines	Gypsum
Carpets and rugs	Ice
Clothing	Metal products
Electric generation	
ESS (dedicated use)	
Food processing > 2,500 sf	
Furniture	
Laundries	
Millwork	
Paper mills or products	
Plastic products	
Printing or publishing	
Refuse incineration	
Textiles	
Water/sewer treatment	
Woodworking	

Classification as a Group F-2 occupancy is strictly limited because of the restrictions placed on such uses. The fabrication or manufacture of noncombustible materials, as well as their finishing, packaging or processing operations, cannot involve a significant fire hazard.

Code Text: *High-hazard Group H occupancy includes, among others, the use of a building or structure, or a portion thereof, that involves the manufacturing, processing, generation or storage of materials that constitute a physical or health hazard in quantities in excess of those allowed in control areas complying with Section 414, based on the maximum allowable quantity limits for control areas set forth in Tables 307.1(1) and 307.1(2).*

Discussion and Commentary: There is only one fundamental type of Group H occupancy—that which is designated based solely on excessive quantities of hazardous materials contained therein. The quantities of hazardous materials that necessitate a Group H classification vary, based on the type, quantity, condition (use or storage) and environment of the materials. Where the use does not exceed the maximum allowable quantities set forth in the code, a classification other than Group H is appropriate.

Where hazardous materials and processes are involved.

References for detailed provisions

Although the *International Building Code* is limited to general construction regulations and occupancy-specific requirements, the *International Fire Code®* (IFC®) sets forth special detailed provisions relating to hazardous materials and the specific conditions of their storage, use and handling.

Code Text: *An occupancy that stores, uses or handles hazardous materials as described in one or more of the following items shall not be classified as Group H, but shall be classified as the occupancy that it most nearly resembles.* See a listing of 19 conditions under which a Group H occupancy is not warranted. *Hazardous materials in any quantity shall conform to the requirements of* the IBC, *including Section 414, and the* International Fire Code.

Discussion and Commentary: Although some degree of hazardous materials is found in most buildings, the occupancy is designated as Group H only where the quantities are excessive and the hazards are not adequately addressed. The most common condition for a non-H classification is where the amount of hazardous materials contained in the building does not exceed the maximum allowable quantities shown in Table 307.1(1) for physical hazards and Table 307.1(2) for health hazards. Footnotes to both tables can be used to increase the permitted quantities.

TABLE 307.1(1)
MAXIMUM ALLOWABLE QUANTITY PER CONTROL AREA OF HAZARDOUS MATERIALS POSING A PHYSICAL HAZARD[a, j, m, n, p]

MATERIAL	CLASS	GROUP WHEN THE MAXIMUM ALLOWABLE QUANTITY IS EXCEEDED	STORAGE[b] Solid pounds (cubic feet)	Liquid gallons (pounds)	Gas cubic feet at NTP	USE-CLOSED SYSTEMS[b] Solid pounds (cubic feet)	Liquid gallons (pounds)	Gas cubic feet at NTP	USE-OPEN SYSTEMS[b] Solid pounds (cubic feet)	Liquid gallons (pounds)
Combustible dust	NA	H-2	See Note q	NA	NA	See Note q	NA	NA	See Note q	NA
Combustible fiber[d]	Loose Baled[o]	H-3	(100) (1,000)	NA	NA	(100) (1,000)	NA	NA	(20) (200)	NA
Combustible liquid[c, i]	II IIIA IIIB	H-2 or H-3 H-2 or H-3 NA	NA	120[d, e] 330[d, e] 13,200[c, f]	NA	NA	120[d] 330[d] 13,200[f]	NA	NA	30[d] 80[d] 3,300[f]
Cryogenic flammable	NA	H-2	NA	45[d]	NA	NA	45[d]	NA	NA	10[d]
Cryogenic inert	NA	NA	NA	NA	NL	NA	NA	NL	NA	NA
Cryogenic oxidizing	NA	H-3	NA	45[d]	NA	NA	45[d]	NA	NA	10[d]
Explosives	Division 1.1 Division 1.2 Division 1.3 Division 1.4 Division 1.4G Division 1.5 Division 1.6	H-1 H-1 H-1 or H-2 H-3 H-3 H-1 H-1	1[e, g] 1[e, g] 5[e, g] 50[e, g] 125[e, l] 1[e, g] 1[e, g]	(1)[e, g] (1)[e, g] (5)[e, g] (50)[e, g] NA (1)[e, g] NA	NA	0.25[g] 0.25[g] 1[g] 50[g] NA 0.25[g] NA	(0.25)[g] (0.25)[g] (1)[g] (50)[g] NA (0.25)[g] NA	NA	0.25[g] 0.25[g] 1[g] NA NA 0.25[g] NA	(0.25)[g] (0.25)[g] (1)[g] NA NA (0.25)[g] NA
Flammable gas	Gaseous Liquefied	H-2	NA	NA (150)[d, e]	1,000[d, e] NA	NA	NA (150)[d, e]	1,000[d, e] NA	NA	NA
Flammable liquid[c]	IA IB and IC	H-2 or H-3	NA	30[d, e] 120[d, e]	NA	NA	30[d] 120[d]	NA	NA	10[d] 30[d]
Flammable liquid, combination (IA, IB, IC)	NA	H-2 or H-3	NA	120[d, e, h]	NA	NA	120[d, h]	NA	NA	30[d, h]

(continued)

Where one of the 19 exemptions is applied, the classification is based on the general use. For example, a warehouse containing quantities below the maximum allowable would simply be classified as Group S-1. A manufacturing facility would be classified as a Group F-1 occupancy.

Code Text: *Institutional Group I occupancy includes, among others, the use of a building or structure, or a portion thereof, in which care or supervision is provided to persons who are or are not capable of self preservation without physical assistance or in which persons are detained for penal or correctional purposes or in which the liberty of the occupants is restricted. Institutional occupancies shall be classified as Group I-1, I-2, I-3 or I-4.*

Discussion and Commentary: The institutional uses classified as Group I occupancies are of three broad types. The first is a facility in which care is provided for the very young, sick or injured. The second category includes those facilities in which the personal liberties of the inmates or residents are restricted. Thirdly, supervised care facilities are regulated. Though the hazard due to combustible contents is quite low in institutional uses, the occupants' lack of mobility limits their egress ability.

Group I-1

Alcohol and drug centers
Assisted living facilities
Congregate care facilities
Group homes
Halfway houses
Residential board and care facilities
Social rehabilitation facilities

Group I-2

Foster care facilities
Detoxification facilities
Hospitals
Nursing homes
Psychiatric hospitals

Group I-3

Correctional centers
Detention centers
Jails
Prerelease centers
Prisons
Reformatories

Group I-4

Adult day care
Child day care

Where the number of children, patients or residents in institutional uses is five or less, the hazards are similar in nature to a residential use. In most cases, an institutional facility with such a low occupant load would be considered a Group R-3 occupancy or regulated under the IRC.

Code Text: *Mercantile Group M occupancy includes, among others, the use of a building or a structure or a portion thereof, for the display and sale of merchandise, and involves stocks of goods, wares or merchandise incidental to such purposes and where the public has access.*

Discussion and Commentary: A Group M occupancy is a retail or wholesale facility, or a store. An entire building can be classified as a Group M occupancy, such as a department store, or a portion of a building can be considered a mercantile use, such as the sales room in a manufacturing facility. A service station, including a canopy over the pump islands, is also classified as a Group M occupancy. In limited instances, a sales operation is designated as a Group B occupancy, as in the case of automobile showrooms.

Group M

Department stores
Drug stores
Greenhouses (display and sale)
Markets
Motor fuel-dispensing facilities
Retail or wholesale stores
Sales rooms

When classifying the occupancy of a storage area accessory to the sales area in a retail store, it is appropriate to apply the provisions that address the specific hazards of the use. In most situations, it is appropriate to classify the incidental storage area as a Group S-1 occupancy.

Code Text: *Residential Group R occupancy includes, among others, the use of a building or structure, or a portion thereof, for sleeping purposes when not classified as an Institutional Group I or when not regulated by the* International Residential Code.

Discussion and Commentary: Residential occupancies are characterized by: (1) their use by people for living and sleeping purposes, (2) a relatively low potential fire severity, and (3) the worst fire record of all structure types. Because occupants of these types of buildings spend up to one-third of each day sleeping, there is a high potential of a fire to rage out of control before the occupants awaken. After awakening, the residents will typically be disoriented for a short period of time, further decreasing the opportunity for immediate egress. A major difference between the Group R-1 and R-2 occupancy classifications is the transient nature of the use. "Transient" is defined as *occupancy of a dwelling unit or sleeping unit for not more than 30 days.*

Group R-1

Boarding houses (transient)
 > 10 occupants
Congregate living
 facilities (transient) > 10 occupants
Hotels (transient)
Motels (transient)

Group R-2

Apartment houses
Congregate living
 facilities (nontransient)
 > 1 6 occupants
Hotels (nontransient)
Live/work units
Motels (nontransient)
Vacation timeshare properties

Group R-3

Buildings with ≤ two dwelling units
Care facilities ≤ 5 persons
 receiving care
Congregate living facilities
 (nontransient) ≤ 16 ocupants
Congregate living facilities
 (transient) ≤ 10 occupants
Lodging houses with
≤ 5 guest rooms and ≤ 10 occupants

Group R-4

Alcohol and drug centers
Assisted living facilities
Congregate care facilities
Convalescent facilities
Group homes
Halfway houses
Residential board and
 custodial care facilities
Social rehabilitation facilities

Detached one- and two-family dwellings, as well as townhouses, are not regulated by the *International Building Code* when limited to the conditions of the exception to Section 101.2. They are to be designed and constructed in accordance with the *International Residential Code.*

Code Text: *Storage Group S occupancy includes among others, the use of a building or structure, or a portion thereof, for storage that is not classified as a hazardous occupancy.*

Discussion and Commentary: Where a warehouse or other storage facility does not contain significant amounts of hazardous commodities (as determined by Section 307), it should be considered a Group S occupancy. A facility used for the storage of combustible goods is classified as Group S-1, whereas a Group S-2 occupancy shall be used only for the storage of noncombustible materials. If it is reasonable to believe that a storage building will house combustible goods for any significant period of time, it would be appropriate to consider the structure a Group S-1 occupancy, designed and constructed accordingly. Motor-vehicle-related uses are also included in the Group S category, with repair garages classified as Group S-1 and parking garages (both open and enclosed) as Group S-2 occupancies.

Group S-1	Group S-2
Aerosols products Level 2 and Level 3 Aircraft repair hangar Bags; cloth, burlap, paper Belting; canvas, leather Books Paper in rolls Cardboard and cardboard boxes Clothing Furniture Grains Lumber Motor vehicle repair garages Self-service storage facility Tires, bulk storage of Tobacco, cigars, cigarettes Upholstery and mattresses	Aircraft hangar Asbestos Cement in bags Chalk and crayons Dairy products Dry cell batteries Electric motors Food products Fresh fruits and vegetables Frozen foods Glass Gypsum board Meats Metals Open parking garages Enclosed parking garages Porcelain and pottery

Although the goods being stored in a Group S-2 occupancy must be noncombustible, the code permits a limited amount of combustibles in the packaging or support materials. Wood pallets, paper cartons, paper wrappings, plastic trim and film wrapping are permitted for such purposes.

Code Text: *Buildings and structures of an accessory character and miscellaneous structures not classified in any specific occupancy shall be constructed, equipped and maintained to conform to the requirements of the IBC commensurate with the fire and life hazard incidental to their occupancy.*

Discussion and Commentary: Those structures not ordinarily occupied by the general public are typically classified as Group U occupancies. The fire load in these structures varies considerably but is usually not excessive. Because these types of uses are not normally occupied, the concern for fire severity is not very great, and as a group they constitute a low hazard. Several of the structures regulated as Group U occupancies are never occupied, such as fences, towers and tanks.

Group U

Agricultural buildings
Barns
Carports
Fences more than 7 feet in height
Livestock shelters
Private garages
Retaining walls
Sheds
Stables
Tanks
Towers

Private garages classified as Group U occupancies are generally limited to 1,000 square feet in floor area. However, such structures are permitted to be increased in size where complying 1-hour separations are provided.

Code Text: *Each portion of a building shall be individually classified in accordance with Section 302.1. Where a building contains more than one occupancy group, the building or portion thereof shall comply with the applicable provisions of Section 508.2 (Accessory Occupancies), 508.3 (Nonseparated Occupancies), 508.4 (Separated Occupancies), or 508.5 (Live/Work Units), or a combination of these sections.* See the exceptions for: (1) occupancies separated in accordance with Section 510 (Special Provisions), and (2) Group H-1, H-2 and H-3 occupancies required by Table 415.6.5 to be located in a separate and detached building.

Discussion and Commentary: It is not uncommon for two or more distinct occupancy classifications to occur in the same building. Where such conditions exist, the code requires that such multiple occupancies be either (1) isolated from each other using fire-resistive separation elements (fire barriers and/or horizontal assemblies), or (2) imposed with special provisions that eliminate the need for such fire separations.

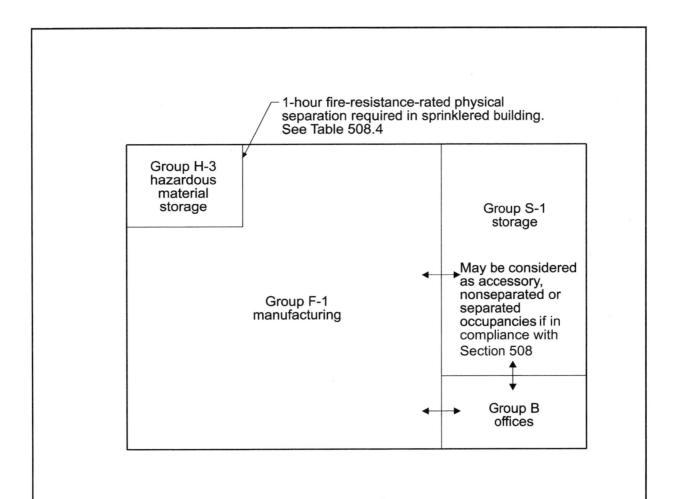

1-hour fire-resistance-rated physical separation required in sprinklered building. See Table 508.4

Group H-3 hazardous material storage

Group S-1 storage

Group F-1 manufacturing

May be considered as accessory, nonseparated or separated occupancies if in compliance with Section 508

Group B offices

Although compliance with only one of the three mixed-occupancy methods is required, it is acceptable to utilize two or even all three methods within the same building.

Code Text: *Accessory occupancies are those occupancies that are ancillary to the main occupancy of the building or portion thereof. Aggregate accessory occupancies shall not occupy more than 10 percent of the area of the story in which they are located and shall not exceed the tabular values for nonsprinklered buildings in Table 506.2 for each such accessory occupancy.*

Discussion and Commentary: The mixed-occupancy method of "Accessory Occupancies" is one of the three design options that the code provides when dealing with mixed-occupancy buildings. This approach is only applicable where one or more of the occupancies is quite small in relationship to the major occupancy in the building. The aggregate floor area of all accessory occupancies is limited to 10 percent of the floor area of the story in which the accessory occupancies are located. In addition, the aggregate floor area of the accessory occupancies cannot exceed the allowable floor area taken from Table 506.2 for a nonsprinklered building.

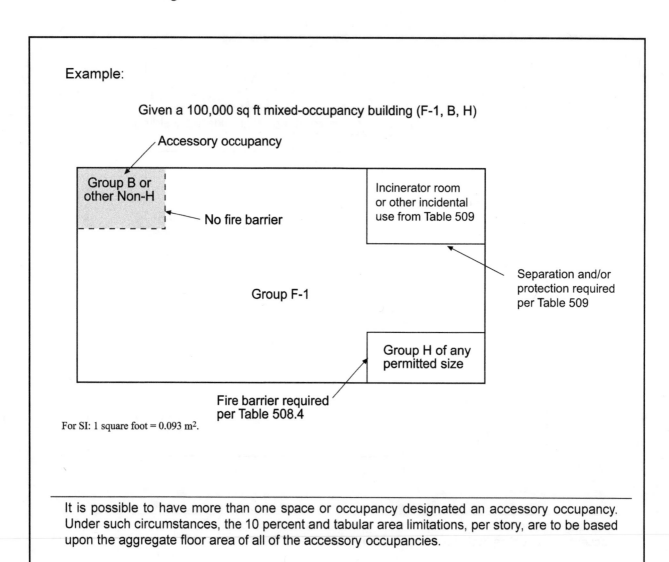

Example:

Given a 100,000 sq ft mixed-occupancy building (F-1, B, H)

Accessory occupancy

Group B or other Non-H

No fire barrier

Incinerator room or other incidental use from Table 509

Separation and/or protection required per Table 509

Group F-1

Group H of any permitted size

Fire barrier required per Table 508.4

For SI: 1 square foot = 0.093 m².

It is possible to have more than one space or occupancy designated an accessory occupancy. Under such circumstances, the 10 percent and tabular area limitations, per story, are to be based upon the aggregate floor area of all of the accessory occupancies.

Code Text: *Accessory occupancies shall be individually classified in accordance with Section 302.1. The requirements of the IBC shall apply to each portion of the building based on the occupancy classification of that space.*

Discussion and Commentary: The occupancy classification of a use that is regulated under the provisions for accessory occupancies is based solely upon the specific use of that area. Although the size of the occupancy may be quite small in comparison with the remainder of the building, the accessory occupancy has its own unique hazards that must be adequately addressed.

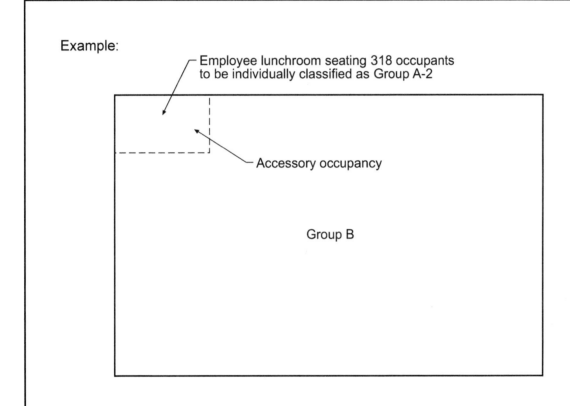

Example:

Employee lunchroom seating 318 occupants to be individually classified as Group A-2

Accessory occupancy

Group B

Unless modified by Section 508.2, requirements of the code apply to each occupancy independently based on their specific uses. For example, the ventilation requirements applicable to the accessory occupancy may not be appropriate for the major occupancy. Each of the occupancies would be regulated based upon their unique classifications.

Code Text: *The allowable height and number of stories of the building containing accessory occupancies shall be in accordance with Section 504 for the main occupancy of the building. No separation is required between accessory occupancies and the main occupancy. See the exceptions for (1) Group H-2, H-3, H-4 and H-5 occupancies; and (2) dwelling and sleeping units in Groups I-1, R-1, R-2 and R-3.*

Discussion and Commentary: Where the methodology of "Accessory Occupancies" is utilized, the allowable height and area of the accessory occupancies, as well as that of the major occupancy, is based solely on the building's major occupancy. There is no mandate to apply the more restrictive height and area provisions of each of the occupancies involved, as required under the "Nonseparated Occupancies" method, nor to go through calculations based on the unity formula as required for "Separated Occupancies."

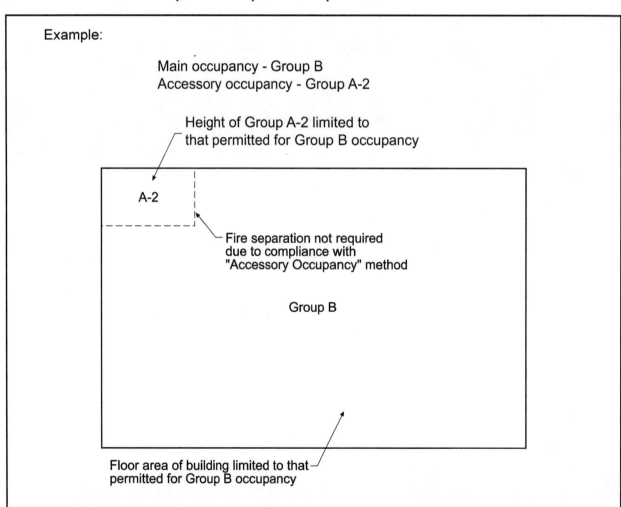

Example:

Main occupancy - Group B
Accessory occupancy - Group A-2

Height of Group A-2 limited to that permitted for Group B occupancy

A-2

Fire separation not required due to compliance with "Accessory Occupancy" method

Group B

Floor area of building limited to that permitted for Group B occupancy

As long as the accessory occupancies involved are not classified as Group H, there is no requirement to separate the accessory occupancies from the major occupancy of the building. In addition, where two or more accessory occupancies are present, they do not need to be separated from each other.

Code Text: *Nonseparated occupancies shall be individually classified in accordance with Section 302.1. The requirements of the IBC shall apply to each portion of the building based on the occupancy classification of that space. In addition, the most restrictive provisions of Chapter 9 that apply to the nonseparated occupancies shall apply to the total nonseparated occupancy area.*

Discussion and Commentary: The allowance for "Nonseparated Occupancies," one of the alternatives to the physical separation of different occupancies, is based on the most limiting requirements for building size (height and area) and fire-protection features such as sprinklers, standpipes and alarm systems. Where occupancies are regulated by the nonseparated occupancy provisions, a physical separation is permitted, but it is not required.

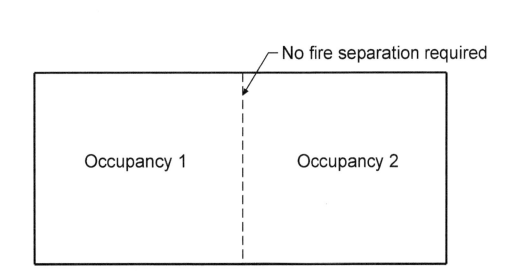

- Type of construction limited by:
  - Lesser height limit of Occupancy 1 or 2
  - Lesser floor area limit of Occupancy 1 or 2

- Most restrictive fire-protection system requirements of Occupancy 1 and 2

Where the provisions for nonseparated occupancies are utilized in a high-rise building as defined by Section 403, the special high-rise provisions that apply to the nonseparated occupancies are applicable to the entire building.

Code Text: *The allowable building area, height and number of stories of the building or portion thereof shall be based on the most restrictive allowances for the occupancy groups under consideration for the type of construction of the building in accordance with Section 503.1. No separation is required between nonseparated occupancies.* See the exceptions for (1) Group H-2, H-3, H-4 and H-5 occupancies; and (2) dwelling and sleeping units in Groups I-1, R-1, R-2 and R-3.

Discussion and Commentary: Where the option for nonseparated occupancies is utilized to address a mixed-occupancy building, it is necessary to determine the maximum building size for each of the occupancies that are not appropriately separated. The maximum allowable height and area for each occupancy would be based upon the building's type of construction. The most restrictive height and area of those nonseparated occupancies would then be the limiting size for the combination of such occupancies.

Example:

Given: A nonsprinklered Type VB building contains both Group B and Group E occupancies.

Determine: The height and area limitations if the occupancies are not separated under the nonseparated occupancies provisions of Section 508.3.

OCCUPANCY	ALLOWABLE HEIGHT[1]	ALLOWABLE AREA[2]
Group B[2]	2 stories	9,000 square feet
Group E[3]	1 story	9,500 square feet

1 Based on Table 504.4

2 Based on Table 506.2 assuming no frontage increase.

3 Most restrictive fire protection requirements of Chapter 9 also applicable to entire building.

^Thus, for nonseparated occupancies, the maximum building size would be 1 story and 9,000 square feet.

Nonseparated Occupancies

The use of the nonseparated occupancies method is not applicable to high-hazard occupancies. Those areas or spaces classified as Group H occupancies must be isolated from other occupancies within the building by fire barriers and/or horizontal assemblies in accordance with Table 508.4 for occupancy separations.

Code Text: *Separated occupancies shall be individually classified in accordance with Section 302.1. Each separated space shall comply with* the IBC *based on the occupancy classification of that portion of the building.*

Discussion and Commentary: Under the provisions for "Separated Occupancies," each of the distinct uses is to be individually classified as to occupancy. This approach is consistent with that for accessory occupancies and nonseparated occupancies. The concept of separated occupancies provides for a fire-resistance-rated separation in order to isolate the hazards associated with a specific occupancy from other portions of the building.

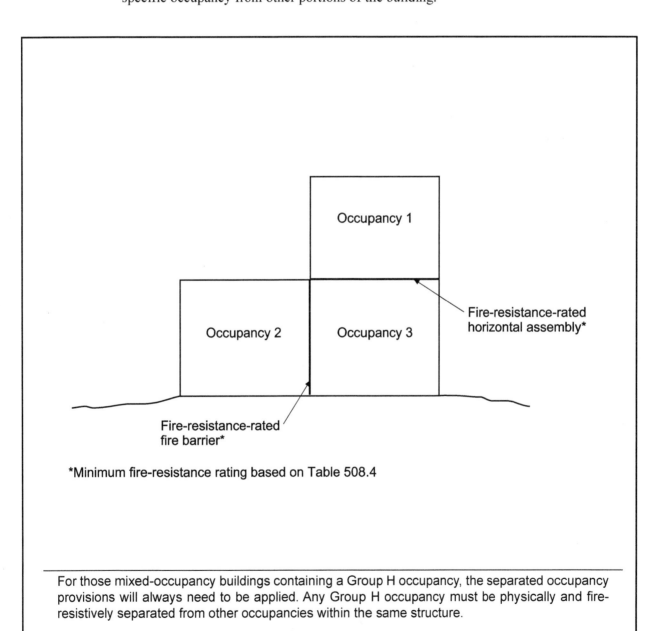

Occupancy 1

Occupancy 2

Occupancy 3

Fire-resistance-rated horizontal assembly*

Fire-resistance-rated fire barrier*

*Minimum fire-resistance rating based on Table 508.4

For those mixed-occupancy buildings containing a Group H occupancy, the separated occupancy provisions will always need to be applied. Any Group H occupancy must be physically and fire-resistively separated from other occupancies within the same structure.

Code Text: *In each story, the building area shall be such that the sum of the ratios of the actual building area of each separated occupancy divided by the allowable area of each separated occupancy shall not exceed 1. Each separated occupancy shall comply with the building height limitations and story limitations based on the type of construction of the building in accordance with Section 503.1. See exception where Section 510 is applied.*

Discussion and Commentary: The approach to separated occupancies mandates that the ratios of the actual and allowable floor areas be calculated in order to determine compliance. Often known as the "unity formula," this calculation recognizes the relationship between the permitted sizes of the various occupancies involved. The unity formula is only applicable where the separated occupancy method is utilized and does not apply to accessory occupancies or non-separated occupancies.

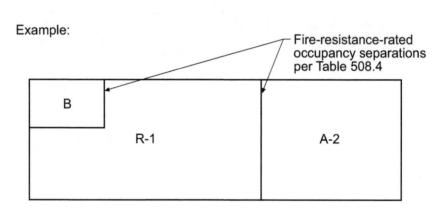

Example:

Fire-resistance-rated occupancy separations per Table 508.4

B

R-1

A-2

Allowable height per Section 504 for each individual occupancy

$$\frac{\text{Actual area A-2}}{\text{Allowable area A-2}} + \frac{\text{Actual area B}}{\text{Allowable area B}} + \frac{\text{Actual area R-1}}{\text{Allowable area R-1}} \leq 1.0$$

The height limitations for separated occupancies are based upon the general provisions of Section 504. The height limit, in both feet and stories, is to be measured from the grade plane, and the measurement must include all intervening fire areas.

Code Text: *Individual occupancies shall be separated from adjacent occupancies in accordance with Table 508.4. Required separations shall be fire barriers constructed in accordance with Section 707 or horizontal assemblies constructed in accordance with Section 711, or both, so as to completely separate adjacent occupancies.*

Discussion and Commentary: A matrix, Table 508.4, has been established to identify any required fire-resistance-rated separation between various occupancies. The table is based on the perceived degree of dissimilarity between the occupancies involved. Where Table 508.4 requires a level of fire-resistance between the adjoining occupancies, fire barriers and/or horizontal separations are to be used. The intended result is that the hazards associated with one occupancy be completely isolated from those present in the remainder of the building.

TABLE 508.4
REQUIRED SEPARATION OF OCCUPANCIES (HOURS)[f]

OCCUPANCY	A, E		I-1ª, I-3, I-4		I-2		Rª		F-2, S-2ᵇ, U		Bᵉ, F-1, M, S-1		H-1		H-2		H-3, H-4		H-5	
	S	NS	S	NS	S	NS	S	NS	S	NS	S	NS	S	NS	S	NS	S	NS	S	NS
A, E	N	N	1	2	2	NP	1	2	N	1	1	2	NP	NP	3	4	2	3	2	NP
I-1ª, I-3, I-4	1	2	N	N	2	NP	1	NP	1	2	1	2	NP	NP	3	NP	2	NP	2	NP
I-2	2	NP	2	NP	N	N	2	NP	2	NP	2	NP	NP	NP	3	NP	2	NP	2	NP
Rª	1	2	1	NP	2	NP	N	N	1ᶜ	2ᶜ	1	2	NP	NP	3	NP	2	NP	2	NP
F-2, S-2ᵇ, U	N	1	1	2	2	NP	1ᶜ	2ᶜ	N	N	1	2	NP	NP	3	4	2	3	2	NP
Bᵉ, F-1, M, S-1	1	2	1	2	2	NP	1	2	1	2	N	N	NP	NP	2	3	1	2	1	NP
H-1	NP	NP	NP	NP	NP	NP	NP	NP	NP	NP	NP	NP	N	NP	NP	NP	NP	NP	NP	NP
H-2	3	4	3	NP	3	NP	3	NP	3	4	2	3	NP	NP	N	NP	1	NP	1	NP
H-3, H-4	2	3	2	NP	2	NP	2	NP	2	3	1	2	NP	NP	1	NP	1ᵈ	NP	1	NP
H-5	2	NP	2	NP	2	NP	2	NP	2	NP	1	NP	NP	NP	1	NP	1	NP	N	NP

S = Buildings equipped throughout with an automatic sprinkler system installed in accordance with Section 903.3.1.1.

NS = Buildings not equipped throughout with an automatic sprinkler system installed in accordance with Section 903.3.1.1.

N = No separation requirement.

NP = Not Permitted.

a. See Section 420.

b. The required separation from areas used only for private or pleasure vehicles shall be reduced by 1 hour but not to less than 1 hour.

c. See Sections 406.3.2 and 406.6.4.

d. Separation is not required between occupancies of the same classification.

e. See Section 422.2 for *ambulatory care facilities*.

f. Occupancy separations that serve to define fire area limits established in Chapter 9 for requiring fire protection systems shall also comply with Section 707.3.10 and Table 707.3.10 in accordance with Section 901.7.

Although the title of Section 508.4 implies that the method described requires a physical and/or fire-resistive separation, that is not always the case. A number of the occupancies do not require such a separation due to the lack of hazard dissimilarity between the uses that occur.

Code Text: *Incidental uses are ancillary functions associated with a given occupancy that generally pose a greater level of risk to that occupancy and are limited to those uses listed in Table 509.1. Incidental uses shall not be individually classified in accordance with Section 302.1. Incidental uses shall be included in the building occupancies within which they are located. Incidental uses shall not occupy more than 10 percent of the building area of the story in which they are located.*

Discussion and Commentary: It is common to find uses that are typical of the general occupancy classification of the building, yet which create a hazard different from the other hazards found in the occupancy. An example would be a chemistry laboratory classroom in a high school building. The code addresses such conditions by requiring incidental uses to be separated from the remainder of the building with fire-resistance-rated construction, or to be protected with an automatic sprinkler system. An incidental use should be assigned an occupancy classification consistent with the portion of the building in which it is located.

[F]TABLE 509.1
INCIDENTAL USES

ROOM OR AREA	SEPARATION AND/OR PROTECTION
Furnace room where any piece of equipment is over 400,000 Btu per hour input	1 hour or provide automatic sprinkler system
Rooms with boilers where the largest piece of equipment is over 15 psi and 10 horsepower	1 hour or provide automatic sprinkler system
Refrigerant machinery room	1 hour or provide automatic sprinkler system
Hydrogen fuel gas rooms, not classified as Group H	1 hour in Group B, F, M, S and U occupancies; 2 hours in Group A, E, I and R occupancies.
Incinerator rooms	2 hours and provide automatic sprinkler system
Paint shops, not classified as Group H, located in occupancies other than Group F	2 hours; or 1 hour and provide automatic sprinkler system
In Group E occupancies, laboratories and vocational shops not classified as Group H	1 hour or provide automatic sprinkler system
In Group I-2 occupancies, laboratories not classified as Group H	1 hour and provide automatic sprinkler system
In *ambulatory care facilities*, laboratories not classified as Group H	1 hour or provide automatic sprinkler system
Laundry rooms over 100 square feet	1 hour or provide automatic sprinkler system
In Group I-2, laundry rooms over 100 square feet	1 hour
Group I-3 cells and Group I-2 patient rooms equipped with padded surfaces	1 hour
In Group I-2, physical plant maintenance shops	1 hour
In ambulatory care facilities or Group I-2 occupancies, waste and linen collection rooms with containers that have an aggregate volume of 10 cubic feet or greater	1 hour
In other than ambulatory care facilities and Group I-2 occupancies, waste and linen collection rooms over 100 square feet	1 hour or provide automatic sprinkler system
In ambulatory care facilities or Group I-2 occupancies, storage rooms greater than 100 square feet	1 hour
Electrical installations and transformers	See Sections 110.26 through 110.34 and Sections 450.8 through 450.48 of NFPA 70 for protection and separation requirements.

For SI: 1 square foot = 0.0929 m², 1 pound per square inch (psi) = 6.9 kPa, 1 British thermal unit (Btu) per hour = 0.293 watts, 1 horsepower = 746 watts, 1 gallon = 3.785 L, 1 cubic foot = 0.0283 m³.

The separation and protection of incinerator rooms is unique in that both methods are required. Although an automatic sprinkler system is required within the incinerator room, it is still necessary to provide a fire-resistance-rated separation utilizing minimum 2-hour fire barriers.

Code Text: *Where Table 509.1 specifies a fire-resistance-rated separation, the incidental uses shall be separated from the remainder of the building by a fire barrier constructed in accordance with Section 707 or a horizontal assembly constructed in accordance with Section 711, or both. Where Table 509.1 permits an automatic sprinkler system without a fire barrier, the incidental uses shall be separated from the remainder of the building by construction capable of resisting the passage of smoke.*

Discussion and Commentary: In utilizing Table 509.1, it is common that two options are available for addressing rooms or areas considered incidental uses. A fire barrier may often be used to isolate the specific hazard from the remainder of the building. As an alternative, a sprinkler system may be used to limit any fire in the incidental use to that space only. By incorporating smoke containment construction, little if any smoke created would be transferred to other portions of the building.

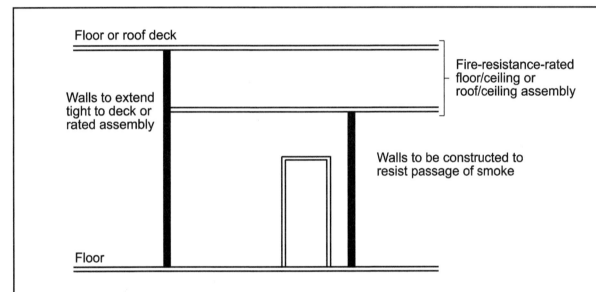

Construction to resist the passage of smoke

Where an automatic sprinkler system is used to provide protection for an incidental use, the area must still be separated from the remainder of the building. The separation must be constructed such that smoke will be contained. Enclosure doors also are regulated.

Quiz

Study Session 2
IBC Chapter 3 and Sections 508 and 509

1. An institutional occupancy is typically considered Group _____ .

    a. A   b. B

    c. I   d. R

    Reference_____

2. A Group _____ occupancy is the general classification for miscellaneous and utility structures.

    a. A   b. M

    c. S   d. U

    Reference_____

3. Accessory religious educational rooms need not be considered separate occupancies where the occupant load is less than _____ occupants.

    a. 100   b. 150

    c. 200   d. 300

    Reference_____

4. An accessory assembly area may be classified as a Group B occupancy where the floor area is a maximum of _____ square feet.

    a. 120   b. 399

    c. 749   d. 1,000

    Reference_____

5. In a Group E middle school, an assembly area associated with the Group E shall be classified as what occupancy?

    a. Group E

    b. Group A-5

    c. Group I-1

    d. Group U

Reference_____

6. Which of the following uses is typically considered a Group A-4 occupancy?

    a. restaurant with a dance floor   b. school library

    c. outdoor football stadium   d. indoor hockey arena

Reference_____

7. Which of the following uses is not considered a Group B occupancy?

    a. convenience store   b. motor vehicle showroom

    c. car wash   d. ambulatory care facility

Reference_____

8. The gaming floor of a large casino shall be classified as a Group _____ occupancy.

    a. A-2   b. A-3

    c. B   d. M

Reference_____

9. A Group _____ occupancy classification is to be assigned to a facility where combustible dusts are generated in a manner that creates a fire or explosion hazard.

    a. H-1   b. H-2

    c. H-4   d. H-5

Reference_____

10. Buildings containing materials that present a detonation hazard are typically considered _____ occupancies.

    a.   Group H-1   b.   Group H-2

    c.   Group H-3   d.   Group H-5

Reference_____

11. A foster-care facility providing care on a 24-hour basis to six or more infants/toddlers ($2^1/_2$ years of age or less) is classified as a Group _____ occupancy.

    a.   E   b.   I-1

    c.   I-2   d.   R-4

Reference_____

12. Prior to any permitted increases, the maximum allowable quantity per control area of a Class IB flammable liquid permitted in a storage condition in a one-story Group F-1 occupancy is _____ gallons.

    a.   15   b.   30

    c.   60   d.   120

Reference_____

13. A facility used for supervised custodial care and housing more than 16 persons in a supervised environment is classified as a Group _____ occupancy.

    a.   I-1   b.   I-4

    c.   R-3   d.   R-4

Reference_____

14. Which one of the following uses is not considered a Group M occupancy?

    a.   wholesale store   b.   retail sales room

    c.   motor vehicle showroom   d.   motor vehicle service station

Reference_____

15. A fraternity house with 40 occupants is considered a Group _____ occupancy.

    a. R-1   b. R-2

    c. R-3   d. R-4

Reference_____

16. Which one of the following facilities with 12 residents living in a supervised environment and receiving custodial care would not be considered a Group R-4 occupancy?

    a. halfway house   b. drug abuse center

    c. group home   d. detoxification facility

Reference_____

17. Which of the following uses is not considered a Group S-2 occupancy?

    a. open parking garage   b. enclosed parking garage

    c. dry cell battery storage   d. stable

Reference_____

18. A food processing establishment not associated with a restaurant or similar dining facility is classified as a Group B occupancy where it is a maximum of _____ square feet in floor area.

    a. 1,000   b. 1,500

    c. 2,000   d. 2,500

Reference_____

19. A manufacturing facility utilizing highly toxic materials exceeding the maximum allowable quantities set forth in Table 307.1(2) is considered a _____ occupancy.

    a. Group F-1   b. Group F-2

    c. Group H-3   d. Group H-4

Reference_____

20. Aerosol product storage buildings shall be classified as Group _____ occupancies when constructed in accordance with the *International Fire Code*.

    a. H-2   b. H-3

    c. S-1   d. S-2

    Reference_____

21. Owner-occupied lodging houses are permitted to be constructed in accordance with the *International Residential Code* where there are a maximum of _____ guest rooms and _____ occupants.

    a. 5, 10   b. 6, 12

    c. 10, 16   d. 12, 20

    Reference _____

22. Where a training and skill development use not classified as a Group A occurs in other than a school or academic program, it is classified as a Group _____ occupancy.

    a. I-3   b. B

    c. E   d. M

    Reference _____

23. A congregate living facility (transient) with an occupant load of 8 persons is to be classified as a Group _____ occupancy.

    a. R-1   b. R-2

    c. R-3   d. R-4

    Reference _____

24. By definition, a transient residential dwelling unit or sleeping unit has a maximum occupancy period of _____ days.

    a. 14   b. 30

    c. 90   d. 180

    Reference _____

25. Unless protected by an automatic sprinkler system, what is the minimum required fire separation between a 350-square-foot laundry room and the manufacturing building it is incidental to?

    a.   no fire separation is required

    b.   1-hour fire partition

    c.   1-hour fire barrier and/or horizontal assembly

    d.   smoke barrier

    Reference_____

26. What minimum level of incidental use protection is required for an incinerator room located in a manufacturing facility?

    a.   1-hour fire partition only

    b.   automatic sprinkler system only

    c.   1-hour fire barrier and an automatic sprinkler system

    d.   separation of two hours and an automatic sprinkler system

    Reference_____

27. What minimum level of incidental use protection is required for a chemistry laboratory/classroom in a high school?

    a.   1-hour fire barrier/horizontal assembly only

    b.   automatic sprinkler system only

    c.   both a 1-hour fire barrier/horizontal assembly and an automatic sprinkler system

    d.   either a 1-hour fire barrier/horizontal assembly or an automatic sprinkler system

    Reference_____

28. Where an automatic sprinkler system without a fire barrier is utilized for the protection of incidental use areas, what minimum level of separation is required?

    a.   1-hour fire partition

    b.   nonrated smoke partition

    c.   1-hour smoke barrier walls and horizontal assemblies

    d.   construction capable of resisting the passage of smoke

    Reference_____

29. Aggregate accessory occupancies are limited to a maximum floor area of
_____ of the area of the story in which they are located.

a. 10 percent   b. 15 percent

c. 25 percent   d. 33 percent

Reference_____

30. Any accessory occupancy area classified as a Group _____ occupancy
must always be separated by a fire barrier and/or horizontal assembly from other
occupancies in the building.

a. A-2   b. E

c. H-3   d. I-1

Reference_____

31. Where the provisions for nonseparated occupancies are used for a mixed-occupancy
building, the most restrictive _____ requirements shall apply to the nonseparated uses.

a. Chapter 9 (fire protection)   b. Chapter 10 (means of egress)

c. Chapter 11 (accessibility)   d. Chapter 8 (interior finish)

Reference_____

32. Where the provisions for separated occupancies are used for a nonsprinklered mixed-
occupancy building, the minimum separation between a Group A-2 and Group B
occupancy shall be a _____ .

a. 1-hour fire partition

b. 1-hour fire barrier/horizontal assembly

c. 2-hour fire barrier/horizontal assembly

d. 2-hour fire wall

Reference_____

33. Where the provisions for separated occupancies are used for a sprinklered mixed-occupancy building, the minimum separation between a Group H-2 and Group F-1 occupancy shall be a _____ .

    a. 1-hour fire partition

    b. 1-hour fire barrier/horizontal assembly

    c. 2-hour fire barrier/horizontal assembly

    d. 2-hour fire wall

Reference_____

34. Where the provisions for separated occupancies are utilized for a fully sprinklered building housing both a Group A-2 occupancy and a Group R-1 occupancy, the minimum required separation between the two occupancies shall be a _____ .

    a. 1-hour fire partition

    b. 1-hour fire barrier/horizontal assembly

    c. 2-hour fire barrier/horizontal assembly

    d. 2-hour fire wall

Reference_____

35. Under the provisions for separated occupancies, what is the minimum hourly fire-resistance-rated separation required between a Group F-1 occupancy and a Group S-1 occupancy where located in a nonsprinklered building?

    a. 0 hours (no separation requirement)

    b. 1-hour

    c. 2-hour

    d. 3-hour

Reference _____

36. Buildings used for the storage of beverages having an alcohol content over 16 percent are to be classified as Group _____ occupancies.

    a. H-2   b. H-3

    c. S-1   d. S-2

Reference _____

37. Fences are to be classified as a Group U occupancy where more than _____ feet in height.

    a.   4   b.   5

    c.   6   d.   7

Reference _____

38. Where mass timber elements serve as fire barriers used as incidental use separations in Type IV-B buildings, gypsum board used as a thermal barrier on the side of the incidental use shall be minimum _____.

    a. $^1/_2$-inch   b. $^1/_2$-inch Type X

    c. $^5/_8$-inch   d. $^5/_8$-inch Type X

Reference _____

39. In the determination of allowable building area for a mixed occupancy building, the _____ occupancies method requires the sum of the ratios of the actual building area of each occupancy divided by the allowable building area of each occupancy to be not greater than 1.0.

    a.   accessory   b.   incidental

    c.   nonseparated   d.   separated

Reference _____

40. Live/work units are to be classified as _____ occupancies.

    a.   Group B   b.   Group R-2

    c.   accessory   d.   mixed

Reference _____

2021 IBC Chapter 6
Types of Construction

OBJECTIVE: To gain an understanding of how a building is classified as a specific type of construction, based on the construction materials and the various building elements' resistance to fire.

REFERENCE: Chapter 6, 2021 *International Building Code*

KEY POINTS:
- What do the various types of construction indicate?
- How are the required fire-resistance ratings of building elements determined?
- Which types of materials are required to be used as building elements of a Type I or II building?
- How do the two different categories of Type I construction differ in fire protection? Type II construction?
- Which types of materials are required for use in the exterior walls of a Type III structure? In the interior building elements?
- What is considered as mass timber construction? How is noncombustible protection used in mass timber construction?
- What are the key elements of buildings classified as Type IV-A construction? Type IV-B? Type IV-C?
- What materials of construction are generally permitted in mass timber buildings? Under what conditions must mass timber elements be protected in buildings of Type IV-A construction? Type IV-B? Type IV-C?
- How are concealed spaces regulated in Type IV buildings?
- How shall exterior walls in Type IV-HT buildings be constructed? Interior building elements?
- What are the minimum construction details for columns used in a building of Type IV-HT construction?
- In Type IV-HT buildings, what is the minimum size of heavy-timber members used in the floor and roof framing? Floors? Roofs? Partitions?

- Where the minimum dimensions for Type IV-HT solid sawn members are prescribed, how are the equivalent sizes established for glued laminated members?

- Which requirements apply to cross-laminated timber used as a Type IV-HT member?

- Type V buildings may be constructed of which building materials?

- How does a Type VA building differ from a Type VB building?

- In noncombustible Type I and II buildings, where may fire-retardant-treated wood be used?

- Which specific allowances are provided for combustible materials in Type I and Type II buildings?

- What are the limitations for the use of fire-retardant-treated wood in the roof construction of noncombustible buildings? In nonbearing partitions? In nonbearing exterior walls?

- Which building elements are considered primary structural frame elements for the determination of fire resistance? Secondary members?

- When are bracing members considered part of the structural frame?

- Under which conditions may the required fire resistance of roof supports be reduced?

- At what height may the required fire resistance of roof construction be eliminated? In which occupancies is the elimination not applicable?

- For which building elements are Type IV-HT members and 1-hour fire-resistance-rated construction interchangeable?

- Does a sprinkler system affect a building's type of construction classification?

- How are interior nonbearing walls regulated for fire resistance based on construction type? Exterior nonbearing walls?

Code Text: *Buildings and structures erected or to be erected, altered or extended in height or area shall be classified in one of the five construction types defined in Sections 602.2 through 602.5.*

Discussion and Commentary: There are two major groupings based on the construction materials: noncombustible construction (Types I and II) and noncombustible or combustible construction (Types III, IV and V). These groupings are divided into two more general categories: protected, where the major structural elements are provided with some degree of fire resistance, and unprotected, where no fire protection of the building elements is typically mandated. Protected construction is further distinguished in Type I buildings where the required protection for many structural elements exceeds a 1-hour fire-resistance rating.

Noncombustible	Exterior and interior (bearing or nonbearing) walls, floors, roofs and structural elements are to be of noncombustible materials	I	A	B		
		II	A	B		
Noncombustible or combustible	Exterior walls are to be of noncombustible materials	III	A	B		
		IV	A	B	C	HT
		V	A	B		

It is the intent of the *International Building Code* that each building be classified as a single type of construction. The construction materials and the degree to which such materials are protected determine the classification based on the criteria of Table 601 and Chapter 6.

Code Text: *Types I and II construction are those types of construction in which the building elements listed in Table 601 are of noncombustible materials, except as permitted in Section 603 and elsewhere in the IBC.*

Discussion and Commentary: Type I buildings are noncombustible, and the building elements are also provided with a mandated degree of fire resistance. This type of construction requires the highest level of fire protection specified in the code. Type II buildings are also of noncombustible construction; however, the level of fire resistance is usually less than that required for Type I structures. Buildings of Type II construction may have a limited degree of fire resistance (Type IIA) or no fire resistance whatsoever (Type IIB). There are limited allowances for the use of fire-retardant-treated wood in nonbearing partitions, nonbearing exterior walls and roof construction.

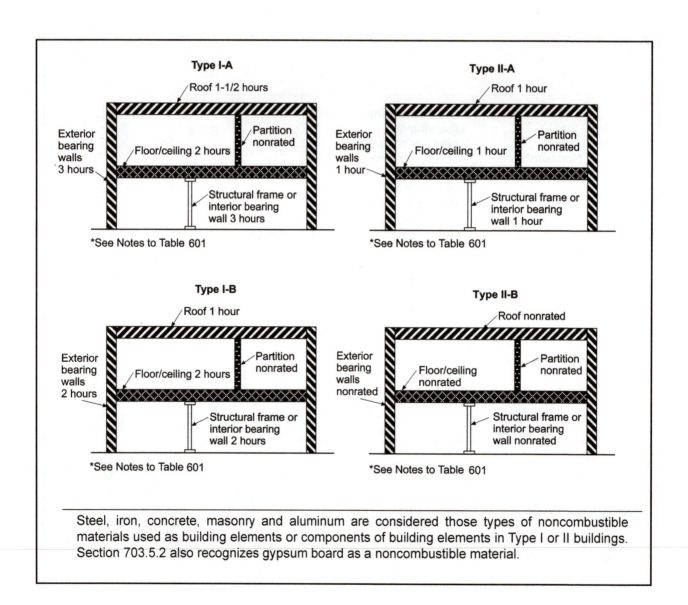

Steel, iron, concrete, masonry and aluminum are considered those types of noncombustible materials used as building elements or components of building elements in Type I or II buildings. Section 703.5.2 also recognizes gypsum board as a noncombustible material.

Code Text: *Type III construction is that type of construction in which the exterior walls are of non-combustible materials and the interior building elements are of any material permitted by the IBC. Fire-retardant-treated wood framing and sheathing complying with Section 2303.2 shall be permitted within exterior wall assemblies of a 2-hour rating or less.*

Discussion and Commentary: Type III buildings are considered combustible buildings and are either protected or unprotected. This building type was developed out of the necessity to prevent conflagrations in heavily built-up areas where buildings were erected side-by-side in congested downtown business districts. To limit the spread of fire from building to building, exterior walls were required to be of both noncombustible and fire-resistant construction.

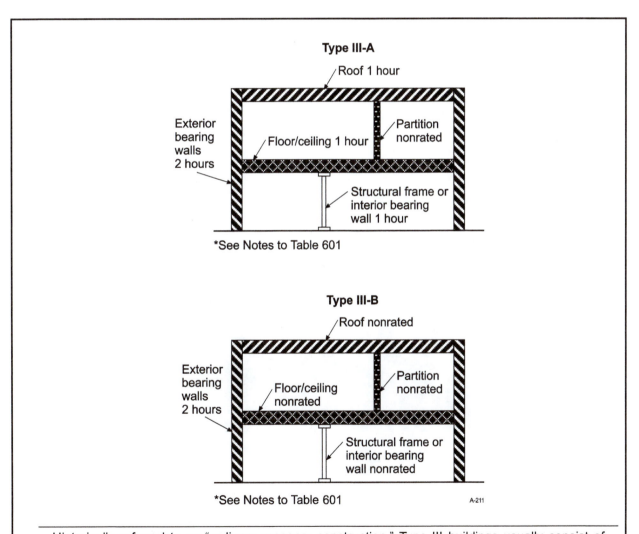

Historically referred to as "ordinary masonry construction," Type III buildings usually consist of concrete or masonry exterior walls with wood floor and roof systems. However, the IBC permits such walls to contain fire-retardant-treated wood as an element of the exterior wall construction.

Code Text: *Type IV construction is that type of construction in which the building elements are mass timber or noncombustible materials and have fire-resistance ratings in accordance with Table 601. Mass timber elements shall meet the fire-resistance rating requirements of Section 602.4 based on either the fire-resistance rating of the noncombustible protection, the mass timber, or a combination of both and shall be determined in accordance with Section 703.2.*

Discussion and Commentary: Mass timber is defined as those *structural elements of Type IV construction primarily of solid, built-up, panelized or engineered wood products that meet minimum cross-section dimensions of Type IV construction.* The term "mass timber" represents the large wood building elements permitted for heavy timber (Type IV-HT) construction and is deemed to meet fire-resistance requirements based solely on the required minimum dimensions of the wood element. It also represents construction Types IV-A, IV-B and IV-C, which are required to have a fire-resistance rating, in many cases provided by both the mass timber element itself and noncombustible protection applied to the mass timber element.

While mass timber can be fully exposed in Type IV-C construction and partially exposed in Type IV-B construction, it must in other cases be protected with a noncombustible material, such as gypsum board. It must also have a protection time assigned based on testing that is prescribed elsewhere in the code.

Code Text: *The outside face of exterior walls of mass timber construction shall be protect with non-combustible protection with a minimum assigned time of 40 minutes, as specified in Table 722.7.1(1). Interior faces of all mass timber elements, including the inside faces of exterior mass timber walls and mass timber roofs, shall be protected with materials complying with Section 703.3. The floor assembly shall contain a noncombustible materials not less than 1 inch (25 mm) in thickness above the mass timber. The interior surfaces of roof assemblies shall be protected in accordance with Section 602.4.1.2 (consistent with protection of interior walls).*

Discussion and Commentary: Type IV-A construction is composed of mass timber elements that are completely protected with noncombustible materials. The contribution of the noncombustible protection to the overall fire-resistance rating of a mass timber member or assembly is established through a performance path set forth in Section 703.6. In addition, noncombustible assemblies such as those of light-gage steel are also permitted. However, light-frame combustible assemblies, including those consisting of wood studs, joists or furring, are specifically prohibited.

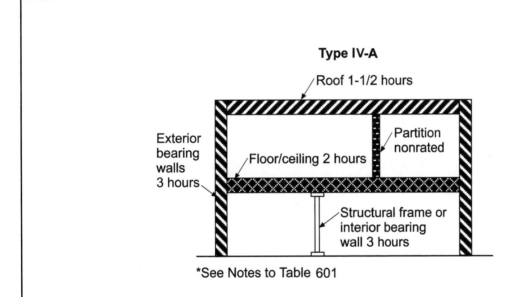

Type IV-A

Roof 1-1/2 hours

Exterior bearing walls 3 hours

Floor/ceiling 2 hours

Partition nonrated

Structural frame or interior bearing wall 3 hours

*See Notes to Table 601

Construction adhesive or other sealant is required at joint and intersections to prevent air flow. Where a wall or horizontal assembly serves as the separation between two atmospheres, it is necessary to properly seal any voids that could serve as a conduit for air movement during a fire.

Code Text: *In Type IV-B construction, interior faces of all mass timber elements, including the inside face of exterior mass timber walls and mass timber roofs, shall be protected, as required by Section 602.4.2.2, with materials complying with Section 707.3. Unprotected portions of mass timber ceilings and walls are permitted when complying with Section 602.4.2.2.4 (separation distance between unprotected mass timber elements) and the following: [see allowances for unprotected portions of mass timber ceilings (limited to 20 percent of floor area in any dwelling unit or fire area) and mass timber walls (limited to 40 percent of floor area in any dwelling unit or fire area)]. In Type IV-C construction, mass timber elements (interior walls, ceilings, columns and beams) are permitted to be unprotected.*

Discussion and Commentary: Type IV-B construction permits portions of interior mass timber surfaces to be exposed. The amount of exposed surface permitted, as well as the required separation between unprotected portions, is regulated to limit potential contribution of the structure to an interior fire. Type IV-C construction permits fully exposed mass timber on the interior of the building except in specific areas such as concealed spaces, shafts, elevator hoistways and interior exit stairway enclosures.

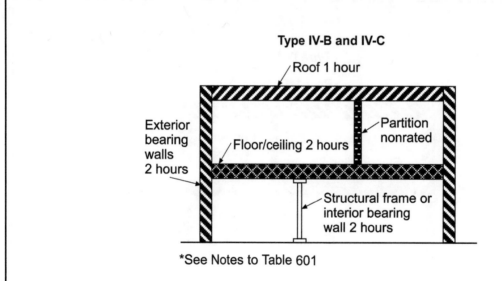

Type IV-B and IV-C

Roof 1 hour

Exterior bearing walls 2 hours

Floor/ceiling 2 hours

Partition nonrated

Structural frame or interior bearing wall 2 hours

*See Notes to Table 601

Exterior walls are required to be protected in the same manner for Types IV-A, IV-B and IV-C construction, which requires noncombustible protection of at least 40 minutes on the exterior side of exterior mass timber walls and prohibits all combustible materials on the exterior side of mass timber walls other than the water-resistive barrier.

Code Text: *Type IV-HT (Heavy Timber) construction is that type of construction in which the exterior walls are of noncombustible materials and the interior building elements are of solid wood, laminated heavy timber or structural composite lumber (SCL), without concealed spaces or with concealed spaces complying with Section 602.4.4.3. The minimum dimensions for permitted materials shall comply with the provisions of Section 602.3.3 and Section 2304.11. Exterior walls complying with Section 602.4.4.1 or 602.4.4.2 shall be permitted. Interior walls and partitions not less than 1-hour fire-resistance rated or heavy timber conforming to Section 2304.11.2.2 shall be permitted.*

Discussion and Commentary: Historically referred to as "heavy-timber," buildings of Type IV-HT construction are essentially Type III buildings with an interior of wood members of significant mass. To conform to Type IV-HT construction, building members must be of substantial thickness. Given the characteristics of massive wood members, there is little chance for sudden structural collapse during or after a fire.

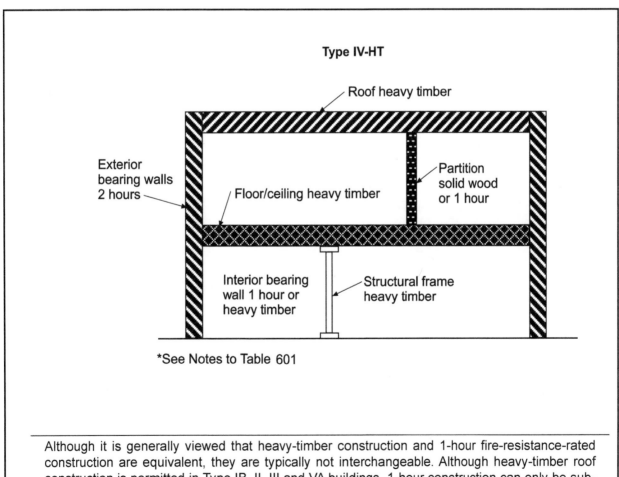

Type IV-HT

Roof heavy timber

Exterior bearing walls 2 hours

Floor/ceiling heavy timber

Partition solid wood or 1 hour

Interior bearing wall 1 hour or heavy timber

Structural frame heavy timber

*See Notes to Table 601

Although it is generally viewed that heavy-timber construction and 1-hour fire-resistance-rated construction are equivalent, they are typically not interchangeable. Although heavy-timber roof construction is permitted in Type IB, II, III and VA buildings, 1-hour construction can only be substituted for heavy-timber construction in interior bearing walls of Type IV buildings.

Code Text: *Where a structure, portion thereof or individual structural elements are required by provisions of the IBC to be of heavy timber, the building elements therein shall comply with the applicable provisions of Sections 2304.11.1 through 2304.11.4. Minimum dimensions of heavy timber shall comply with the applicable requirements in Table 2304.11 based on roofs or floors supported and the configuration of each structural element, or in Sections 2304.11.2 through 2304.11.4.*

Discussion and Commentary: Solid-sawn wood members, glued-laminated timbers and structural composite lumber are manufactured with different methods and procedures: therefore, they do not have the same dimensions. However, they both have the same inherent fire-resistive capability that has been long recognized in the code.

TABLE 2304.11
MINIMUM DIMENSIONS OF HEAVY TIMBER STRUCTURAL MEMBERS

SUPPORTING	HEAVY TIMBER STRUCTURAL ELEMENTS	MINIMUM NOMINAL SOLID SAWN SIZE		MINIMUM GLUED-LAMINATED NET SIZE		MINIMUM STRUCTURAL COMPOSITE LUMBER NET SIZE	
		Width, inch	Depth, inch	Width, inch	Depth, inch	Width, inch	Depth, inch
Floor loads only or combined floor and roof loads	Columns; Framed sawn or glued-laminated timber arches that spring from the floor line; Framed timber trusses	8	8	$6^3/_4$	$8^1/_4$	7	$7^1/_2$
	Wood beams and girders	6	10	5	$10^1/_2$	$5^1/_4$	$9^1/_2$
Roof loads only	Columns (roof and ceiling loads); Lower half of: wood-frame or glued-laminated arches that spring from the floor line or from grade	6	8	5	$8^1/_4$	$5^1/_4$	$7^1/_2$
	Upper half of: wood-frame or glued-laminated arches that spring from the floor line or from grade	6	6	5	6	$5^1/_4$	$5^1/_2$
	Framed timber trusses and other roof framing; [a] Framed or glued-laminated arches that spring from the top of walls or wall abutments	4^b	6	3^b	$6^7/_8$	$3^1/_2$[b]	$5^1/_2$

For SI: 1 inch = 25.4 mm.

a. Spaced members shall be permitted to be composed of two or more pieces not less than 3 inches nominal in thickness where blocked solidly throughout their intervening spaces or where spaces are tightly closed by a continuous wood cover plate of not less than 2 inches nominal in thickness secured to the underside of the members. Splice plates shall be not less than 3 inches nominal in thickness.

b. Where protected by approved automatic sprinklers under the roof deck, framing members shall be not less than 3 inches nominal in width.

Table 2304.11 in the IBC, which sets forth the minimum net sizes for glued-laminated members necessary to comply as Type IV construction elements, also identifies the minimum net sizes for structural composite lumber (SCL).

Topic: Cross-Laminated Timber	**Category:** Types of Construction
Reference: IBC 602.4.4.2, 2304.11.3.1	**Subject:** Type IV Construction

Code Text: *Cross-laminated timber (CLT) not less than 4 inches (102 mm) in thickness complying with Section 2303.1.4 shall be permitted within exterior wall assemblies with a 2-hour rating or less,* provided *the exterior surface of the cross-laminated timber and heavy timber elements are protected by (1) fire-retardant-treated wood not less than $^{15}/_{32}$ inch (12 mm) thick, (2) gypsum board not less than $^{1}/_{2}$ inch (12.7 mm) thick, or (3) a noncombustible material. Cross-laminated timber floors shall be not less than 4 inches (102 mm) in actual thickness. Cross-laminated timber roofs shall be not less than 3 inches (76 mm) nominal in thickness.*

Discussion and Commentary: Cross-laminated timber (CLT) is a prefabricated engineered wood product consisting of not less than three layers of solid-sawn lumber or structural composite lumber where the adjacent layers are cross oriented and bonded with structural adhesive to form a solid wood element. First developed in Europe, CLT has been used extensively there for a large section of structural lumber. When of the specified size, it is considered as Type IV heavy-timber construction.

Cross-laminated timber floors regulated as Type IV heavy-timber construction must be continuous from support to support and mechanically fastened to one another. Unlike sawn or glued-laminated plank floors, CLT is permitted to be connected to walls without a shrinkage gap if swelling or shrinking is considered in the design.

Code Text: *Type V construction is that type of construction in which the structural elements, exterior walls and interior walls are of any materials permitted by the IBC.*

Discussion and Commentary: Type V buildings are essentially construction systems that will not fit into any of the other higher types of construction specified by the IBC. Although the construction normally considered Type V is the conventional light-frame wood building, any combination of approved materials can be considered Type V construction. Section 602.1.1 indicates that a building is not required to conform to the details of a type of construction higher than the type that meets the minimum requirements based on occupancy, even though certain features of such a building actually conform to a higher construction type.

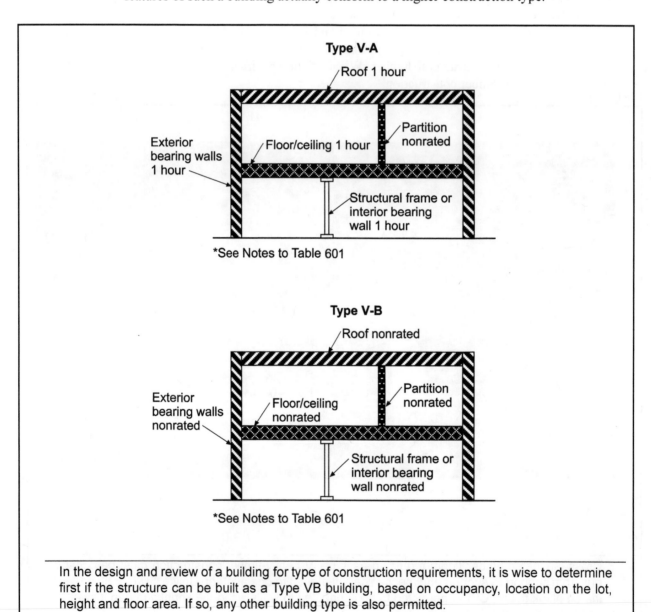

In the design and review of a building for type of construction requirements, it is wise to determine first if the structure can be built as a Type VB building, based on occupancy, location on the lot, height and floor area. If so, any other building type is also permitted.

Code Text: *The building elements shall have a fire-resistance rating not less than that specified in Table 601. The protection of openings, ducts and air transfer openings in building elements shall not be required unless required by other provisions of the IBC.*

Discussion and Commentary: The building elements regulated by Table 601 for types of construction include primary structural frame members, such as columns, girders and trusses; bearing walls, both interior and exterior; floor construction, including supporting beams and joists; and roof construction, consisting of supporting beams, joists, rafters and other members. The required fire-resistance rating for each of these elements is based on the specific type of construction assigned to the building. The required fire-resistance rating can be as high as a 3-hour or as little as a 0-hour (no fire-resistance rating required).

TABLE 601
FIRE-RESISTANCE RATING REQUIREMENTS FOR BUILDING ELEMENTS (HOURS)

BUILDING ELEMENT	TYPE I		TYPE II		TYPE III		TYPE IV				TYPE V	
	A	B	A	B	A	B	A	B	C	HT	A	B
Primary structural frame[f] (see Section 202)	$3^{a,b}$	$2^{a,b,c}$	$1^{b,c}$	0^c	$1^{b,c}$	0	3^a	2^a	2^a	HT	$1^{b,c}$	0
Bearing walls												
Exterior[e,f]	3	2	1	0	2	2	3	2	2	2	1	0
Interior	3^a	2^a	1	0	1	0	3	2	2	$1/HT^g$	1	0
Nonbearing walls and partitions Exterior	See Table 705.5											
Nonbearing walls and partitions Interior[d]	0	0	0	0	0	0	0	0	0	See Section 2304.11.2	0	0
Floor construction and associated secondary structural members (see Section 202)	2	2	1	0	1	0	2	2	2	HT	1	0
Roof construction and associated secondary structural members (see Section 202)	$1^1/_2{}^b$	$1^{b,c}$	$1^{b,c}$	0^c	$1^{b,c}$	0	$1^1/_2$	1	1	HT	$1^{b,c}$	0

For SI: 1 foot = 304.8 mm.

a. Roof supports: Fire-resistance ratings of primary structural frame and bearing walls are permitted to be reduced by 1 hour where supporting a roof only.

b. Except in Group F-1, H, M and S-1 occupancies, fire protection of structural members in roof construction shall not be required, including protection of primary structural frame members, roof framing and decking where every part of the roof construction is 20 feet or more above any floor immediately below. Fire-retardant-treated wood members shall be allowed to be used for such unprotected members.

c. In all occupancies, heavy timber complying with Section 2304.11 shall be allowed for roof construction, including primary structural frame members, where a 1-hour or less fire-resistance rating is required.

d. Not less than the fire-resistance rating required by other sections of this code.

e. Not less than the fire-resistance rating based on fire separation distance (see Table 705.5).

f. Not less than the fire-resistance rating as referenced in Section 704.10.

g. Heavy timber bearing walls supporting more than two floors or more than a floor and a roof shall have a fire resistance rating of not less than 1 hour.

Where a structure is separated by one or more fire walls, the code treats those individual compartments created by the fire walls as separate buildings for the purpose of classification by type of construction.

Code Text: *The primary structural frame shall include all of the following structural members: (1) the columns; (2) structural members having direct connections to the columns, including girders, beams, trusses and spandrels; (3) members of the floor construction and roof construction having direct connections to the columns; and (4) members that are essential to the vertical stability of the primary structural frame under gravity loading.*

Discussion and Commentary: To maintain stability of the building as a whole, the major structural elements are regulated for endurance when subjected to a fire. In addition to the columns, beams and girders, both interior bearing walls and exterior bearing walls are regulated to a level of fire resistance equal to or greater than that of other structural elements. Secondary members, such as floor joists, roof joists or rafters, are protected within the rated floor-ceiling or roof-ceiling assemblies.

Primary Structural Frame Considered to be

- **Columns**

- **Girders**

- **Beams**

- **Trusses**

- **Spandrels**

- **Floor Construction**

- **Roof Construction**

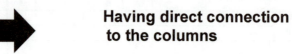

Having direct connection to the columns

- **Members essential to vertical stability of primary structural frame under gravity loading**

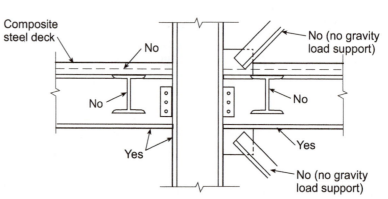

Components of primary structural frame

Lateral force bracing is not considered part of the structural frame where it serves no other purpose than to resist the lateral loads. For example, lateral load bracing within exterior nonbearing walls or interior partitions would be protected by the wall or partition construction. Such bracing elements would be considered secondary members.

Topic: Roof Construction

Category: Types of Construction

Reference: IBC Table 601, Note b

Subject: Building Elements

Code Text: *Except in Group F-1, H, M and S-1 occupancies, fire protection of structural members shall not be required, including protection of primary structural frame members, roof framing and decking, where every part of the roof construction is 20 feet or more above any floor immediately below. Fire-retardant-treated wood members shall be allowed to be used for such unprotected members.*

Discussion and Commentary: Where there is limited potential for a fire to be of a severe nature at the roof structure due to its height above the floor below, an elimination of the required fire-resistance rating of the roof construction is permitted in construction of Types I, IIA, IIIA and VA. Elimination of the required fire resistance is not allowed where combustible or hazardous materials are located adjacent to the roof.

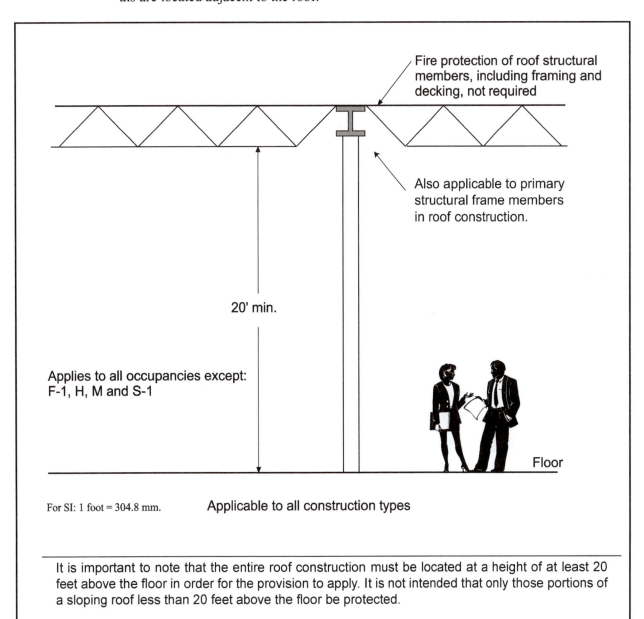

Fire protection of roof structural members, including framing and decking, not required

Also applicable to primary structural frame members in roof construction.

20' min.

Applies to all occupancies except:
F-1, H, M and S-1

Floor

For SI: 1 foot = 304.8 mm.   Applicable to all construction types

It is important to note that the entire roof construction must be located at a height of at least 20 feet above the floor in order for the provision to apply. It is not intended that only those portions of a sloping roof less than 20 feet above the floor be protected.

Code Text: *Combustible materials shall be permitted in buildings of Type I and II construction in the following applications:* (27 applications listed).

Discussion and Commentary: Materials used in the construction of buildings classified as either Type I or Type II are intended to be noncombustible, thereby not increasing the potential fire loading (fuel contribution). There are, however, a number of applications where the presence of combustible building materials is desirable in otherwise noncombustible structures. Such materials are typically permitted where they are adequately protected, limited in use or amount, or installed in accordance with the *International Fire Code, International Mechanical Code*®, or other provisions of the *International Building Code.*

Combustible materials permitted in buildings of Type I and Type II construction in the following applications:

- Fire-retardant-treated wood in

    – Roof construction of most buildings.

    – Nonbearing partitions with fire-resistance rating ≤ 2 hours.

    – Nonbearing exterior walls requiring no fire rating.

- Thermal and acoustical insulation with limited flame spread.

- Foam plastics per Chapter 26.

- A, B or C roof coverings.

- Interior floor finish, trim, millwork such as, doors, frames, etc.

- Stages and platforms per Section 410.

- Blocking for handrails, fixtures, windows and door frames, etc.

- Light-transmitting plastics per Chapter 26.

- Nailing or furring strips per Section 803.15.

- Heavy timber for specific components.

- Additional applications as specified.

In Type I and II construction, the use of fire-retardant-treated wood is permitted in roof construction of all Type IB and II buildings and those buildings of Type IA construction that do not exceed two stories or have a top-story height of at least 20 feet.

Code Text: *Combustible materials shall be permitted in buildings of Type I or II construction in accordance with Sections 603.1.1 through 603.1.3. The use of nonmetallic ducts shall be permitted when installed in accordance with the limitations of the* International Mechanical Code. *The use of combustible piping materials shall be permitted when installed in accordance with the limitations of the* International Mechanical Code *and the* International Plumbing Code®. *The use of electrical wiring methods with combustible insulation, tubing, raceways and related components shall be permitted when installed in accordance with the limitations of the IBC.*

Discussion and Commentary: The IMC contains requirements for nonmetallic ducts that address the issues of flammability, flame spread and smoke development. The IPC regulates the use of combustible piping materials, such as plastic, and also addresses those same characteristics applicable to nonmetallic ducts. Similar regulations apply to combustible wiring materials. These provisions in Chapter 6 clarify that such combustible materials are acceptable for installation in buildings of Type I and II construction, provided they meet the limitations set forth in the appropriate code.

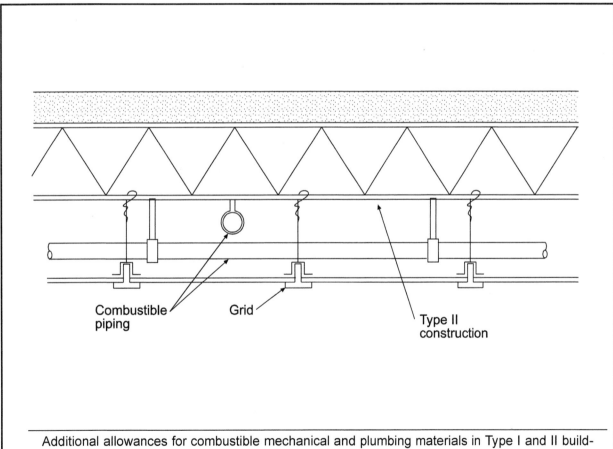

Combustible piping   Grid   Type II construction

Additional allowances for combustible mechanical and plumbing materials in Type I and II buildings are established by Exception 24 of Section 603. Specified combustible materials are permitted in concealed spaces under the provisions of Section 718.5.

Quiz

Study Session 3

IBC Chapter 6

1. What types of construction are considered "noncombustible"?

    a. I, II   b. I, II, III, IV

    c. III, IV   d. III, IV, V

    Reference_____

2. Type III buildings are constructed with _____ or fire-retardant-treated wood exterior walls and interior elements _____.

    a. fire-resistant, of noncombustible materials

    b. noncombustible, of noncombustible materials

    c. noncombustible, of any material permitted by the code

    d. fire-resistant, of any material permitted by the code

    Reference_____

3. The type of construction where building elements are mass timber or noncombustible is _____.

    a. Type I   b. Type II

    c. Type III   d. Type IV

    Reference_____

4. In buildings of Type III construction, under what condition is fire-retardant-treated wood framing permitted within an exterior wall assembly?

    a. the wall has a 2-hour rating or less

    b. the fire separation distance exceeds 10 feet

    c. wood columns of heavy-timber sizes are used

    d. the wall is a nonbearing element

    Reference_____

5. Where supporting floor loads, solid sawn wood columns of Type IV-HT construction shall be of what minimum nominal size?

    a. 5 inches by 5 inches   b. 6 inches by 6 inches

    c. 6 inches by 8 inches   d. 8 inches by 8 inches

    Reference_____

6. Where used in floor framing, solid sawn wood beams of Type IV-HT construction shall be of what minimum nominal size?

    a. 4 inches by 8 inches   b. 4 inches by 10 inches

    c. 6 inches by 10 inches   d. 8 inches by 10 inches

    Reference_____

7. Combustible concealed spaces in buildings of Type _____ construction must be protected.

    a. I   b. III

    c. IV   d. V

    Reference_____

8. Which of the following materials is permitted in a building of Type VB construction?

    a. wood   b. steel

    c. masonry   d. all of the above

    Reference_____

9. In a building of Type IB construction, what is the minimum required fire-resistance rating of the floor construction?

    a. 3 hours   b. 2 hours

    c. 1 hour   d. 0 hours (no rating required)

    Reference_____

10. Which one of the following members is not considered to be a part of the primary structural frame?

    a. columns supporting only a roof load

    b. girders supporting no more than a floor and a roof

    c. members essential to the vertical stability of the frame under gravity loads

    d. floor joists not having direct connections to the columns

    Reference_____

11. In a building of Type IIB construction, what is the minimum required fire-resistance rating of the roof construction?

    a.   0 hours (no rating required)   b.   1 hour

    c. $1^1/_2$ hours   d.   2 hours

Reference_____

12. In a building of Type VA construction, which of the following building elements does not require a minimum 1-hour fire-resistance rating?

    a.   primary structural frame   b.   exterior bearing wall

    c.   interior nonbearing wall   d.   roof construction

Reference_____

13. In a one-story Type IA building, what is the minimum required fire-resistance rating for the interior bearing walls supporting the roof only?

    a.   3 hours   b.   2 hours

    c. $1^1/_2$ hours   d.   1 hour

Reference_____

14. In Type IA buildings limited to two stories in height, what building element is permitted to be constructed of fire-retardant-treated wood?

    a.   structural frame   b.   bearing walls

    c.   floor construction   d.   roof construction

Reference_____

15. In a Type IB building housing a Group A-4 occupancy, fire protection of the roof structural members, framing and decking is not required where every portion of the roof construction is a minimum of _____ feet above the floor below.

    a.   18   b.   20

    c.   25   d.   35

Reference_____

16. What is the minimum required fire-resistance rating for interior bearing walls in a building of Type IV-A construction?

    a. 3 hours   b. 2 hours

    c. 1 hour   d. 0 hours (no rating required)

Reference_____

17. Complying heavy-timber columns and arches are permitted to be used externally where a minimum _____-foot horizontal separation is provided.

    a. 5   b. 10

    c. 20   d. 30

Reference_____

18. In a Type IIIA building housing a Group A-1 occupancy, what is the minimum required rating for an exterior bearing wall located with a fire separation distance of 10 feet?

    a. 3 hours   b. 2 hours

    c. 1 hour   d. 0 hours (no rating required)

Reference_____

19. In a Type VB building housing a Group B occupancy, what is the minimum required rating for an exterior bearing wall located with a fire separation distance of 10 feet?

    a. 3 hours   b. 2 hours

    c. 1 hour   d. 0 hours (no rating required)

Reference_____

20. What is the minimum required fire-resistance rating for roof construction in a building of Type IA construction?

    a. 0 hours (no rating required) b. 1 hour

    c. $1^1/_2$ hours   d. 2 hours

Reference_____

21. In a building of Type I or II construction, nonbearing partitions having a maximum fire-resistance rating of _____ are permitted to be constructed of fire-retardant-treated wood.

    a.   0 hours (no rating required)   b.   1 hour

    c. $1^1/_2$ hours   d.   2 hours

Reference_____

22. When used in Type IV-HT floor construction, cross-laminated timber shall be a minimum of _____ inches in actual thickness.

    a.   3   b. $3^1/_2$

    c.   4   d. $4^1/_2$

Reference_____

23. In a building of Type I or II construction, nonbearing exterior walls having a maximum fire-resistance rating of _____ are permitted to be constructed of fire-retardant-treated wood.

    a.   0 hours (no rating required)   b.   1 hour

    c. $1^1/_2$ hours   d.   2 hours

Reference_____

24. Show windows may be of combustible construction in Type I and II construction where located a maximum of _____ above grade.

    a.   15 feet   b.   35 feet

    c.   one story   d.   three stories

Reference_____

25. Which type of roof covering is not permitted on an office building of Type IIB construction?

    a.   Class A   b.   Class B

    c.   Class C   d.   nonclassified

Reference_____

26. Which of the following methods of construction is not permitted for interior partitions in Type IV-HT structures?

    a. two layers of $^1/_2$-inch fire-retardant-treated structural wood panels

    b. 4 inches of laminated solid-wood construction

    c. two layers of 1-inch matched boards

    d. one-hour fire-resistance-rated construction

Reference_____

27. What is the minimum fire-resistive rating required for interior metal stud partitions in Type IIB construction?

    a. 0, no rating is required   b. 1 hour

    c. 2 hours   d. 3 hours

Reference_____

28. What is the minimum required vertical distance between the upper floor and the roof to allow the use of fire-retardant-treated wood in the roof construction of an eight-story Type IA building?

    a. 20 feet

    b. 25 feet

    c. there is no minimum distance required

    d. FRT wood is never permitted in such a case

Reference_____

29. For an office building of Type IB construction, what is the minimum required fire-resistance rating for an exterior bearing wall located on an interior lot line?

    a. 0, no rating is required   b. 1 hour

    c. 2 hours   d. 3 hours

Reference_____

30. In a building of Type IIA construction, heavy timber members may be used in lieu of one-hour fire-resistance-rated construction for which building element?

    a. structural frame members   b. interior bearing walls

    c. floor construction   d. roof construction

Reference_____

31. In a building of Type IV-HT construction, 1-hour combustible construction is permitted in lieu of heavy-timber construction for which of the following building elements?

    a.   floor construction
    b.   exterior bearing walls
    c.   interior bearing walls
    d.   roof construction

Reference _____

32. What is the minimum required fire-resistance rating for floor construction in a building of Type IV-C construction?

    a.   2 hours
    b. $1\frac{1}{2}$ hours
    c.   1 hour
    d.   0 hours (no rating required)

Reference _____

33. What is the minimum required fire-resistance rating for the floor construction in a Type IIIB building?

    a.   2 hours
    b. $1\frac{1}{2}$ hours
    c.   1 hour
    d.   0 hours (no rating required)

Reference _____

34. A glued-laminated beam, where utilized in a Type IV-HT building requiring a 6-inch by 10-inch solid-sawn member of nominal size, shall have a minimum net finished size of _____ .

    a. $5\frac{1}{4}$ inches by $9\frac{1}{4}$ inches
    b.   6 inches by 10 inches
    c. $6\frac{3}{4}$ inches by $10\frac{1}{2}$ inches
    d.   5 inches by $10\frac{1}{2}$ inches

Reference _____

35. Under general conditions, thermal and acoustical insulation other than foam plastic is permitted to be installed in buildings of Type I or II construction, provided the insulation has a maximum flame spread index of _____ .

    a.   25
    b.   75
    c.   200
    d.   450

Reference _____

36. In buildings of Type I and II construction, fire-retardant-treated wood may be used in the construction of balconies not used for egress purposes where the building is a maximum of _____ stories above grade plane.

    a. 6   b. 4

    c. 3   d. 2

Reference _____

37. In a building of Type IV-A construction, floor assemblies that contain mass timber elements shall include a minimum of _____ inch(es) of noncombustible material above the mass timber.

    a. $^5/_8$ b. $^3/_4$

    c. 1   d. $1^1/_2$

Reference _____

38. In an office building of Type IV-B construction, unprotected portions of mass timber walls shall be limited to a maximum area of _____ percent of the floor area in any fire area.

    a. 10   b. 20

    c. 25   d. 40

Reference _____

39. In Type IV-C construction, shafts shall be protected with noncombustible protection with a minimum assigned time of _____ minutes on both the inside and outside of the shaft.

    a. 0 (no protection required)   b. 30

    c. 40   d. 60

Reference _____

40. In a fully-sprinklered Type IIB building, freezer wall construction may be of combustible materials where the freezer is a maximum of _____ square feet in size and the walls are lined with noncombustible materials on both sides.

    a. 399   b. 999

    c. 1,499   d. 1,999

Reference _____

2021 IBC Chapter 5
General Building Heights and Areas

OBJECTIVE: To gain an understanding of how a building is classified and regulated based on its floor area, height and number of stories.

REFERENCE: Chapter 5, 2021 *International Building Code*

KEY POINTS:
- How and why must buildings be identified by their address?
- How is the maximum floor area of a building determined? The height in feet and number of stories?
- How must multiple buildings located on the same lot be handled?
- What types of special industrial occupancies are exempt from the height and area limitations of Sections 504 and 506?
- Under which conditions may the basic allowable height of a building be increased? How much of an increase is permitted?
- Which special provisions address the construction of towers, spires, steeples and other roof structures?
- What is a mezzanine?
- Under which conditions may a floor level be considered a mezzanine?
- Under what conditions is a mezzanine permitted to be enclosed or in some manner separated from the room in which it is located?
- Which conditions provide for an increase in the allowable floor areas specified in Table 506.2?
- What is the minimum width of a yard or public way that can provide for a floor area increase?
- How much of a building's perimeter must be considered "open" for the area increase to apply?
- How is a basement viewed in the calculation of maximum allowable floor area?
- How is the maximum total combined floor area for a multistory building determined?

- Which occupancy groups are eligible for unlimited floor area in a one-story nonsprinklered building?

- Which criteria must be met for buildings of Groups A-4, B, F, M or S to be unlimited in floor area? Groups A-1 and A-2?

- What is the minimum width required for open space surrounding an unlimited area building?

- Under which conditions may that width be reduced?

- Under what limitations is a Group A-3 occupancy permitted to be of unlimited area?

- How may high-hazard occupancies be accommodated in an unlimited area building?

- Which limitations are placed on motion picture theaters of unlimited area?

- Where the special provisions for a horizontal building separation allowance are applied, what criteria must be met?

- Which special provisions address the situation where an enclosed or open parking garage is located below another occupancy group? Below an open parking garage?

- What are the height limitations for apartment houses and other Group R-2 occupancies where the special provisions are met?

- How is an open parking garage regulated where located below Groups A, B, I, M or R?

Code Text: *New and existing buildings shall be provided with approved address identification. Each character shall be a minimum of 4 inches (102 mm) high with a minimum stroke width of $^1/_2$ inch (12.7 mm). Where required by the fire code official, address identification shall be provided in additional approved locations to facilitate emergency response. Where access is by means of a private road and the building address cannot be viewed from the public way, a monument, pole or other approved sign or means shall be used to identify the structure. Address identification shall be maintained.*

Discussion and Commentary: Buildings must be provided with plainly visible and legible address numbers posted on the building or in such a place on the property that the building may be identified by emergency services such as fire, medical and police.

As a fundamental requirement, the approved street numbers are to be placed in a location readily visible from the street fronting the property. The fire code official has the authority to require that the address numbers be posted in more than one location to help eliminate any confusion or delay in identifying the location of the emergency.

Code Text: Building area is *the area included within surrounding exterior walls (or exterior walls and fire walls) exclusive of vent shafts and courts. Areas of the building not provided with surrounding walls shall be included in the building area if such areas are included within the horizontal projection of the roof or floor above.*

Discussion and Commentary: The building area must be determined in order to verify that it does not exceed the maximum allowable area as determined by Section 503.1. The building area is considered, in very general terms, the "footprint" of the building, excluding those unroofed areas and any projections that may extend beyond the exterior walls. Where complying mezzanines are located within a building, they are not assumed to contribute to the building area.

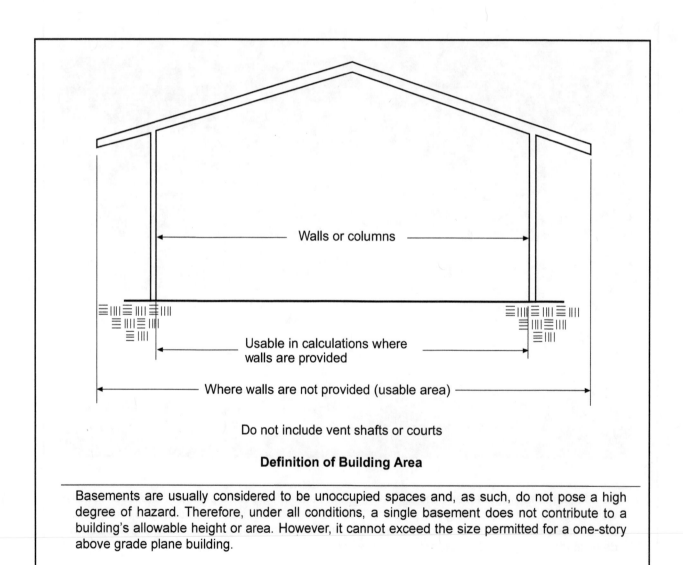

Walls or columns

Usable in calculations where walls are provided

Where walls are not provided (usable area)

Do not include vent shafts or courts

Definition of Building Area

Basements are usually considered to be unoccupied spaces and, as such, do not pose a high degree of hazard. Therefore, under all conditions, a single basement does not contribute to a building's allowable height or area. However, it cannot exceed the size permitted for a one-story above grade plane building.

Code Text: A "story above grade plane" is *any story having its finished floor surface entirely above grade plane, or in which the finished surface of the floor next above is (1) more than 6 feet (1829 mm) above grade plane, or (2) more than 12 feet (3658 mm) above the finished ground level at any point.* A "basement" is *a story that is not a story above grade plane.*

Discussion and Commentary: A number of provisions in the IBC are applicable based on the location of the floor under consideration, relative to the exterior ground level. Therefore, it is necessary to define specifically the circumstances under which a floor level is considered a story above grade plane.

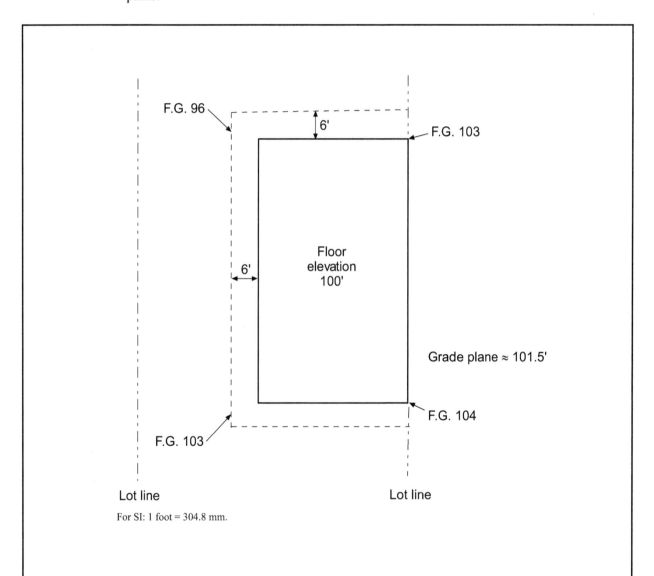

For SI: 1 foot = 304.8 mm.

The "grade plane" is defined as a reference plane representing the average of finished ground level adjoining the building at exterior walls. It is measured at the lowest point between the building and the lot line, though never more than 6 feet from the building.

Code Text: *Buildings and structures designed to house special industrial processes that require large areas and unusual building heights to accommodate craneways or special machinery and equipment, including among others, rolling mills; structural metal fabrication shops and foundries; or the production and distribution of electric, gas or steam power, shall be exempt from the building height, number of stories and building area limitations specified in Sections 504 and 506.*

Discussion and Commentary: A limited number of buildings that house special industrial processes need extensive heights and/or areas for their operations. The activities that occur are generally of moderate to low hazard, and the buildings are not typically accessible to the public. Therefore, it has been deemed appropriate that no type of construction limitations should be placed on these unique structures.

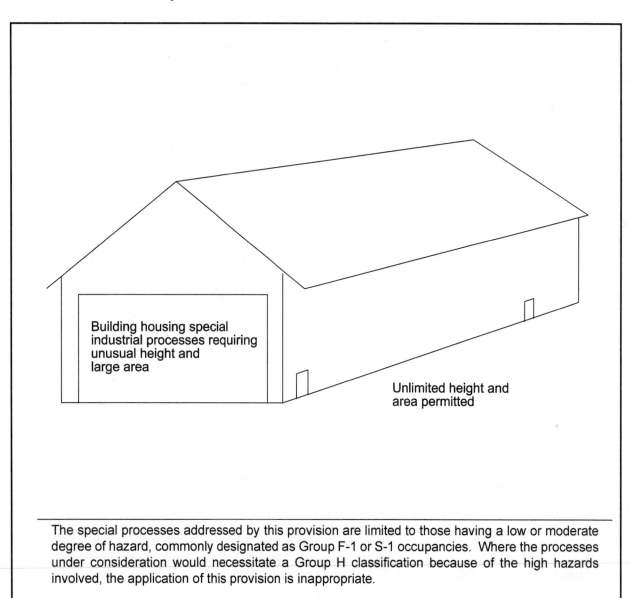

Building housing special industrial processes requiring unusual height and large area

Unlimited height and area permitted

The special processes addressed by this provision are limited to those having a low or moderate degree of hazard, commonly designated as Group F-1 or S-1 occupancies. Where the processes under consideration would necessitate a Group H classification because of the high hazards involved, the application of this provision is inappropriate.

Code Text: *Two or more buildings on the same lot shall be regulated as separate buildings or shall be considered as portions of one building where the building height, number of stories of each building and the aggregate building area of the buildings are within the limitations specified in Sections 504 and 506. The provisions of* the IBC *applicable to the aggregate building shall be applicable to each building.*

Discussion and Commentary: In general, the provisions of Section 705.3 require an assumed imaginary line to be located between two buildings on the same site to regulate exterior wall and opening protection, as well as projection and roof-covering requirements. This method would provide protection equivalent to that of buildings on adjoining lots.

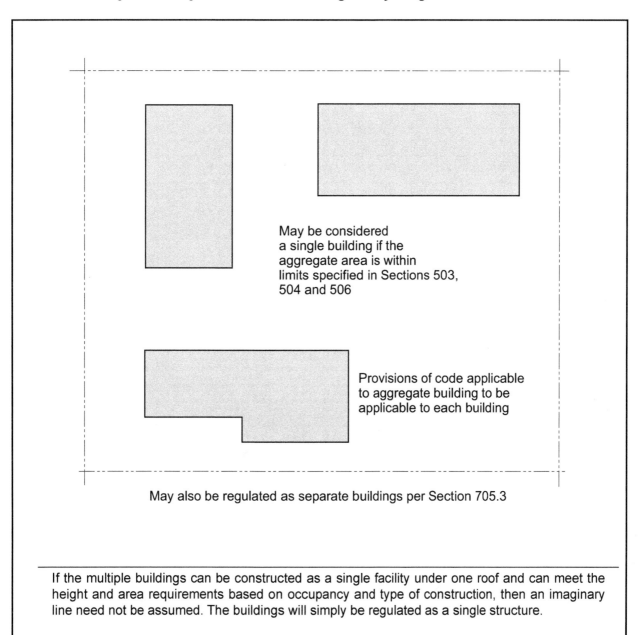

May be considered
a single building if the
aggregate area is within
limits specified in Sections 503,
504 and 506

Provisions of code applicable
to aggregate building to be
applicable to each building

May also be regulated as separate buildings per Section 705.3

If the multiple buildings can be constructed as a single facility under one roof and can meet the height and area requirements based on occupancy and type of construction, then an imaginary line need not be assumed. The buildings will simply be regulated as a single structure.

Code Text: *The maximum height, in feet, of a building shall not exceed the limits specified in Table 504.3.* See the exception for towers, spires, steeples and other roof structures.

Discussion and Commentary: The allowable height of a building in feet is based on three fundamental aspects of building classification and fire protection: occupancy classification, type of construction classification and the presence of an automatic sprinkler system. The limitation on building height recognizes the concern of property damage, along with the concerns of dealing with egress and fire department access. Table 504.3 typically reflects an increased allowable height for sprinklered buildings of 20 feet over the height permitted for nonsprinklered buildings. Also reflected in the table is the allowance for unlimited height in most buildings of Type IA construction.

TABLE 504.3
ALLOWABLE BUILDING HEIGHT IN FEET ABOVE GRADE PLANE[a]

OCCUPANCY CLASSIFICATION	See Footnotes	Type I		Type II		Type III		Type IV				Type V	
		A	B	A	B	A	B	A	B	C	HT	A	B
A, B, E, F, M, S, U	NS[b]	UL	160	65	55	65	55	65	65	65	65	50	40
	S	UL	180	85	75	85	75	270	180	85	85	70	60
H-1, H-2, H-3, H-5	NS[c,d]	UL	160	65	55	65	55	120	90	65	65	50	40
	S												
H-4	NS[c,d]	UL	160	65	55	65	55	65	65	65	65	50	40
	S	UL	180	85	75	85	75	140	100	85	85	70	60
I-1 Condition 1, I-3	NS[d,e]	UL	160	65	55	65	55	65	65	65	65	50	40
	S	UL	180	85	75	85	75	180	120	85	85	70	60
I-1 Condition 2, I-2	NS[d,e,f]	UL	160	65	55	65	55	65	65	65	65	50	40
	S	UL	180	85									
I-4	NS[d,g]	UL	160	65	55	65	55	65	65	65	65	50	40
	S	UL	180	85	75	85	75	180	120	85	85	70	60
R[h]	NS[d]	UL	160	65	55	65	55	65	65	65	65	50	40
	S13D	60	60	60	60	60	60	60	60	60	60	50	40
	S13R	60	60	60	60	60	60	60	60	60	60	60	60
	S	UL	180	85	75	85	75	270	180	85	85	70	60

For SI: 1 foot = 304.8 mm.

UL = Unlimited; NS = Buildings not equipped throughout with an automatic sprinkler system; S = Buildings equipped throughout with an automatic sprinkler system installed in accordance with Section 903.3.1.1; S13R = Buildings equipped throughout with an automatic sprinkler system installed in accordance with Section 903.3.1.2; S13D = Buildings equipped throughout with an automatic sprinkler system installed in accordance with Section 903.3.1.3.

a. See Chapters 4 and 5 for specific exceptions to the allowable height in this chapter.
b. See Section 903.2 for the minimum thresholds for protection by an automatic sprinkler system for specific occupancies.
c. New Group H occupancies are required to be protected by an automatic sprinkler system in accordance with Section 903.2.5.
d. The NS value is only for use in evaluation of existing building height in accordance with the *International Existing Building Code*.
e. New Group I-1 and I-3 occupancies are required to be protected by an automatic sprinkler system in accordance with Section 903.2.6. For new Group I-1 occupancies Condition 1, see Exception 1 of Section 903.2.6.
f. New and existing Group I-2 occupancies are required to be protected by an automatic sprinkler system in accordance with Section 903.2.6 and Section 1103.5 of the *International Fire Code*.
g. For new Group I-4 occupancies, see Exceptions 2 and 3 of Section 903.2.6.
h. New Group R occupancies are required to be protected by an automatic sprinkler system in accordance with Section 903.2.8.

Where an NFPA 13R, *Standard for the Installation of Sprinkler Systems in Low Rise Residential Occupancies*, sprinkler system is installed in a residential building, the table reflects a maximum building height of 60 feet, regardless of the building's type of construction.

Topic: Allowable Height in Stories	**Category:** Building Heights and Areas
Reference: IBC 504.4, Table 504.4	**Subject:** Building Height in Stories

Code Text: *The maximum number of stories of a building shall not exceed the limits specified in Table 504.4.*

Discussion and Commentary: The maximum number of stories permitted in a building is generally represented in Table 504.4. However, the table only regulates the number of stories that are considered above grade plane. Basements are selectively permitted under various provisions throughout the code and regulated accordingly. The conditions that affect the allowable number of stories are consistent with those for the allowable height in feet: occupancy classification, type of construction classification and sprinkler protection. Table 504.4 typically reflects an increased allowable number of stories for sprinklered buildings of one story above the number permitted for nonsprinklered buildings. Also reflected in the table is the allowance for an unlimited number of stories in most buildings of Type IA construction.

TABLE 504.4
ALLOWABLE NUMBER OF STORIES ABOVE GRADE PLANE[a, b]

OCCUPANCY CLASSIFICATION	See Footnotes	Type I A	Type I B	Type II A	Type II B	Type III A	Type III B	Type IV A	Type IV B	Type IV C	HT	Type V A	Type V B
A-1	NS	UL	5	3	2	3	2	3	3	3	3	2	1
A-1	S	UL	6	4	3	4	3	9	6	4	4	3	2
A-2	NS	UL	11	3	2	3	2	3	3	3	3	2	1
A-2	S	UL	12	4	3	4	3	18	12	6	4	3	2
A-3	NS	UL	11	3	2	3	2	3	3	3	3	2	1
A-3	S	UL	12	4	3	4	3	18	12	6	4	3	2
A-4	NS	UL	11	3	2	3	2	3	3	3	3	2	1
A-4	S	UL	12	4	3	4	3	18	12	6	4	3	2
A-5	NS	UL	UL	UL	UL	UL	UL	1	1	1	UL	UL	UL
A-5	S	UL	UL	UL	UL	UL	UL	UL	UL	UL	UL	UL	UL
B	NS	UL	11	5	3	5	3	5	5	5	5	3	2
B	S	UL	12	6	4	6	4	18	12	9	6	4	3
E	NS	UL	5	3	2	3	2	3	3	3	3	1	1
E	S	UL	6	4	3	4	3	9	6	4	4	2	2
F-1	NS	UL	11	4	2	3	2	3	3	3	4	2	1
F-1	S	UL	12	5	3	4	3	10	7	5	5	3	2
F-2	NS	UL	11	5	3	4	3	5	5	5	5	3	2
F-2	S	UL	12	6	4	5	4	12	8	6	6	4	3
H-1	NS[c, d]	1	1	1	1	1	1	NP	NP	NP	1	1	NP
H-1	S	1	1	1	1	1	1	1	1	1	1	1	NP
H-2	NS[c, d]	UL	3	2	1	2	1	1	1	1	2	1	1
H-2	S	UL	3	2	1	2	1	2	2	2	2	1	1
H-3	NS[c, d]	UL	6	4	2	4	2	3	3	3	4	2	1
H-3	S	UL	6	4	2	4	2	4	4	4	4	2	1
H-4	NS[c, d]	UL	7	5	3	5	3	5	5	5	5	3	2
H-4	S	UL	8	6	4	6	4	8	7	6	6	4	3
H-5	NS[c, d]	4	4	3	3	3	3	2	2	2	3	3	2
H-5	S	4	4	3	3	3	3	3	3	3	3	3	2
I-1 Condition 1	NS[d, e]	UL	9	4	3	4	3	4	4	4	4	3	2
I-1 Condition 1	S	UL	10	5	4	5	4	10	7	5	5	4	3
I-1 Condition 2	NS[d, e]	UL	9	4	3	4	3	3	3	3	4	3	2
I-1 Condition 2	S	UL	10	5	3	4	3	10	6	4	4	3	2
I-2	NS[d, f]	UL	4	2	1	1	NP	NP	NP	NP	1	1	NP
I-2	S	UL	5	3	1	1	NP	7	5	1	1	1	NP
I-3	NS[d, e]	UL	4	2	1	2	1	2	2	2	2	2	1
I-3	S	UL	5	3	2	3	2	7	5	3	3	3	2
I-4	NS[d, g]	UL	5	3	2	3	2	3	3	3	3	1	1
I-4	S	UL	6	4	3	4	3	9	6	4	4	2	2
M	NS	UL	11	4	2	4	2	4	4	4	4	3	1
M	S	UL	12	5	3	5	3	12	8	6	5	4	2

(continued)

Where an NFPA 13R, *Standard for the Installation of Sprinkler Systems in Low Rise Residential Occupancies*, sprinkler system is installed in a residential building, the table reflects an allowable number of stories above grade plane of four or less for buildings of any occupancy classification and construction type.

Code Text: *Towers, spires, steeples and other roof structures shall be constructed of materials consistent with the required type of construction of the building except where other construction is permitted by Section 1511.2.4. Such structures shall not be used for habitation or storage. The structures shall be unlimited in height if of noncombustible materials and shall not extend more than 20 feet (6096 mm) above the allowable building height if of combustible materials* (see Chapter 15 for additional requirements).

Discussion and Commentary: The types of structures addressed by this provision are intended to be unoccupied with no significant fire loading. It would seem logical that the height of such structures could be increased over that required for typical buildings. The only limitation occurs where the structure is of combustible materials, which would create a higher hazard.

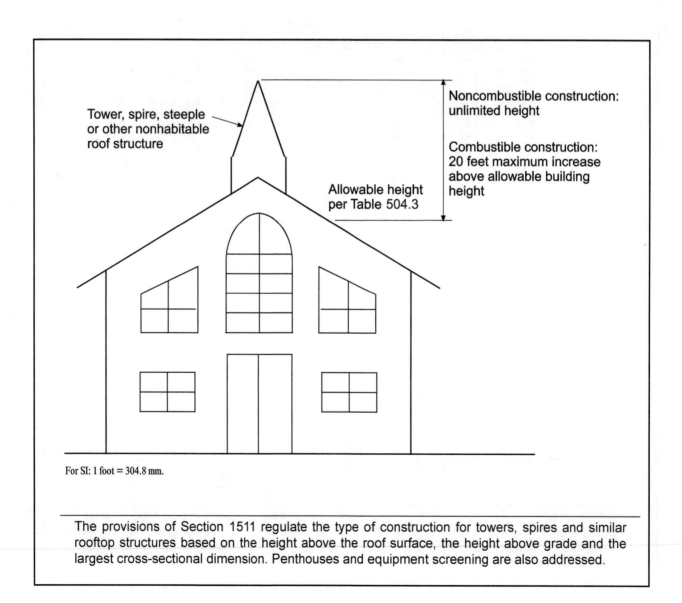

Tower, spire, steeple or other nonhabitable roof structure

Noncombustible construction: unlimited height

Combustible construction: 20 feet maximum increase above allowable building height

Allowable height per Table 504.3

For SI: 1 foot = 304.8 mm.

The provisions of Section 1511 regulate the type of construction for towers, spires and similar rooftop structures based on the height above the roof surface, the height above grade and the largest cross-sectional dimension. Penthouses and equipment screening are also addressed.

Code Text: A mezzanine is *an intermediate level or levels between the floor and ceiling of any story and in accordance with Section 505. The aggregate area of a mezzanine or mezzanines within a room shall not exceed one-third of the floor area of that room or space in which they are located.* See the exceptions that allow for increased mezzanine sizes in (1) special industrial occupancies of Type I or II construction, (2) fully sprinklered Type I or II buildings provided with an approved emergency voice/alarm communication system, and (3) dwelling units.

Discussion and Commentary: Because of size limitation and openness (a mezzanine is open to the room in which it is located, with exceptions), an intermediate floor level within a room adds minimal hazard to the building and its occupants. The occupants of the mezzanine by means of sight, smell or hearing will be able to determine if there is some emergency or fire taking place either on the mezzanine or in the room in which the mezzanine is located.

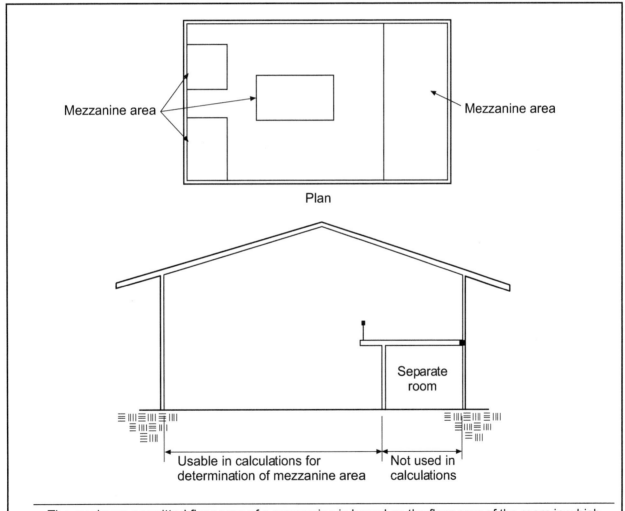

The maximum permitted floor area of a mezzanine is based on the floor area of the room in which it is located. Only those portions of the lower room that are unenclosed may be considered in the calculation of maximum mezzanine size.

Code Text: *A mezzanine or mezzanines in compliance with Section 505.2 shall be considered a portion of the story below. Such mezzanines shall not contribute to either the building area or number of stories as regulated by Section 503.1. The area of a mezzanine shall be included in determining the fire area.*

Discussion and Commentary: There are two distinct benefits derived from the qualification of a floor level as a mezzanine. One, the mezzanine is not considered in the allowable number of stories, and two, for allowable area purposes, the mezzanine floor area does not increase the building area of the story in which it is located. However, in the determination of fire area size for sprinkler requirements, the floor area must be considered. The requirements for sprinkler systems are generally based on the fire load expected in an occupancy; thus, an increased floor area would increase the potential fire loading.

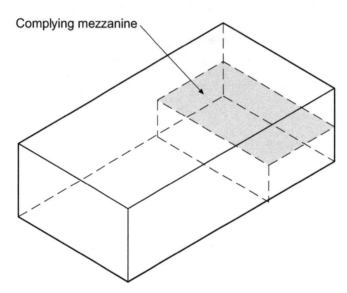

Complying mezzanine

Mezzanine:
- Does <u>not</u> contribute to floor area for maximum allowable area
- Does <u>not</u> contribute as an additional story
- Does contribute to floor area for fire area size determination

Example:
For 8,000 sq ft first floor as shown with 2,000 sq ft mezzanine, building area is 8,000 sq ft, building is one story in height, and fire area is 10,000 sq ft

For SI: 1 square foot = 0.093 m^2

Although it is quite possible that an individual floor level within a building can meet all of the provisions of the IBC and qualify as a mezzanine, its actual designation is the choice of the designer. It may be more advantageous to treat the floor level simply as an additional story.

Code Text: *A mezzanine shall be open and unobstructed to the room in which such mezzanine is located except for walls not more than 42 inches high, columns and posts.* See the exceptions addressing mezzanines, including (1) where the enclosed area has a maximum occupant load of 10, (2) having two or more means of egress, (3) where the aggregate floor area of the enclosed space does not exceed 10 percent of the mezzanine area, and (4) in industrial facilities.

Discussion and Commentary: By definition, a mezzanine is intended to be open to the room or space below. This common environment allows individuals on either floor level to be aware of the conditions and hazards that may affect their safety. The IBC, through the application of one of the exceptions, permits the mezzanine to be enclosed when it has been determined that the enclosure creates little, if any concern.

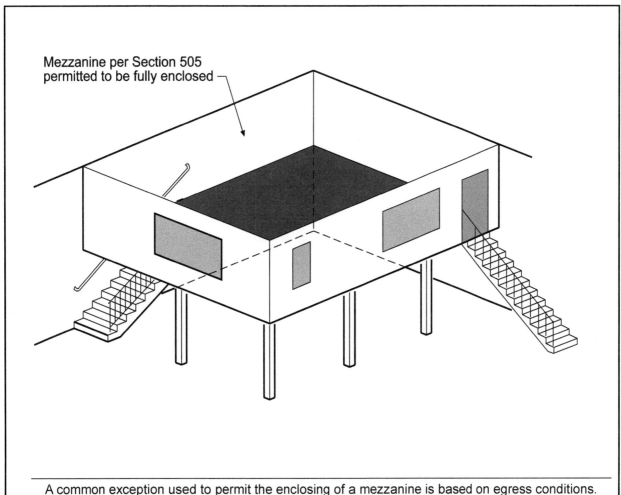

Mezzanine per Section 505 permitted to be fully enclosed

A common exception used to permit the enclosing of a mezzanine is based on egress conditions. If a minimum of two means of egress are provided from the mezzanine level, then the mezzanine is not required to be open to the room or space below.

Code Text: *The allowable area of each story of a single-occupancy building shall be determined in accordance with Equation 5-1:*

$A_a = A_t + (NS \times I_f)$ *where:*

$A_a = $ *Allowable area (square feet)*

$A_t = $ *Tabular allowable area factor (NS, S1, S13R or S13D value, as applicable) in accordance with Table 506.2.*

$NS = $ *Tabular allowable area factor in accordance with Table 506.2 for nonsprinklered building (regardless of whether the building is sprinklered).*

$I_f = $ *Area factor increase due to frontage (percent) as calculated in accordance with Section 506.3.*

Discussion and Commentary: The allowable building areas determined in accordance with Section 506.2 are based on the allowable area factors of Table 506.2, along with any available frontage increase as calculated by Section 506.3. The presence of sufficient open space adjacent to a building provides for an increase above the tabular value. The protection afforded by an automatic sprinkler system, as addressed in Table 506.2, justifies a significant allowable area increase.

EXAMPLE:

GIVEN: A fully sprinklered Group A-2 restaurant in a building of Type VB construction. Building has two stories above grade plane with 8,500 square feet per story. A 25% increase is permitted due to open frontage.

DETERMINE: If in compliance with maximum allowable building area.

2021 IBC Procedure for Determining Allowable Area and Compliance Review:

Step 1: Review and apply applicable provisions of Section 503 for general building area determination.

Step 2: Review and apply applicable provisions of Section 506 regarding the determination of allowable area.

Step 3: Determine allowable building area factor (A_t) as established in Table 506.2, based upon SM value (sprinklered, multi-story condition).

Allowable area factor in square feet from Table 506.2: $A_t = 18,000$ square feet

Step 4: Determine applicable allowable area frontage increase as established in Section 506.3.

Frontage increased based on example: $I_f = 0.25$

Step 5: Determine maximum building allowable area using Equation 5-2, $A_a = [A_t + (NS \times I_f)] \times S_a$

$[18,000 + (6,000 \times 0.25)] \times 2 = (18,000 + 1,500) \times 2 = 39,000$ square feet　　　　OK

Step 6: Determine maximum allowable area per story using Equation 5-2, with $S_a = 1$

$[18,000 + (6,000 \times 0.25)] \times 1 = (18,000 + 1,500) \times 1 = 19,500$ square feet　　　　OK

Specific methods of determining allowable area are also established for mixed-occupancy buildings.

Code Text: *Every building shall adjoin or have access to a public way to receive an area factor increase based on frontage. The area factor increase based on frontage shall be determined in accordance with Sections 506.3.1 through 506.3.3. The area factor increase based on frontage shall be determined in accordance with Table 506.3.3.*

Discussion and Commentary: It is assumed that every building will adjoin a street, alley or yard on at least one side. Therefore, no frontage increase is given where less than 25 percent of a building's perimeter is open. Credit is provided, however, where additional frontage is considered open (20 feet or more in width). The benefit of increased allowable building area is accrued based on better access for the fire department, as well as decreased exposure to adjoining properties. The frontage increase is based on the smallest public way or open space that is 20 feet or greater, as well as the percentage of the building perimeter having a minimum 20-foot public way or open space.

Entire perimeter considered for frontage increase

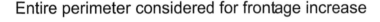
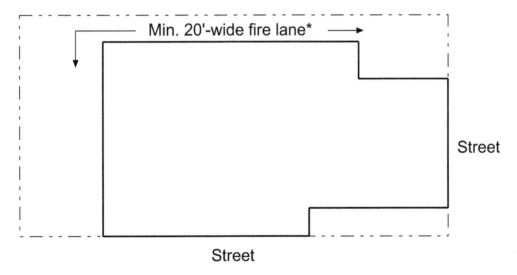

Min. 20'-wide fire lane*

Street

Street

Open space to be on same lot or dedicated for public use, and accessed from a street or approved fire lane

*Fire lane need only be provided to within 150 feet of exterior wall per Section 503.1.1 of the IFC.

Access must be provided from a street or an approved fire lane for any open space that is used for a frontage increase in allowable floor area. The *International Fire Code* mandates that a fire lane for fire apparatus be maintained with an unobstructed width of at least 20 feet.

Code Text: *The public ways or yards of 60 feet (18 288 mm) in width required in Sections 507.3, 507.4, 507.5, 507.6 and 507.12 shall be permitted to be reduced to not less than 40 feet (12 192 mm) in width provided all of the following requirements are met: (1) the reduced open space shall not be allowed for more than 75 percent of the perimeter of the building, (2) the exterior walls facing the reduced open space shall have a minimum fire-resistance rating of not less than 3 hours, and (3) openings in the exterior walls facing the reduced open space shall have opening protectives with a minimum fire-resistance rating of not less than 3 hours.*

Discussion and Commentary: When it is necessary or desirable to reduce the open space around the perimeter of an unlimited area building, the code provides an alternative. An equivalent level of protection can be provided by increasing the level of exterior wall and opening protection.

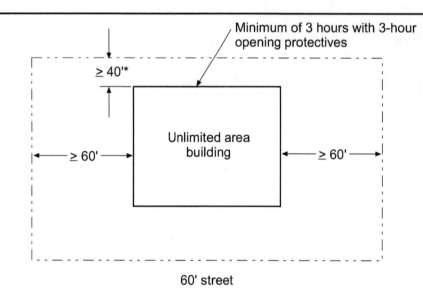

Minimum of 3 hours with 3-hour opening protectives

≥ 40'*

Unlimited area building

≥ 60'   ≥ 60'

60' street

*Reduced open space permitted:

- Up to 75% of building perimeter

- Where exterior wall facing reduced open space has minimum 3-hour fire-resistance rating

- Openings in such walls are protected for 3 hours

For SI: 1 foot = 304.8 mm.

This provision is designed for warehouses, factories, retail stores, office buildings, Group A-3 uses and movie theaters where fire resistance at the exterior wall is easily accomplished. The reduction does not apply to other buildings permitted to be unlimited in area, such as educational uses and aircraft paint hangars.

Code Text: *The area of a Group A-4 building no more than one story above grade plane of other than Type V construction, or the area of a Group B, F, M or S building no more than one story above grade plane of any construction type, shall not be limited when the building is provided with an automatic sprinkler system throughout in accordance with Section 903.3.1.1, and is surrounded and adjoined by public ways or yards not less than 60 feet (18 288 mm) in width. Provisions also apply to two-story buildings of such occupancies other than Group A-4.*

Discussion and Commentary: It is often beneficial to have very large, undivided floor areas for facilities such as arenas, office buildings, factories, retail centers and warehouses. The unlimited area provisions allow for an alternative to the higher types of construction that would normally be required. The installation of a sprinkler system and sufficient open space around the building reduce the potential fire severity to a reasonable level in these moderate-hazard occupancies.

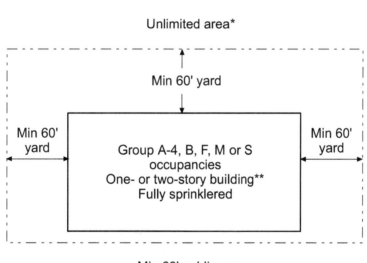

Unlimited area*

Min 60' yard

Min 60' yard

Group A-4, B, F, M or S occupancies
One- or two-story building**
Fully sprinklered

Min 60' yard

Min 60' public way

*Any type of construction permitted (other than Type V for Group A-4)

**Limited to one story for Group A-4

For SI: 1 foot = 304.8 mm.

Low-hazard manufacturing and storage occupancies of any construction type are permitted to be unlimited in area where they are only one story in height and are provided on all sides with public ways or yards at least 60 feet in width. Installation of an automatic sprinkler system is not required.

| **Topic:** Group A-3 Buildings | **Category:** Building Heights and Areas |
| **Reference:** IBC 507.6, 507.7 | **Subject:** Unlimited Area Buildings |

Code Text: *The area of a Group A-3 building no more than one story above grade plane used as a place of religious worship, community hall, dance hall, exhibition hall, gymnasium, lecture hall, indoor swimming pool or tennis court of Type II construction, shall not be limited when all of the following criteria are met:* See three conditions for allowance of unlimited area. The provisions are also applicable to buildings of Type III and IV construction, provided four conditions are met.

Discussion and Commentary: The Group A-3 occupancy classification includes the most diverse types of assembly uses assigned by the code. Traditionally, the allowable area of Group A occupancies is greatly limited as compared to most other occupancy groups. However, those assembly uses expected to have a relatively low fire load are permitted in unlimited area buildings subject to the special conditions prescribed by the code.

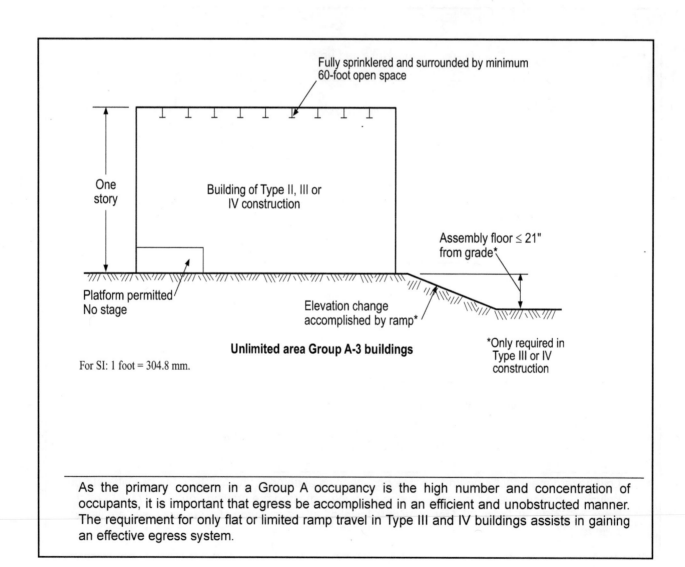

Fully sprinklered and surrounded by minimum 60-foot open space

One story

Building of Type II, III or IV construction

Assembly floor ≤ 21" from grade*

Platform permitted No stage

Elevation change accomplished by ramp*

*Only required in Type III or IV construction

Unlimited area Group A-3 buildings

For SI: 1 foot = 304.8 mm.

As the primary concern in a Group A occupancy is the high number and concentration of occupants, it is important that egress be accomplished in an efficient and unobstructed manner. The requirement for only flat or limited ramp travel in Type III and IV buildings assists in gaining an effective egress system.

Code Text: *Group H-2, H-3 and H-4 occupancies shall be permitted in unlimited area buildings containing Group F or S occupancies, in accordance with Sections 507.4 and 507.5 and the provisions of Sections 507.8.1 through 507.8.4. The aggregate floor area of the Group H occupancies located in an unlimited area building shall not exceed 10 percent of the area of the building or the area limitations for the Group H occupancies as specified in Section 506, based upon the perimeter of each Group H floor area that fronts on a public way or open space. The aggregate floor area of Group H occupancies not located at the perimeter of the building shall not exceed 25 percent of the area limitations for the Group H occupancies as specified in Section 506.*

Discussion and Commentary: The aggregate allowable area of the permitted Group H occupancies in a factory or warehouse regulated as an unlimited area building is dependent on the type of construction of the building and the location of the Group H occupancies in the building.

Example:

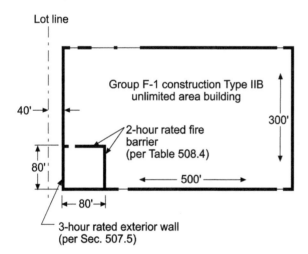

Lot line

Group F-1 construction Type IIB
unlimited area building

40'

2-hour rated fire
barrier
(per Table 508.4)

300'

80'

500'

80'

3-hour rated exterior wall
(per Sec. 507.5)

- Group H-2
- Per Table 506.3.3
  50% of perimeter
  Open space of 40'
  I_f = 0.50

- Allowable area for H-2 = 7,000 + (0.50)(7,000)
  = 10,500 sq ft
- Check 10% of floor area criterium:
  (500)(300) = 150,000 sq ft
  150,000/10 = 15,000 sq ft
  15,000 >10,500, ∴ 10,500 maximum allowable

- Actual area = 6,400, which is less than 10,500,
  therefore OK

For **SI:** 1 inch = 25.4 mm, 1 foot = 304.8 mm
1 square foot = 0.0929 m²

Group H-2 at the corner of an unlimited area Group F or S building

More ready access to the Group H from the exterior of the building provides the fire department with an opportunity to respond more effectively to an incident. As such, the allowable floor area of the Group H can be far greater than where completely surrounded by the Group F or S use.

Code Text: *A building shall be considered as separate and distinct buildings for the purpose of determining area limitations, continuity of fire walls, limitation of number of stories and type of construction where all of the following conditions are met:* See the list of seven criteria.

Discussion and Commentary: The special provisions of Section 510 are intended to modify the specific requirements of Chapter 5 regarding allowable heights and areas of buildings. The allowances granted in Section 510.2 address those structures typically referred to as "podium" or "pedestal" buildings. Compliance with the multiple conditions results in consideration of the structure as two separate and distinct buildings for four distinct issues. Similar provisions are established in Sections 510.3, 510.4, 510.7 and 510.8 where complying horizontal separations, along with other requirements, permit modifications to the general allowable height and area limitations.

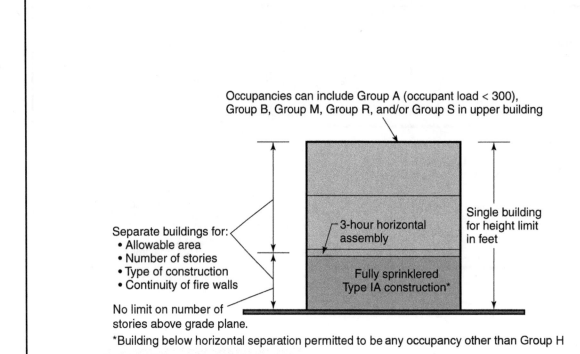

Although this provision is often utilized where the lower building contains a parking garage, such parking facilities are not required to take advantage of the benefits. A variety of uses are permitted both above and below the fire-resistance-rated horizontal separation.

Code Text: *Open parking garages constructed under Groups A, I, B, M and R shall not exceed the height and area limitations permitted under Section 406.5. The height and area of the portion of the building above the open parking garage shall not exceed the limitations in Section 503 for the upper occupancy. The height, in both feet and stories, of the portion of the building above the open parking garage shall be measured from grade plane and shall include both the open parking garage and the portion of the building above the parking garage.*

Discussion and Commentary: In the more common types of occupancies, it is desirable at times to provide tiers of parking below the major use of the building. In this special mixed-use condition, two different types of construction are permitted for determining the maximum allowable height and area. This special allowance is just one of several special provisions established in Section 510 that modify the general requirements of the code.

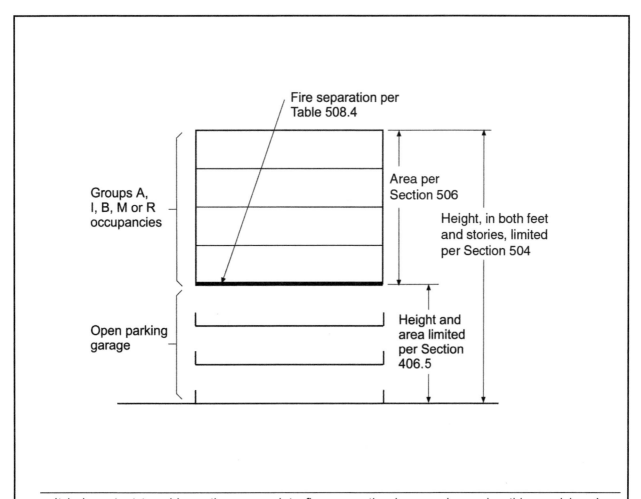

It is important to address the appropriate fire separation issues when using this provision. In addition, the structural members supporting the upper occupancy must be protected by the more restrictive fire-resistant assemblies of all of the occupancies involved.

Quiz

Study Session 4
IBC Chapter 5

1. Premises must be identified by numbers or addresses visible from the street, with a minimum character height of at least _____ inches.

    a. three   b. four

    c. six   d. eight

    Reference_____

2. Building height is measured to the _____.

    a. average height of the highest roof surface

    b. highest point of the highest roof surface

    c. average height of all of the roof surfaces

    d. highest point of the lowest roof surface

    Reference _____

3. The tabular allowable building height for a fully-sprinklered single-occupancy Type IB building housing a Group I-2 occupancy is _____ stories and _____ feet.

    a. 4, 160   b. 3, 85

    c. 5, 180   d. unlimited, unlimited

    Reference_____

4. What is the tabular allowable height, in feet, for a single-occupancy nonsprinklered Group B building of Type IIA construction?

    a. 50   b. 55

    c. 65   d. 85

Reference_____

5. Basements do not need to be included in the total allowable area of a single-occupancy building, provided the total area of such basements do not exceed _____.

    a. one-third the floor area permitted for any single story

    b. the area permitted for a one-story above grade plane building

    c. twice the area permitted for a single story

    d. the tabular area based on construction type and occupancy group

Reference_____

6. A story is considered a story above grade plane where the finished surface of the floor above is more than _____ feet above grade plane.

    a. 3   b. 4

    c. 5   d. 6

Reference _____

7. The maximum building area of a six-story single-occupancy building is limited to _____ times the allowable area permitted per story.

    a. two   b. three

    c. four   d. six

Reference_____

8. What is the maximum allowable height in feet above grade plane for a fully sprinklered single-occupancy Type IIA building housing a Group A-2 occupancy?

    a. 55 feet   b. 65 feet

    c. 75 feet   d. 85 feet

Reference_____

9. What is the maximum allowable number of stories above grade plane for a fully-sprinklered single-occupancy IIIB building housing a Group I-2 occupancy?

    a. 0, it is not permitted   b. 1

    c. 2   d. 3

Reference_____

10. Combustible steeples are limited to a maximum height of _____ feet above the allowable building height.

    a. 15   b. 20

    c. 30   d. 40

Reference_____

11. The area of a mezzanine is not to be included in the determination of the _____.

    a. fire area   b. building area

    c. occupant load   d. plumbing fixture count

Reference_____

12. A minimum clear height of _____ is required above and below mezzanine floor construction.

    a. 6 feet, 8 inches   b 7 feet

    c. 7 feet, 6 inches   d. 8 feet

Reference_____

13. In general, the aggregate area of mezzanines within a room is limited to _____ of the area of the room in which the mezzanines are located.

    a. 10 percent   b. 25 percent

    c. $33^1/_3$ percent   d. 50 percent

Reference_____

14. Portions of a mezzanine need not be open to the room in which the mezzanine is located, provided the enclosed space is limited in size to a maximum of _____ of the mezzanine area.

    a. 10 percent   b. 25 percent

    c. $33^{1}/_{3}$ percent   d. 50 percent

    Reference_____

15. A mezzanine is not required to be open to the room in which it is located where the occupant load of the enclosed space does not exceed _____.

    a. 10   b. 20

    c. 30   d. 50

    Reference_____

16. An allowable area increase for frontage is not permitted unless a minimum of _____ of the building perimeter is sufficiently open.

    a. 10 percent   b. 25 percent

    c. $33^{1}/_{3}$ percent   d. 40 percent

    Reference_____

17. In order to be considered as sufficiently open for an allowable area increase for frontage, the public way or open space must have a minimum width of _____ feet.

    a. 10   b. 20

    c. 25   d. 30

    Reference_____

18. What is the allowable tabular height, in number of stories above grade plane, for a Group R-1 single-occupancy building of Type IIB construction where the building is protected by an NFPA 13R sprinkler system?

    a. 3   b. 4

    c. 5   d. 6

    Reference _____

19. What is the allowable building area factor for a nonsprinklered Type VB building housing a Group B occupancy?

    a. 9,000 square feet

    b. 12,000 square feet

    c. 27,000 square feet

    d. 36,000 square feet

Reference _____

20. The maximum permitted aggregate area of mezzanines, per story, in a Type IIB building provided with a sprinkler system and an emergency voice/alarm communication system is _____ of the floor area of the room.

    a. one-third

    b. 50 percent

    c. two-thirds

    d. 75 percent

Reference_____

21. What is the maximum allowable number of stories above grade plane permitted for a single-occupancy Type IIIA building housing a Group R-2 occupancy that is provided with a 13R sprinkler system throughout?

    a. 2

    b. 3

    c. 4

    d. 5

Reference_____

22. In order for a Group E building to comply with the unlimited area allowances of Section 507, the building's construction type cannot be Type _____ .

    a. IIA

    b. IIB

    c. IIIA

    d. IIIB

Reference_____

23. In order to reduce the required open space surrounding certain unlimited area buildings from 60 feet to 40 feet, walls facing the reduced open space shall have a minimum fire-resistance rating of _____ .

    a. 45 minutes

    b. 1 hour

    c. 2 hours

    d. 3 hours

Reference_____

24. A complying Group H-2 aircraft paint hangar may be unlimited in floor area when limited to one story, provided the hangar is surrounded by yards or public ways having a minimum width of _____.

    a.   40 feet

    b.   60 feet

    c.   twice the height of the hangar

    d.   one and one-half times the height of the hangar

Reference_____

25. Where using the special provisions of Section 510.2 for the horizontal building separation allowance, the horizontal separation between buildings shall be provided with a horizontal assembly having a minimum _____ fire-resistance rating.

    a.   1-hour   b.   2-hour

    c.   3-hour   d.   4-hour

Reference _____

26. What is the maximum allowable height permitted for a noncombustible communications tower located on the roof of a Type IIB office building?

    a.   55 feet   b.   65 feet

    c.   75 feet   d.   unlimited

Reference_____

27. In order for a Type IIIB office building to be considered for unlimited area under Section 507, it must be limited to a maximum height of _____ above grade plane.

    a.   one story   b.   two stories

    c.   50 feet   d.   40 feet

Reference_____

28. A one-story Group A-3 gymnasium building of Type IIIA construction may be considered under the unlimited area provisions, provided the gymnasium floor is located a maximum of _____ above or below grade level.

    a.   21 inches   b.   24 inches

    c.   30 inches   d.   48 inches

Reference_____

29. A Group H-3 storage room located within a 100,000-square foot unlimited area manufacturing building of Type IIB construction is limited to_____ square feet where not located on the building's perimeter.

    a. 3,125   b. 3,500

    c. 12,500   d. 14,000

    Reference_____

30. A nine-story apartment building of Type IIA construction, where permitted, shall be located a minimum of _____ feet from any other building on the lot and from all lot lines.

    a. 10 feet   b. 30 feet

    c. 50 feet   d. 60 feet

    Reference_____

31. In buildings of Type I or II construction housing special industrial occupancies in accordance with Section 503.1.1, the aggregate floor area of mezzanines is limited to a maximum of _____ of the area of the room in which they are located.

    a. $^1/_4$ b. $^1/_3$

    c. $^1/_2$ d. $^2/_3$

    Reference _____

32. Where the aggregate area of all equipment platforms within a room is limited to a maximum of _____ of the area of the room in which they are located, the equipment platforms shall not be considered a portion of the floor below.

    a. $^1/_4$ b. $^1/_3$

    c. $^1/_2$ d. $^2/_3$

    Reference _____

33. The area of a complying covered mall building and any anchor stores is not limited where their maximum height is _____ stories.

    a. 2   b. 3

    c. 4   d. 5

    Reference _____

34. A Group E building of unlimited area under the conditions of Section 507 shall be surrounded and adjoined by public ways and yards a minimum of _____ feet in width.

    a. 30   b. 40

    c. 60   d. 75

Reference _____

35. What is the maximum allowable building height in feet above grade plane for a single-occupancy nonsprinklered IIIB building housing a Group B occupancy?

    a. 55   b. 65

    c. 75   d. 85

Reference _____

36. What is the maximum allowable building height, in number of stories above grade plane, for a Group B single-occupancy fully sprinklered building of Type IV-A construction?

    a. unlimited   b. 18

    c. 12   d. 9

Reference _____

37. What is the frontage increase factor for a Group I-2 building having a percentage of building perimeter of 65 percent and the smallest open space of 20 feet or more is 28 feet?

    a. 0.21   b. 0.42

    c. 0.50   d. 0.75

Reference _____

38. Where a building meets the requirements of Section 507 except for compliance with the open frontage requirement, what is the frontage increase factor where the percentage of building perimeter is 75 percent and the smallest open space of 30 feet or more is 50 feet?

    a. 0.75   b. 0.83

    c. 1.25   d. 1.38

Reference _____

39. What is the allowable area factor for a Group R-2 single-occupancy building of Type IV-C construction with multiple stories above grade plane and an NFPA 13 sprinkler system?

    a. 25,625 square feet   b. 61,500 square feet

    c. 76,875 square feet   d. 102,500 square feet

Reference _____

40. Regardless of other conditions, mezzanines used for control equipment are permitted to be glazed on all sides in _____ facilities.

    a. fully-sprinklered   b. industrial

    c. detention   d. single-story

Reference _____

2021 IBC Sections 701 through 705
Fire and Smoke Protection Features I

OBJECTIVE: To gain an understanding of the fundamentals of fire-resistance-rated construction, the methods for the determination of fire resistance, and the regulation of exterior walls for fire-resistance rating and opening protection.

REFERENCE: Sections 701 through 705, 2021 *International Building Code*

KEY POINTS:
- Why are fire-resistance-rated materials and systems used in the construction of buildings?
- What is a fire-resistance rating? How is such a rating determined?
- What referenced standards are the basis for determining fire-resistance ratings?
- What is nonsymmetrical wall construction?
- How must interior walls and partitions of nonsymmetrical construction be tested? Exterior walls?
- Which alternative methods are available for determining the fire-resistance rating of different building elements?
- What is a prescriptive design of fire-resistance-rated building elements? What specific types of elements are addressed?
- Which types of materials can be evaluated for fire-resistance ratings through calculations?
- When is a material considered noncombustible? Is gypsum board considered a noncombustible material?
- Under what conditions is the use of fire-resistance-rated glazing permitted? How must such glazing be identified?
- What fire-resistance-rated walls must be identified by signs or stenciling? Where is the identification required to be located? What minimum lettering size is required?
- Under what conditions must fire-resistance-rated columns be individually protected? Other primary structural frame members?
- How are secondary members required to be protected for fire-resistance purposes?

KEY POINTS
(Cont'd)

- How must the fire protective covering of a structural member be protected from impact that is due to moving vehicles?
- How is the minimum fire-resistance rating determined for structural members located within exterior walls?
- What are the general requirements applicable to sprayed fire-resistant materials?
- How is a projection defined? What types of building elements are considered projections?
- What limits the extent of a projection?
- Which types of projections are permitted from walls of Type I and II buildings? Type III, IV and V buildings?
- When must combustible projections be protected? What other options are available?
- How are multiple buildings on the same lot addressed in regard to exterior wall and opening protection?
- Under which conditions must fire-resistance-rated exterior walls be rated for fire exposure from both sides?
- Why are exterior walls protected differently based on fire separation distance?
- At what minimum distance is the protection of exterior walls unnecessary?
- Under which conditions are openings in exterior walls prohibited? What are the limitations where protected openings are provided? Unprotected openings?
- How are protected and unprotected openings regulated in the same exterior wall?
- How does the presence of a sprinkler system affect the amount of unprotected openings?
- Which special provisions apply to openings in the first story of exterior walls?
- When must exterior openings in adjacent stories be protected? Where required, what methods of protection are available?
- What is a parapet? Where are parapets required?
- What fire-resistance rating is mandated for required parapets?
- What is the minimum required height of a parapet? How does the slope of the roof affect the minimum required height?
- Why are exterior walls protected based on fire separation distance?
- At what minimum distance is the protection of exterior walls unnecessary?

Code Text: *The provisions of* Chapter 7 *shall govern the materials, systems and assemblies used for structural fire resistance and fire-resistance-rated construction separation of adjacent spaces to safeguard against the spread of fire and smoke within a building and the spread of fire to or from buildings.*

Discussion and Commentary: There are basically two reasons for the protection of various building elements with construction resistant to fire. One, structural elements such as columns, girders, bearing walls and other load-bearing members are often required by the code to maintain their structural integrity under fire conditions for a prescribed time period. Two, horizontal and vertical assemblies are used to create compartments, including control areas, or to isolate portions of the building, such as exitways, through fire-resistant construction.

FIRE RESISTANCE. That property of materials or their assemblies that prevents or retards the passage of excessive heat, hot gases or flames under conditions of use.

In addition to limiting or resisting the spread of fire and heat within a building, certain provisions are intended to provide protection for adjoining structures. The code also addresses construction utilized to restrict the passage of smoke to specific areas.

Code Text: Fire-resistance rating is *the period of time a building element, component or assembly maintains the ability to confine a fire, continues to perform a given structural function, or both as determined by the tests, or the methods based on tests, prescribed in Section 703. A fire-resistance rating of building elements, components or assemblies shall be determined by the test procedures set forth in ASTM E119 or UL 263* or by analytic methods set forth in Section 703.2.2.

Discussion and Commentary: ASTM E119 is the referenced standard, *Standard Test Methods for Fire Tests of Building Construction and Materials.* These test methods are used for the great majority of building components or assemblies that are mandated by the code to have a fire-resistance rating. Assemblies tested under the criteria of UL 263 are also considered to have the fire-resistance rating as assigned.

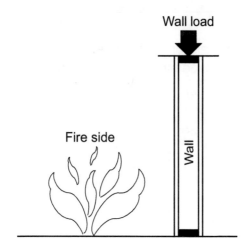

Wall load

Fire side

Wall

Assembly must:

sustain applied load,

have no passage of flame or gases hot enough to ignite cotton waste,

have average temperature rise on unexposed surface not more than 250°F above initial temperature or more than 325°F at any point, and

have no water pass through during hose-stream test.

Conditions of acceptance - wall fire test

For nonsymmetrical wall construction, where interior walls and partitions are provided with differing membranes on opposing sides, the IBC mandates that tests be performed from both sides. The side with the shortest test duration is the basis for the fire-resistance rating.

Code Text: *The fire resistance of building elements, components or assemblies established by an analytical method shall be of any of the following methods listed in Section 703.2.2, based on the fire exposure and acceptance criteria specified in ASTM E119 or UL 263: (1) fire-resistance designs documented in approved sources; (2) prescriptive designs of fire-resistance-rated building elements as prescribed in Section 721; (3) calculations in accordance with Section 722; (4) engineering analysis based on a comparison of building element, component or assembly designs having fire-resistance ratings as determined by the test procedures set forth in ASTM E119 or UL 263; or (5) fire-resistance designs certified by an approved agency.*

Discussion and Commentary: Prescriptive details of fire-resistance-rated building elements are contained in Section 721. Generic listings for structural parts, walls, partitions, floor systems and roof systems are addressed.

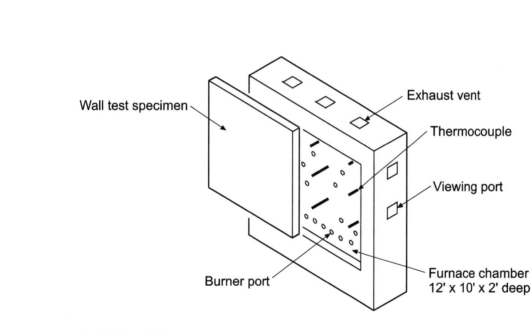

For SI: 1 foot = 304.8 mm.   **Wall test furnace**

Section 722 provides methods of calculated fire resistance for concrete, masonry, steel, wood assemblies or members, and mass timber elements. The procedures and calculations are limited to the specific information set forth in this section and are not to be used in any other manner.

Code Text: *The provisions of* Section 721 *contain prescriptive details of fire-resistance-rated building elements. The materials of construction listed in Tables 721.1(1), 721.1(2) and 721.1(3) shall be assumed to have the fire-resistance ratings prescribed therein. Where materials that change the capacity for heat dissipation are incorporated into a fire-resistance-rated assembly, fire test results or other substantiating data shall be made available to the building official to show that the required fire-resistance rating time period is not reduced.*

Discussion and Commentary: The tables in Section 721 provide the details for obtaining desired fire-resistance ratings for structural parts, walls and partitions, and floor and roof systems. The methods and materials found in the tables are to be used in the same manner as any listed assembly.

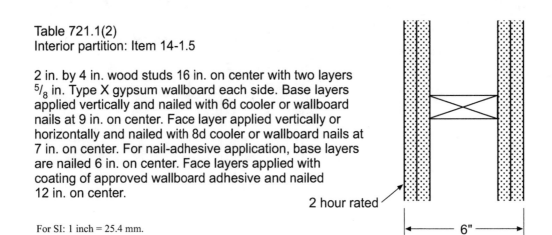

Table 721.1(2)
Interior partition: Item 14-1.5

2 in. by 4 in. wood studs 16 in. on center with two layers $^5/_8$ in. Type X gypsum wallboard each side. Base layers applied vertically and nailed with 6d cooler or wallboard nails at 9 in. on center. Face layer applied vertically or horizontally and nailed with 8d cooler or wallboard nails at 7 in. on center. For nail-adhesive application, base layers are nailed 6 in. on center. Face layers applied with coating of approved wallboard adhesive and nailed 12 in. on center.

For SI: 1 inch = 25.4 mm.

2 hour rated

6"

When insulation or a similar material is added to a fire-resistance-rated assembly, it may change the assembly's capacity to dissipate heat. Particularly in noncombustible horizontal assemblies, the fire-resistance rating may be diminished to some degree.

Code Text: *The provisions of Section 722 contain procedures by which the fire resistance of specific materials or combinations of materials is established by calculations. The procedures apply only to the information contained in Section 722 and shall not be otherwise used.*

Discussion and Commentary: Another method used to obtain the necessary fire-resistance ratings mandated by the code is calculation. The provisions for calculating fire resistance are applicable to concrete assemblies, concrete masonry, clay brick and tile masonry, steel assemblies, wood assemblies and mass timber elements.

TABLE 722.6.2(1)
TIME ASSIGNED TO WALLBOARD MEMBRANES[a, b, c, d]

DESCRIPTION OF FINISH	TIME[e](minutes)
$^3/_8$-inch wood structural panel bonded with exterior glue	5
$^{15}/_{32}$-inch wood structural panel bonded with exterior glue	10
$^{19}/_{32}$-inch wood structural panel bonded with exterior glue	15
$^3/_8$-inch gypsum wallboard	10
$^1/_2$-inch gypsum wallboard	15
$^5/_8$-inch gypsum wallboard	30
$^1/_2$-inch Type X gypsum wallboard	25
$^5/_8$-inch Type X gypsum wallboard	40
Double $^3/_8$-inch gypsum wallboard	25
$^1/_2$-inch + $^3/_8$-inch gypsum wallboard	35
Double $^1/_2$-inch gypsum wallboard	40

For SI: 1 inch = 25.4 mm.

a. These values apply only when membranes are installed on framing members which are spaced 16 inches o.c. or less.

b. Gypsum wallboard installed over framing or furring shall be installed so that all edges are supported, except $^5/_8$-inch Type X gypsum wallboard shall be permitted to be installed horizontally with the horizontal joints staggered 24 inches each side and unsupported but finished.

c. On wood frame floor/ceiling or roof/ceiling assemblies, gypsum board shall be installed with the long dimension perpendicular to framing members and shall have all joints finished.

d. The membrane on the unexposed side shall not be included in determining the fire resistance of the assembly. When dissimilar membranes are used on a wall assembly, the calculation shall be made from the least fire-resistant (weaker) side.

e. The time assigned is not a finished rating.

TABLE 722.6.2(2)
TIME ASSIGNED FOR CONTRIBUTION OF WOOD FRAME [a, b, c]

DESCRIPTION	TIME ASSIGNED TO FRAME (minutes)
Wood studs 16 inches o.c.	20
Wood floor and roof joists 16 inches o.c.	10

For SI: 1 inch = 25.4 mm.

a. This table does not apply to studs or joists spaced more than 16 inches o.c.

b. All studs shall be nominal 2 × 4 and all joists shall have a nominal thickness of at least 2 inches.

c. Allowable spans for joists shall be determined in accordance with Sections 2308.8, 2308.10.2 and 2308.10.3.

Applicable to both load-bearing and nonload-bearing assemblies, the calculated fire resistance for wood-framed walls, floor/ceiling assemblies and roof/ceiling assemblies is limited to a 1-hour rating.

Code Text: *The term "noncombustible" does not apply to the flame spread characteristics of interior finish or trim materials. A material shall not be classified as a noncombustible building construction material if it is subject to an increase in combustibility or flame spread beyond the limitations herein established through the effects of age, moisture, or other atmospheric conditions.*

Discussion and Commentary: In buildings of Types I, II, III and IV construction, specific elements are required to be constructed of noncombustible materials. Such materials are desirable because they do not aid combustion, nor do they add appreciable heat to an ambient fire. Under conditions of the test, a material may have a limited amount of combustible content and still qualify as noncombustible. Materials required to be noncombustible are to be tested in accordance with ASTM E136, or ASTM E2652 using the acceptance criteria of ASTM E136.

Vertical Tube Furnace for ASTM E136 Test

Thermocouple leads T₃ and T₄ (thermocouple T₂ placed at location of T₃ for initial heating of furnace)

Suspension wire

6.4 cm² area opening

Glass cover (in halves to facilitate access)

Thermocouple T₁ (204 mm down)

Terminals for 50 turn No. 16 nichrome wire heating element

Air inlet provides flow tangential to inner cylinder

Heating element protected by alundum cement

High temperature insulation

102 mm I.D. outer cylinder

76 mm I.D. inner cylinder

Spacing and support blocks (3) for inner cylinder

254 mm diameter outer cover 273 mm long

Metal ring to hold legs

Inspection plug retained by turnbuttons

Legs provides 152 mm minimum clearance

T₃

T₄

Gypsum wallboard and similar products are also acceptable as noncombustible materials. They must have a structural base of noncombustible materials, a surface material no more than $1/_8$-inch in thickness and a maximum flame-spread index of 50.

Code Text: *Fire-resistance-rated glazing, when tested in accordance with ASTM E119 or UL 263 and complying with the requirements of Section 707, shall be permitted. Fire-resistance-rated glazing shall bear a label marked in accordance with Table 716.1(1) issued by an agency and shall be permanently identified on the glazing.*

Discussion and Commentary: Under the provisions of Table 716.1(3), fire windows are not permitted in fire walls and most fire barriers having a required fire-resistance rating of 1 hour or greater. Therefore, glazing in such fire separations must either be protected by complying fire shutters or be in compliance with the requirements of Section 703.4. The fire-resistance-rated glazing permitted by this section is acceptable because it is tested to the same criteria as any fire wall or fire barrier.

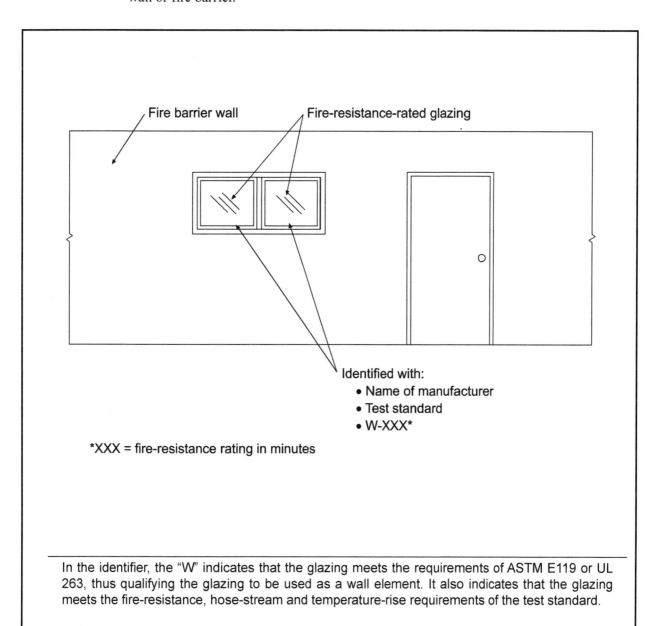

Fire barrier wall

Fire-resistance-rated glazing

Identified with:
- Name of manufacturer
- Test standard
- W-XXX*

*XXX = fire-resistance rating in minutes

In the identifier, the "W" indicates that the glazing meets the requirements of ASTM E119 or UL 263, thus qualifying the glazing to be used as a wall element. It also indicates that the glazing meets the fire-resistance, hose-stream and temperature-rise requirements of the test standard.

Code Text: *Where there is an accessible concealed floor, floor-ceiling or attic space, fire walls, fire barriers, fire partitions, smoke barriers and smoke partitions or any other wall required to have protected openings or penetrations shall be effectively and permanently identified with signs or stenciling in the concealed space.*

Discussion and Commentary: The integrity of fire and/or smoke separation walls is subject to compromise during the life of a building. During maintenance and remodel activities, it is not uncommon for new openings and penetrations to be installed in a fire separation wall without recognition that the integrity of the construction must be maintained or that some type of fire or smoke protective is required. Provisions mandating the appropriate identification of such walls under certain conditions have been established to better ensure that tradespeople, maintenance workers and inspectors will recognize the required level of protection that must be maintained.

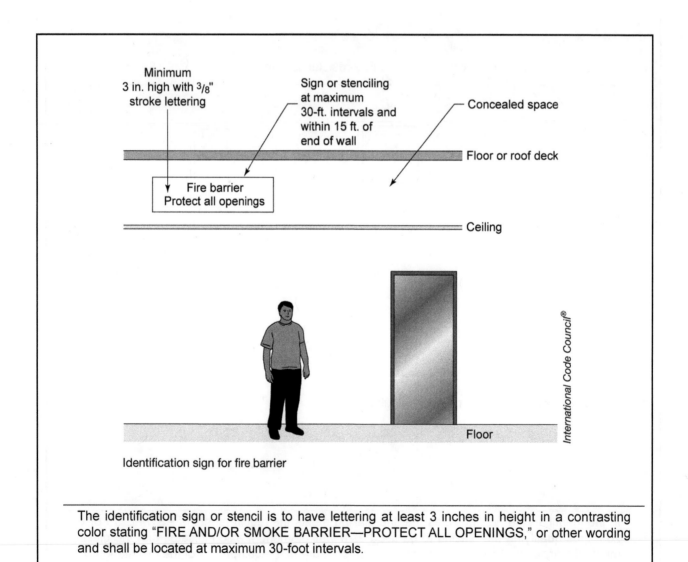

Identification sign for fire barrier

The identification sign or stencil is to have lettering at least 3 inches in height in a contrasting color stating "FIRE AND/OR SMOKE BARRIER—PROTECT ALL OPENINGS," or other wording and shall be located at maximum 30-foot intervals.

Code Text: *Members of the primary structural frame other than columns that are required to have protection to achieve a fire-resistance rating and support more than two floors or one floor and roof, or support a load-bearing wall or a nonload-bearing wall more than two stories high, shall be provided individual encasement protection by protecting them on all sides for their full length, including connections to other structural members, with materials having the required fire-resistance rating. Secondary members that are required to have protection to achieve a fire-resistance rating shall be protected by individual encasement protection.* Light-frame construction elements and horizontal assemblies are permitted to be protected by membrane protection.

Discussion and Commentary: Because of the differences in both the testing procedure and the conditions of acceptance, primary structural frame members carrying significant portions of the structure cannot simply be protected by enclosure within a fire-resistance-rated wall, floor/ceiling or roof/ceiling assembly. Therefore, under specific conditions, individual encasement is required.

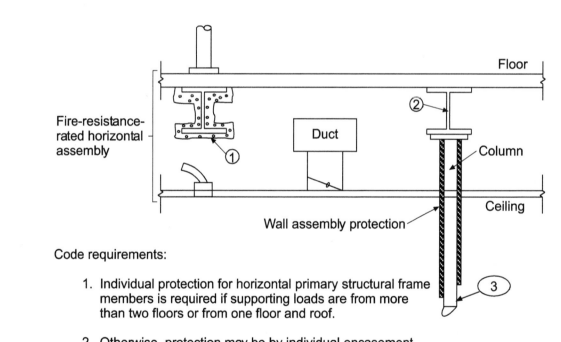

Code requirements:

1. Individual protection for horizontal primary structural frame members is required if supporting loads are from more than two floors or from one floor and roof.

2. Otherwise, protection may be by individual encasement, membrane or ceiling protection per Sec. 711, or combination of both.

3. Columns must always be individually encased and protected for full height (Sec. 704.2) unless in compliance with Section 704.4.1 when within walls of light-frame construction.

When a column requires a fire-resistance rating, it must always be fully protected by individual encasement, including its connections to beams or girders. If the column extends above a ceiling, the fire protection must continue through the above-ceiling space to the top of the column.

Code Text: *Load-bearing structural members located within the exterior walls or on the outside of a building or structure shall be provided with the highest fire-resistance rating as determined in accordance with the following: (1) as required by Table 601 for the type of building element based on the type of construction of the building, (2) as required by Table 601 for exterior bearing walls based on the type of construction, and (3) as required by Table 705.5 for exterior walls based on the fire separation distance.*

Discussion and Commentary: Structural frame members such as columns that are placed inside an exterior wall assembly, or are located on the outside of a building, must be evaluated for fire-resistance purposes. Three criteria are to be evaluated, with the minimum required fire-resistance rating of the structural members based on the highest rating of the three criteria.

GIVEN: An exterior nonbearing wall in a Type IIIB building housing a Group M occupancy. The wall has a fire separation distance of 15 feet to an interior lot line.

DETERMINE: The minimum required fire-resistance rating for structural columns located within the exterior wall.

SOLUTION:

Per Table 601 for structural frame members, a minimum of 0 hours

Per Table 601 for exterior bearing walls, a minimum of 2 hours

Per Table 705.5 for a FSD of 15 feet, a minimum of 1 hour

∴ The columns shall have a minimum fire-resistance rating of 2 hours

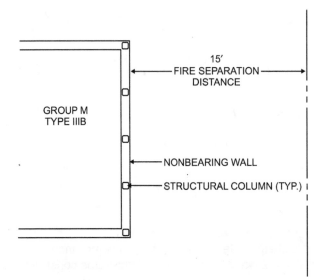

Any structural frame members located within, or on the outside of, an exterior wall should never have a lower fire-resistance rating than that required to protect the members from an internal fire. However, if the exposure hazard from an external source is so great as to require exterior wall protection, a higher rating may be required.

Code Text: *Cornices, eave overhangs, exterior balconies and similar projections extending beyond the exterior wall shall conform to the requirements of Sections 705 and 1405. Exterior egress balconies and exterior exit stairways and ramps shall also comply with Sections 1021 and 1027, respectively. Projections shall not extend any closer to the line used to determine the fire separation distance than shown in Table 705.2. See the exception for projections beyond opposing walls of two buildings on the same lot.*

Discussion and Commentary: Where a building projection is located in close proximity to another building, either on the same lot or an adjoining lot, there is significant potential under fire conditions for convected heat to be trapped. The requirement for some degree of physical separation between any adjacent building and the edge of a projection allows for open space to assist in the heat's dissipation.

TABLE 705.2
MINIMUM DISTANCE OF PROJECTION

FIRE SEPARATION DISTANCE-FSD (feet)	MINIMUM DISTANCE FROM LINE USED TO DETERMINE FSD
0 to less than 2	Projections not permitted
2 to less than 3	24 inches
3 to less than 5	Two-thirds of FSD
5 or greater	40 inches

For SI: 1 foot = 304.8 mm; 1 inch = 25.4 mm.

The allowable projection length is based upon the fire separation distance related to the exterior wall. Where the fire separation distance is less than 2 feet, no projection is permitted. If the fire separation distance is at least 2 feet, some amount of projection is allowed up to the limit established by Table 705.2.

Topic: Construction of Projections **Category:** Fire and Smoke Protection Features
Reference: IBC 705.2.1, 705.2.2, 705.2.3 **Subject:** Exterior Walls

Code Text: *Projections from walls of Type I or II construction shall be of noncombustible materials or combustible materials as allowed by Sections 705.2.3.1 and 705.2.4. Projections from walls of Type III, IV or V construction shall be of any approved material. Projections extending to within 5 feet (1524 mm) of the line used to determine the fire separation distance shall be of one of the following: noncombustible materials, combustible materials of not less than 1-hour fire-resistance-rated construction, heavy timber construction, fire-retardant-treated wood or as permitted by Section 705.2.3.1. See the exception for Group R-3 and U occupancies.*

Discussion and Commentary: In noncombustible buildings, those of Type I and II construction, projections must also be noncombustible in order to maintain the limited fire loading created by the building's construction features. In buildings where combustible construction is permitted—Types III, IV and V—combustible projections typically pose no greater hazard than the other combustible elements in the building.

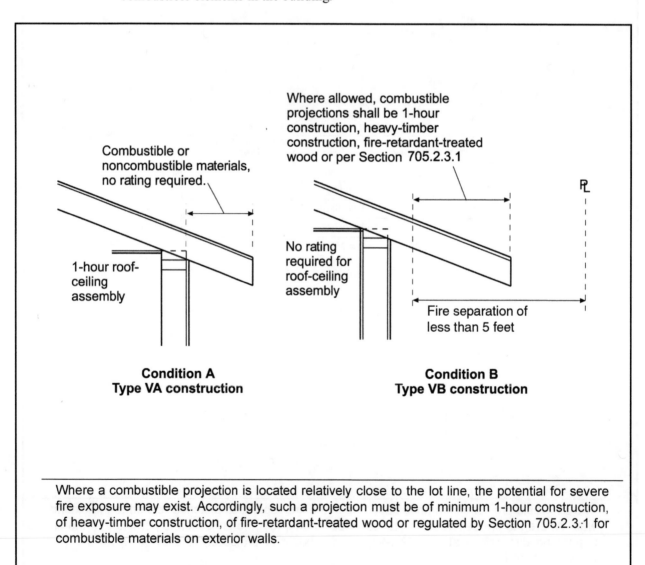

Where a combustible projection is located relatively close to the lot line, the potential for severe fire exposure may exist. Accordingly, such a projection must be of minimum 1-hour construction, of heavy-timber construction, of fire-retardant-treated wood or regulated by Section 705.2.3.1 for combustible materials on exterior walls.

2021 IBC Study Companion

Code Text: *For the purposes of determining the required wall and opening protection, projections and roof-covering requirements, buildings on the same lot shall be assumed to have an imaginary line between them.* See the exception where aggregate area of multiple buildings is within limits specified in Chapter 5 for a single building.

Discussion and Commentary: Where two or more buildings are placed on the same piece of property, their exterior walls and openings must be regulated in the same manner as if they were on separate lots. However, if the buildings could be constructed as a single structure under one roof and meet the size requirements based on occupancy and type of construction, then an assumed imaginary line is not required.

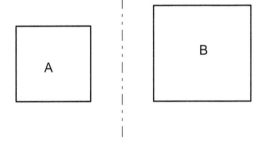

Assumed imaginary line

A

B

Case I: an assumed imaginary line between buildings

    A. Fire resistance and opening protection for walls adjacent to the imaginary line must comply with the code

    B. Imaginary line may be placed to take best advantage of wall and opening protection

Case II: as a single building

    A. Allowable area and type of construction are based on the most restrictive requirements for the occupancies housed

    B. Total floor area may not exceed that allowed for a single building

Buildings on the same lot

Where a new building is to be constructed on the same lot as an existing building, the assumed imaginary line must be placed in a location where it will not cause the exterior wall and opening protection of the existing building to become noncompliant.

Code Text: *Exterior walls shall be fire-resistance rated in accordance with Table 601, based on the type of construction, and Table 705.5, based on the fire separation distance.*

Discussion and Commentary: The rationale behind exterior wall protection is that an owner has no control over what occurs on an adjacent lot. The lot line concept provides a convenient means of protecting one building from another insofar as radiant heat could potentially be transmitted from one building to another during a fire. The requirements are based on "fire separation distance," which must be considered for all exterior walls. Where such walls are also bearing walls, the provisions of Table 601 also apply, governed by the more restrictive of the hourly ratings.

Table 705.5 Regulates Exterior Walls Only

- Table 705.5 used in conjunction with Table 601 for fire resistance of exterior bearing walls
- Only Table 705.5 used for nonbearing exterior walls
- Based on occupancy and type of construction
- Highest required rating for exterior wall is 3 hours
- Final threshold at ≥ 30'
- Additional provisions for exterior walls and openings throughout Section 705

TABLE 705.5
FIRE-RESISTANCE RATING REQUIREMENTS FOR EXTERIOR WALLS BASED ON FIRE SEPARATION DISTANCE[a, d, g]

FIRE SEPARATION DISTANCE = X (feet)	TYPE OF CONSTRUCTION	OCCUPANCY GROUP H[e]	OCCUPANCY GROUP F-1, M, S-1[f]	OCCUPANCY GROUP A, B, E, F-2, I, R[i], S-2, U[h]
X < 5[b]	All	3	2	1
5 ≤ X < 10	IA, IVA	3	2	1
	Others	2	1	1
10 ≤ X < 30	IA, IB, IVA, IVB	2	1	1[c]
	IIB, VB	1	0	0
	Others	1	1	1[c]
X ≥ 30	All	0	0	0

For SI: 1 foot = 304.8 mm.
a. Load-bearing exterior walls shall also comply with the fire-resistance rating requirements of Table 601.
b. See Section 706.1.1 for party walls.
c. Open parking garages complying with Section 406 shall not be required to have a fire-resistance rating.
d. The fire-resistance rating of an exterior wall is determined based upon the fire separation distance of the exterior wall and the story in which the wall is located.
e. For special requirements for Group H occupancies, see Section 415.6.
f. For special requirements for Group S aircraft hangars, see Section 412.3.1.
g. Where Table 705.8 permits nonbearing exterior walls with unlimited area of unprotected openings, the required fire-resistance rating for the exterior walls is 0 hours.
h. For a building containing only a Group U occupancy private garage or carport, the exterior wall shall not be required to have a fire-resistance rating where the fire separation distance is 5 feet (1523 mm) or greater.
i. For a Group R-3 building of Type II-B or Type V-B construction, the exterior wall shall not be required to have a fire-resistance rating where the fire separation distance is 5 feet (1523 mm) or greater.

In addition to establishing the required fire-resistive rating of exterior walls due to their location on the lot, the "fire separation distance" is also often utilized in the regulation of two or more buildings on the same lot, projections beyond the exterior wall, and parapet requirements.

Topic: Fire Separation Distance
Reference: IBC Table 705.5, 202

Category: Type of Construction
Subject: Exterior Walls

Code Text: Fire separation distance *is the distance measured from the building face to one of the following: (1) the closest interior lot line; (2) to the centerline of a street, alley or public way; or (3) to an imaginary line between two buildings on the lot. The distance shall be measured at right angles from the face of the wall.*

Discussion and Commentary: The atmospheric separation provided between a building and an adjoining structure provides resistance to fire spread due to radiant heat transfer. Many provisions throughout the IBC, such as those regulating projections and parapets, are based upon the degree of separation provided. A measurement at a right angle from the building face addresses heat transfer from the building of fire incident toward other structures and properties.

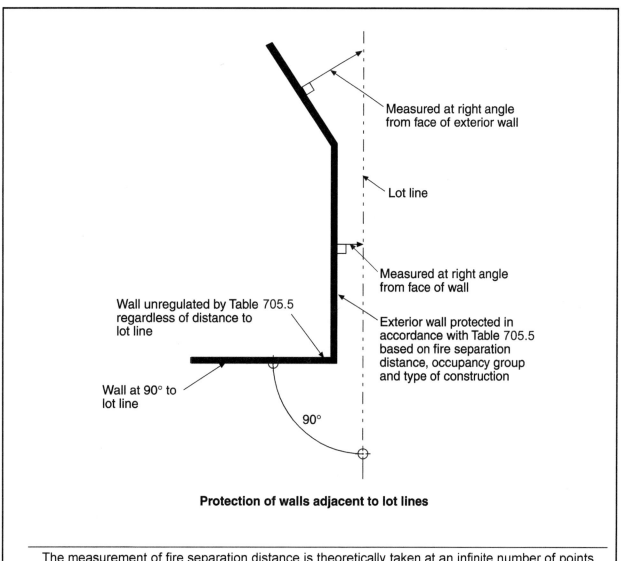

Protection of walls adjacent to lot lines

The measurement of fire separation distance is theoretically taken at an infinite number of points along the exterior wall. In reality, zones are created adjacent to the building under consideration, with higher degrees of regulation mandated for those zones closest to the building.

Code Text: The minimum fire-resistance rating for exterior bearing walls shall be *not less than the fire-resistance rating based on fire separation distance.* In addition to the fire-resistance rating requirements for exterior walls based on fire separation distance, *load-bearing exterior walls shall also comply with the fire-resistance rating requirements of Table 601.*

Discussion and Commentary: When analyzing an exterior wall for its required level of fire resistance, it is necessary to use both Tables 601 and 705.5. Table 601 addresses the potential need for structural stability of exterior bearing walls under fire conditions. Exterior nonbearing walls are not regulated by this table. The concern of radiant heat transfer from an adjoining burning building results in Table 705.5 regulating the exterior wall rating based upon its fire separation distance (typically the distance from the building face to the lot line). This concern exists for both bearing and nonbearing exterior walls.

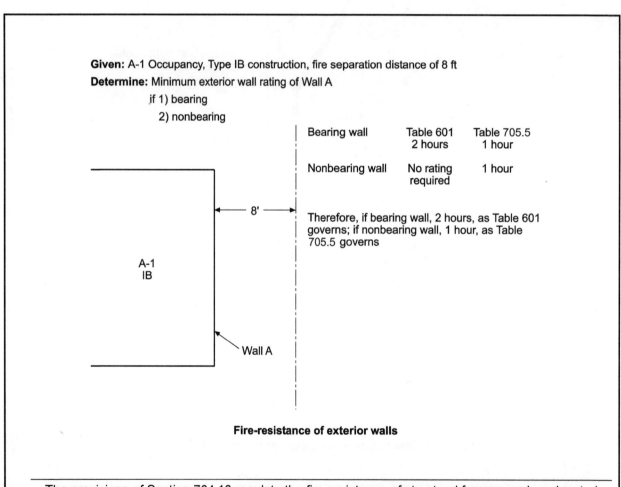

Given: A-1 Occupancy, Type IB construction, fire separation distance of 8 ft

Determine: Minimum exterior wall rating of Wall A

if 1) bearing

2) nonbearing

	Table 601	Table 705.5
Bearing wall	2 hours	1 hour
Nonbearing wall	No rating required	1 hour

Therefore, if bearing wall, 2 hours, as Table 601 governs; if nonbearing wall, 1 hour, as Table 705.5 governs

A-1
IB

8'

Wall A

Fire-resistance of exterior walls

The provisions of Section 704.10 regulate the fire resistance of structural frame members located within nonbearing exterior walls. The required fire rating is based on the highest of ratings found in Table 601 (structural frame, exterior bearing wall) and Table 705.5 (fire separation distance).

Code Text: *Exterior walls shall be fire-resistance rated in accordance with Table 601, based on the type of construction, and Table 705.5, based on fire separation distance. The required fire-resistance rating of exterior walls with a fire separation distance of greater than 10 feet (3048 mm) shall be rated for exposure to fire from the inside. The required fire-resistance rating of exterior walls with a fire separation distance of less than or equal to 10 feet (3048 mm) shall be rated for exposure to fire from both sides.*

Discussion and Commentary: Exposure of the exterior wall to an interior fire does not vary based on the distance of the wall from the lot line. However, exterior fire exposure decreases with an increase in the distance between the lot line and the exterior wall (fire separation distance). A fire separation distance of 10 feet is considered by the IBC to be a reasonable limit of flame impingement (direct exterior fire exposure) from an adjacent building.

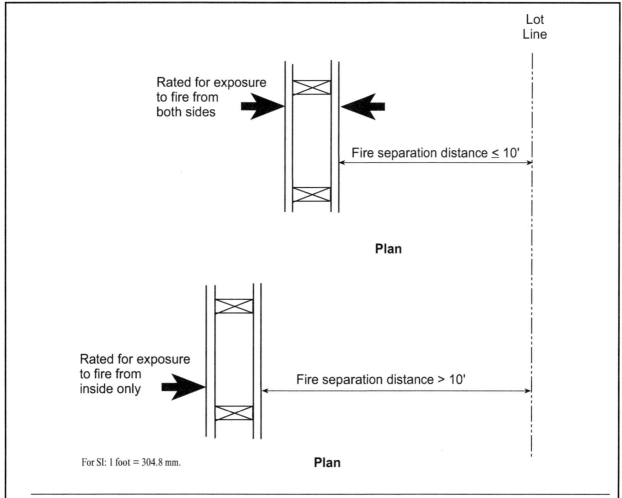

The determination of the minimum fire-resistance-rating for an exterior wall is typically based on two conditions: (1) the type of construction of the building, and (2) the fire separation distance. The higher of the two ratings regulates the minimum level of fire resistance.

Topic: Allowable Area of Openings   **Category:** Fire and Smoke Protection Features
Reference: IBC 705.8.1, 705.8.4   **Subject:** Exterior Walls

Code Text: *The maximum area of unprotected and protected openings permitted in an exterior wall in any story shall not exceed the percentages specified in Table 705.8 based on the fire separation distance of each individual story.* See the exceptions for (1) openings on the first story, and (2) stories where the exterior wall is not required to have a fire-resistance rating. *Where both unprotected and protected openings are located in the exterior wall in any story of a building, the total area of the openings shall comply with the following formula:* $A_p/a_p + A_u/a_u \le 1$.

Discussion and Commentary: Based on the fire separation distance, the amount of openings in an exterior wall is regulated on a floor-by-floor basis. Where all of the exterior openings are protected, a higher percentage of the exterior wall surface may be provided with openings, whereas a lesser amount is permitted if all openings are unprotected. The IBC also permits both protected and unprotected openings in an exterior wall, provided they comply with the unity formula. In a fully-sprinklered building, the maximum allowable area of unprotected openings is the same as that allowed for protected openings.

TABLE 705.8
MAXIMUM AREA OF EXTERIOR WALL OPENINGS BASED ON FIRE SEPARATION DISTANCE AND DEGREE OF OPENING PROTECTION

FIRE SEPARATION DISTANCE (feet)	DEGREE OF OPENING PROTECTION	ALLOWABLE AREA[a]
0 to less than 3[b, c]	Unprotected, Nonsprinklered (UP, NS)	Not Permitted
	Unprotected, Sprinklered (UP, S)[i]	Not Permitted
	Protected (P)	Not Permitted
3 to less than 5[d, e]	Unprotected, Nonsprinklered (UP, NS)	Not Permitted
	Unprotected, Sprinklered (UP, S)[i]	15%
	Protected (P)	15%
5 to less than 10[e, f]	Unprotected, Nonsprinklered (UP, NS)	10%[h]
	Unprotected, Sprinklered (UP, S)[i]	25%
	Protected (P)	25%
10 to less than 15[e, f, g]	Unprotected, Nonsprinklered (UP, NS)	15%[h]
	Unprotected, Sprinklered (UP, S)[i]	45%
	Protected (P)	45%
15 to less than 20[f, g]	Unprotected, Nonsprinklered (UP, NS)	25%
	Unprotected, Sprinklered (UP, S)[i]	75%
	Protected (P)	75%

If a building's exterior wall is not required to be fire-resistance rated by Table 705.5, then an unlimited percentage of unprotected openings is permitted regardless of fire separation distance.

Code Text: *In other than Group H occupancies, unlimited unprotected openings are permitted in the first story above grade either: (1.1) where the wall faces a street and has a fire separation distance of more than 15 feet (4572 mm), or (1.2) where the wall faces an unoccupied space. The unoccupied space shall be on the same lot or dedicated for public use, shall not be less than 30 feet (9144 mm) in width and shall have access from a street by a posted fire lane in accordance with the* International Fire Code.

Discussion and Commentary: Because the first story of a building is generally readily available for fire department access and manual suppression efforts, unprotected openings are not restricted, provided a moderate amount of open space is provided adjacent to the exterior wall. It is expected that the fire department can quickly mitigate the potential radiant heat exposure to surrounding buildings or structures.

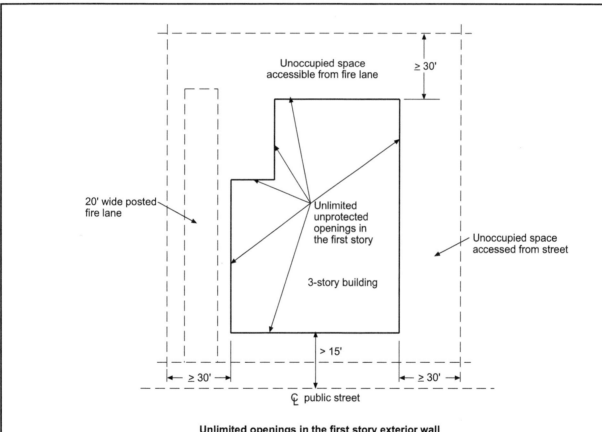

Unlimited openings in the first story exterior wall

For SI: 1 foot = 304.8 mm.

As the primary allowance for unlimited unprotected openings is the ability of the fire service to easily access and suppress at the ground level, it is critical that adequate open space be available for such purposes. Where not accessed directly from a street, a fire lane must be provided.

Topic: Vertical Separation of Openings	**Category:** Fire and Smoke Protection Features
Reference: IBC 705.8.5	**Subject:** Exterior Walls

Code Text: *Openings in exterior walls in adjacent stories shall be separated vertically to protect against fire spread on the exterior of the buildings where the openings are within 5 feet (1524 mm) of each other horizontally and the opening in the lower story is not a protected opening with a fire protection rating of not less than $^3/_4$ hour. Such openings shall be separated vertically not less than 3 feet (914 mm) by spandrel girders, exterior walls or other similar assemblies that have a fire-resistance rating of not less than 1 hour or by flame barriers than extend horizontally not less than 30 inches (762 mm) beyond the exterior wall. Flame barriers shall have a fire-resistance rating of not less than 1 hour.* See the exceptions for buildings no more than three stories in height, buildings that are fully sprinklered and open parking garages.

Discussion and Commentary: Where unprotected openings occur in adjacent stories, a fire that breaks out of an opening in a lower story can spread vertically to upper stories of the building. Two methods of flame resistance are available to restrict such fire spread.

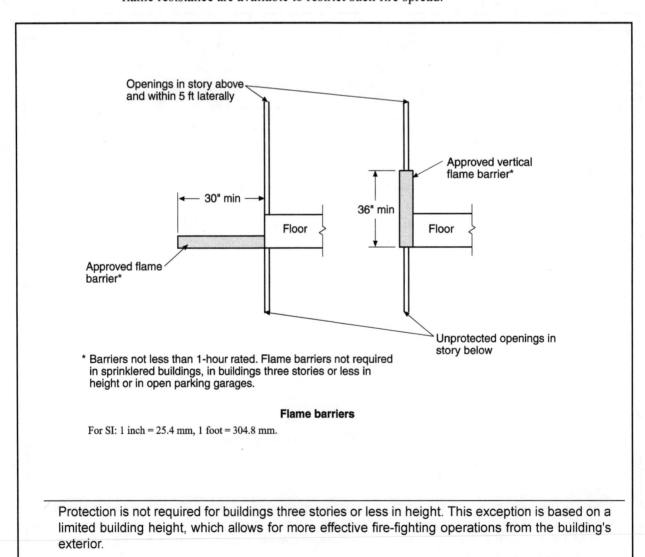

Openings in story above and within 5 ft laterally

Approved vertical flame barrier*

30" min

36" min

Floor

Floor

Approved flame barrier*

Unprotected openings in story below

* Barriers not less than 1-hour rated. Flame barriers not required in sprinklered buildings, in buildings three stories or less in height or in open parking garages.

Flame barriers

For SI: 1 inch = 25.4 mm, 1 foot = 304.8 mm.

Protection is not required for buildings three stories or less in height. This exception is based on a limited building height, which allows for more effective fire-fighting operations from the building's exterior.

Code Text: *Parapets shall be provided on exterior walls of buildings.* See the six exceptions for construction methods or locations that would eliminate the requirement for parapets. *Parapets shall have the same fire-resistance rating as that required for the supporting wall, and on any side adjacent to a roof surface, shall have noncombustible faces for the uppermost 18 inches (457 mm), including counterflashing and coping materials. The height of the parapet shall not be less than 30 inches (762 mm) above the point where the roof surface and the wall intersect.*

Discussion and Commentary: A parapet wall is defined as the part of any wall entirely above the roof line. Its purpose is to prevent the spread of fire from the roof of the subject building to an adjacent building and to protect the roof of a building from exposure to a fire in an adjacent building.

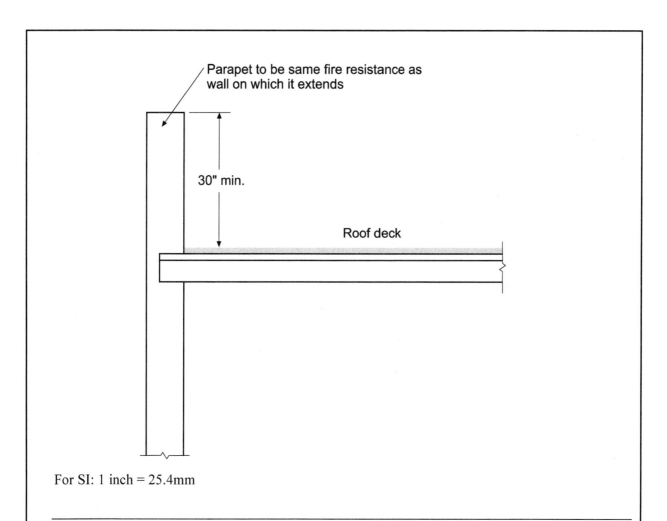

Parapet to be same fire resistance as wall on which it extends

30" min.

Roof deck

For SI: 1 inch = 25.4mm

As very few buildings actually provide exterior parapet walls for fire protection, it is evident that the exceptions are widely used. In many situations, a parapet is provided only to hide the roof slope or to screen rooftop equipment, in which case the requirements do not apply.

Code Text: *A parapet need not be provided on an exterior wall where 1-hour fire-resistance-rated exterior walls terminate at the underside of the roof sheathing, deck or slab, provided: four conditions are met.*

Discussion and Commentary: Limited to walls having a 1-hour fire-resistance rating, Exception 4 permits exterior walls to terminate at the underside of the roof sheathing as an alternative to the use of parapets. Protection of the roof construction is provided from the interior of the building rather than at the exterior side. In addition to the restrictions on roof covering materials and openings in the roof, roof framing elements are addressed where installed parallel or perpendicular to their supporting walls.

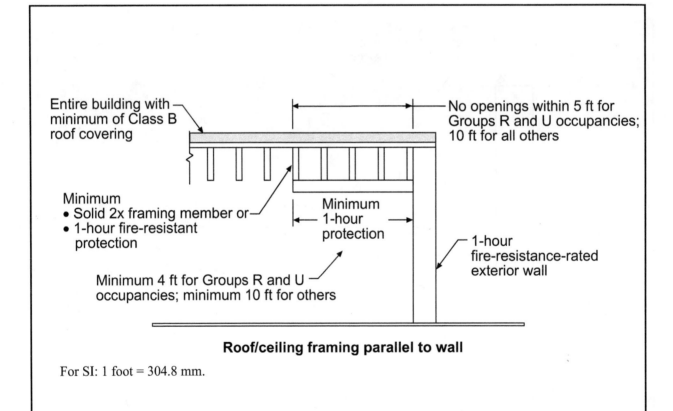

Roof/ceiling framing parallel to wall

For SI: 1 foot = 304.8 mm.

Other parapet exceptions are applicable where (1) the wall is not required to be fire-resistance-rated by Table 602; (2) no story exceeds 1,000 square feet in floor area; (3) the wall terminates at a minimum 2-hour fire-resistance-rated roof; (4) the roof is constructed of noncombustible materials, including the deck and supporting construction; (5) the wall is permitted to have a minimum of 25 percent unprotected openings per Section 705.8; or (6) in Groups R-2 and R-3, a number of special conditions are met.

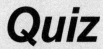

Quiz

Study Session 5
IBC Sections 701 through 705

1. An opening around a penetrating item is a(n) _____.

    a. annular space   b. penetration

    c. through penetration   d. joint

    Reference_____

2. A _____ is a listed device installed in a ceiling membrane of a fire-resistance-rated floor/ceiling or roof/ceiling assembly to limit automatically the radiative heat transfer through an air inlet/outlet opening.

    a. horizontal fire damper

    b. ceiling radiation damper

    c. combination fire/smoke damper

    d. horizontal access door

    Reference_____

3. The time period that a through-penetration firestop system or perimeter fire containment system limits the spread of fire through a penetration or void is considered

    _____.

    a. a fire protection rating   b. an F rating

    c. a T rating   d. a fire-resistance rating

    Reference_____

4. _____ consists of building materials installed to resist the free passage of flame to other areas of the building through concealed spaces.

    a. Draftstopping   b. Fireblocking

    c. Firestopping   d. Opening protectives

Reference_____

5. The measurement between the face of an exterior wall and the closest interior lot line is described as the _____.

    a. fire separation distance   b. fire exposure setback

    c. clearance to construction   d. exterior fire exposure

Reference_____

6. A _____ must have sufficient structural stability under fire conditions to allow collapse of construction on either side without collapse of the wall.

    a. fire wall   b. fire separation wall

    c. fire barrier   d. smoke barrier

Reference_____

7. A smoke compartment is a space within a building separated from other interior areas of the building by _____, including interior walls and horizontal assemblies.

    a. smoke partitions   b. smoke barriers

    c. shaft enclosure construction   d. fire partitions

Reference_____

8. The T rating for a penetration firestop system is based on a maximum temperature rise of _____ °F above its initial temperature through the penetration on the nonfire side when tested in accordance with ASTM E184 or UL 1479.

    a. 250   b. 325

    c. 375   d. 400

Reference_____

9. Where a fire-resistance rating of building elements, components or assemblies is determined by test procedures, the procedures set forth in ASTM E119 or_____ shall be applicable.

    a. ANSI Z 97.1   b. ASCE 5

    c. UL 263   d. UL 555

    Reference_____

10. Where a fire barrier is required to be identified by signage in an accessible concealed attic space, the identification shall occur at maximum intervals of _____ feet measured horizontally along the wall.

    a. 15   b. 20

    c. 30   d. 40

    Reference_____

11. Composite materials with a noncombustible structural base are considered noncombustible where the surface material is limited to _____ inch in thickness and has a maximum flame spread index of _____.

    a. $^{1}/_{2}$, 25   b. $^{1}/_{16}$, 50

    c. $^{1}/_{8}$, 25   d. $^{1}/_{8}$, 50

    Reference_____

12. A projection extending beyond an exterior wall located 6 feet from an interior lot line shall be located such that a minimum of_____ inches is provided between the lot line and the edge of the projection.

    a. 12   b. 24

    c. 40   d. 48

    Reference_____

13. Projections beyond an exterior wall are permitted where the exterior wall has a minimum fire separation distance of _____ inches.

    a. 12   b. 24

    c. 30   d. 36

    Reference_____

14. In a building of Type III construction, projections may be _____.

    a. of noncombustible construction

    b. of combustible construction

    c. of minimum one-hour fire-resistance-rated construction

    d. of any approved materials

Reference_____

15. For wall and opening protection, projections and roof covering requirements, an assumed imaginary line shall be placed between _____ unless they are considered a single building.

    a. court walls   b. fire areas

    c. buildings on the same lot   d. different occupancies

Reference_____

16. The fire-resistance rating for an exterior wall shall be based on both interior and exterior fire exposure where the wall is located a maximum of _____ feet from an interior lot line.

    a. 3   b. 5

    c. 10   d. 20

Reference_____

17. In a nonsprinklered Type VB building, what is the maximum permissible area of unprotected exterior wall openings for a fire separation distance of 8 feet?

    a. 10 percent   b. 25 percent

    c. unlimited   d. unprotected openings are prohibited

Reference_____

18. In a nonsprinklered Type IIIA building, what is the maximum allowable area of protected exterior wall openings for a fire separation distance of 20 feet?

    a. 25 percent   b. 45 percent

    c. 75 percent   d. unlimited

Reference_____

19. In a fully-sprinklered Type IIB office building, what is the maximum allowable area of unprotected exterior wall openings for a fire separation distance of 5 feet?

   a. 10 percent

   b. 15 percent

   c. 25 percent

   d. unprotected openings are prohibited

   Reference_____

20. In other than Group H occupancies, unlimited unprotected exterior openings are permitted in the first story above grade of exterior walls facing an unoccupied space of at least _____ feet in width.

   a. 15

   b. 20

   c. 30

   d. 40

   Reference_____

21. Where flame barriers are required for the vertical separation of exterior openings in adjacent stories, horizontal barriers must extend at least _____ inches beyond the exterior wall.

   a. 12

   b. 24

   c. 30

   d. 36

   Reference_____

22. Flame barriers protecting openings in exterior walls in adjacent stories shall have a minimum fire-resistance rating of _____.

   a. 20 minutes

   b. 45 minutes

   c. 1 hour

   d. 2 hours

   Reference_____

23. A parapet is not required at an exterior wall of a building having a maximum floor area of _____ square feet on each floor.

   a. 400

   b. 1,000

   c. 1,500

   d. 3,000

   Reference_____

24. Where required at exterior walls, parapets must extend a minimum of
_____ inches above the point where the roof surface and wall intersect.

    a. 30   b. 32

    c. 36   d. 42

Reference_____

25. The uppermost portion of parapet walls must have noncombustible faces for a minimum of _____ inches.

    a. 12   b. 18

    c. 24   d. 30

Reference_____

26. To obtain a fire-resistance rating, all nonsymmetrical walls except for _____ shall be tested with both faces exposed to the furnace.

    a. fire walls   b. fire barriers

    c. smoke barriers   d. exterior walls

Reference_____

27. A roof eave extending to within 5 feet of the line used to determine fire separation distance may be constructed of all of the following materials except _____ .

    a. heavy-timber construction

    b. noncombustible materials

    c. fire-retardant-treated wood

    d. $^1/_2$-hour fire-resistance-rated combustible construction

Reference_____

28. In a fully sprinklered Type IIA building, the maximum allowable area of protected exterior wall openings is _____ where the fire separation distance is 12 feet.

    a. 15 percent   b. 25 percent

    c. 45 percent   d. 60 percent

Reference_____

29. A parapet is not required on the exterior wall of a nonsprinklered building located a minimum of _____ feet from an interior lot line.

    a. 5   b. 10

    c. 15   d. 20

Reference_____

30. Unprotected openings are not permitted in the exterior wall of a Group H-3 warehouse where the fire separation distance is less than _____ feet.

    a. 15   b. 20

    c. 25   d. 30

Reference_____

31. Materials are considered to be _____ when tested and in compliance with ASTM E136.

    a. fire-resistive   b. noncombustible

    c. fire-retardant   d. nonflammable

Reference_____

32. The area of openings in an exterior wall of an open parking garage is permitted to be unlimited where there is a minimum fire separation distance of _____ feet.

    a. 5   b. 10

    c. 20   d. 30

Reference_____

33. A parapet is not required on an exterior wall where the wall terminates at a roof with a minimum fire-resistance rating of _____ .

    a. 45 minutes   b. 1 hour

    c. $1^{1}/_{2}$ hour   d. 2 hours

Reference_____

34. A projection extending beyond an exterior wall that is located 4 feet from an interior lot line shall be located such that a minimum of _____ inches is provided between the lot line and the edge of the projection.

    a. 12   b. 24

    c. 32   d. 40

Reference _____

35. In other than Group H occupancies, unlimited unprotected openings are permitted in a first-story exterior wall that faces a street, provided the minimum fire separation distance is greater than _____ feet.

    a. 5   b. 10

    c. 15   d. 20

Reference _____

36. In a Type IIB building housing a Group I-2 occupancy, what is the minimum required rating for an exterior nonbearing wall located with a fire separation distance of 8 feet?

    a. 3 hours   b. 2 hours

    c. 1 hour   d. 0 hours (no rating required)

Reference _____

37. In a Type IIA building housing a Group R-2 occupancy, what is the minimum required rating for an exterior nonbearing wall located with a fire separation distance of 3 feet?

    a. 3 hours   b. 2 hours

    c. 1 hour   d. 0 hours (no rating required)

Reference _____

38. Where an exterior bearing wall of a Group M occupancy of Type IIB construction is located 3 feet from an interior lot line, the wall must have a minimum fire-resistance rating of _____ hour(s).

    a. 0 hours (no rating required)   b. 1

    c. 2   d. 3

Reference _____

39. A nonbearing exterior wall of a Type IB open parking garage complying with Section 406 shall have a minimum fire-resistance rating of _____ hour(s) where the fire separation distance is 10 feet.

    a. 0 hours (no rating required)   b. 1

    c. 2   d. 3

    Reference _____

40. Fire protection is not required at the bottom flange of a lintel that is part of the primary structural frame provided the maximum lintel span is _____.

    a. 4 feet, 0 inches   b. 5 feet, 0 inches

    c. 5 feet, 6 inches   d. 6 feet, 4 inches

    Reference _____

2021 IBC Sections 706 through 712
Fire and Smoke Protection Features II

OBJECTIVE: To gain an understanding of the fire-resistance-rated building components such as fire walls, fire barriers, fire partitions, smoke barriers, smoke partitions, and horizontal assemblies and vertical openings.

REFERENCE: Sections 706 through 712, 2021 *International Building Code*

KEY POINTS:
- What is the purpose of a fire wall?
- Where is a party wall located? How is it to be constructed?
- How must a fire wall perform structurally?
- What is the relationship between NFPA 221 and Section 706 of the IBC?
- Which types of materials are permitted in a fire wall? How is the minimum fire-resistance rating of a fire wall determined?
- How must the horizontal continuity of a fire wall be accomplished? Vertical continuity?
- Which options are possible where a fire wall serves a stepped building?
- How shall the penetration of combustible framing members entering into a masonry or concrete fire wall be addressed?
- What are the limitations on openings in a fire wall?
- Where are fire barriers utilized?
- How must a fire barrier be constructed? What restrictions are placed on openings?
- What is a fire area? What is its purpose? How is the minimum fire-resistance rating for fire barrier assemblies separating fire areas determined?
- How is a joint made at the intersection of a fire barrier and the underside of a fire-resistance-rated floor or roof deck above to be regulated? At the intersection of a fire barrier and a nonfire-resistance-rated roof assembly?
- Where are fire partitions required to be installed?

- What minimum fire-resistance rating is required for fire partitions? What rating is required in a sprinklered hotel or apartment building?

- To what extent must a fire partition extend above a ceiling?

- What is the function of a smoke barrier?

- What fire-resistance rating is mandated for smoke barriers?

- How must openings in a smoke barrier be protected?

- Where are smoke barriers required?

- How is a smoke partition to be constructed? How are door openings, penetrations, ducts and air transfer openings regulated?

- How is the required rating of a horizontal assembly determined?

- What is the minimum fire-resistance rating for floor assemblies separating dwelling units in apartment buildings? Sleeping units in Group R-1 occupancies?

- What weight of ceiling panel requires no additional devices for the prevention of lateral displacement?

- When may the ceiling membrane in a fire-resistance-rated horizontal assembly be omitted? Floor membrane?

- How are skylights regulated in fire-resistance-rated roof construction?

- What various methods are permitted to address a joint in or between floor assemblies without a required fire-resistance rating?

- What are the various methods that have been established to address vertical openings between stories in a building?

Code Text: A fire wall is *a fire-resistance-rated wall having protected openings, which restricts the spread of fire and extends continuously from the foundation to or through the roof, with sufficient structural stability under fire conditions to allow collapse of construction on either side without collapse of the wall.*

Discussion and Commentary: By placing one or more fire walls in a large-area building, multiple smaller-area buildings are created. Each of these smaller spaces can then be considered a unique building for the purposes of allowable height, allowable area, construction type and number of control areas. Under various conditions, fire walls are also recognized for use in the creation of horizontal exits, as well as other applications.

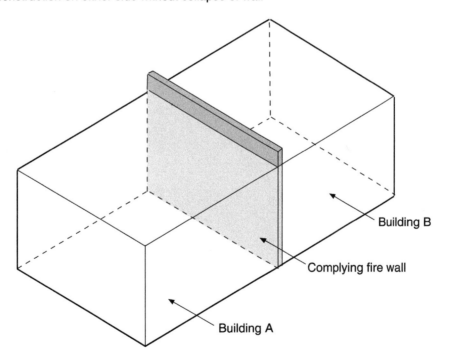

Fire wall to have sufficient structural stability under fire conditions to allow collapse of construction on either side without collapse of wall

Building B

Complying fire wall

Building A

In a situation where a fire wall separates distinct occupancy groups that are required to be separated by a fire barrier wall, the most restrictive requirements of each separation apply. This includes both the wall's continuity and the required fire-resistance rating.

Code Text: *Fire walls shall be of any approved noncombustible materials.* See the exception for Type V construction. *Fire walls shall have a fire-resistance rating of not less than that required by Table 706.4.*

Discussion and Commentary: A fire wall is designed to act in a manner similar to an exterior wall, as a barrier to prevent a fire in one building from spreading to the other building. Accordingly, construction of the fire wall must be commensurate with the exterior wall requirements for the construction type. In addition, the fire-resistance rating of the wall must be considerable in order to provide the necessary level of protection based on the anticipated fire loading that is due to the uses of the separate buildings. The required ratings vary based on occupancy and, to some degree, type of construction.

TABLE 706.4
FIRE WALL FIRE-RESISTANCE RATINGS

GROUP	FIRE-RESISTANCE RATING (hours)
A, B, E, H-4, I, R-1, R-2, U	3[a]
F-1, H-3[b], H-5, M, S-1	3
H-1, H-2	4[b]
F-2, S-2, R-3, R-4	2

a. In Type II or V construction, walls shall be permitted to have a 2-hour fire-resistance rating.

b. For Group H-1, H-2 or H-3 buildings, also see Sections 415.4 and 415.5.

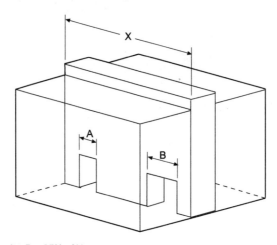

A + B ≤ 25% of X

Each opening limited to 156 square feet unless both buildings are sprinklered

Fire-protection rating based on Tables 706.4 and 715.4

For SI: 1 square foot = 0.093m²

Per Section 706.8, the total width of all openings in a fire wall is limited to 25 percent of the length of the wall in each story. There is no limit on the amount of total wall area containing openings; however, each opening is limited to 156 square feet in nonsprinklered buildings.

Code Text: *Fire walls shall be continuous from exterior wall to exterior wall and shall extend not less than 18 inches (457 mm) beyond the exterior surface of exterior walls.* See the three exceptions for various methods of terminating the fire wall at the interior surface of the exterior sheathing or finish materials.

Discussion and Commentary: Historically, the code has addressed the hazards of fire exposure at the fire wall from a vertical perspective, at the roof. There is also concern of a similar hazard from the horizontal perspective, at the intersection of the fire wall and the exterior wall. The 18-inch extension is intended to abate the potential for fire to travel from one building to the other around the fire wall. The 18-inch extension must extend the full height of the fire wall.

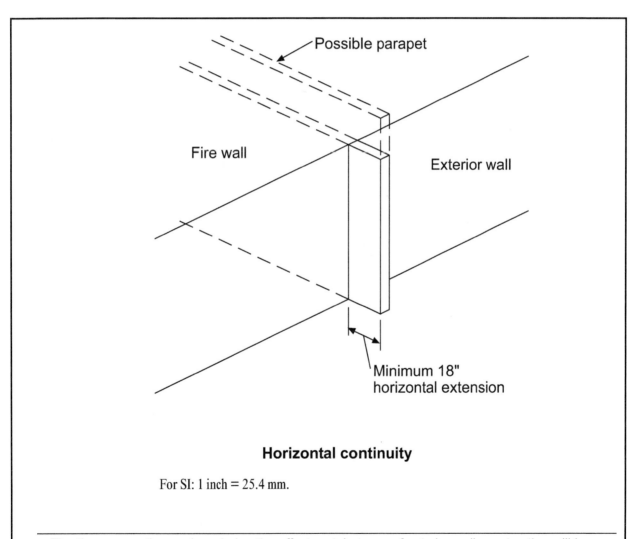

Horizontal continuity

For SI: 1 inch = 25.4 mm.

The three exceptions acknowledge the effect certain types of exterior wall construction will have on fire breaching the exterior of the building and exposing the adjacent building. These methods of protection are similar to those used at the roof construction where a parapet is not provided.

Code Text: *Fire walls shall extend from the foundation to a termination point not less than 30 inches (762 mm) above both adjacent roofs.* See the exceptions for buildings with different roof levels, those with noncombustible roof construction, and those constructed under special provisions.

Discussion and Commentary: To ensure the *separate building* concept, a fire wall must be continuous vertically with no horizontal offsets from the foundation, through the roof to a point at least 30 inches above. Various exceptions to the parapet requirement allow the fire wall to terminate at the bottom of the roof deck or sheathing. According to many of the exceptions, the roof covering must be minimum Class B, and no openings in the roof are permitted within 4 feet of the fire wall.

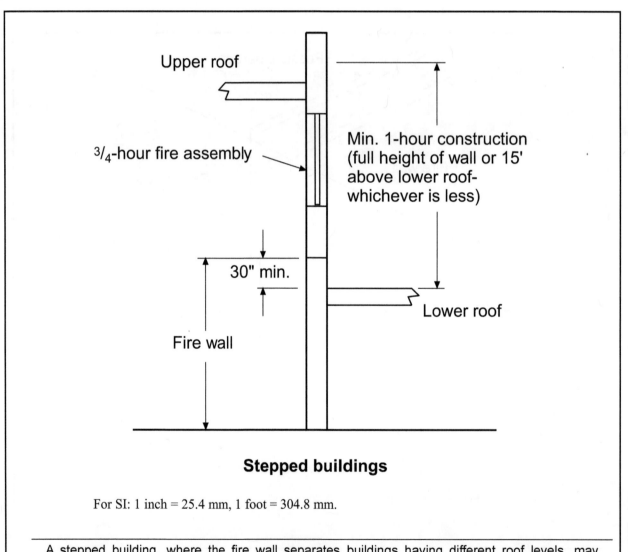

Upper roof

³/₄-hour fire assembly

Min. 1-hour construction (full height of wall or 15' above lower roof- whichever is less)

30" min.

Lower roof

Fire wall

Stepped buildings

For SI: 1 inch = 25.4 mm, 1 foot = 304.8 mm.

A stepped building, where the fire wall separates buildings having different roof levels, may require additional fire resistance to a point 15 feet above the lower roof. An alternative method provides for minimum 1-hour horizontal protection of the lower roof assembly.

Code Text: A fire barrier is *a fire-resistance-rated wall assembly of materials designed to restrict the spread of fire in which continuity is maintained. Fire barriers installed as required elsewhere in the* International Building Code *or the* International Fire Code *shall comply with* Section 707.

Discussion and Commentary: The term *fire barrier* is specific in the IBC and is used to describe a unique type of vertical fire separation element. Many of the building elements required to be constructed as fire barriers are listed in Section 707.3, including shaft enclosures, enclosures for interior exit stairways and exit access stairways, exit passageways, horizontal exits, atriums, incidental uses, control areas, separation of mixed occupancies and separation of fire areas.

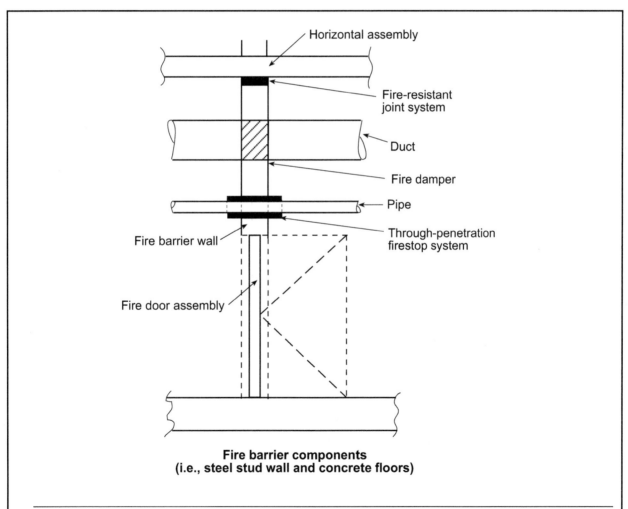

**Fire barrier components
(i.e., steel stud wall and concrete floors)**

Fire barriers may also be mandated for specific conditions not specifically mentioned in Section 707. Throughout the IBC, as well as the other *International Codes*, fire barriers are identified as the element used to provide the necessary fire separation for compartmentation of building spaces.

Code Text: *The fire barriers, fire walls or horizontal assemblies, or combination thereof, separating a single occupancy into different fire areas shall have a fire-resistance rating of not less than that indicated in Table 707.3.10. The fire barriers, fire walls or horizontal assemblies, or combination thereof, separating fire areas of mixed occupancies shall have a fire-resistance rating of not less than the highest value indicated in Table 707.3.10 for the occupancies under consideration.*

Discussion and Commentary: The code recognizes that in many buildings there are two methods to limit the spread of fire, either: (1) the use of an automatic sprinkler system, or (2) the creation of fire-resistive compartments that contain a fire's movement (fire areas). Section 903.2 identifies those occupancies where compartmentation is an acceptable alternative to a sprinkler system. Table 707.3.10 then mandates the minimum level of fire resistance of the fire barriers utilized to separate the building into two or more compartments (fire areas). As a result, the use of Table 707.3.10 is only applicable in buildings not protected by an automatic sprinkler system.

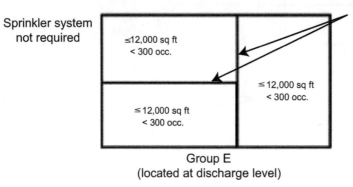

Example of the use of fire area concept

Sprinkler system not required

≤12,000 sq ft < 300 occ.

≤ 12,000 sq ft < 300 occ.

≤ 12,000 sq ft < 300 occ.

Minimum 2-hour fire barriers from Table 707.3.10

Group E
(located at discharge level)

For SI: 1 square foot = 0.093 m²

TABLE 707.3.10
FIRE-RESISTANCE RATING REQUIREMENTS FOR
FIRE BARRIERS, FIRE WALLS OR HORIZONTAL
ASSEMBLIES BETWEEN FIRE AREAS

OCCUPANCY GROUP	FIRE-RESISTANCE RATING (hours)
H-1, H-2	4
F-1, H-3, S-1	3
A, B, E, F-2, H-4, H-5, I, M, R, S-2	2
U	1

A fire area is considered the aggregate floor area enclosed and bounded by fire walls, fire barriers, exterior walls or horizontal assemblies of a building. The floor area under a canopy or similar horizontal projection is also included in the fire area determination.

Topic: Continuity	**Category:** Fire and Smoke Protection Features
Reference: IBC 707.5, 707.5.1	**Subject:** Fire Barriers

Code Text: *Fire barrier walls shall extend from the top of the floor/ceiling assembly below to the underside of the floor or roof sheathing, slab or deck above and shall be securely attached thereto. Such fire barriers shall be continuous through concealed spaces, such as the space above a suspended ceiling.* See the exceptions for shaft, stairway and ramp, and exit passageway enclosures. *The supporting construction for fire barrier walls shall be protected to afford the required fire-resistance rating of the fire barrier supported.* See the exceptions for fire barriers: (1) separating tank storage in accordance with Section 415.9.1.2, and (2) enclosing incidental uses.

Discussion and Commentary: Where a wall is required to serve as a fire barrier, it must be tight from floor deck to floor or roof deck in order to provide a full separation. A fire barrier is often used in conjunction with a horizontal assembly in a multistory building to provide a complete separation.

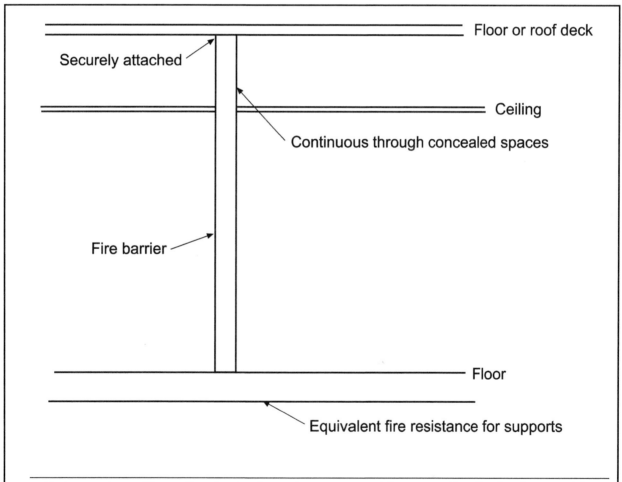

Under most conditions, the structural members or assemblies supporting fire barriers must be provided with equivalent or better fire resistance. It is important that the integrity of fire barriers supported by other building elements be maintained for the mandated time period.

Code Text: *Openings in a fire barrier shall be protected in accordance with Section 716. Openings shall be limited to a maximum aggregate width of 25 percent of the length of the wall, and the maximum area of any single opening shall not exceed 156 square feet (15 m²). Openings in enclosures for exit access stairways and ramps, interior exit stairways and ramps and exit passageways shall also comply with Sections 1019, 1023.4 and 1024.5, respectively. See the exceptions for (1) sprinklered adjoining floor areas, (2) fire doors serving an interior exit stairway or exit access stairway, (3) openings tested per ASTM E119 or UL 263, (4) fire windows in atrium separation walls and (5) fire doors separating an interior exit stairway/ramp or exit access stairway/ramp from an exit passageway.*

Discussion and Commentary: As openings in a fire barrier create a potential breach in the integrity of the fire-resistive separation, a limit is placed on the amount of permitted openings. The limitation allows for design flexibility without compromising the necessary level of fire separation. The aggregate area of such openings is not limited; however, each opening is limited to 156 square feet.

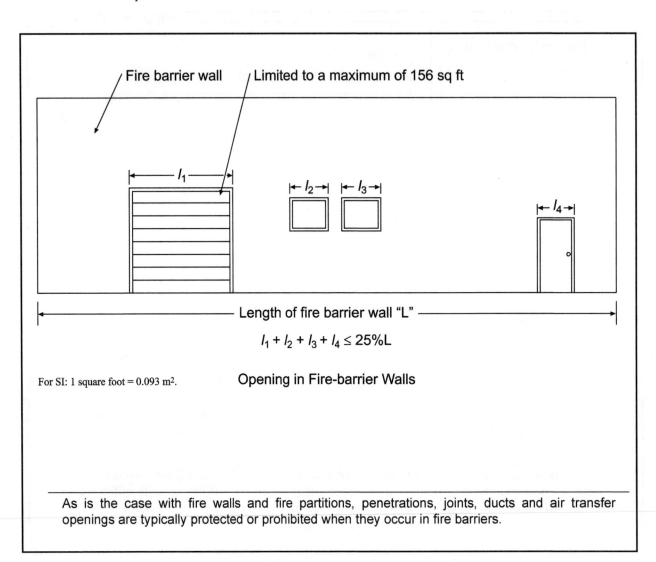

For SI: 1 square foot = 0.093 m².

Fire barrier wall

Limited to a maximum of 156 sq ft

Length of fire barrier wall "L"

$$l_1 + l_2 + l_3 + l_4 \leq 25\%L$$

Opening in Fire-barrier Walls

As is the case with fire walls and fire partitions, penetrations, joints, ducts and air transfer openings are typically protected or prohibited when they occur in fire barriers.

Code Text: A fire partition is *a vertical assembly of materials designed to restrict the spread of fire in which openings are protected. The following wall assemblies shall comply with* Section 708: *(1) separation walls as required by Section 420.2 for Group I-1 and Group R occupancies; (2) walls separating tenant spaces in covered and open mall buildings as required by Section 402.4.2.1, (3) corridor walls as required by Section 1020.3, (4) enclosed elevator lobby separation as required by Section 3006.3, (5) egress balconies as required by Section 1021.2, (6) walls separating ambulatory care facilities from adjacent spaces, and (7) vestibules per Section 1028.2. Fire partitions shall have a fire-resistance rating of not less than 1 hour.* See the exceptions for ratings reductions for corridor walls and dwelling unit/sleeping unit separations.

Discussion and Commentary: Typically required to have a fire-resistance-rating of one-hour, fire partitions provide a moderate level of separation that is necessary under certain conditions. Although fire partitions have limited applications, they are important elements in the specific uses and areas in which they are mandated.

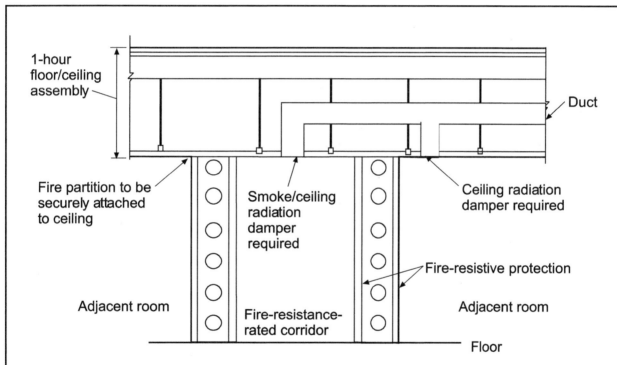

1-hour floor/ceiling assembly

Duct

Fire partition to be securely attached to ceiling

Smoke/ceiling radiation damper required

Ceiling radiation damper required

Fire-resistive protection

Adjacent room

Adjacent room

Fire-resistance-rated corridor

Floor

The suspended ceiling is used to provide fire protection for the structural members above. Dampers are required wherever ducts pierce the rated ceiling.

Corridor fire partitions

In sprinklered buildings of Types IIB, IIIB and VB construction, the 1-hour fire-resistance rating for dwelling unit and guestroom separations may be reduced to $1/_2$ hour. For a typical wood-stud wall system, this separation could be satisfied with $1/_2$-inch gypsum board installed on each side.

Code Text: *Fire partitions shall extend from the top of the foundation or floor/ceiling assembly below and be securely attached to one of the following: (1) the underside of the floor or roof sheathing, deck or slab above; or (2) the underside of a fire-resistance-rated floor/ceiling or roof/ceiling assembly having a fire-resistance rating that is not less than the fire-resistance rating of the fire partition.* See four exceptions to these continuity options. *The supporting construction for a fire partition shall have a fire-resistance rating that is equal to or greater than the required fire-resistance rating of the supported fire partition.* See exception for conditions where rating is not required.

Discussion and Commentary: The method of continuity is a primary difference between fire barriers and fire partitions. Fire partitions need not extend through a concealed space, such as the one above a suspended ceiling, provided that the ceiling is a portion of a fire-resistance-rated floor/ceiling or roof/ceiling assembly.

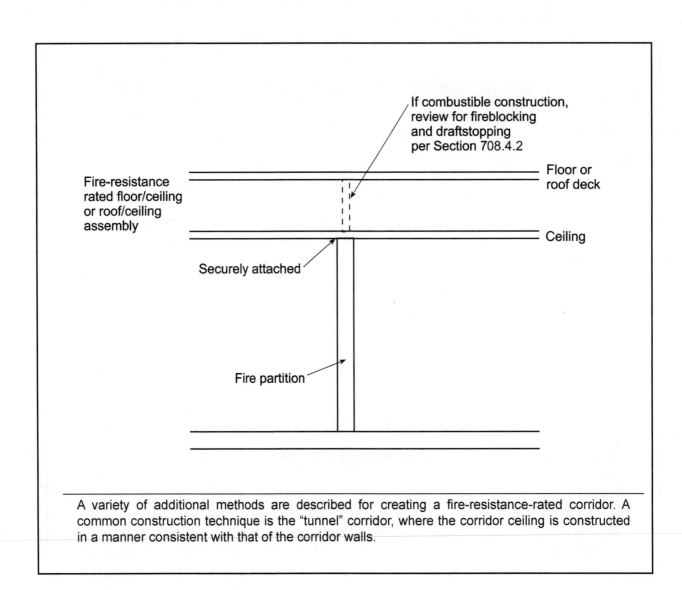

A variety of additional methods are described for creating a fire-resistance-rated corridor. A common construction technique is the "tunnel" corridor, where the corridor ceiling is constructed in a manner consistent with that of the corridor walls.

Code Text: A smoke barrier is *a continuous membrane, either vertical or horizontal, such as a wall, floor, or ceiling assembly, that is designed and constructed to restrict the movement of smoke. Smoke barriers shall form an effective membrane continuous from the top of the foundation or floor/ceiling assembly below to the underside of the floor or roof sheathing, deck or slab above, including continuity through concealed spaces, such as those found above suspended ceilings, and including interstitial structural and mechanical spaces.* See the exceptions where ceilings or exterior walls provide resistance to fire and smoke equivalent to the resistance provided by smoke barrier walls.

Discussion and Commentary: Where the primary concern of the code is the containment of smoke, the use of a smoke barrier is mandated. The locations for smoke barriers are found in various provisions in the IBC, including Section 407.5 for Group I-2 occupancies and Section 1009.6.4 for areas of refuge.

Required Use of Smoke Barriers

- Compartmentation of underground buildings (Sec. 405.4.2)
- Compartmentation of Group I-2 (Sec. 407.5)
- Compartmentation of Group I-3 (Sec. 408.6)
- Compartmentation of ambulatory care facilities (Sec. 422.3)
- Compartmentation of Group I-1, Condition 2 (Sec. 420.6)
- Smoke control systems (Sec. 402.7.2, 404.5 and 909.5)
- Areas of refuge (Sec. 1009.6.4)

A smoke barrier must have a minimum 1-hour fire-resistance rating. Openings, penetrations, joints, ducts and transfer openings must also be protected to minimize the passage of smoke through the barrier. Opening protectives must have a minimum 20-minute fire-protection rating.

Code Text: *Smoke partitions installed as required elsewhere in the IBC shall comply with Section 710. The walls shall be of materials permitted by the building type of construction. Unless required elsewhere in the IBC, smoke partitions are not required to have a fire-resistance rating. Smoke partitions shall extend from the top of the foundation or floor below to the underside of the floor or roof sheathing, deck or slab above or to the underside of the ceiling above where the ceiling membrane is constructed to limit the transfer of smoke.*

Discussion and Commentary: A smoke partition is designed for a singular purpose, to limit the movement of smoke from one area to another. Therefore, windows in smoke partitions must be sealed, penetrations and joints must be adequately filled, and smoke dampers used to protect air transfer openings. The most common application of smoke partitions is corridor walls of Group I-2 occupancies.

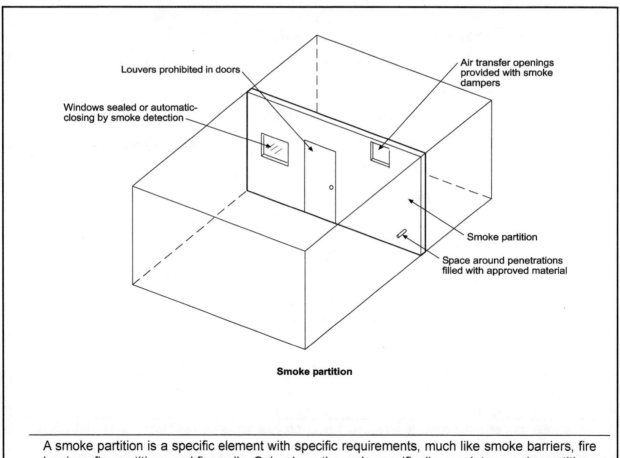

Smoke partition

A smoke partition is a specific element with specific requirements, much like smoke barriers, fire barriers, fire partitions and fire walls. Only where the code specifically mandates smoke partitions are the requirements of Section 710 applicable.

Code Text: *Assemblies shall be continuous without vertical openings, except as permitted by Sections 711 and 712. The supporting construction shall be protected to afford the required fire-resistance rating of the horizontal assembly supported.* See the exception for incidental uses, dwelling and sleeping unit separations and smoke barriers. *The fire-resistance rating of horizontal assemblies shall comply with Sections 711.2.4.1 through 711.2.4.6 but shall be not less than that required by the building type of construction.*

Discussion and Commentary: Table 601 regulates the minimum fire-resistance ratings for floor construction based on the building's type of construction. This minimum level of fire-resistance must always be maintained. Other provisions of the code must also be considered where a horizontal separation is needed within a multistory building, such as for control areas or occupancy separations.

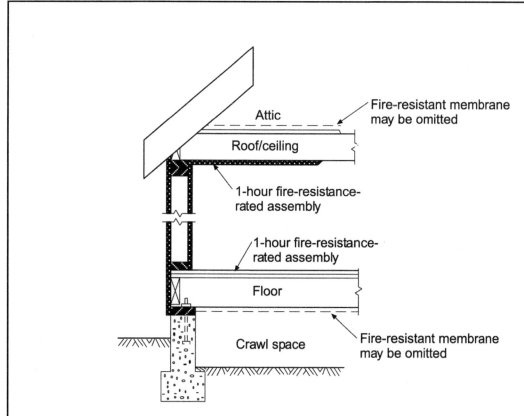

Omission of ceiling and flooring in horizontal assemblies per Section 711.2.6

Other than permitted openings, penetrations or joints, horizontal assemblies must be continuous in order to isolate totally one floor from another. An allowance is permitted for fire-resistance-rated roof construction, where skylights and other penetrations may be unprotected.

Code Text: *Each vertical opening shall comply in accordance with one of the protection methods in Sections 712.1.1 through 712.1.16.*

Discussion and Commentary: In multistory buildings, the upward transmission of fire, smoke and toxic gases through openings in the floor/ceiling assemblies continues to be a hazard of the highest degree. For many years, a shaft enclosure was considered the appropriate method to protect openings within a floor/ceiling assembly. Over time, other methods of protection have been identified as acceptable alternatives to the shaft enclosure approach. The IBC now places the emphasis on the presence of vertical openings while identifying the use of shaft enclosures as one of many protective measures that can be utilized to address the concern related to the vertical spread of fire, smoke and toxic gases.

Shaft Enclosures	**712.1.1**
Individual Dwelling Units	**712.1.2**
Escalator Openings	**712.1.3**
Penetrations	**712.1.4**
Joints	**712.1.5**
Ducts	**712.1.6**
Atriums	**712.1.7**
Masonry Chimneys	**712.1.8**
Two-Story Openings	**712.1.9**
Parking Garages	**712.1.10**
Mezzanines	**712.1.11**
Exit Access Stairs and Ramps	**712.1.12**
Floor Fire Doors and Access Doors	**712.1.13**
Group I-3 Occupancies	**712.1.14**
Skylights	**712.1.15**
Openings Otherwise Permitted	**712.1.16**

In addition to a general reference to any other code provisions that might address the protection of vertical openings between stories, seventeen specific conditions—including shaft enclosures—are listed that identify various methods of compliance.

Quiz

Study Session 6
IBC Sections 706 through 712

1. Fire walls must be constructed of noncombustible materials unless separating buildings of Type _____ construction.

    a. I   b. III

    c. IV   d. V

    Reference_____

2. A fire wall separating Type VA buildings housing Group M occupancies must have a minimum fire-resistance rating of _____ hour(s).

    a. 1   b. 2

    c. 3   d. 4

    Reference_____

3. In a Type IIB building containing a Group B occupancy, what is the minimum required fire-resistance rating for a fire wall?

    a. 1 hour   b. 2 hour

    c. 3 hour   d. 4 hour

    Reference_____

4. As a general provision, what minimum distance must a fire wall extend horizontally beyond the exterior surface of exterior walls?

    a. 18 inches   b. 20 inches

    c. 30 inches   d. 4 feet

    Reference_____

5. In general, what minimum distance above the roof must a fire wall extend?

    a. 18 inches   b. 30 inches

    c. 3 feet   d. 4 feet

Reference_____

6. Where a fire wall occurs at a location where the roof levels differ, the fire wall may terminate at the underside of the lower roof slab, provided three conditions are met, including _____ .

    a. the lower roof is of noncombustible construction

    b. the lower roof assembly within 10 feet of the fire wall has a minimum 1-hour rating

    c. the exterior wall of the higher portion is 1-hour to a height of 10 feet

    d. openings in the lower roof have a minimum 45-minute fire-protective rating

Reference_____

7. Embedded ends of combustible members entering masonry or concrete fire walls shall be separated a minimum distance of _____ inch(es).

    a. 1   b. 2

    c. 4   d. 6

Reference_____

8. The aggregate width of openings in a fire wall is limited to a maximum of _____ of the length of the wall.

    a. 10 percent   b. 25 percent

    c. $33^1/_3$ percent   d. 50 percent

Reference_____

9. Fire barriers are required for the separation of all of the following building elements, except _____ .

    a. shaft enclosures   b. exit passageways

    c. incidental uses   d. fire-resistance-rated corridors

Reference_____

10. In Type VB buildings, construction supporting fire barriers need not be protected by equivalent fire resistance where the fire barriers are used for _____ .

    a. 1-hour occupancy separations

    b. 1-hour interior exit stairways

    c. 1-hour incidental use separations

    d. 2-hour horizontal exits

    Reference_____

11. In a nonsprinklered building, any single opening in a fire barrier used for separating control areas is limited to a maximum area of _____ square feet.

    a. 20   b. 100

    c. 120   d. 156

    Reference_____

12. Openings for the fire door assemblies in a fire barrier are permitted to be unlimited in area and aggregate width where the fire barrier is utilized as a(n) _____ .

    a. interior exit stairway enclosure

    b. horizontal exit wall

    c. incidental use separation

    d. control area separation

    Reference_____

13. Where vertical openings are created for an escalator system in a fully sprinklered hotel, special opening protection methods are established , other than automatic shutters, where the openings connect a maximum of _____ stories.

    a. two   b. three

    c. four   d. six

    Reference_____

14. A floor opening is permitted between a maximum of two stories without vertical opening protection, under specified conditions, in all but which one of the following occupancies?

    a.   Group A-2   b.   Group H-2

    c.   Group I-2   d.   Group S-2

Reference_____

15. Fire walls shall be designed and constructed for structural stability in accordance with IBC Section 706 or _____.

    a.   NFPA 286   b.   NFPA 221

    c.   UL 1040   d.   UL 2079

Reference_____

16. A fire barrier used as a horizontal exit shall have a minimum fire-resistance rating of _____.

    a.   1 hour   b. $1^1/_2$ hours

    c.   2 hours   d.   3 hours

Reference_____

17. A fire partition is not the appropriate wall assembly for walls separating _____ .

    a.   sleeping units in a Group R-1 hotel

    b.   tenant spaces in a covered mall building

    c.   control areas in a manufacturing occupancy

    d.   dwelling units in an apartment building

Reference_____

18. What is the minimum required fire-resistance rating for a fire partition separating sleeping units in a Group I-1 occupancy housed in a Type IIA building?

    a.   20 minutes   b.   30 minutes

    c.   1 hour   d.   no rating is required

Reference_____

19. Where a fire-resistance-rated corridor ceiling is constructed as required for the corridor walls, the walls shall not terminate before reaching _____ .

    a. the lower membrane of the ceiling assembly

    b. the upper membrane of the ceiling assembly

    c. the underside of the floor or roof deck above

    d. an approved fire-resistant joint system

    Reference_____

20. In other than a Group I-3 occupancy, what is the minimum required fire-resistance rating for a smoke barrier?

    a. no rating is required   b. 30 minutes

    c. 45 minutes   d. 1 hour

    Reference_____

21. In which one of the following types of construction must a smoke barrier be supported by fire-resistance-rated construction having at least an equivalent rating to the smoke barrier supported?

    a. Type IIB   b. Type IIIA

    c. Type IIIB   d. Type VB

    Reference_____

22. Automatic shutters utilized to protect escalator openings between stories shall have a minimum fire-resistance rating of _____.

    a. 45 minutes   b. 1 hour

    c. $1^{1}/_{2}$ hours   d. 2 hours

    Reference_____

23. Wire or other approved devices shall be installed above lay-in ceiling panels in a fire-resistance-rated floor/ceiling assembly to prevent vertical displacement where the weight of the panels is not adequate to resist a minimum upward force of

_____ .

    a. 1 psf   b. 2 psf

    c. 5 psf   d. 15 psf

    Reference_____

24. Under which of the following conditions may the ceiling membrane of a fire-resis-tance-rated horizontal assembly be omitted?

    a.   where usable attic space occurs above

    b.   where the assembly has a minimum fire-resistance rating of 2 hours

    c.   where the floor construction is limited to combustible construction

    d.   where an unusable crawl space occurs below

Reference_____

25. Unprotected skylights are permitted through a fire-resistance-rated roof deck, pro-vided _____ .

    a.   the skylights were tested as a part of the roof assembly

    b.   the roof construction has not less than a 1-hour fire-resistance rating

    c.   the structural integrity of the roof construction is maintained

    d.   they are limited to 10 percent of the total roof area

Reference_____

26. Where a fire barrier is utilized to separate a Group M occupancy into multiple fire areas, the minimum fire-resistance rating of the fire barrier shall be _____ hour(s).

    a. 1   b. 2

    c. 3   d. 4

Reference_____

27. The voids created at the intersection of a fire barrier and a nonfire-resistance-rated roof assembly _____ .

    a.   are not regulated by the code

    b.   shall be filled by an approved material or system

    c.   shall be sealed with a noncombustible material

    d.   must be protected with a fire-resistive joint system

Reference_____

28. What hourly rating is mandated for the construction of smoke partitions?

    a.   0, no rating is required   b. $^1/_2$ hour

    c. $^3/_4$ hour   d.   1 hour

    Reference_____

29. Windows in smoke partitions shall have a minimum fire-protection rating of

    _____ .

    a.   0, no rating is required   b.   20 minutes

    c.   45 minutes   d.   1 hour

    Reference_____

30. In a Type IIB hotel that is sprinklered in accordance with NFPA 13, what is the minimum fire-resistance rating for the fire partitions and horizontal assemblies that separate sleeping units?

    a.   0, no rating is required   b. $^1/_2$ hour

    c.   1 hour   d.   2 hours

    Reference_____

31. In general, fire walls shall extend to the outer edge of horizontal projecting elements that are located within _____ feet of the fire wall.

    a.   4   b.   5

    c.   8   d.   10

    Reference _____

32. In which of the following uses must cross-corridor doors be provided with a vision panel?

    a.   ambulatory care facilities   b.   large assembly facilities

    c.   hotels   d.   day-care facilities

    Reference _____

33. In other than Group _____ occupancies, the vertical openings created by an atrium condition are regulated under the provisions of IBC Section 404.

    a. A   b. H

    c. I   d. R

Reference _____

34. Unless the installation of a damper will interfere with the operation of a smoke control system, air transfer openings in smoke partitions shall be provided with what type of damper?

    a. smoke damper only

    b. fire damper only

    c. combination fire/smoke damper

    d. no damper is required

Reference _____

35. In a Group I-2 occupancy where a pair of opposite-swinging doors without a center mullion is installed in a smoke barrier across a corridor, the doors are permitted maximum undercuts of _____ inch.

    a. $1/_4$ b. $3/_8$

    c. $1/_2$ d. $3/_4$

Reference _____

36. A wall located on a lot line between adjacent buildings that is used for joint service between the two buildings shall be constructed as a _____.

    a. fire partition   b. fire barrier

    c. fire wall   d. exterior wall

Reference _____

37. Where double fire walls are used in accordance with NFPA 221 in a building assigned to Seismic Design Category D, floor and roof sheathing having a maximum thickness of _____ inch is permitted to be continuous through the wall assemblies of light frame construction.

    a. $1/_4$ b. $1/_2$

    c. $5/_8$ d. $3/_4$

Reference _____

38. In Group R-2 occupancies of combustible construction where fire partitions do not extend to the underside of the floor sheathing above, fireblocking and draftstopping are not required where the building has a maximum of _____ dwelling units.

    a. 3   b. 4

    c. 5   d. 8

Reference _____

39. Where pass-through openings are provided in smoke partitions in Group I-2, Condition 2 occupancies, the maximum aggregate area of all pass-through openings permitted within a single room is _____ square inches.

    a. 16   b. 64

    c. 80   d. 144

Reference _____

40. Unconcealed vertical openings are permitted within an individual dwelling unit where connecting a maximum of _____ stories.

    a. 2   b. 3

    c. 4   d. 5

Reference _____

2021 IBC Sections 713 through 720
Fire and Smoke Protection Features III

OBJECTIVE: To gain an understanding of shaft enclosures, fireblocking and draftstopping, as well as the methods of protecting fire-resistance-rated building components where they contain doors, windows, ducts, air transfer openings and penetrations.

REFERENCE: Sections 713 through 720, 2021 *International Building Code*

KEY POINTS:
- What is the purpose of a shaft enclosure? Where are such enclosures required?
- What type of fire-resistance-rated assemblies are used to construct shaft enclosures?
- How does the height of a building affect the fire-resistance ratings of shaft enclosures? How does the fire-resistance rating of the floor construction apply?
- Which methods are mandated for construction of a shaft enclosure?
- Which types of openings are permitted to penetrate a shaft enclosure? How must they be protected?
- How must shafts be enclosed at the top? At the bottom?
- Which special provisions govern refuse, recycling and laundry chutes?
- Which two types of penetrations are regulated by the code?
- What are the appropriate installation details where sleeves are used in penetrating a fire-resistance-rated assembly?
- What is a through penetration? Membrane penetration?
- Penetrating items of steel, ferrous or copper may be protected in what manner?
- What is an F rating and a T rating? What minimum fire-resistance rating is required of a through-penetration firestop system?
- How can the membrane penetration by a steel outlet box be addressed? A listed electrical box? A fire sprinkler?
- Which limitations are placed on noncombustible penetrating items connecting to combustible items?

KEY POINTS:
(Cont'd)

- How are fire-resistance-rated horizontal assemblies penetrated? Nonfire-resistance-rated horizontal assemblies?

- What is the purpose of a fire-resistance-rated joint system? When is such a system required?

- How should the intersection of an exterior curtain wall and a fire-resistance-rated floor assembly be accomplished? An exterior curtain wall and a nonrated floor assembly?

- How is the required fire-protection rating of an opening protective determined?

- What are the characteristics of a fire-resistance-rated corridor door or smoke barrier door?

- In what locations must a fire door be rated to a maximum transmission temperature end point?

- What are the labeling requirements for fire doors? Smoke and draft control doors? Fire-protection-rated glazing?

- Where are self-closing door assemblies mandated? Automatic-closing assemblies?

- What is the maximum fire-protection rating assigned to fire-protection-rated glazing?

- What are the different types of dampers? How should they be actuated?

- How must fire and smoke dampers be identified and accessed?

- Where are fire dampers required? Smoke dampers? Ceiling radiation dampers? Corridor dampers?

- In what specific locations are fire dampers not required for penetrations of shaft enclosures? Where smoke dampers are not required?

- Why is draftstopping and fireblocking unnecessary in noncombustible construction?

- Where is fireblocking required to be installed? Draftstopping?

- Which materials are acceptable as fireblocks? Draftstops?

Code Text: A shaft is *an enclosed space extending through one or more stories of a building, connecting vertical openings in successive floors, or floors and roof.* A shaft enclosure is *the walls or construction forming the boundaries of a shaft. The provisions of* Section 713 *shall apply to shafts required to protect openings and penetrations through floor/ceiling and roof/ceiling assemblies.*

Discussion and Commentary: It is not uncommon in multistory buildings to have openings that are provided to accommodate elevators, mechanical equipment or similar devices, and to transmit light or ventilation air. Because of the potential for the rapid spread of fire, smoke and gases vertically through buildings, such vertical openings must be protected with fire-resistance-rated shaft enclosures or otherwise addressed in accordance with Section 712.

Shaft enclosure utilized to enclose interior space extending through floors and may accommodate:

- Elevators
- Dumbwaiters
- Mechanical equipment
- Ventilation air
- Exterior light

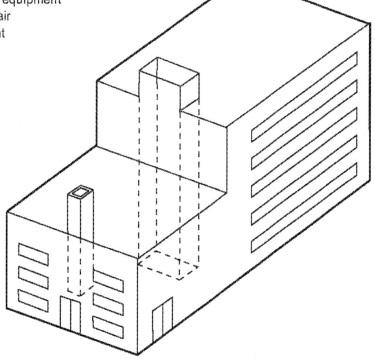

The fire-resistance rating required for a shaft enclosure is based on the building height, with 2 hours being required where four stories or more are connected. Where less than four stories are connected, 1 hour is required. The enclosure rating cannot be less than that of any floor penetrated.

Code Text: *Shaft enclosures shall be constructed as fire barriers in accordance with Section 707 or horizontal assemblies constructed in accordance with Section 711, or both. Openings in a shaft enclosure shall be protected in accordance with Section 716 as required for fire barriers. Doors shall be self- or automatic-closing by smoke detection in accordance with Section 716.2.6.6. Openings other than those necessary for the purpose of the shaft shall not be permitted in shaft enclosures.*

Discussion and Commentary: The general provisions dictate that a shaft be completely enclosed with fire-resistance-rated construction. However, there are conditions that modify this rule. The protection of exterior shaft walls is often unnecessary. Additionally, for those shafts that do not extend to the bottom of the building, the code provides three methods of maintaining the integrity of the shaft enclosure.

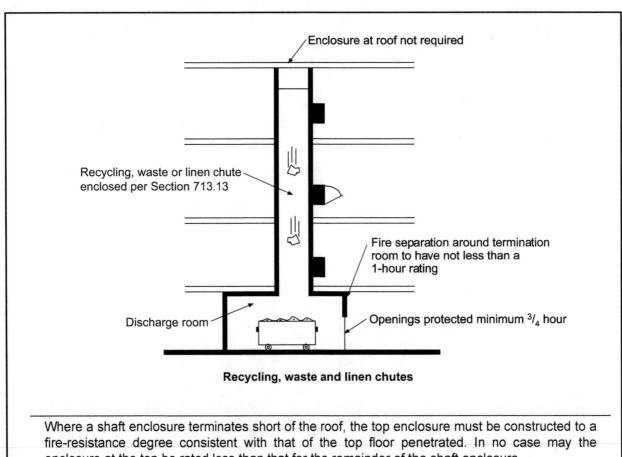

Enclosure at roof not required

Recycling, waste or linen chute enclosed per Section 713.13

Fire separation around termination room to have not less than a 1-hour rating

Discharge room

Openings protected minimum ³/₄ hour

Recycling, waste and linen chutes

Where a shaft enclosure terminates short of the roof, the top enclosure must be constructed to a fire-resistance degree consistent with that of the top floor penetrated. In no case may the enclosure at the top be rated less than that for the remainder of the shaft enclosure.

Code Text: A through penetration is *a breach in both sides of a floor, floor-ceiling or wall assembly to accommodate an item passing through the breaches.* A membrane penetration is *a breach in one side of a floor-ceiling, roof-ceiling or wall assembly to accommodate an item installed into or passing through the breach. The provisions of Section 714 shall govern the materials and methods of construction used to protect through penetrations and membrane penetrations of horizontal assemblies and fire-resistance-rated wall assemblies.*

Discussion and Commentary: Fire-resistance-rated walls and horizontal assemblies are usually penetrated, both fully and partially, with piping, conduit, outlet boxes, cable, vents and similar penetrating items. The IBC regulates both the materials and the methods of penetration based on the specific conditions that exist. Where sleeves are used, they must be fastened securely in place, and all open space within and around the sleeve must be appropriately protected.

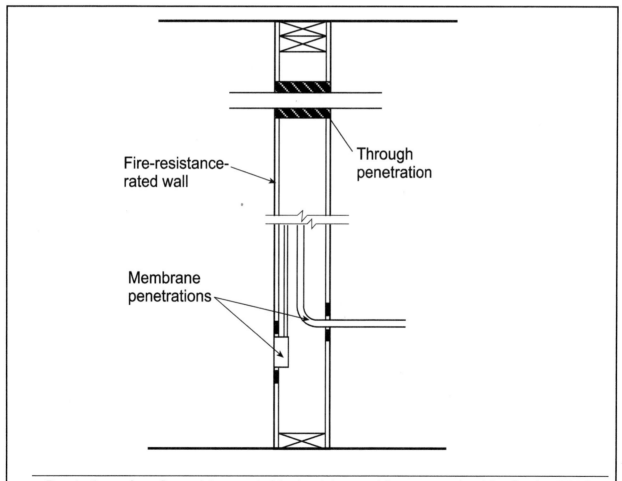

Fire-resistance-rated wall

Through penetration

Membrane penetrations

Penetrations of nonfire-resistance-rated horizontal assemblies are regulated by Section 714.6. Although some horizontal assemblies may not require a fire-resistance rating, the code intends that some degree of separation (compartmentalization) be provided from one story to another.

Code Text: *Penetrations into or through fire walls, fire barriers, smoke barrier walls, and fire partitions shall comply with Sections 714.4.1 through 714.4.3. Penetrations in smoke barrier walls shall also comply with Section 714.5.4.*

Discussion and Commentary: In general, penetrations into or through fire-resistance-rated walls must be either protected with an approved through-penetration firestop system or installed as a tested component of an approved fire-resistance-rated assembly. These methods are considered proprietary, with each penetration being regulated by the specifics of the installation. Two generic methods are identified as exceptions to the general requirements; however, both methods are based on the penetration only of steel, ferrous or copper pipes or steel conduits. Under such conditions, the annular space around the penetrating items shall be filled with an appropriate material.

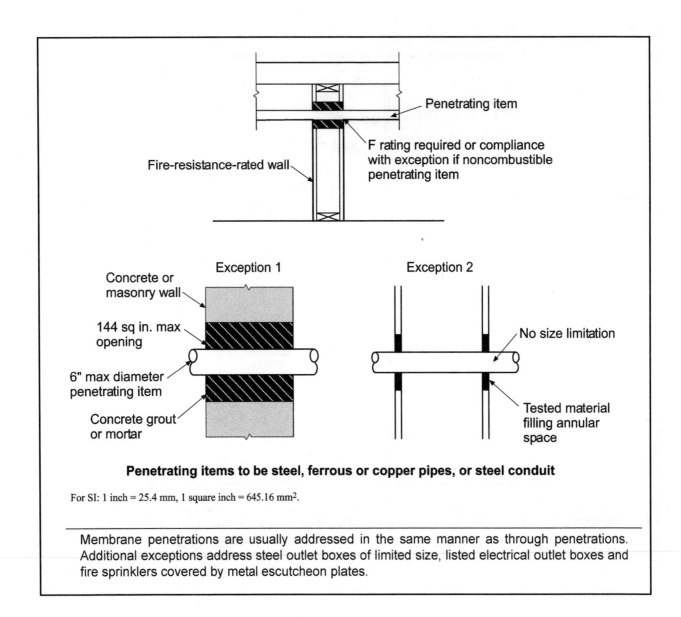

Penetrating items to be steel, ferrous or copper pipes, or steel conduit

For SI: 1 inch = 25.4 mm, 1 square inch = 645.16 mm².

Membrane penetrations are usually addressed in the same manner as through penetrations. Additional exceptions address steel outlet boxes of limited size, listed electrical outlet boxes and fire sprinklers covered by metal escutcheon plates.

Code Text: *Noncombustible penetrating items shall not connect to combustible items beyond the point of firestopping unless it can be demonstrated that the fire-resistance integrity of the wall is maintained. Ducts that penetrate fire-resistance-rated assemblies and are not required by Section 717 to have fire dampers shall comply with the requirements of Sections 714.3 through 714.4.3.*

Discussion and Commentary: Duct penetrations of fire-resistance-rated wall assemblies are typically protected with fire dampers in accordance with Section 717.5. However, in those locations where dampers are not required, it is still necessary to address the structural integrity of the fire-resistive-rated wall where it is penetrated. Thus, the space between the duct and the wall must be protected in a manner consistent with that used for pipes, conduits and similar items.

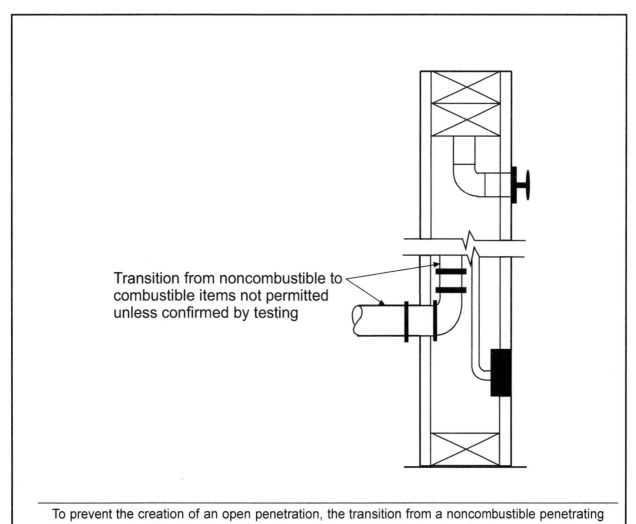

Transition from noncombustible to combustible items not permitted unless confirmed by testing

To prevent the creation of an open penetration, the transition from a noncombustible penetrating item to a combustible item is prohibited beyond the point of firestopping. Such a condition is only permitted when its suitability has been demonstrated through testing.

Code Text: *Penetrations of a fire-resistance-rated floor, fire-resistance-rated floor/ceiling assembly or the ceiling membrane of a roof/ceiling assembly not required to be enclosed in a shaft by Section 712.1 shall be protected in accordance with Sections 714.5.1 through 714.5.4. Through penetrations of horizontal assemblies shall comply with Section 714.5.1.1 or 714.5.1.2.*

Discussion and Commentary: Where horizontal construction is penetrated by a duct, pipe, tube, wire, conduit, cable, vent or similar item, the primary requirements are based on Section 713 for shaft enclosures. However, Section 712.1.4 permits the use of Section 714 for both through penetrations and membrane penetrations. The provisions for horizontal assemblies are very similar to those for walls, with special allowances for steel, copper or ferrous penetrating items. Where the penetrations occur in smoke barriers, any firestop system must also be tested for air leakage and provided with the appropriate L rating.

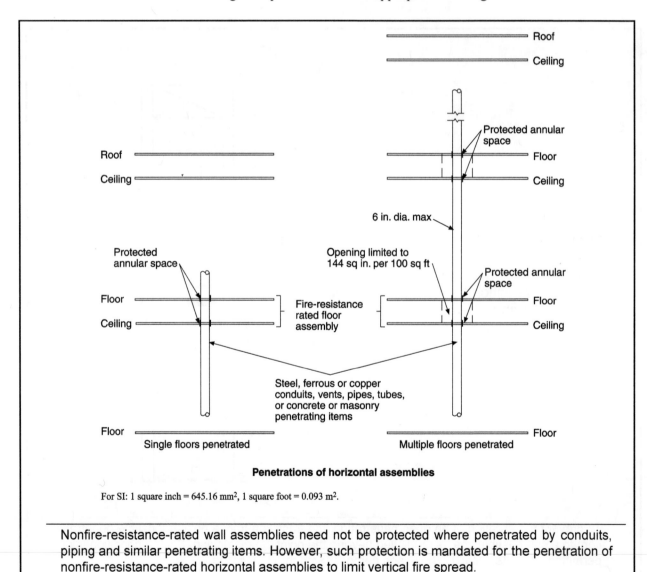

Penetrations of horizontal assemblies

For SI: 1 square inch = 645.16 mm², 1 square foot = 0.093 m².

Nonfire-resistance-rated wall assemblies need not be protected where penetrated by conduits, piping and similar penetrating items. However, such protection is mandated for the penetration of nonfire-resistance-rated horizontal assemblies to limit vertical fire spread.

Code Text: *Joints installed in or between fire-resistance-rated walls, floor or floor/ceiling assemblies and roofs or roof/ceiling assemblies shall be protected by an approved fire-resistant joint system designed to resist the passage of fire for a time period not less than the required fire-resistance rating of the wall, floor or roof in or between which it is installed.* See the exception for 10 locations where joint systems are not required. *Systems or materials protecting joints and voids shall be securely installed in accordance with the manufacturer's installation instructions in or on the joint or void for its entire length so as not to dislodge, loosen, or otherwise impair its ability to accommodate expected building movements and to resist the passage of fire and hot gases.*

Discussion and Commentary: Joints are created where the structural design of a building necessitates a separation between building components in order to accommodate anticipated structural displacements caused by thermal expansion and contraction, seismic activity, wind or other loads. The integrity of the fire-resistant separation must be maintained where such joints occur.

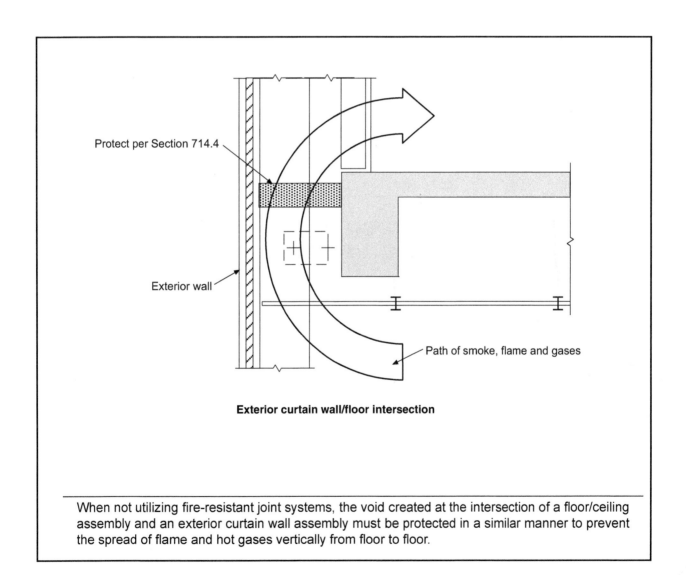

Protect per Section 714.4

Exterior wall

Path of smoke, flame and gases

Exterior curtain wall/floor intersection

When not utilizing fire-resistant joint systems, the void created at the intersection of a floor/ceiling assembly and an exterior curtain wall assembly must be protected in a similar manner to prevent the spread of flame and hot gases vertically from floor to floor.

Code Text: *Approved fire door and fire shutter assemblies shall be constructed of any material or assembly of component materials that conforms to the test requirements of Section 716.2.1.1 (side-hinged or pivoted swinging doors), 716.2.1.2 (other types of assemblies) or (glazing in transom lights and sidelights in corridors and smoke barriers), and 716.2.1.4 (smoke and draft control) and the fire-protection rating indicated in Table 716.1(2).* See the exceptions for tin-clad fire doors and floor fire doors.

Discussion and Commentary: The level of protection required for a fire door is commensurate with that required for the wall or partition in which it is installed. The minimum fire protection rating varies based on the wall's required rating as well as the type and use of the wall assembly under consideration. In addition to establishing the minimum fire-protection rating required for fire door assemblies. Table 716.1(2) also provides information on door vision panels, sidelights and transoms.

TABLE 716.1(2)
OPENING FIRE PROTECTION ASSEMBLIES, RATINGS AND MARKINGS

TYPE OF ASSEMBLY	REQUIRED WALL ASSEMBLY RATING (hours)		MINIMUM FIRE DOOR AND FIRE SHUTTER ASSEMBLY RATING (hours)	DOOR VISION PANEL SIZE[a]	FIRE-RATED GLAZING MARKING DOOR VISION PANEL[b,c]	MINIMUM SIDELIGHT/ TRANSOM ASSEMBLY RATING (hours)		FIRE-RATED GLAZING MARKING SIDELIGHT/ TRANSOM PANEL	
						Fire protection	Fire resistance	Fire protection	Fire resistance
Fire walls and fire barriers having a required fire-resistance rating greater than 1 hour	4		3	See Note a	D-H-W-240	Not Permitted	4	Not Permitted	W-240
	3		3[d]	See Note a	D-H-W-180	Not Permitted	3	Not Permitted	W-180
	2		$1^1/_2$	100 sq. in.	≤100 sq. in. = D-H-90 >100 sq. in.=D-H-W-90	Not Permitted	2	Not Permitted	W-120
	$1^1/_2$		$1^1/_2$	100 sq. in.	≤100 sq. in. = D-H-90 >100 sq. in.= D-H-W-90	Not Permitted	$1^1/_2$	Not Permitted	W-90
Double fire walls constructed in accordance with NFPA 221	Single-wall assembly rating (hours)[e]	Each wall of the double-wall assembly (hours)[f]	—						
	4	3	3	See Note a	D-H-W-180	Not Permitted	3	Not Permitted	W-180
	3	2	$1^1/_2$	100 sq. in.	≤ 100 sq. in. = D-H-90 >100 sq. in.= D-H-W-90	Not Permitted	2	Not Permitted	W-120
	2	1	1	100 sq. in.	≤ 100 sq. in. = D-H-60 > 100 sq. in. = D-H-W-60	Not Permitted	1	Not Permitted	W-60

(continued)

A fire door assembly installed in a fire-rated corridor wall or smoke barrier must have a minimum fire protection rating of 20 minutes. In addition, the door must pass an air leakage test to verify that it provides the necessary level of smoke protection.

Code Text: *Fire doors shall be labeled showing the name of the manufacturer or other identification readily traceable back to the manufacturer, the name or trademark of the third-party inspection agency, the fire-protection rating, and where required for fire doors in interior exit stairways and ramps and exit passageways by Section 716.2.2.3, the maximum transmitted temperature end point. Smoke and draft control doors complying with UL 1784 shall be labeled as such and shall also comply with Section 716.2.9.3. Labels shall be approved and permanently affixed. The label shall be applied at the factory or location where fabrication and assembly are performed.*

Discussion and Commentary: To be certain that the proper protective assembly is installed in the proper location, it is critical that the assembly be listed and labeled. Field alteration of a fire door assembly is not permitted, because the assembly is usually only listed for use in the condition it was in when it left the factory.

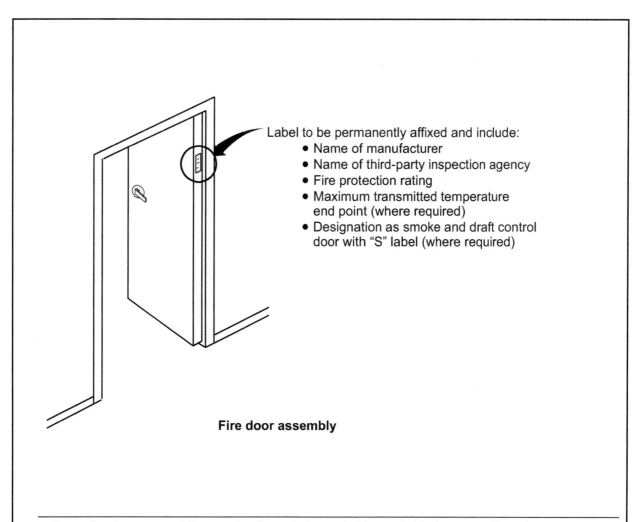

Label to be permanently affixed and include:
- Name of manufacturer
- Name of third-party inspection agency
- Fire protection rating
- Maximum transmitted temperature end point (where required)
- Designation as smoke and draft control door with "S" label (where required)

Fire door assembly

Some fire door assemblies are too large to be tested in available furnaces. Therefore, the code recognizes a certificate of inspection as proof that the oversized doors comply with the requirements for materials, design and construction for a comparable fire door.

Code Text: *Fire-rated glazing assemblies shall be marked in accordance with Tables 716.1(1), 716.1(2) and 716.1(3). For fire-rated glazing, the label shall bear the identification required in Tables 716.1(1) and 716.1(2). "D" indicates that the glazing is permitted to be used in fire door assemblies and meets the fire protection requirements of NFPA 252, UL 10B or UL 10C. "H" indicates that the glazing meets the hose stream requirements of NFPA 252, UL 10B or UL 10C. "T" indicates that the glazing meets the temperature requirements of Section 716.2.2.3.1. The placeholder "XXX" represents the fire rating period, in minutes*

Discussion and Commentary: Glazing utilized in fire door assemblies can be easily identified for verification of its appropriate application. Such glazing must also be provided with the proper identification indicating its compliance as safety glazing in conformance with Section 2406.4.

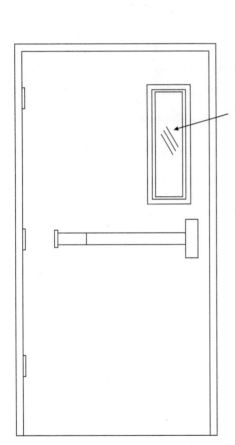

Glazing to be labeled with 4-part identifier:

- "D": applicable for fire-door assemblies and meets applicable fire-resistance requirements

- "H": meets hose stream requirements

- "T": meets temperature requirements

- "XXX": fire-protection rating in minutes

The identification methods for glazing found in Table 716.1(1) are also applicable to fire-resistance-rated glazing utilized as wall assemblies as well as fire-protection-rated glazing used in fire window assemblies as established in Table 716.1(3).

Topic: Door Closing	Category: Fire and Smoke Protection Features
Reference: IBC 716.2.6.1, 716.2.6.2	Subject: Fire Door Assemblies

Code Text: *Fire doors shall be latching and self- or automatic-closing in accordance with* Section 716. See the exceptions for fire doors in common walls between Group R-1 guestrooms, and elevator car and associated hoistway doors. *Unless otherwise specifically permitted, single side-hinged swinging fire doors and both leaves of pairs of side-hinged swinging fire doors shall be provided with an active latch bolt that will secure the door when it is closed.*

Discussion and Commentary: Fire doors must close and latch to be effective during a fire. The expectation is that the doors will normally be in a closed position and that the self-closing device will cause the door to close after use. Where specifically mandated by the code, automatic-closing devices must be installed. Such devices are intended for doors normally held in an open position.

Per Section 716.2.6.6, automatic-closing doors shall be actuated by smoke detection at:

- Doors in walls of incidental uses required to resist the passage of smoke (Sec. 509.4);
- Doors installed in smoke barriers (Sec. 709.5);
- Doors installed in fire partitions (Sec. 708.6);
- Doors installed in fire walls (Sec. 706.8);
- Doors installed in shaft enclosures (Sec. 713.7);
- Doors installed in waste and linen chutes and access and discharge rooms (Sec. 713.13);
- Doors installed in smoke partitions (Sec. 710.5.2.3);
- Doors installed in fire barriers (Sec. 707.6).

Automatic-closing fire door assemblies are required only where specifically addressed, such as in Section 709.5.1 for cross-corridor doors in Group I-2 occupancies and ambulatory care facilities. Where automatic-closing fire doors are provided, including nonrequired locations, they must typically be smoke activated.

Code Text: A fire damper is *a listed device, installed in ducts and air transfer openings designed to close automatically upon detection of heat and resist the passage of flame.* A smoke damper is *a listed device installed in ducts and air transfer openings that is designed to resist the passage of smoke.* A ceiling radiation damper is *a listed device installed in a ceiling membrane of a fire-resistance-rated floor/ceiling or roof/ceiling assembly to limit automatically the radiative heat transfer through an air inlet/outlet opening.*

Discussion and Commentary: The IBC identifies several types of dampers, each of which performs a specific function. The required type of damper is based on the function of the building element that is being penetrated by the duct or air transfer opening.

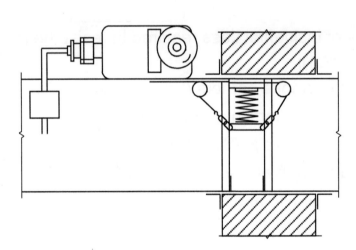

Figure courtesy
Sheet Metal and Air Conditioning Contractors National Association

Note: This illustration is not intended to exclusively endorse or indicate preference for a combination fire and smoke damper. Two separate dampers that satisfy the requirements for the respective functions may also be used for fire and smoke control.

Combination fire and smoke dampers

Where both a fire and a smoke damper are mandated, the use of a combination damper is permitted. This type of listed device is designed to close automatically upon detecting heat and to resist the passage of air and smoke.

Topic: Damper Testing and Ratings	**Category:** Fire-Resistance-Rated Construction
Reference: IBC 717.3.1	**Subject:** Ducts and Air Transfer Openings

Code Text: *Dampers shall be listed and labeled in accordance with the standards in* Section 717.3. *Fire dampers shall comply with the requirements of UL 555. Smoke dampers shall comply with the requirements of UL 555S. Combination fire/smoke dampers shall comply with the requirements of both UL 555 and UL 555S. Ceiling radiation dampers shall comply with the requirements of UL 555C* (or tested as a part of a horizontal assembly). *Corridor dampers shall comply with requirements of both UL 555 and UL 555S. Fire dampers shall have the minimum fire-protection rating specified in Table 717.3.2.1. Smoke damper leakage ratings shall be Class I or II. Elevated temperature ratings shall not be less than 250°F (121°C).*

Discussion and Commentary: Consistent with other openings that penetrate a fire-resistance-rated assembly, fire and smoke dampers must be provided where it is necessary to maintain the integrity of the assembly. The minimum damper rating is based on the rating of the assembly penetrated. Where corridor dampers are required, they shall have a minimum one-hour fire-resistance rating and a Class I or II leakage rating.

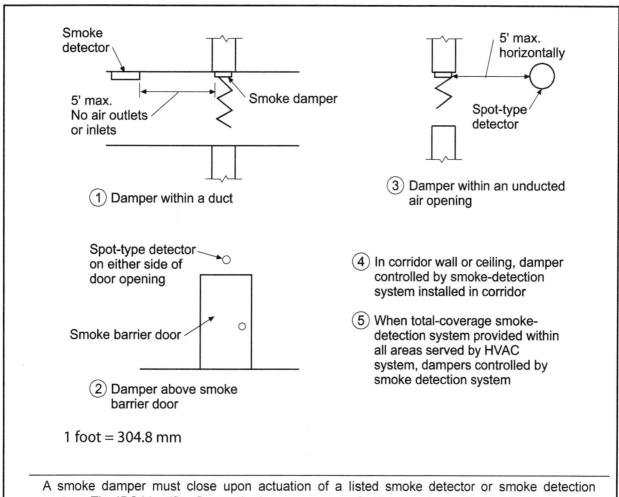

① Damper within a duct

Smoke detector

5' max. No air outlets or inlets

Smoke damper

③ Damper within an unducted air opening

5' max. horizontally

Spot-type detector

Spot-type detector on either side of door opening

Smoke barrier door

② Damper above smoke barrier door

④ In corridor wall or ceiling, damper controlled by smoke-detection system installed in corridor

⑤ When total-coverage smoke-detection system provided within all areas served by HVAC system, dampers controlled by smoke detection system

1 foot = 304.8 mm

A smoke damper must close upon actuation of a listed smoke detector or smoke detection system. The IBC identifies five methods, one or more of which may be applicable, for the detector location and/or actuation.

Code Text: *Fire dampers, smoke dampers, combination fire/smoke dampers, ceiling radiation dampers and corridor dampers shall be provided at the locations prescribed in Sections 717.5.1 through 717.5.7 and 717.6. Where an assembly is required to have both fire dampers and smoke dampers, combination fire/smoke dampers or a fire damper and a smoke damper shall be provided.*

Discussion and Commentary: Only those specific building elements identified in the code need to be protected by fire and/or smoke dampers where penetrated by ducts or air transfer openings. As a general rule, fire dampers protect such openings in fire walls, fire barriers, shaft enclosures and fire partitions. Fire dampers may also be installed in some of those locations where a shaft enclosure is otherwise required. Smoke dampers are generally required for openings in shaft enclosures, smoke- and draft-control corridor enclosures, and smoke barriers.

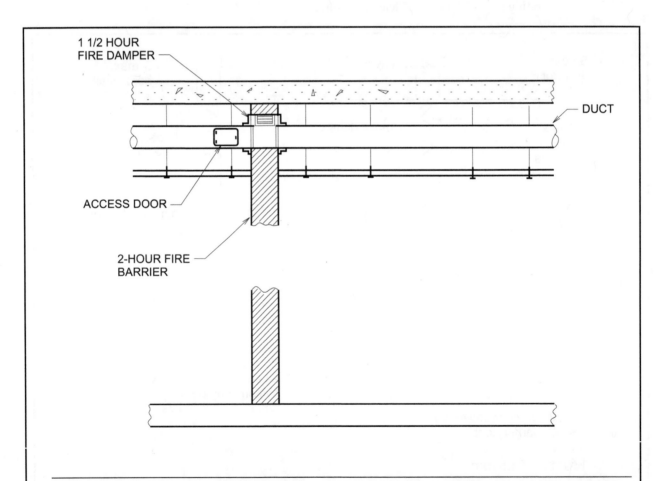

There will be times when a fire-resistance-rated assembly is penetrated by a duct or transfer opening that is not required to be protected by a fire or smoke damper. In such situations, the condition will be regulated and protected as a penetration in accordance with Section 714.

Code Text: *Duct systems constructed of approved materials in accordance with the* International Mechanical Code *that penetrate nonfire-resistance-rated floor assemblies shall be protected by any of the following methods.* See three methods addressing (1) shaft enclosures, (2) ducts connecting only two stories, and (3) ducts connecting a maximum of three stories where floor assemblies are noncombustible construction.

Discussion and Commentary: It is important when addressing the vertical spread of fire, smoke and gases—even in buildings where the floor assemblies are not required to have a fire-resistance rating—that some level of compartmentation is provided between stories.

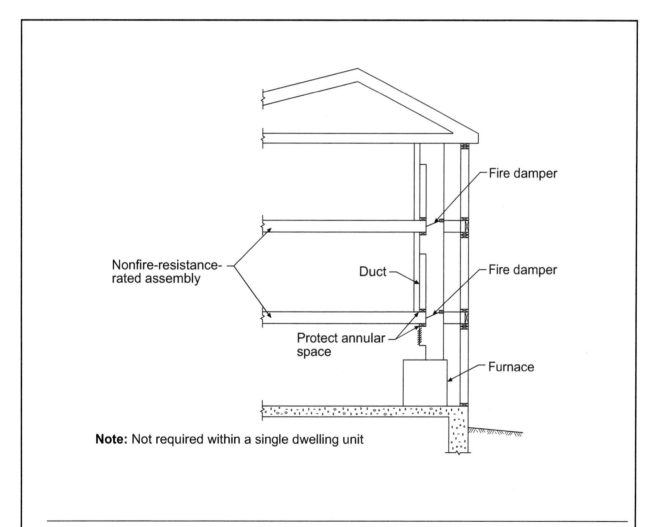

Note: Not required within a single dwelling unit

Where Item 3 is utilized for a duct that connects three stories, a minimum 1¹⁄₂-hour fire damper is required at each floor line even though the floor or floor/ceiling assembly is not required to have a fire-resistance rating, because the damper is an alternative to a 1-hour shaft enclosure.

Code Text: Fireblocking consists of *materials installed to resist the free passage of flame to other areas of the building through concealed spaces. In combustible construction, fireblocking shall be installed to cut off concealed draft openings (both vertical and horizontal) and shall form an effective barrier between floors, between a top story and a roof or attic space. Fireblocking shall be installed in the locations specified in Sections 718.2.2 through 718.2.7.*

Discussion and Commentary: Experience has shown that the greatest fire damage to conventional light-framed wood buildings occurs when the fire travels unimpeded through concealed draft openings. Virtually any concealed air space within a building will provide an open channel through which high-temperature air and gases can spread. Fireblocking is invaluable to the control of fire prior to active fire suppression activities.

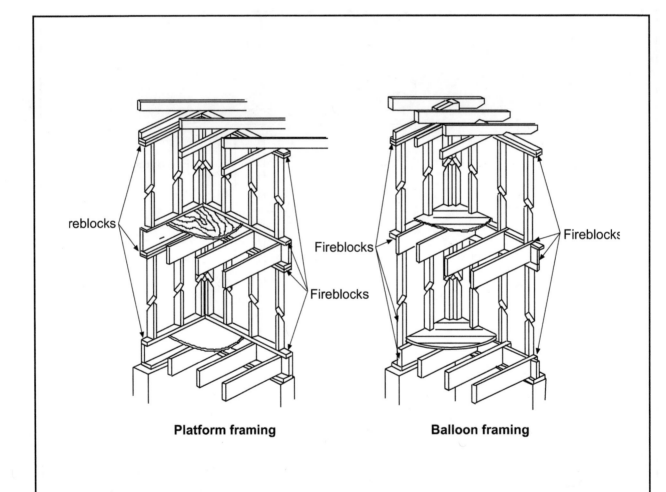

Platform framing

Balloon framing

reblocks

Fireblocks

Fireblocks

Fireblocks

In noncombustible construction, building materials located in concealed areas of the building construction do not contribute to the spread of fire. Therefore, fireblocking and draftstopping are required only in buildings of combustible construction.

Code Text: *Fireblocking shall be provided in concealed spaces of stud walls and partitions, including furred spaces, and parallel rows of studs or staggered studs, as follows: (1) vertically at the ceiling and floor levels, and (2) horizontally at intervals not exceeding 10 feet (3048 mm). Fireblocking shall be provided at interconnections between concealed vertical . . . and horizontal spaces . . . such as occur at soffits, drop ceilings, cove ceilings and similar locations.* See additional provisions for fireblocking at stairways; openings around vents, ducts and chimneys; concealed spaces of exterior architectural trim; and concealed sleeper spaces in floors.

Discussion and Commentary: The platform framing techniques that are typically used in light-frame wood construction provide adequate fireblocking between stories in the stud walls. However, furred spaces and openings for penetrating elements such as vents should be addressed carefully as avenues for fire transmission between stories or along a wall.

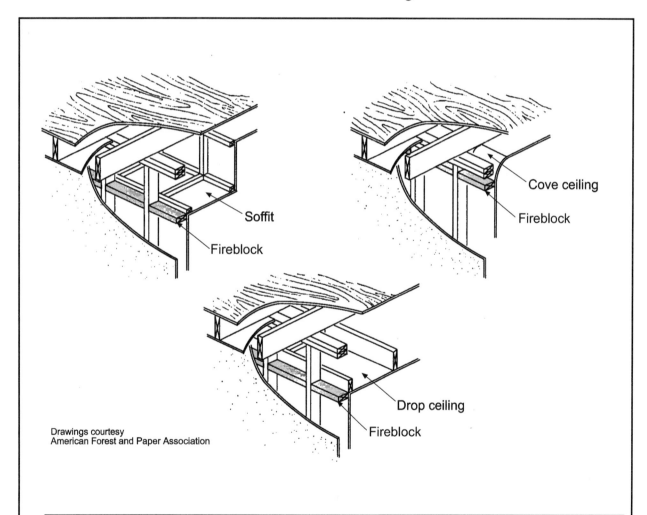

Soffit
Fireblock
Cove ceiling
Fireblock
Drop ceiling
Fireblock

Drawings courtesy
American Forest and Paper Association

In general, fireblocking materials must consist of lumber or wood structural panels of the thicknesses specified, gypsum board, cement fiber board, batts or blankets of mineral wool or glass fiber, or any other approved materials securely fastened in place.

Code Text: A draftstop is *a material, device or construction installed to restrict the movement of air within open spaces of concealed areas of building components such as crawl spaces, floor/ceiling assemblies, roof/ceiling assemblies and attics. Draftstopping materials shall not be less than $^1/_2$-inch (12.7 mm) gypsum board, $^3/_8$-inch (9.5 mm) wood structural panel, $^3/_8$-inch (9.5 mm) particleboard, 1-inch (25 mm) nominal lumber, cement fiberboard, batts or blankets of mineral wool or glass fiber, or other approved materials adequately supported. The integrity of draftstops shall be maintained.*

Discussion and Commentary: Draftstopping, like fireblocking, is required only in combustible construction. Although the role of draftstopping is important, it is less critical than that of fireblocking. Therefore, the protective materials used in draftstopping construction are permitted to be less substantial.

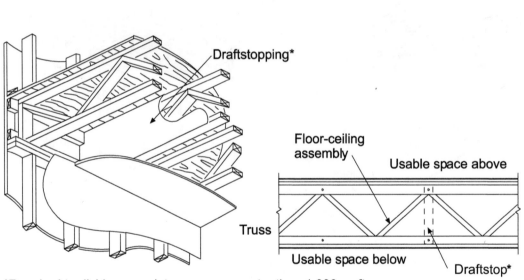

Draftstopping*

Floor-ceiling assembly

Usable space above

Truss

Usable space below

Draftstop*

*Required to divide space into areas no greater than 1,000 sq ft

Drawings courtesy
American Forest and Paper Association

For SI: 1 square foot = 0.093 m².

The provisions for draftstops are categorized for two general occupancy categories: residential and all uses other than residential. Both floor/ceiling assemblies and attics are addressed for each category. Many of the requirements are eliminated in fully sprinklered buildings.

Study Session 7

IBC Sections 713 through 720

1. A shaft enclosure shall have a minimum 2-hour fire-resistance rating where connecting a minimum of _____ stories.

    a. two
             b. three

    c. four
            d. six

    Reference_____

2. Where the annular space at the penetration of horizontal assemblies is filled with an approved material, noncombustible piping may connect a maximum of _____ stories, provided the horizontal assemblies require no fire-resistance rating.

    a. 2
             b. 3

    c. 4
            d. 5

    Reference_____

3. In which of the following locations is a fire-resistant joint system required to protect all joints?

    a. floors within malls
         b. horizontal exit walls

    c. mezzanine floors
         d. roofs where openings are permitted

    Reference_____

4. Fire-resistant joint systems are not required for control joints having a maximum width of _____ inch when tested in accordance with ASTM E119 or UL 263.

    a. 0.25
         b. 0.375

    c. 0.5
         d. 0.625

    Reference _____

5. In a nonsprinklered building, a fire door assembly in an exit passageway shall have a maximum transmitted temperature end point of _____ above ambient at the end of 30 minutes of standard fire test exposure.

a. 250°F

b. 450°F

c. 600°F

d. 650°F

Reference _____

6. An opening into a linen chute access room shall be protected by an opening protective having a minimum fire protection rating of _____ .

a. 20 minutes

b. 45 minutes

c. 1 hour

d. $1\frac{1}{2}$ hours

Reference _____

7. A fire door assembly in a 1-hour fire barrier used in an interior exit stairway enclosure shall have a minimum fire protection rating of _____ hour.

a. $\frac{1}{3}$

b. $\frac{1}{2}$

c. $\frac{3}{4}$

d. 1

Reference _____

8. Fire door assemblies required in a 2-hour exterior wall shall have a minimum fire protection rating of _____ .

a. 20 minutes

b. 45 minutes

c. 1 hour

d. 90 minutes

Reference_____

9. Penetrations in _____ shall be tested for air leakage in accordance with the requirements of UL 1479.

a. smoke partitions

b. smoke barriers

c. fire barriers

d. fire walls

Reference _____

10. Where an elevator lobby is used to provide hoistway protection required in a non-sprinklered building, it shall be separated from the floor level through the use of

_____ .

    a.   smoke barriers   b.   fire barriers

    c.   fire partitions   d.   smoke partitions

Reference_____

11. In which one of the following locations may self-closing or automatic-closing devices be omitted from required fire doors?

    a.   Group E corridor doors

    b.   doors in common walls separating Group R-1 sleeping units

    c.   doors between interior exit stairways and exit passageways

    d.   Group I-2 smoke barrier doors

Reference_____

12. Which one of the following fire-rated glazing markings is required for a sidelight adjacent to a 1-hour interior exit stairway door assembly?

    a.   D-H-45   b.   D-H-O-H-20

    c.   D-H-O-H-45   d.   W-60

Reference_____

13. Where automatic-closing fire doors are installed, which one of the following locations does not require closing upon actuation of smoke detectors?

    a.   cross-corridor doors in an office building

    b.   doors in a fire barrier separating control areas

    c.   a pair of doors installed in a fire wall

    d.   a single door installed in a smoke partition

Reference_____

14. Access openings for waste or linen chutes shall be located in rooms enclosed by minimum _____ fire barriers.

    a.   1   b. $1^1/_2$

    c.   2   d.   3

Reference_____

15. What is the minimum required fire-protection rating for a fire window assembly located in a 2-hour fire barrier?

    a. $^3/_4$ hour

    b. 1 hour

    c. $1^1/_2$ hours

    d. fire windows are not permitted

    Reference _____

16. The total area of interior fire window assemblies located in fire partitions and fire barriers is limited to a maximum of _____ percent of the area of the common wall within any room.

    a. 10

    b. 20

    c. 25

    d. 50

    Reference _____

17. What is the minimum required fire damper rating for a damper located in a 1-hour fire barrier?

    a. 20 minutes

    b. 45 minutes

    c. 1 hour

    d. $1^1/_2$ hour

    Reference _____

18. Where a spot-type detector is used to actuate a smoke damper installed within an air transfer opening in a wall, the detector shall be located within _____ of the damper.

    a. 12 inches vertically

    b. 30 inches vertically

    c. 3 feet horizontally

    d. 5 feet horizontally

    Reference _____

19. Where a duct passes through a fire wall used as a horizontal exit, which of the following dampers is/are required?

    a. fire damper only

    b. smoke damper only

    c. both a fire damper and a smoke damper

    d. neither a fire damper nor a smoke damper

    Reference _____

20. In general, which of the following dampers is/are required where an air transfer opening penetrates a shaft enclosure?

    a. fire damper only

    b. smoke damper only

    c. both fire and smoke dampers

    d. neither a fire damper nor a smoke damper

    Reference_____

21. Fire window assemblies identified with a fire-rated glazing marking of OH-45 or W-60 are permitted for use in all but which one of the following wall assemblies?

    a. incidental use areas

    b. smoke barriers

    c. 2-hour fire barriers

    d. 1-hour fire partitions

    Reference_____

22. The maximum spacing of fireblocking within concealed spaces of exterior architectural elements erected with combustible framing shall be _____ feet.

    a. 10   b. 20

    c. 60   d. 100

    Reference_____

23. Which of the following materials is not specifically listed by the code as an acceptable draftstopping material?

    a. $^3/_8$-inch gypsum board

    b. $^3/_8$-inch wood structural panels

    c. $^3/_8$-inch particleboard

    d. glass fiber batts

    Reference_____

24. In a nonsprinklered office building having combustible attic spaces, the maximum attic area permitted between draftstops is _____ .

    a.   1,000 square feet   b.   3,000 square feet

    c.   100 feet in any direction   d.   unlimited

Reference_____

25. Other than for cellulose loose-fill insulation that is not spray applied, the maximum flame spread index of insulating materials concealed within a Type II building shall be _____ .

    a.   25   b.   50

    c.   75   d.   unlimited

Reference_____

26. A through-penetration firestop system, where used to protect a through penetration in a fire barrier wall, shall at minimum have a(n) _____ rating of not less than the rating of the wall penetrated.

    a.   F   b.   L

    c.   T   d.   F and T

Reference_____

27. A firestop system may not be required for the protection of a membrane penetration by an unlisted steel electrical box in a 1-hour fire partition, provided the box has a maximum individual size of _____ square inches.

    a.   16   b.   25

    c.   100   d.   144

Reference_____

28. What is the minimum required fire protection rating for a fire window located in a $^1/_2$-hour fire-resistance-rated fire partition?

    a.   0, no rating is required   b.   20 minutes

    c.   30 minutes   d.   45 minutes

Reference_____

29. Where wood sleepers are installed for the installation of wood flooring in a church sanctuary, the maximum size of any open spaces under the flooring shall be _____ square feet unless the entire underfloor space is filled with an approved material.

    a. 10   b. 20

    c. 100   d. 144

    Reference_____

30. Where plaster is used for fire-resistance purposes, it shall be reinforced with an additional layer of approved lath where its thickness exceeds _____ inch.

    a. $^3/_8$ b. $^1/_2$

    c. $^3/_4$ d. 1

    Reference_____

31. The operating temperature of a ceiling radiation damper actuation device shall be _____ above the normal temperature within the duct system, but not less than _____ .

    a. 40°F, 160°F   b. 50°F, 160°F

    c. 50°F, 175°F   c. 55°F, 175°F

    Reference_____

32. Draftstopping shall be installed in combustible floor/ceiling spaces of a nonsprinklered Group E occupancy such that the horizontal floor areas are a maximum of _____ square feet.

    a. 100   b. 400

    c. 1,000   d. 3,000

    Reference_____

33. A required smoke damper shall have a leakage rating of Class _____ .

    a. I only   b. II only

    c. III only   d. I or II

    Reference_____

34. Fireblocking shall be installed within concealed spaces of exterior wall coverings erected with combustible framing so that any open spaces will be a maximum of _____ square feet in area.

    a. 100   b. 200

    c. 1,000   d. 3,000

Reference _____

35. For fire-resistance purposes, $1/2$ inch of unsanded gypsum plaster is deemed to be equivalent to _____ inch of Portland cement sand plaster.

    a. $1/4$ b. $3/8$

    c. $3/4$ d. 1

Reference _____

36. Shaft enclosures are to be constructed as _____ or horizontal assemblies, or both.

    a. fire partitions   b. fire barriers

    c. fire walls   d. smoke barriers

Reference _____

37. Combustible penetrating items are permitted to connect a maximum of _____ stories provided the annular space is filled with an approved material to resist the passage of flame and the products of combustion.

    a. two   b. three

    c. four   d. five

Reference _____

38. A(n) _____ marking on a fire-rated glazing assembly indicates the glazing meets the fire window assembly criteria, including the _____ test.

    a. FW, air leakage

    b. W, impact

    c. OH, hose stream

    d. FC, fire protection

Reference _____

39. Unless provided with a removable duct section, a fire damper equipped with a fusible link shall be provided with an access door a minimum of _____ inches square.

    a. 10   b. 12

    c. 14   d. 15

Reference _____

40. Access points to smoke dampers shall be permanently identified on the exterior by a label having letters a minimum of _____ inch in height.

    a. $^1/_2$ b. $^5/_8$

    c. $^3/_4$ d. 1

Reference _____

2021 IBC Chapter 9
Fire Protection and Life Safety Systems

OBJECTIVE: To obtain an understanding of the design and installation of fire protection systems, including automatic sprinkler systems, standpipe systems, fire alarm and detection systems, smoke control systems, and smoke and heat vents.

REFERENCE: Chapter 9, 2021 *International Building Code*

KEY POINTS:
- What are the quality standards for fire protection systems?
- How shall fire alarm systems be monitored?
- What are the different classifications for standpipe systems? For other types of systems?
- For Group A-1, A-3 and A-4 occupancies, what size fire area requires the installation of an automatic sprinkler system? How many occupants? What location in the building?
- When must a restaurant or café be sprinklered?
- Under what conditions does an assembly occupancy on a roof require the installation of a sprinkler system in a building?
- Under what conditions must an ambulatory care facility be provided with an automatic sprinkler system?
- Which conditions would allow Group E occupancies to be nonsprinklered?
- A sprinkler system is required in Groups F-1, M and S-1 occupancies when the floor area within any fire area exceeds what size?
- Which high-hazard occupancies require installation of a sprinkler system? Institutional occupancies?
- Which residential occupancies require the installation of an automatic sprinkler system? In which portions of the building must the sprinkler system be located?
- When must an open parking garage be sprinklered? An enclosed parking garage?
- Under what conditions must sprinkler protection be provided for exterior balconies and ground-floor patios of dwelling units?
- For the purpose of fire department access, what is considered a "windowless" building?

KEY POINTS:
(Cont'd)

- In "windowless" buildings, how are basements regulated as compared to above-grade levels?
- When must buildings be sprinklered due to their height?
- Which locations or uses are exempt from the sprinkler requirements?
- What are the different classes of standpipe systems? How do they differ?
- When are standpipes required?
- When a standpipe system is mandated, where must the hose connections be located?
- In what locations must portable fire extinguishers be installed? How is the size and distribution of portable fire extinguishers to be determined?
- In which occupancies are manual fire alarm systems required? Automatic fire alarm systems?
- Where are smoke alarms mandated?
- Where fire alarms are required, where must visible appliances be installed?
- What is the scope and purpose of a smoke-control system?
- What are the three different methods of mechanical smoke control? Which of the three is the primary means of controlling smoke?
- What are the critical elements for the acceptance of a smoke-control system?
- What are the different means of providing a smokeproof enclosure? How do they differ from each other?
- In which occupancies are smoke and heat vents required?
- When smoke and heat vents are provided, what are their minimum size and spacing requirements?
- Under which conditions can a mechanical smoke exhaust system be substituted for smoke and heat vents?
- What buildings must be provided with a fire command center? What are the requirements for a fire command center?
- Where must fire department connections be located? What degree of fire department access is required to the connections?
- How are fire pump rooms required to be protected?
- What identification is required for shaftways accessible to the fire department from the exterior? From the interior?
- What types of buildings must be provided with emergency responder radio coverage?
- How are vertical shafts and fire protection equipment rooms to be identified?
- In what occupancies is carbon monoxide detection required? Under what conditions?
- How are gas detection systems to be regulated?
- Under what conditions are university and college buildings required to have an approved mass notification system?

Code Text: A fire protection system consists of *approved devices, equipment and systems or combinations of systems used to detect a fire, activate an alarm, extinguish or control a fire, control or manage smoke and products of a fire or any combination thereof. The provisions of* Chapter 9 *shall specify where fire protection systems are required and shall apply to the design, installation and operation of fire protection and life safety systems. Fire protection and life safety systems shall be installed, repaired, operated and maintained in accordance with the* International Building Code *and the* International Fire Code.

Discussion and Commentary: The code provides requirements for three distinct systems considered vital to a safe building environment. The first system is intended to control and limit fire spread and to provide building occupants and fire personnel with the means of fighting a fire. The second system provides for detection of a fire condition and a means of notification. The third system is intended to control smoke migration.

General requirements for fire protection systems:

- Systems to be installed, repaired, operated and maintained in accordance with the *International Building Code* and *International Fire Code.*

- Systems not required by the IBC are permitted to be installed for partial or complete protection, provided such systems meet the requirements of the IBC.

- Any system for which an exception to, or reduction in, the provisions of the IBC has been granted shall be considered a required system.

- No person shall remove or modify any system installed or maintained under the provisions of either code without approval of the building official.

- All systems shall be tested in accordance with the requirements of the IBC and IFC, in the presence of the building official and at the expense of the owner or owner's representative.

- It is unlawful to occupy portions of a structure until the required fire protection systems within that portion have been tested and approved.

Unless specifically excepted, approved supervising stations in accordance with NFPA 72 are mandated for automatic sprinkler systems, fire alarm systems and Group H occupancy emergency alarm, detection and automatic fire-extinguishing systems.

Code Text: A fire area is *the aggregate floor area enclosed and bounded by fire walls, fire barriers, exterior walls or horizontal assemblies of a building. Where buildings, or portions thereof, are divided into fire areas so as not to exceed the limits established for requiring a fire protection system in accordance with* Chapter 9, *such fire areas shall be separated by fire walls, fire barriers or horizontal assemblies, or a combination thereof, having a fire-resistance rating of, not less than that determined in accordance with Section 707.3.10.*

Discussion and Commentary: The concept behind fire areas is that of compartmentalization. As a building is subdivided into smaller spaces through the use of fire-resistance-rated elements, the potential hazards tend to be confined to each compartment. Therefore, as the level of hazards decreases, the need for protection diminishes. In the IBC, this reduced level of protection is reflected in the fact that an automatic sprinkler system may not be required. The primary purpose for the creation of fire areas is to address the requirements of Section 903.2 for sprinkler protection.

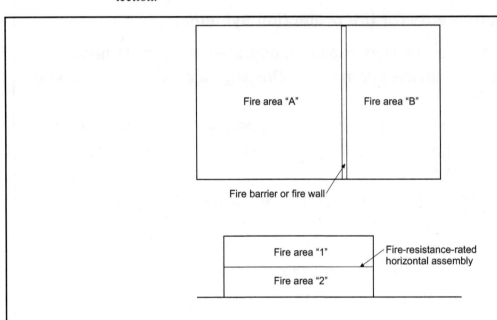

TABLE 707.3.10
FIRE-RESISTANCE RATING REQUIREMENTS FOR FIRE BARRIER ASSEMBLIES OR HORIZONTAL ASSEMBLIES BETWEEN FIRE AREAS

OCCUPANCY GROUP	FIRE-RESISTANCE RATING (hours)
H-1, H-2	4
F-1, H-3, S-1	3
A, B, E, F-2, H-4, H-5, I, M, R, S-2	2
U	1

To determine the appropriate level of fire resistance for fire barriers used to create one or more fire areas, refer to Table 707.3.10. This table mandates the minimum hourly rating for fire barriers separating one or more occupancies into different fire areas.

Code Text: *An automatic sprinkler system shall be provided throughout buildings and portions thereof used as Group A occupancies as provided in* Section 903.2.1. *For Group A-1, A-2, A-3 and A-4 occupancies, the automatic sprinkler system shall be provided throughout stories containing the Group A-1, A-2, A-3 or A-4 occupancy and throughout all stories from the Group A occupancy to, and including, the levels of exit discharge serving the Group A occupancy.*

Discussion and Commentary: Although most Group A occupancies lack the combustible loading that creates a high degree of fire severity, protection provided by an automatic sprinkler system is deemed necessary due to the hazards of having large numbers of people in concentrated areas. Based on varying thresholds, a sprinkler system may be required in any of the five assembly occupancies.

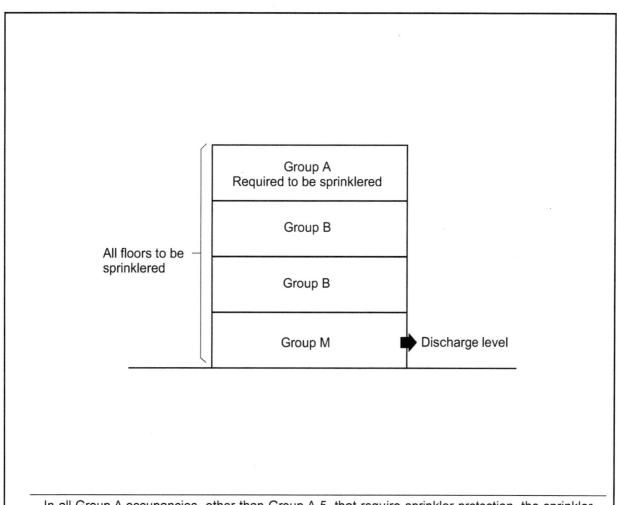

In all Group A occupancies, other than Group A-5, that require sprinkler protection, the sprinkler system must be provided throughout the entire story on which the Group A is located. In multistory buildings, the sprinkler system must also be provided on all stories between, and including, the Group A occupancy and the level of exit discharge.

Code Text: *An automatic sprinkler system shall be provided throughout stories containing Group A-1 occupancies and throughout all stories from the Group A-1 occupancy to and including the levels of exit discharge serving that occupancy where one of the following conditions exists: (1) the fire area exceeds 12,000 square feet (1115 m²), (2) the fire area has an occupant load of 300 or more, or (3) the fire area is located on a floor other than a level of exit discharge serving such occupancies.* The same criteria apply to Group A-3 and A-4 occupancies. *An automatic sprinkler system shall be provided for fire areas containing Group A-2 occupancies where one of the following conditions exist: (1) the fire area exceeds 5,000 square feet (465 m²), (2) the fire area has an occupant load of 100 or more, or (3) the fire area is located on a floor other than a level of exit discharge serving such occupancies. An automatic sprinkler system shall be provided for all enclosed Group A-5 accessory use areas in excess of 1,000 square feet (93 m²).*

Discussion and Commentary: The thresholds at which Group A occupancies are required to be sprinklered vary based upon fire records and the hazards associated with the different types of assembly uses.

Automatic sprinkler system required where:

A-1 A-3 A-4	> 12,000 sq ft, or ≥ 300 occupants, or located above or below discharge level

A-2	> 5,000 sq ft, or ≥ 100 occupants, or located above or below discharge level

For SI: 1 square foot = 0.093 m²

Sprinkler protection may also be required in a building where a Group A occupancy occurs on the roof, with a threshold of 100 or more occupants in a Group A-2 occupancy and 300 or more occupants in other Group A occupancies.

Code Text: *An automatic sprinkler system shall be provided for Group E occupancies as follows: (1) throughout all Group E fire areas greater than 12,000 square feet (1115 m²) in area, (2) the Group E fire area is located on a floor other than a level of exit discharge serving such occupancies* (see exception), *or (3) the Group E fire area has an occupant load of 300 or more.*

Discussion and Commentary: As a group, educational occupancies tend to have a very good fire record. This stems from the ongoing supervision of activities in the building, as well as the rapid egress of students in response to emergencies. However, because of the amount of combustibles in Group E occupancies and the potentially high occupant load, it is typically necessary to provide sprinkler systems for those undivided floor areas in a manner somewhat consistent with Group A-1, A-2 and A-4 occupancies.

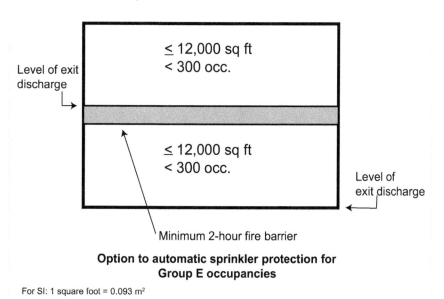

Automatic fire sprinkler system required throughout all Group E fire areas exceeding 12,000 square feet or 299 occupants in fire area

Option to automatic sprinkler protection for Group E occupancies

For SI: 1 square foot = 0.093 m²

Minimum 2-hour fire-resistance-rated fire barriers (Table 707.3.10) can be used to subdivide the building into small fire areas, thereby eliminating the sprinkler requirement. Direct egress at ground level from each classroom in the building is considered as an alternative to basement sprinkler protection.

Code Text: *An automatic sprinkler system shall be provided throughout all buildings containing a Group F-1 occupancy where one of the following conditions exists: (1) where a Group F-1 fire area exceeds 12,000 square feet (1115 m²); (2) where a Group F-1 fire area is located more than three stories above grade plane; or (3) where the combined area of all Group F-1 fire areas on all floors, including any mezzanines, exceeds 24,000 square feet (2230 m²).* Same criteria applies to Group M and S-1 occupancies. A sprinkler system is also required in such occupancies where the manufacture, storage or display and sale of upholstered furniture or mattresses occurs in a significant amount. In addition, a sprinkler system is required in Group F-1 and S-1 fire areas where distilled spirits are manufactured or stored.

Discussion and Commentary: Because of the potential presence of high levels of combustible materials in factories, sales buildings and warehouses, the IBC limits the size and location of fire areas not protected by an automatic sprinkler system. If any fire area in the building exceeds the threshold, the sprinkler system must be provided throughout the entire building, not just in the fire area that exceeds the area or height limitations.

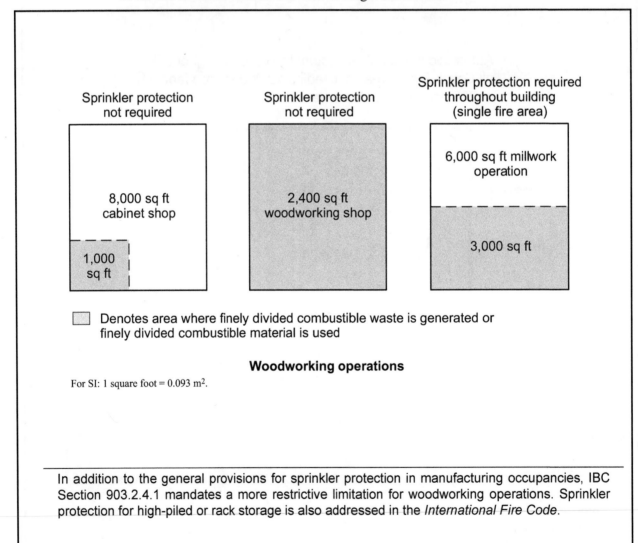

Sprinkler protection
not required

8,000 sq ft
cabinet shop

1,000
sq ft

Sprinkler protection
not required

2,400 sq ft
woodworking shop

Sprinkler protection required
throughout building
(single fire area)

6,000 sq ft millwork
operation

3,000 sq ft

☐ Denotes area where finely divided combustible waste is generated or
finely divided combustible material is used

Woodworking operations

For SI: 1 square foot = 0.093 m².

In addition to the general provisions for sprinkler protection in manufacturing occupancies, IBC Section 903.2.4.1 mandates a more restrictive limitation for woodworking operations. Sprinkler protection for high-piled or rack storage is also addressed in the *International Fire Code*.

Code Text: *An automatic sprinkler system shall be installed in Group H occupancies. An automatic sprinkler system shall be provided throughout buildings with a Group I fire area.* See the exceptions for Group I-1 and day-care facilities.

Discussion and Commentary: Hazardous occupancies require automatic sprinkler systems to protect not only the building's occupants and contents, but also the surrounding property. The sprinkler system only need be provided in the portion of the building classified as Group H. Buildings containing institutional uses must be protected throughout due to the lack of mobility of the occupants. The sprinkler system is intended to limit the size and the spread of a fire, thereby allowing extra time for moving occupants of the institutional building into an adjoining smoke compartment or through a horizontal exit.

[F] TABLE 903.2.5.2
GROUP H-5 SPRINKLER DESIGN CRITERIA

LOCATION	OCCUPANCY HAZARD CLASSIFICATION
Fabrication areas	Ordinary Hazard Group 2
Service corridors	Ordinary Hazard Group 2
Storage rooms without dispensing	Ordinary Hazard Group 2
Storage rooms with dispensing	Extra Hazard Group 2
Corridors	Ordinary Hazard Group 2

In a semiconductor fabrication facility classified as a Group H-5 occupancy, the sprinkler system must be installed throughout the entire building. For sprinkler design criteria, the code identifies the occupancy hazard classifications based on the various areas and locations.

Code Text: *An automatic sprinkler system installed in accordance with Section 903.3 shall be provided throughout all buildings with a Group R fire area.*

Discussion and Commentary: Statistics bear out that the majority of fire deaths and injuries occur in residential occupancies. It has also been statistically shown that buildings provided with sprinkler systems perform quite well under fire conditions. This mandate for the installation of automatic sprinkler systems in all buildings containing any Group R occupancy is based upon the desire to reduce such fire deaths and injuries in all residential buildings regulated by the *International Building Code*. This provision, like most requirements found in Chapter 9, is also found in the *International Fire Code*.

The scope of the IBC, *Section 101.2*, defers certain residential occupancies to the construction regulations of the *International Residential Code*. As such, this sprinkler requirement applies only to those residential structures constructed under the requirements of the *International Building Code*.

Code Text: *An automatic sprinkler system shall be provided throughout buildings classified as enclosed parking garages where any of the following conditions exist: (1) where the fire area of the enclosed parking garage exceeds 12,000 square feet (1115 m²), (2) where the enclosed parking garage is located beneath other groups (see the exception for enclosed parking garages located beneath Group R-3 occupancies), or (3) where the fire area of the open parking garage exceeds 48,000 square feet (4460 m²).*

Discussion and Commentary: Although parking garages are shown to have a very good fire record, the fire behavior in an enclosed parking garage is of greater concern than in an open parking garage. Because of the lack of exterior openings, smoke ventilation will be more difficult in the enclosed environment. Therefore, an automatic sprinkler system is required once the enclosed garage is sizeable in fire area. An additional concern occurs where the parking facility is in a mixed-occupancy building. If another occupancy group is located above the enclosed parking area, a sprinkler system is mandated regardless of the garage's fire area size. Sprinkler requirements also apply to open parking garages, but at a much higher threshold.

Sprinkler system required
throughout building where:

Fire area exceeds
12,000 sq ft

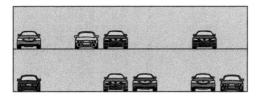

2-story Group S-2
enclosed parking garage

OR

Enclosed parking garage of any size
located beneath another occupancy

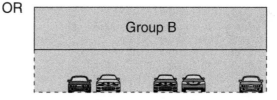

Group B

Group B office building with Group S-2
enclosed parking garage below

Sprinkler protection of Group S-2 enclosed parking garages

Where the vehicles being stored consist of commercial trucks or buses, a more stringent fire area threshold is appropriate. The limitation of 5,000 square feet without sprinkler protection is typically applied to garages housing larger vehicles rather than pick-up trucks and similar-sized vehicles used for business activities.

Code Text: *An automatic sprinkler system shall be installed throughout all stories, including basements of all buildings where the floor area exceeds 1,500 square feet (139.4 m²) and where the story does not comply with the criteria for exterior wall openings.* The criteria addresses the minimum size and required locations of such openings.

Discussion and Commentary: The IBC considers those structures with inadequate exterior openings for fire department access and/or rescue to be "windowless buildings," which require the installation of an automatic sprinkler system. Two methods of providing appropriate openings are set forth; one method is for openings below grade, and the other is for openings entirely above adjoining ground level. In all cases, at least one side of the building must be provided with complying openings in each 50 lineal feet of exterior wall. Basements are more highly regulated than floors above grade.

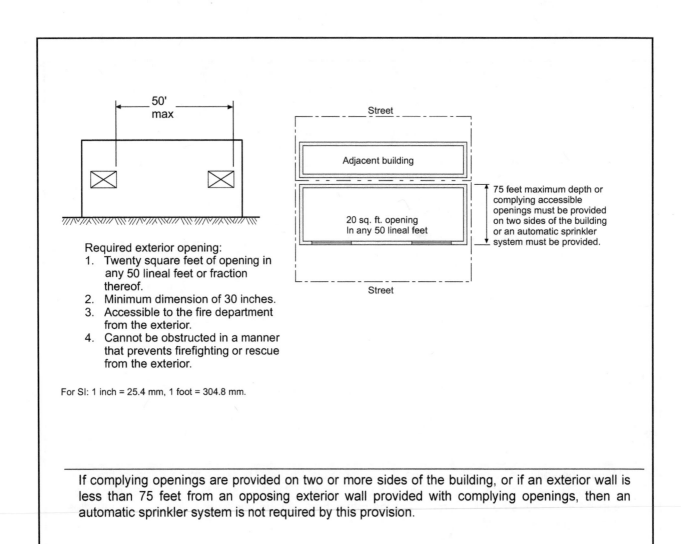

Required exterior opening:
1. Twenty square feet of opening in any 50 lineal feet or fraction thereof.
2. Minimum dimension of 30 inches.
3. Accessible to the fire department from the exterior.
4. Cannot be obstructed in a manner that prevents firefighting or rescue from the exterior.

For SI: 1 inch = 25.4 mm, 1 foot = 304.8 mm.

If complying openings are provided on two or more sides of the building, or if an exterior wall is less than 75 feet from an opposing exterior wall provided with complying openings, then an automatic sprinkler system is not required by this provision.

Code Text: *An automatic sprinkler system shall be installed throughout buildings that have one or more stories with an occupant load of 30 or more located 55 feet (16 764 mm) or more above the lowest level of fire department vehicle access, measured to the finished floor. See the exception that exempts Group F-2 occupancies.*

Discussion and Commentary: Because of difficulties associated with manual suppression of a fire in buildings constructed a substantial height above the fire department's point of attack, an automatic sprinkler system is required throughout the building, regardless of occupancy. Note that buildings that qualify for a sprinkler system by this provision, often termed "mid-rise" buildings, are not necessarily high-rise buildings as defined in Section 202.

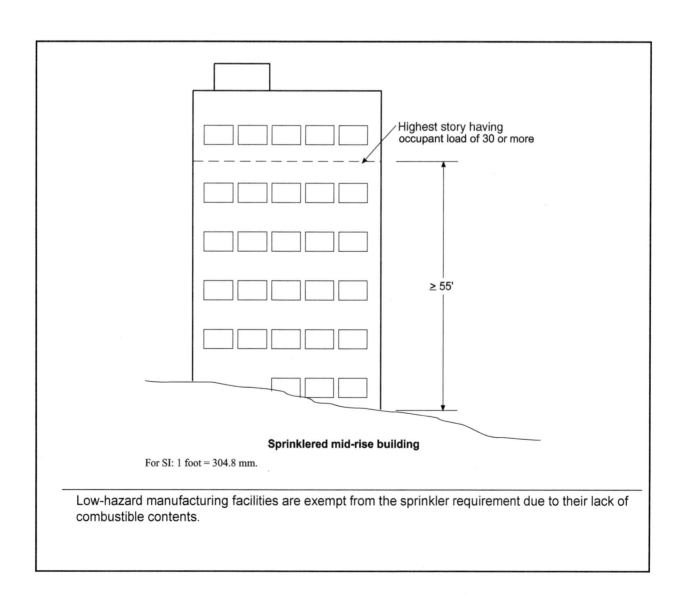

Highest story having occupant load of 30 or more

≥ 55'

Sprinklered mid-rise building

For SI: 1 foot = 304.8 mm.

Low-hazard manufacturing facilities are exempt from the sprinkler requirement due to their lack of combustible contents.

Code Text: *Standpipe systems shall be installed where required by Sections 905.3.1 through 905.3.8. See the exception for Group R-3 occupancies. Standpipe systems are allowed to be combined with automatic sprinkler systems.*

Discussion and Commentary: Installed exclusively for the fighting of fires, a standpipe system is a wet or dry system composed of piping, valves, outlets and related equipment designed to provide water at specified pressures. Standpipe systems are permitted to be combined with automatic sprinkler systems. Divided into Classes I, II and III, standpipe systems are generally required in structures of substantial height. Connections for Class I standpipes, which are solely for use by the fire department, shall be located in protected areas to allow for staging operations. Enclosures for interior exit stairways are typical locations for Class I connections.

REQUIRED STANDPIPE INSTALLATIONS

LOCATION OR USE	NONSPRINKLERED BUILDING	SPRINKLERED BUILDING
Buildings of 4 or more stories above grade plane or with floor level of the highest story located at more than 30 feet above lowest level of fire department vehicle access	Class III [1,2,5,6]	Class I
Buildings of 4 or more stories below grade plane or with floor level of the lowest story located at more than 30 feet below highest level of fire department vehicle access	Class III [1,2,5,6]	Class I
Group A occupancies with occupant load exceeding 1,000	Class I [4]	No requirement
Covered mall buildings	—	Class I
Stages more than 1,000 square feet	Class III	Class III [5]
Underground buildings	—	Class I

1 Class I standpipes permitted in basements equipped with automatic sprinkler system

2 Class I standpipes permitted in parking garages

3 Not required in open-air seating spaces without enclosed spaces

4 Hose connections permitted to be supplied by sprinkler system

5 Class I standpipes permitted in Groups B and E

6 Class I standpipes permitted in buildings where occupant-use hose lines will not be utilized by trained personnel or the fire department

Fire hose cabinets in which hoses are attached to outlets on Class II standpipes (as well as the use of portable fire extinguishers) are provided as a means by which the building occupants can control the fire prior to either sprinkler activation or fire personnel arrival.

Code Text: *Portable fire extinguishers shall be installed in all of the following locations: (1) in Group A, B, E, F, H, I, M, R-1, R-2, R-4 and S occupancies* (see exceptions for Group E, R-2 and S occupancies); *(2) within 30 feet (9144 mm) of commercial cooking equipment and from domestic cooking equipment in Group I-1, I-2 Condition 1, and R-2 college dormitory occupancies; (3) in areas where flammable or combustible liquids are stored, used or dispensed; (4) on each floor of structures under construction, except Group R-3 occupancies, in accordance with Section 3315.1 of the IFC; (5) where required by the IFC sections indicated in Table 906.1; and (6) special-hazard areas, including but not limited to laboratories, computer rooms and generator rooms, where required by the fire code official.*

Discussion and Commentary: Portable fire extinguishers are typically required in all but Group R-3 and U occupancies to give occupants the means to suppress a fire in its incipient stage. The capability for manual fire suppression can contribute to the protection of the occupants by controlling the fire in its early stages.

In addition to portable fire extinguishers, many of the other fire protection components and systems found in the IBC are also replicated directly from the *International Fire Code* (IFC). IFC provisions addressing automatic sprinkler systems, standpipe systems, fire alarm systems, smoke and heat vents, fire pumps and emergency responder safety features are also inserted into the IBC to provide for greater convenience to the code user.

Code Text: *An approved fire alarm system installed in accordance with the provisions of the IBC and NFPA 72 shall be provided in new buildings and structures in accordance with Sections 907.2.1 through 907.2.23 and provide occupant notification in accordance with Section 907.5, unless other requirements are provided by another section of the IBC. Not fewer than one manual fire alarm box shall be provided at an approved location to initiate a fire alarm signal for fire alarm systems employing automatic fire detectors or waterflow detection devices.* See exceptions for elevator recall control and Group R-2.

Discussion and Commentary: For many of the occupancies identified by the IBC, it is necessary to provide some level of notification to the building occupants and/or a supervised location reserved for a fire emergency. The threshold at which an alarm and/or detection system is required varies according to the occupancy classification.

Audible alarm notification appliances are to be provided and shall create a distinctive sound that is used for no other purpose. Visual alarm notification appliances are also required, to varying degrees, in public and common areas, employee work areas, and Group I-1, R-1 and R-2 occupancies.

Code Text: *Manual fire alarm boxes shall be located not more than 5 feet (1524 mm) from the entrance to each exit. In buildings not protected by an automatic sprinkler system in accordance with Section 903.3.1.1 or 903.3.1.2, additional manual fire alarm boxes shall be located so that the distance of travel to the nearest box does not exceed 200 feet (60 960 mm). The height of the manual fire alarm boxes shall be not less than 42 inches (1067 mm) and not more than 48 inches (1219 mm), measured vertically, from the floor level to the activating handle or lever of the box. Manual fire alarm boxes shall be red in color.*

Discussion and Commentary: The required location of fire alarm boxes adjacent to exit doors provides an opportunity for the alarm to be transmitted in a timely manner. In multistory buildings, such locations also encourage the actuation of a manual fire alarm box on the fire floor prior to entering the stair enclosure, resulting in the alarm being received from the actual fire floor and not another floor along the path of egress.

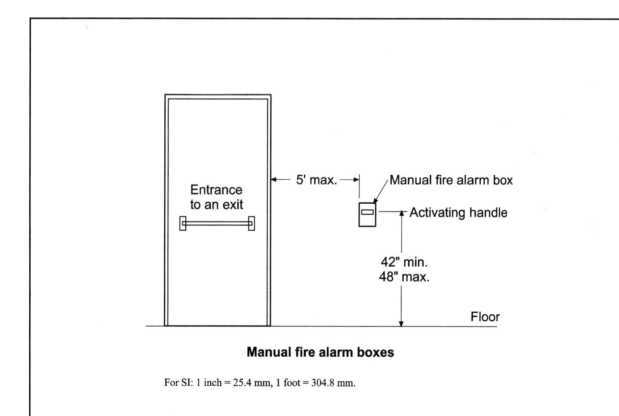

Manual fire alarm boxes

For SI: 1 inch = 25.4 mm, 1 foot = 304.8 mm.

Where a manual fire alarm system is required, manual fire alarm boxes (pull stations) must be installed. However, in some occupancies the code permits the elimination of such boxes if water flow in an automatic sprinkler system installed throughout the building activates the notification appliances.

Code Text: Section 909 *applies to mechanical or passive smoke control systems when they are required by some other provision of* the IBC. *The purpose of* Section 909 *is to provide a tenable environment for the evacuation or relocation of occupants. Smoke control systems regulated by* Section 909 *serve a different purpose than the smoke- and heat-venting provisions found in Section 910.*

Discussion and Commentary: The provisions Section 909 do not apply unless specifically mandated for a special use, such as an atrium. It is the intent that none of the requirements apply unless directed by other provisions of the code. Where a smoke control system is provided, it may be either passive or mechanical, or a combination of the two systems. A mechanical system is an engineered system that uses mechanical fans either to produce pressure differences across smoke barriers or to establish airflows to limit and direct smoke movement. A passive system is a system of smoke barriers arranged to limit the migration of smoke.

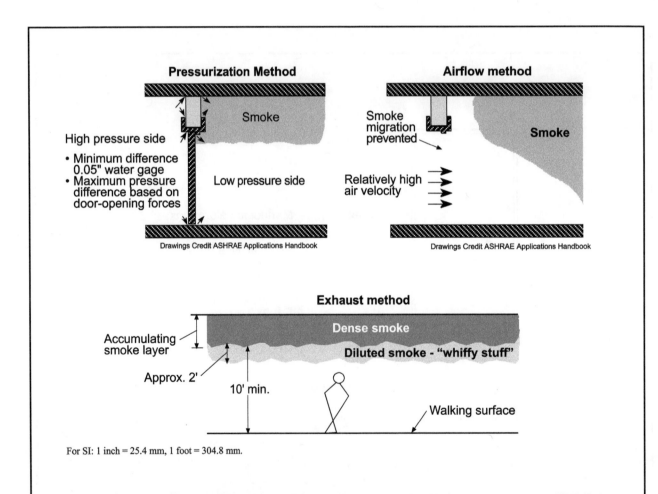

Pressurization Method

Smoke

High pressure side

- Minimum difference 0.05" water gage
- Maximum pressure difference based on door-opening forces

Low pressure side

Drawings Credit ASHRAE Applications Handbook

Airflow method

Smoke migration prevented

Smoke

Relatively high air velocity

Drawings Credit ASHRAE Applications Handbook

Exhaust method

Accumulating smoke layer

Dense smoke

Diluted smoke - "whiffy stuff"

Approx. 2'

10' min.

Walking surface

For SI: 1 inch = 25.4 mm, 1 foot = 304.8 mm.

Three methods of mechanical smoke control are addressed: pressurization, airflow and exhaust. Pressure differences across smoke barriers shall be the primary means of smoke control. The building official may accept the airflow or exhaust methods in specific situations.

Code Text: *Smoke and heat vents or a mechanical smoke removal system shall be installed as required by Sections 910.2.1 and 910.2.2.* See the exceptions for (1) frozen food warehouses, and (2) buildings equipped with ESFR sprinklers. *The vents or smoke removal system shall be installed in buildings and portions thereof: (1) used as Group F-1 or S-1 occupancies having more than 50,000 square feet (4645 m²) in undivided area* (see the exception for aircraft repair hangars), *(2) containing high-piled combustible storage, and (3) buildings equipped with control mode special application sprinklers.*

Discussion and Commentary: Smoke and heat vents shall be uniformly located within the roof in the areas of the building where the vents are required to be installed. Those areas of buildings that are equipped with early suppression fast response (ESFR) sprinklers are not required to be provided with automatic smoke and heat vents.

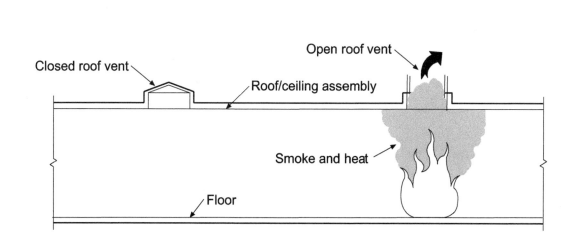

Note: In general, several small vents are more effective than a larger vent of equal area.

Roof vents

A mechanical smoke exhaust system is also permitted to ventilate the building as an alternative to smoke and heat vents. In addition to other conditions of acceptance, the exhaust fans in such a system are regulated for size, location, operation, wiring, control, supply air and interlocks.

Quiz

Study Session 8
IBC Chapter 9

1. Where a fire protection system is required to be monitored, the approved supervising station must comply with _____.

    a. NFPA 4   b. NFPA 13

    c. NFPA 70   d. NFPA 72

    Reference_____

2. Which one of the following classes of standpipe systems is intended primarily for the use of building occupants or the fire department during initial response?

    a. Class I   b. Class II

    c. Class III   d. Class IV

    Reference_____

3. Which one of the following types of standpipe systems requires water from a fire department pumper to be pumped into the system in order to supply the system demand?

    a. automatic dry   b. automatic wet

    c. manual wet   d. semi-automatic dry

    Reference_____

4. In a Group A-2 occupancy, an automatic sprinkler system shall be provided throughout any fire area having a minimum occupant load of _____.

    a. 50   b. 60

    c. 100   d. 3,000

    Reference_____

5. A stadium press box in a Group A-5 occupancy having a maximum floor area of
_____ square feet need not be sprinklered.

    a. 400   b. 1,000

    c. 5,000   d. 12,000

Reference_____

6. A sprinkler system is required for Group E fire areas having a minimum floor area of
_____ square feet.

    a. 2,501   b. 5,001

    c. 12,001   d. 20,001

Reference_____

7. Where woodworking operations in a Group F-1 occupancy generate finely divided
combustible waste, an automatic sprinkler system is required where such operations
occupy a minimum size floor area of _____ square feet.

    a. 1,001   b. 2,501

    c. 5,001   d. 12,001

Reference_____

8. In a single-story ambulatory care facility, an automatic sprinkler system is required
where a minimum of _____ care recipients are incapable of self-preservation at any time.

    a. 4   b. 6

    c. 10   d. 20

Reference_____

9. An automatic sprinkler system shall be provided throughout a building with a Group
M fire area located a minimum of _____ stories above grade plane.

    a. 2   b. 3

    c. 4   d. 6

Reference_____

10. Buildings containing which of the following residential occupancies must be sprinklered under all conditions?

    a. Groups R-1 and R-2 only   b. Groups R-1, R-2 and R-4 only

    c. Groups R-2 and R-4 only   d. All Group R occupancies

Reference_____

11. A building shall be fully sprinklered where the combined area of all Group S-1 fire areas exceeds _____ square feet.

    a. 2,500   b. 5,000

    c. 12,000   d. 24,000

Reference_____

12. A single-story above grade plane Group S-1 repair garage need not be fully sprinklered where the fire area contains a maximum of _____ square feet.

    a. 2,500   b. 10,000

    c. 12,000   d. 24,000

Reference_____

13. A Group S-2 parking garage used to store commercial buses need not be sprinklered where the fire area has a maximum size of _____ square feet.

    a. 2,500   b. 5,000

    c. 10,000   d. 12,000

Reference_____

14. Where any portion of a basement is located more than a minimum of _____ feet from complying exterior openings, the basement shall be provided with an automatic sprinkler system.

    a. 50   b. 75

    c. 100   d. 150

Reference_____

15. An NFPA 13D sprinkler system is permitted to be installed in all but which one of the following uses?

    a. townhouse

    b. Group R-3

    c. Group R-4, Condition 1

    d. Group R-2

    Reference_____

16. Which of the following spaces requiring sprinkler system protection is not required to use quick-response or residential sprinklers?

    a. light-hazard occupancies

    b. sleeping units in Group R-1

    c. care recipient sleeping units in Group I-2

    d. sales rooms of Group M

    Reference_____

17. A minimum of _____ clearance shall be maintained between automatic sprinklers and the top of piles of combustible fibers.

    a. 12 inches

    b. 18 inches

    c. 3 feet

    d. 5 feet

    Reference_____

18. Limited area sprinkler systems are only permitted to protect areas classified as _____.

    a. Light Hazard

    b. Light Hazard or Ordinary Hazard Group 1

    c. Ordinary Hazard Group 1 or 2

    d. Light Hazard, Ordinary Hazard Group 1 or Ordinary Hazard Group 2

    Reference_____

19. The manual actuation device for a fire-extinguishing system for a commercial cooking system shall be located a minimum of _____ feet and a maximum of _____ feet from the kitchen exhaust system.

    a. 3, 6

    b. 5, 10

    c. 6, 12

    d. 10, 20

    Reference_____

20. Connections for Class II standpipe systems shall be located so that all portions of the building are within _____ feet of a nozzle attached to _____ feet of hose.

    a. 20, 50   b. 30, 100

    c. 40, 125   d. 40, 150

Reference_____

21. In a nonsprinklered Group B occupancy, a manual fire alarm system shall be installed where there are a minimum of _____ occupants above or below the level of exit discharge.

    a. 101   b. 201

    c. 301   d. 501

Reference_____

22. A manual fire alarm system is not required in a Group E occupancy with a maximum occupant load of _____ persons.

    a. 30   b. 50

    c. 300   d. 500

Reference_____

23. Manual fire alarm boxes, where required, shall be located a maximum of _____ feet from the entrance to each exit.

    a. 5   b. 10

    c. 12   d. 20

Reference_____

24. In a Group R-1 hotel providing 220 sleeping units, a minimum of _____ such units shall be provided with visible alarm notification devices.

    a. 3   b. 11

    c. 17   d. 22

Reference_____

25. The maximum total sound pressure level for audible alarm notification appliances shall be _____ dBA at the minimum hearing distance from the audible appliance.

    a. 60   b. 75

    c. 90   d. 110

Reference_____

26. The manual actuation device for an automatic fire-extinguishing system serving a commercial cooking system shall be installed a minimum of _____ inches and a maximum of _____ inches above the floor.

    a. 38, 42   b. 34, 48

    c. 38, 48   d. 42, 48

Reference_____

27. A Class III wet standpipe is not required for stages having a maximum size of _____ square feet.

    a. 100   b. 400

    c. 500   d. 1,000

Reference_____

28. Where natural ventilation is utilized for venting a smokeproof enclosure, each vestibule shall be provided with a minimum _____ -square-foot opening in the exterior wall.

    a. 9   b. 16

    c. 24   d. 35

Reference_____

29. Other than for an aircraft repair hangar, a one-story Group S-1 occupancy shall be provided with smoke and heat vents or a mechanical smoke removal system where it exceeds _____ square feet in undivided area.

    a. 8,000   b. 10,000

    c. 15,000   d. 50,000

Reference_____

30. Carbon monoxide detection, when required, shall be provided in all but which one of the following locations?

    a. Group E classrooms   b. Group I-1 group home sleeping units

    c. Group I-3 housing units   d. Group R-1 sleeping units

Reference_____

31. Sprinkler protection is required for exterior balconies, decks and ground floor patios of dwelling units where the building is of _____ construction and a roof or deck exists above.

    a. combustible   b. Type III

    c. Type IV   d. Type V

Reference _____

32. A manual fire alarm system shall be installed in all multistory Group F occupancies having a minimum combined occupant load of _____ above or below the lowest level of exit discharge.

    a. 50   b. 100

    c. 300   d. 500

Reference _____

33. The vestibule space in a smokeproof enclosure shall have a minimum width of _____ inches and a minimum length in the direction of egress travel of _____ inches.

    a. 44, 60   b. 44, 72

    c. 60, 60   d. 60, 84

Reference _____

34. Fire pump rooms, where required, shall be provided with a suitable means for maintaining the temperature above _____.

    a. 40°F   b. 50°F

    c. 55°F   d. 68°F

Reference _____

35. A fire command center in a high-rise building shall be a minimum of
_____ square feet in area.

    a. 96   b. 100

    c. 144   d. 200

    Reference _____

36. An automatic sprinkler system is not required in a Group F-1 fire area used for the manufacture of distilled spirits where the fire area is a maximum of _____ square feet.

    a. 12,000

    b. 5,000

    c. 2,500

    d. 0 (a sprinkler system is required regardless of fire area size)

    Reference _____

37. An automatic sprinkler system is required in a Group S-2 open parking garage where the fire area exceeds _____ square feet.

    a. 5,000   b. 12,000

    c. 20,000   d. 48,000

    Reference _____

38. Where a fire alarm system is required in a Group _____ occupancy, the audible alarm activated by the system shall be a 520-Hz low-frequency signal.

    a. I-1   b. I-2

    c. R-1   d. R-4

    Reference _____

39. Where smoke and heat vents operated by fusible links are installed in areas protected by automatic fire sprinklers, the fusible link shall have a temperature rating of _____ F.

    a. 250°   b. 320°

    c. 360°   d. 400°

    Reference _____

40. A fire command center is required in Group F-1 and S-1 occupancies with a minimum building footprint of _____ square feet.

    a. 250,001   b. 500,001

    c. 600,001   d. 750,001

Reference _____

2021 IBC Sections 1001 through 1005, 1008, 1009, 1013 and 1015

Means of Egress I

OBJECTIVE: To obtain an understanding of the general system design requirements of a means of egress system, including the determination of occupant load, the required width and capacity of egress components, means of egress identification and illumination, accessible means of egress and the provisions regulating guards.

REFERENCE: Sections 1001 through 1005, 1008, 1009, 1013 and 1015, 2021 *International Building Code*

KEY POINTS:
- What is the definition of a means of egress system? What are its three distinct elements?
- What is the minimum ceiling height permitted along a means of egress?
- What limitations are placed on protruding objects extending below the minimum ceiling height? Projecting horizontally over a walking surface?
- For an elevation change along the egress path, at what point is a ramp required rather than a step or stairway?
- In areas without fixed seats, what is the correct method of determining occupant load?
- What method shall be used to calculate the occupant load in areas with fixed seating, such as benches, pews or booths?
- How may the design occupant load be increased over what is calculated?
- In which types of rooms or spaces must the maximum occupant load be posted?
- How is exiting addressed where stairways serve more than one floor?
- How is exiting from a mezzanine regulated?
- Are yards, patios and courts regulated in the same manner as interior areas?
- How shall the minimum width and capacity of different egress components be determined?
- What is the maximum allowable encroachment of a door into the required egress width?

KEY POINTS:
(Cont'd)

- When must the means of egress be illuminated? What is the minimum required illumination at the floor level?
- Which locations must be provided with emergency power for egress illumination?
- For what duration is an emergency power system for means of egress illumination required to provide power?
- What is considered an accessible means of egress? How many are required in a building?
- When is an area of refuge needed? How are they to be constructed?
- Under what conditions is a two-way communication system required? What are the minimum system requirements?
- How must an accessible means of egress be identified?
- What is the purpose of an exterior area for rescue assistance? How must this area be separated from the interior of the building it serves?
- Where are exit signs required? When must they be illuminated? What level of illumination is required? Which types of power sources are necessary?
- Under what conditions are low-level exit signs required? Where are such signs to be located?
- What is the definition of a guard?
- When are guards required? What is the minimum height requirement from the walking surface to the top of a guard?
- How must guards be constructed to limit passage through the protective barrier?
- How is window sill height regulated in Group R-2 and R-3 occupancies where openings are located more than 72 inches above grade? What are window fall prevention devices? Window opening control devices?

Topic: General	**Category:** Means of Egress
Reference: IBC 1001.1	**Subject:** Administration

Code Text: *Buildings or portions thereof shall be provided with a means of egress system as required by* Chapter 10. *The provisions of* Chapter 10 *shall control the design, construction and arrangement of means of egress components required to provide an approved means of egress from structures and portions thereof.*

Discussion and Commentary: The *International Building Code* regulates the design, construction and maintenance of an exiting system through two general categories—system design and egress components. Any building elements that are a part of the system must be reviewed for compliance with the criteria for the number, location, width or capacity, height, continuity and arrangement of egress components, and all other applicable provisions.

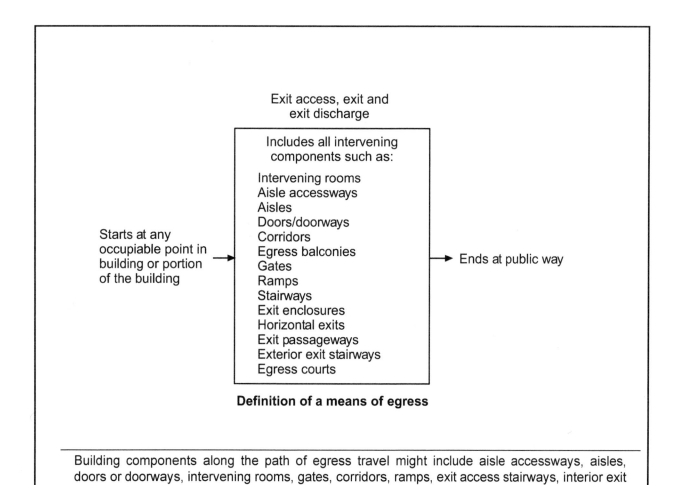

Definition of a means of egress

Building components along the path of egress travel might include aisle accessways, aisles, doors or doorways, intervening rooms, gates, corridors, ramps, exit access stairways, interior exit stairways, exit passageways, horizontal exits, exterior balconies, exterior exit stairways and egress courts.

Code Text: A means of egress is *a continuous and unobstructed path of vertical and horizontal egress travel from any occupied portion of a building or structure to a public way. A means of egress consists of three separate and distinct parts: the exit access, the exit, and the exit discharge.*

Discussion and Commentary: The exit access begins at any occupied location within the building and does not end until it reaches the door to an interior exit stairway or ramp, a horizontal exit or exit passageway, an exterior exit stairway or ramp, or an exterior exit door at the level of exit discharge. Travel distance is regulated throughout the exit access, and the path of travel is seldom a fire-protected environment. At the exit discharge, which begins where the exit ends, egress remains regulated until the public way is reached.

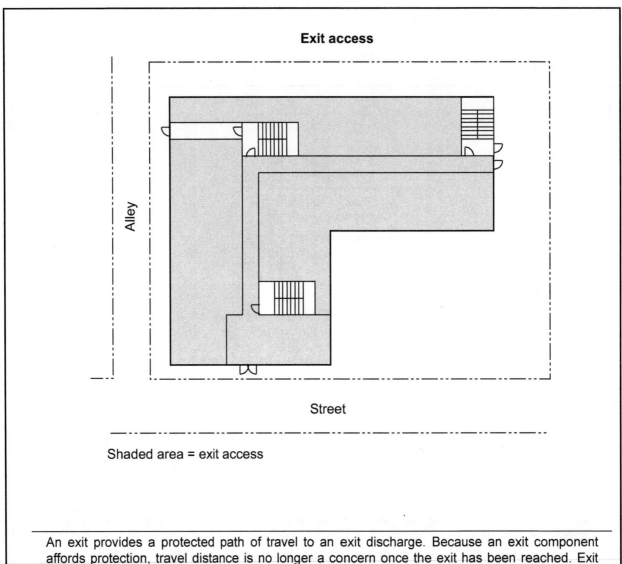

Shaded area = exit access

An exit provides a protected path of travel to an exit discharge. Because an exit component affords protection, travel distance is no longer a concern once the exit has been reached. Exit discharge travel distance to the public way is also unlimited.

Code Text: *The means of egress shall have a ceiling height of not less than 7 feet 6 inches (2286 mm) above the finished floor.* See the exceptions for sloped ceilings, ceilings of dwelling units and sleeping units, allowable projections, stair and ramp headroom, door height, mezzanines and parking garages.

Discussion and Commentary: In addition to providing a travel path of adequate width, the code requires that the clear height of the means of egress be maintained at least $7^1/_2$ feet above the walking surface. There are several exceptions to this general requirement that permit limited reductions in the mandated height. Under most conditions, the vertical clearance at a stairway or doorway may be reduced to 80 inches. Protruding objects, such as sprinklers and light fixtures, are also permitted to extend below the minimum required ceiling height for up to 50 percent of ceiling area of the means of egress, provided such objects maintain a headroom clearance of at least 80 inches. Special provisions are applicable to sloped ceilings.

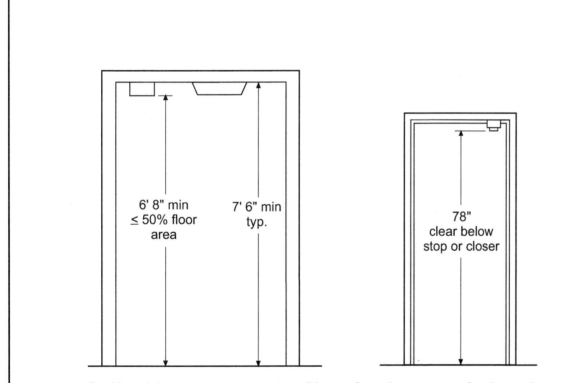

6' 8" min
≤ 50% floor
area

7' 6" min
typ.

78"
clear below
stop or closer

Corridor, aisle, passageway or any walking surface along egress of path travel

For SI: 1 inch = 25.4 mm, 1 foot = 304.8 mm.

The minimum ceiling heights established for environmental concerns are addressed in Section 1208.2. Habitable spaces, such as bedrooms and living rooms in residential occupancies, occupiable spaces and corridors must be at least 7 feet 6 inches in height. In other areas, reduced headroom is permitted.

Code Text: *Where changes in elevation of less than 12 inches (305 mm) exist in the means of egress, sloped surfaces shall be used. Where the slope is greater than 1 unit vertical in 20 units horizontal (5-percent slope), ramps complying with Section 1012 shall be used. Where the difference in elevation is 6 inches (152 mm) or less, the ramp shall be equipped with either handrails or floor finish materials that contrast with adjacent floor finish materials. See the exceptions for (1) a single 7-inch maximum step in Groups F, H, R-2, R-3, S and U; (2) a stair with one or two risers with a handrail provided; and (3) steps at exterior doors that comply with Section 1010.1.4 (Floor elevation).*

Discussion and Commentary: Along the egress path, there is a concern about slight changes in elevation that are not readily apparent to persons seeking to exit under emergency conditions. Therefore, a single riser or a pair of shallow risers is not permitted. Steps used to achieve minor differences in elevation frequently go unnoticed, and as such, can cause accidents.

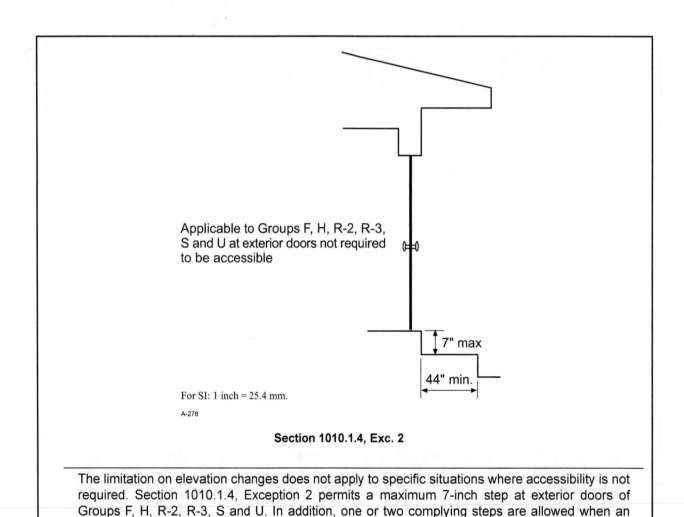

Applicable to Groups F, H, R-2, R-3, S and U at exterior doors not required to be accessible

7" max

44" min.

For SI: 1 inch = 25.4 mm.

A-278

Section 1010.1.4, Exc. 2

The limitation on elevation changes does not apply to specific situations where accessibility is not required. Section 1010.1.4, Exception 2 permits a maximum 7-inch step at exterior doors of Groups F, H, R-2, R-3, S and U. In addition, one or two complying steps are allowed when an additional handrail is provided.

Code Text: *In determining means of egress requirements, the number of occupants for whom means of egress facilities shall be provided shall be determined in accordance with Section 1004. The number of occupants shall be computed at the rate of one occupant per unit of area as prescribed in Table 1004.5. For areas without fixed seating, the occupant load shall not be less than that number determined by dividing the floor area under consideration by the occupant load factor assigned to the function of the space as set forth in Table 1004.5. See the exception where the building official is authorized to reduce occupant load below that calculated.*

Discussion and Commentary: For occupant load determination, it must be assumed that under normal conditions all portions of a building are fully occupied at the same time. The density characteristics of the various uses identified in Table 1004.5 are considered "occupant load factors." For most occupancies, the gross floor area is to be considered. However, a few of the occupant load factors are based on net floor area, which allows the deduction of areas such as corridors, stairways, toilet rooms, equipment rooms and closets.

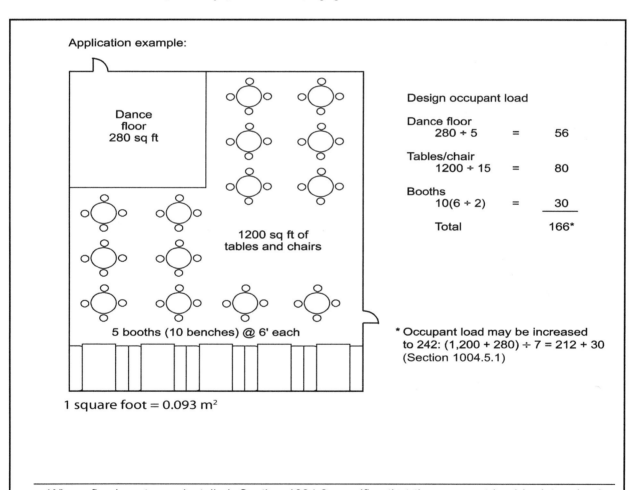

Application example:

Dance floor 280 sq ft

1200 sq ft of tables and chairs

5 booths (10 benches) @ 6' each

1 square foot = 0.093 m²

Design occupant load

Dance floor
    280 ÷ 5   =   56

Tables/chair
    1200 ÷ 15   =   80

Booths
    10(6 ÷ 2)   =   30

    Total   166*

* Occupant load may be increased to 242: (1,200 + 280) ÷ 7 = 212 + 30 (Section 1004.5.1)

Where fixed seats are installed, Section 1004.6 specifies that the occupant load is determined simply by counting the number of seats. For benches and pews, the factor is one occupant per 18 inches of width. For booth seating, the factor is 24 inches per occupant.

Code Text: *Yards, patios, occupied roofs, courts and similar outdoor areas accessible to and usable by the building occupants shall be provided with means of egress as required by* Chapter 10. *Where outdoor areas are to be used by persons in addition to the occupants of the building, and the path of egress travel from the outdoor areas passes through the building, means of egress requirements shall be based on the sum of the occupant loads of the building plus the outdoor areas.* See the exceptions for service areas and dwellings.

Discussion and Commentary: Although not limited in application, the regulation of egress from outdoor areas often addresses the use of exterior spaces for dining and/or drinking in restaurants and similar establishments. In addition, the means of egress required from occupied roofs is determined based upon the requirements for outdoor areas. The building official is authorized to establish an occupant load for the outdoor space in accordance with its anticipated use and to apply all means of egress provisions that would be appropriate.

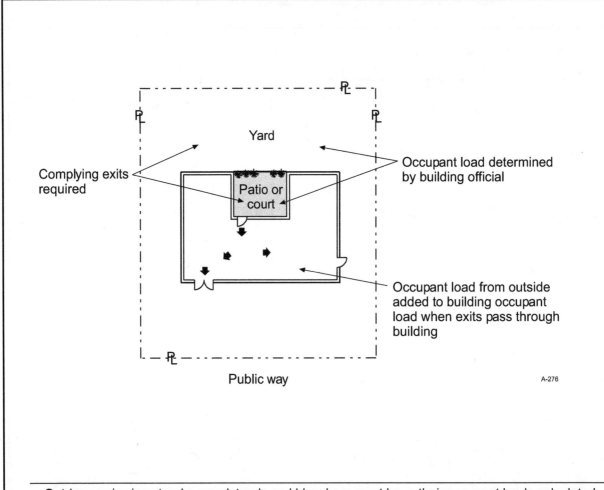

Outdoor reviewing stands, grandstands and bleachers must have their occupant loads calculated according to the specific types of seating arrangements, such as chair backs, benches, loose chairs, etc. Additional specific requirements are contained in Section 1030.

Code Text: *The minimum width, in inches, of any means of egress components shall not be less than that specified for such component, elsewhere in* the IBC. *The capacity, in inches, of means of egress stairways shall be calculated by multiplying the occupant load served by such stairway by a means of egress capacity factor of 0.3 inches (7.6 mm) per occupant. The capacity, in inches, of means of egress components other than stairways shall be calculated by multiplying the occupant load served by such component by a means of egress capacity factor of 0.2 inches (5.1 mm) per occupant.* See the exceptions that reduce the capacity factors to 0.2 inches and 0.15 inches, respectively, for buildings equipped throughout with an automatic sprinkler system and an emergency voice/alarm communication system.

Discussion and Commentary: In a given means of egress system, different components will afford different capacities. The most restrictive component will establish the capacity of the overall system. Doorways, aisles, stairways and corridors also have minimum established widths that must be provided.

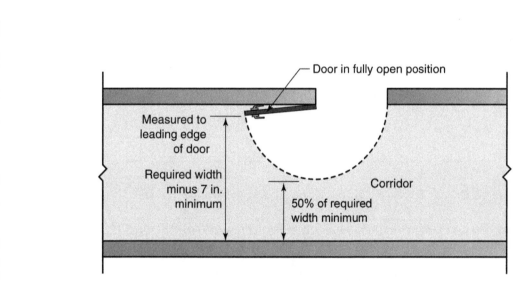

Measurement of minimum required egress width
Section 1005.7.1

Width, in terms of a means of egress system or component, is the clear, unobstructed usable width afforded along the exit path by the individual components. Unless the code provides for a permitted projection, the minimum required clear width may not be reduced throughout the travel path.

Code Text: *Where more than one exit, or access to more than one exit, is required, the means of egress shall be configured such that the loss of any one exit, or access to one exit, shall not reduce the available capacity or width to less than 50 percent of the required capacity or width.*

Discussion and Commentary: Where two complying means of egress are provided, the occupant load is to be distributed evenly between the two means of egress. However, where three or more means of egress are available, it is permissible to size one of the egress points for up to 50 percent of the occupant load, while distributing the remaining occupant load among the other means of egress. This distribution is not required to be equally applied; however, a dramatic imbalance of egress component capacities relative to occupant load distribution should be avoided.

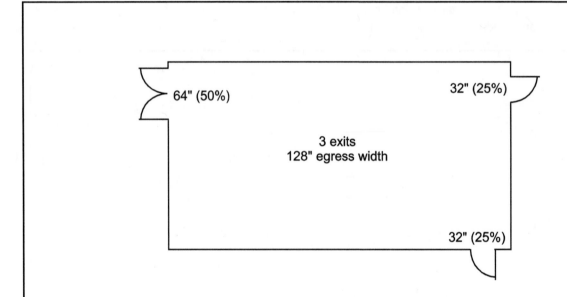

Given: A retail store having three exits, with a total required exit width of 128 in.
Determine: The manner in which the exit width may be distributed.

Any manner is acceptable that does not assign more than 50% (64 in.) of the required width to any single exit.

Egress width distribution

For SI: 1 inch = 25.4 mm.

One of the fundamental concepts in the design of the means of egress is that the capacity of the egress path not be diminished until the public way is reached. Regardless of minimum required component width, the calculated width based on the occupant load served must be maintained.

Code Text: *Where stairways serve more than one story, only the occupant load of each story considered individually shall be used in computing the required capacity of the stairway serving that story. The minimum width or required capacity of the means of egress required from any story of a building shall not be reduced along the path of egress travel until arrival at the public way. Where the means of egress from stories above and below converge at an intermediate level, the capacity of the means of egress from the point of convergence shall not be less than the largest minimum width or the sum of the required capacities for the stairways serving the two adjacent stories, whichever is larger.*

Discussion and Commentary: It is not necessary to add occupants together for required capacity calculations as they travel vertically from one story to the next. Only the capacity for each individual story is utilized in establishing the minimum required stairway width at each flight. However, once a minimum required width has been established along the stair path, it cannot be reduced.

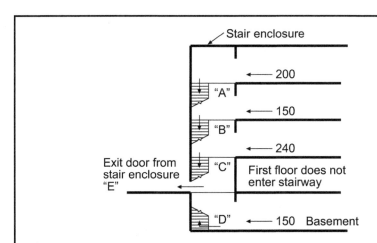

Given:
- A nonsprinklered four-story office building with basement

- Occupant load exiting into stair enclosure at each level as indicated

- First floor occupants exit to exterior without entering the stair enclosure

Exit element	Occupant load served	Required width
Stair-point "A"	200	60"
Stair-point "B"	150	60"[1]
Stair-point "C"	240	72"
Stair-point "D"	150	45"
Stair-point "E"	390[2]	78"

[1]Required width from above must be maintained
[2]Door at point "E" serves occupants from "C" and "D" egress convergence per Section 1005.6

There is an allowance for adding the occupant loads of floors above and below an intermediate level together where they converge along the exit path. The aggregate occupant load of such converging floors is to be used in determining the minimum required exit width.

Code Text: *The means of egress serving a room or space shall be illuminated at all times that the room or space is occupied.* See the exceptions for (1) Group U occupancies; (2) aisle accessways in Group A; (3) dwelling and sleeping units in Groups R-1, R-2 and R-3; and (4) sleeping units of Group I. *The power supply for means of egress illumination shall normally be provided by the premises electrical supply. In the event of power supply failure in rooms and spaces that require two or more means of egress, an emergency electrical system shall automatically illuminate all of the following areas: (1) aisles, (2) corridors and (3) exit access stairways and ramps.* Additional requirements for emergency power for illumination is required for buildings that require at least two means of egress and for special spaces such as fire pump rooms and large public restrooms.

Discussion and Commentary: Often identified as emergency lighting, a completely separate source of power from the premise's wiring system is required when the life-safety risk in a building becomes sufficiently great. This threshold is recognized as the point at which the occupant load of the room, area or building is high enough so that two means of egress are required.

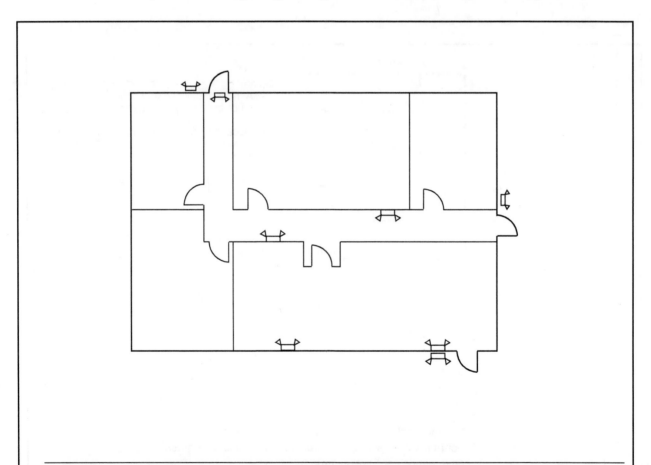

For the building occupant to be able to negotiate safely the means of egress system, the entire system must be illuminated any time the building is occupied. The illumination must provide an intensity of at least one foot-candle at the floor level. Stairway walking surfaces must be provided with at least 10 footcandles of illumination when the stairway is in use.

Code Text: *Accessible spaces shall be provided with not less than one accessible means of egress. Where more than one means of egress is required by Sections 1006.2 or 1006.3 from any accessible space, each accessible portion of the space shall be served by not less than two accessible means of egress.* See the exceptions for (1) accessible mezzanines and (2) assembly spaces with sloped floors. *Each required accessible means of egress shall be continuous to a public way and shall consist of one or more of the following components: accessible routes, interior exit stairways, exit access stairways, exterior exit stairways, elevators, platform lifts, horizontal exits, ramps, areas of refuge and exterior areas for assisted rescue.*

Discussion and Commentary: An accessible means of egress is a continuous and unobstructed way of egress travel, from any accessible point in a building or facility to a public way.

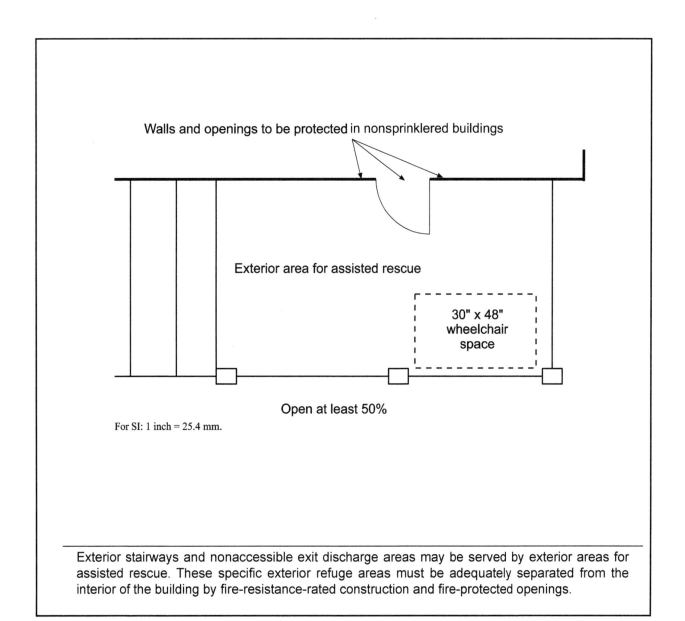

Walls and openings to be protected in nonsprinklered buildings

Exterior area for assisted rescue

30" x 48" wheelchair space

Open at least 50%

For SI: 1 inch = 25.4 mm.

Exterior stairways and nonaccessible exit discharge areas may be served by exterior areas for assisted rescue. These specific exterior refuge areas must be adequately separated from the interior of the building by fire-resistance-rated construction and fire-protected openings.

Code Text: *Every required area of refuge shall be accessible from the space it serves by an accessible means of egress. Every required area of refuge shall have direct access to a stairway complying with Sections 1009.3 and 1023 or an elevator complying with Section 1009.4.*

Discussion and Commentary: An area of refuge is defined as an area where persons unable to use stairways can remain temporarily to await instructions or assistance during emergency evacuation. An area of refuge needs to be separated from the remainder of the story by a smoke barrier or horizontal exit unless the refuge area is located within an enclosure for an exit access stairway or an interior exit stairway. A two-way communication system with appropriate instructions must be provided in each area of refuge and must also be identified by complying signs. There are several conditions under which areas of refuge are not required. The most commonly utilized exception to areas of refuge applies to buildings that are fully sprinklered.

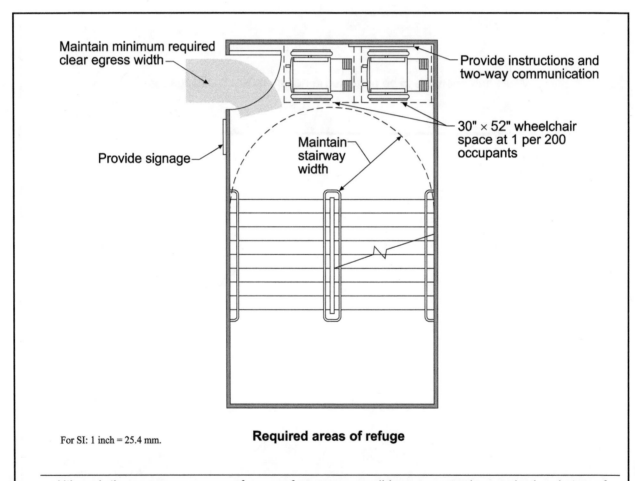

Maintain minimum required clear egress width

Provide instructions and two-way communication

Provide signage

Maintain stairway width

30" × 52" wheelchair space at 1 per 200 occupants

For SI: 1 inch = 25.4 mm.

Required areas of refuge

Although three or more means of egress from an accessible space may be required, only two of the exitways must be accessible. However, where an area of refuge is used as part of the egress system, the maximum travel distance set forth in Section 1017.2 must be maintained.

Code Text: *A two-way communication system complying with Sections 1009.8.1 and 1009.8.2 shall be provided at the landing serving each elevator or bank of elevators on each accessible floor that is one or more stories above or below the level of exit discharge.* See the exceptions where (1) the two-way communication system is provided within complying areas of refuge, (2) the floor level is provided with complying exit ramps, (3) landings serve only service elevators, (4) landings serve only freight elevators, (5) a landing serves a private residence elevator, or (6) the facility is a Group I-2 or I-3 occupancy.

Discussion and Commentary: In multistory buildings, two-way communication systems must be located at the elevator landing on each accessible floor level, with the exception of the level of exit discharge. The system is intended to offer a means of communication to disabled individuals who need assistance during an emergency situation. Such a system can be useful not only in the event of a fire but also in the case of a natural or technological disaster by providing emergency responders with the location of individuals who will require assistance to be safely evacuated from floor levels above or below the discharge level.

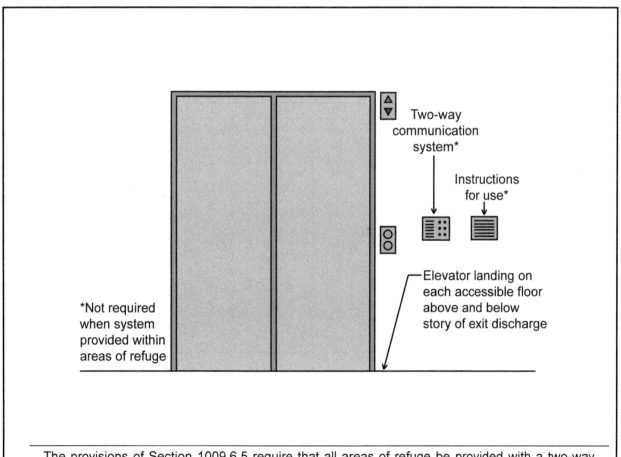

Two-way communication system*

Instructions for use*

Elevator landing on each accessible floor above and below story of exit discharge

*Not required when system provided within areas of refuge

The provisions of Section 1009.6.5 require that all areas of refuge be provided with a two-way communication system. The specific requirements for the system are the same as those for the two-way communication systems mandated at elevator landings as set forth in Section 1009.8.

Code Text: *Exit and exit access doors shall be marked by an approved exit sign readily visible from any direction of egress travel. The path of egress travel to exits and within exits shall be marked by readily visible exit signs to clearly indicate the direction of egress travel in cases where the exit or the path of egress travel is not immediately visible to the occupants.* See the five exceptions for uses or conditions where exit signs are not required.

Discussion and Commentary: Exit signs are only mandated when the room or area under consideration is required to have multiple exits or exit access doors. Other locations are also specified where the presence of an exit sign is deemed unnecessary, such as clearly identifiable main exterior doors. Although the appropriate locations for exit signs should be identified during the plan review phase of a project, the true evaluation of their effectiveness should be done just prior to occupancy, when the correct location and orientation of the signs can be checked.

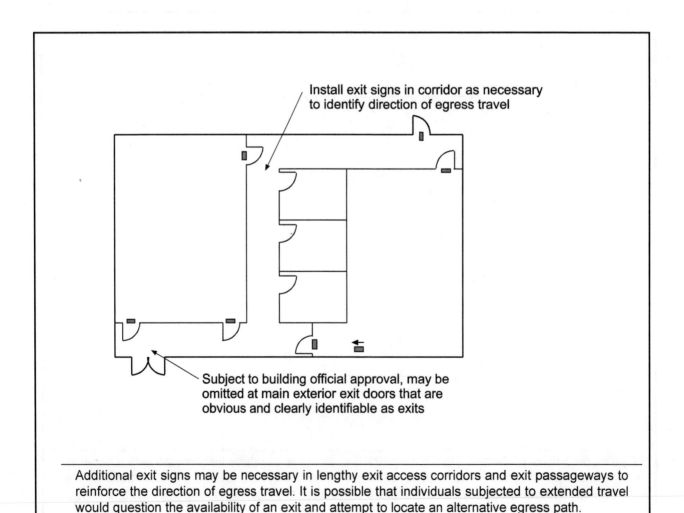

Install exit signs in corridor as necessary to identify direction of egress travel

Subject to building official approval, may be omitted at main exterior exit doors that are obvious and clearly identifiable as exits

Additional exit signs may be necessary in lengthy exit access corridors and exit passageways to reinforce the direction of egress travel. It is possible that individuals subjected to extended travel would question the availability of an exit and attempt to locate an alternative egress path.

Code Text: *Where exit signs are required in Group R-1 occupancies by Section 1013.1, additional low-level exit signs shall be provided in all areas serving guest rooms in Group R-1 occupancies and shall comply with Section 1013.5. The bottom of the sign shall be not less than 10 inches (254 mm) nor more than 18 inches (455 mm) above the floor level. The sign shall be flush mounted to the door or wall. Where mounted on the wall, the edge of the sign shall be within 4 inches (102 mm) of the door frame on the latch side.*

Discussion and Commentary: In the means of egress system for Group R-1 occupancies, additional exit signs are mandated for those portions of the system serving the guest rooms. Occupants of such facilities are transient and typically not familiar with their surroundings. If a corridor or other egress component serving the guest rooms were to fill with smoke, the general exit signs located high in the space could quickly become obscured. The installation of additional signs at floor level provides for a secondary identification of the egress path.

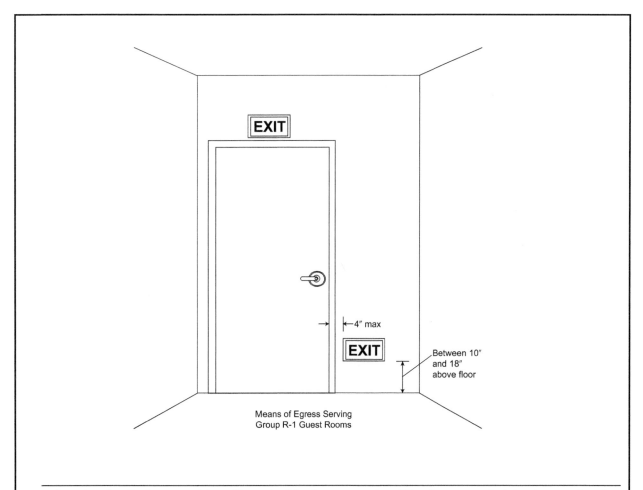

EXIT

←4″ max

EXIT

Between 10″
and 18″
above floor

Means of Egress Serving
Group R-1 Guest Rooms

Low-level exit signs must be either electrically powered, self-luminous or photoluminescent exit signs that are listed and labeled in accordance with UL 924 and installed in accordance with the manufacturer's instructions. Consistent with the requirements for all other exit signs, low-level signs shall be illuminated at all times.

Code Text: *Exit signs shall be internally or externally illuminated.* See the exception for tactile signs. *Exit signs shall be illuminated at all times. To ensure continued illumination for a duration of not less than 90 minutes in case of primary power loss, the sign illumination means shall be connected to an emergency system provided from storage batteries, unit equipment or an on-site generator.*

Discussion and Commentary: To ensure visibility under all conditions, required exit signs must always be illuminated. For those signs that are internally illuminated, which make up the vast majority of exit signs, compliance with UL 924 is mandated. Such exit signs, which includes electrically-powered, self-luminous and photo luminescent signs, must be listed and labeled. In addition, they must be installed in accordance with the manufacturer's installation instructions.

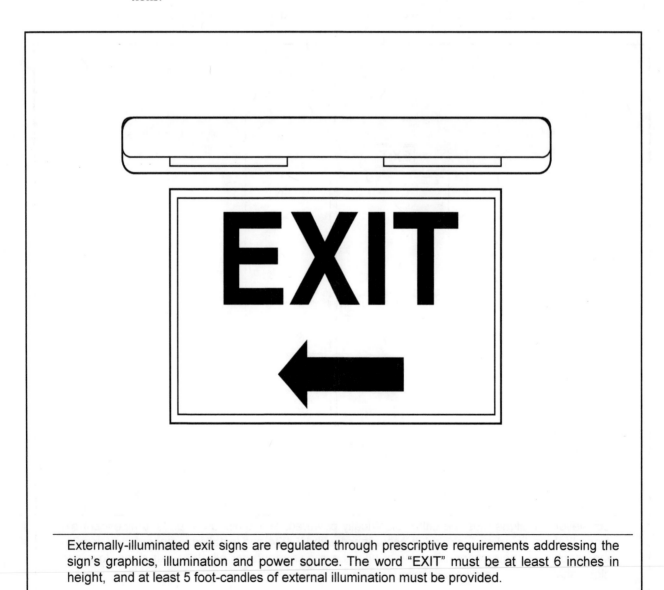

Externally-illuminated exit signs are regulated through prescriptive requirements addressing the sign's graphics, illumination and power source. The word "EXIT" must be at least 6 inches in height, and at least 5 foot-candles of external illumination must be provided.

Code Text: *Guards shall be located along open-sided walking surfaces, including mezzanines, equipment platforms, aisles, stairs, ramps and landings that are located more than 30 inches (762 mm) measured vertically to the floor or grade below at any point within 36 inches (914 mm) horizontally to the edge of the open side.* See the exceptions. *Required guards shall be not less than 42 inches (1067 mm) high, measured vertically (1) from the adjacent walking surfaces; (2) on stairways and stepped aisles, from the line connecting the leading edges of the tread nosings; and (3) on ramps and ramped aisles, from the ramp surface at the guard.* See the exceptions. *Required guards shall not have openings which allow passage of a sphere 4 inches (102 mm) in diameter from the walking surface to the required guard height.* See the exceptions.

Discussion and Commentary: Guards must be of adequate height and structural stability to prevent an individual from accidentally falling from the protected area. They must also be designed also to prevent small children from intentionally crawling through the barrier.

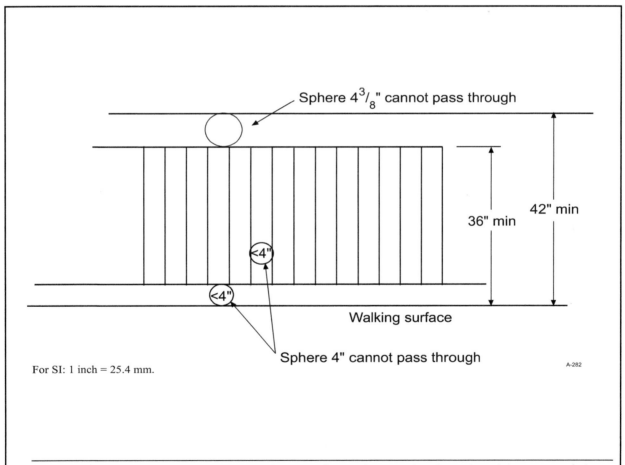

Sphere $4^3/_8$" cannot pass through

42" min

36" min

<4"

<4"

Walking surface

Sphere 4" cannot pass through

For SI: 1 inch = 25.4 mm.

A-282

In certain industrial-type areas, the degree of guard protection is reduced because of the nonpublic uses involved. In addition, guards are not mandated in specific applications relating to loading docks, stages, platforms and vehicle service pits.

Code Text: *Guards shall be provided where various components that require service are located within 10 feet (3048 mm) of a roof edge or open side of a walking surface and such edge or open side is located more than 30 inches (762 mm) above the floor, roof or grade below. The guard shall extend not less than 30 inches (762 mm) beyond each end of such components. The guard shall be constructed so as to prevent the passage of a sphere 21 inches in diameter (533 mm).* See the exception for locations where personal fall arrest/ restraint anchorage connector devices are installed.

Discussion and Commentary: The requirement for guards primarily addresses the hazard created when service personnel are working on rooftop equipment. Where such activity occurs close to a roof edge, it is critical that guards be provided to prevent an accidental fall.

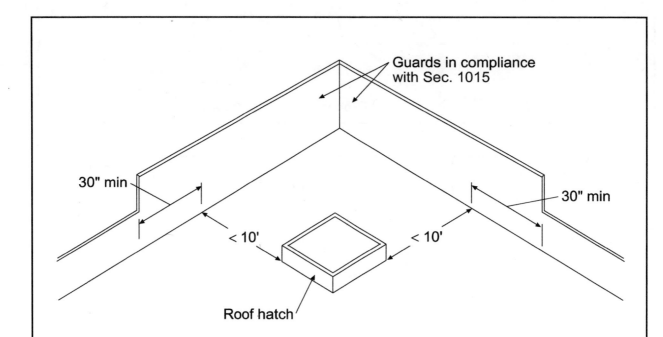

For SI: 1 inch = 25.4 mm, 1 foot = 304.8 mm

A guard is also mandated where a roof hatch is located near a roof edge. At times, these roof accesses are used during inclement weather, emergency situations or times of darkness. The area around roof hatch openings is also often utilized as a staging area or work area.

Code Text: *Windows in Group R-2 and R-3 buildings including dwelling units, where the bottom of the clear opening of an operable window opening is located less than 36 inches (914 mm) above the finished floor and more than 72 inches (1829 mm) above the finished grade or other surface below on the exterior of the building, shall comply with one of the following:* See the four options, including limited-size openings or the use of window fall-prevention devices or window opening-control devices.

Discussion and Commentary: The opening height for operable windows located a considerable height above the surface below is intended to reduce the number of falls by children from such windows. The minimum height is established at a point above the center of gravity of most children.

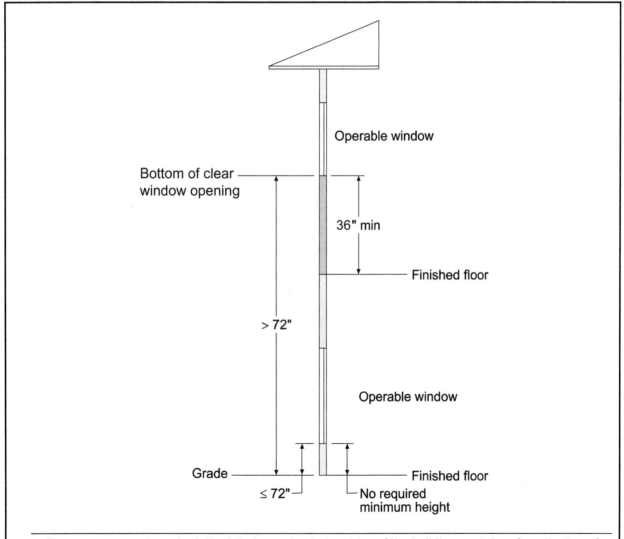

The measurements on both the interior and exterior sides of the building are taken from the top of the clear opening of the operable window, providing for consistent application. Where the lower window panel is inoperable, the measurement is to be taken to the lowest point of the lowest operable panel.

Quiz

Study Session 9
IBC Sections 1001 through 1005, 1008, 1009, 1013 and 1015

1. A court or yard that provides access to a public way for one or more exits is considered a(n) _____ .

    a. exit access way   b. egress court

    c. public way   d. horizontal exit

Reference_____

2. Which of the following elements is not a distinct and separate part of the means of egress?

    a. exit discharge   b. exit access

    c. exit   d. exit convergence

Reference_____

3. That portion of exit access travel distance measured from the most remote point of each room, area or space to that point where the occupants have separate and distinct access to two exits or exit access doorways is considered a _____.

    a. means of egress   b. single egress path

    c. common path of egress travel   d. limited egress travel distance

Reference_____

4. Panic hardware that is listed for use on fire door assemblies is considered to be _____ hardware.

    a. fire egress   b. fire exit

    c. panic   d. panic and fire

Reference_____

5. An alternating tread device has a series of steps that are positioned a minimum of _____ degrees and maximum of _____degrees from horizontal.

    a. 30, 45   b. 45, 60

    c. 50, 70   d. 60, 75

    Reference_____

6. In determining the design occupant load for the sales area of a mercantile facility, the floor area shall be divided by a factor of one occupant per _____ square feet.

    a. 20   b. 30

    c. 50   d. 60

    Reference_____

7. A 1,500-square-foot (net) woodworking shop classroom in a high school is considered to have a design occupant load of _____ persons.

    a. 25   b. 30

    c. 75   d. 100

    Reference_____

8. For areas having fixed seats and aisles, the occupant load for bench seating without dividing arms is based on one occupant for each _____ inches of seating length.

    a. 15   b. 18

    c. 24   d. 30

    Reference_____

9. In a fully-sprinklered Group M retail sales building having an occupant load of 3,200 occupants, the minimum total calculated means of egress width for egress elements other than stairways shall be _____ inches if an emergency voice/alarm communication system is provided.

    a. 960   b. 640

    c. 480   d. 320

    Reference_____

10. A stairway serving 160 occupants in a fully-sprinklered Group I-2 hospital shall be a minimum of _____ inches in width.

    a. 42   b. 44

    c. 48   d. 60

Reference_____

11. Multiple means of egress shall be sized so that the loss of any one means of egress shall not reduce the available capacity to less than _____ of the required capacity.

    a. 10 percent   b. 25 percent

    c. $33^1/_3$ percent   d. 50 percent

Reference_____

12. When fully open, a door is permitted to project into the required width of the path of egress travel a maximum of _____ .

    a. one-half the required width   b. one-half the actual width

    c. $3^1/_2$ inches   d. 7 inches

Reference_____

13. Up to 50 percent of the ceiling area of a means of egress may have a minimum ceiling height of _____ where reduced by protruding objects.

    a. 78 inches   b. 80 inches

    c. 84 inches   d. 90 inches

Reference_____

14. At a doorway, the minimum headroom clearance below any door closer or stop shall be _____ inches.

    a. 76   b. 78

    c. 80   d. 84

Reference_____

15. Other than handrails protruding from a wall or guard, the maximum projection into the travel path of a horizontal projection located between 27 and 80 inches above the walking surface shall be _____ inches.

    a. $1\frac{1}{2}$ b. $3\frac{1}{2}$

    c. 4   d. $4\frac{1}{2}$

Reference_____

16. At an exterior door not required to be accessible in a Group F-1 occupancy, what is the maximum permitted elevation change?

    a. $\frac{1}{2}$ inch   b. 1 inch

    c. 7 inches   d. 8 inches

Reference_____

17. Exit signs shall be located so that the maximum distance from any point in an exit access corridor or exit passageway to the nearest visible exit sign is _____ feet, or the listed viewing distance for the sign, whichever is less.

    a. 50   b. 75

    c. 100   d. 150

Reference_____

18. Externally-illuminated exit signs shall have a minimum intensity at the face of the sign of _____ foot-candles.

    a. 1   b. 5

    c. 10   d. 12

Reference_____

19. Emergency lighting facilities for means of egress illumination shall initially provide_____ along the path of egress at floor level.

    a. at least 1 foot-candle   b. an average of 1 foot-candle

    c. at least 5 foot-candles   d. an average of 0.2 foot-candle

Reference_____

20. A guard need not be located along an open-sided walking surface located a maximum of _____ inches vertically above the floor below.

    a. 15   b. 30

    c. 36   d. 42

Reference_____

21. In a mercantile occupancy, a required guard shall form a protective barrier a minimum of _____ inches in height.

    a. 36   b. 38

    c. 42   d. 44

Reference_____

22. In areas of a Group S-1 occupancy not open to the public, horizontal intermediate rails in a required guard shall be constructed so that a _____ sphere cannot pass through any opening.

    a. 4-inch   b. 6-inch

    c. 12-inch   d. 21-inch

Reference_____

23. Unless a roof-top HVAC unit requiring occasional service and maintenance is located a minimum of _____ from the roof edge, a complying guard shall be provided where complying personal fall arrest anchorage connector devices are not installed.

    a. 10 feet   b. 5 feet

    c. 3 feet   d. 30 inches

Reference_____

24. In a nonsprinklered building, a stairway utilized as an accessible means of egress shall be a minimum of _____ inches in clear width between handrails.

    a. 36   b. 44

    c. 48   d. 60

Reference_____

25. An area of refuge serving 450 occupants shall be provided with a minimum of
_____ wheelchair space(s).

    a. 1   b. 2

    c. 3   d. 5

Reference_____

26. Where a barrier is installed below a protruding object having a vertical clearance of
less than 80 inches, the leading edge of the barrier shall be located a maximum of
_____ inches above the floor.

    a. 27   b. 30

    c. 36   d. 42

Reference_____

27. In all cases, the occupant load in a room or building shall not be increased beyond a
maximum of one occupant per _____ square feet.

    a. 3   b. 5

    c. 6   d. 7

Reference_____

28. Emergency power for means of egress illumination is required in public restrooms
where the area is a minimum of _____ square feet.

    a. 1 (required in all public restrooms)

    b. 201

    c. 301

    d. 401

Reference_____

29. The exterior wall adjacent to an exterior area for assisted rescue landing does not
require a fire-resistance rating where the wall is located a minimum of
_____ feet horizontally from the landing.

    a. 5   b. 10

    c. 15   d. 20

Reference_____

30. A sign stating EXIT in visual characters, raised characters and braille shall be provided adjacent to each door providing direct access to all of the following means of egress components, except for _____.

    a.   an exit stairway
    b.   an exterior area for assisted rescue

    c.   an exit access corridor
    d.   an exit passageway

Reference_____

31. Where seating booths are provided, the occupant load shall be based on one person for each _____ inches of booth length.

    a.   18
    b.   20

    c.   21
    d.   24

Reference_____

32. In any position during the course of the door swing, a door is permitted to project into the required width of the path of egress travel a maximum of _____.

    a.   one-half the required width
    b.   one-half the actual width

    c.   4 inches
    d. $4^1/_2$ inches

Reference_____

33. Under general conditions, the means of egress illumination level shall not be less than _____ foot-candle(s) at the walking surface level.

    a.   0.1
    b.   1

    c.   5
    d.   10

Reference_____

34. From a height of 36 inches to 42 inches in a required guard, a sphere with a maximum diameter of _____ inches shall not pass through.

    a.   4
    b. $4^3/_8$

    c.   6
    d.   8

Reference_____

35. Within an individual dwelling unit of a Group R-2 occupancy, openings in required guards on the open sides of stairs shall not allow the passage of a maximum _____-inch-diameter sphere.

    a. 4   b. $4^3/_8$

    c. 6   d. 8

Reference _____

36. When computing the occupant load of a business area, an occupant load factor of _____square feet per occupant shall be applied.

    a. 100 net   b. 150 net

    c. 100 gross   d. 150 gross

Reference _____

37. Where approved by the building official, the occupant load for concentrated business use areas shall be one occupant per a minimum of _____ square feet of gross occupiable floor space.

    a. 50   b. 80

    c. 100   d. 125

Reference _____

38. Along exit access stairways, a minimum illumination level of _____ footcandles is required at the walking surface when the stairway is in use.

    a. 1   b. 2

    c. 5   d. 10

Reference _____

39. Low-level exit signs required in Group R-1 occupancies shall be located a minimum of _____ inches and a maximum of _____ inches above the floor level.

    a. 10, 14   b. 10, 18

    c. 12, 18   d. 16, 20

Reference _____

40. Decks enclosed with insect screening are not required to be provided with guards where the walking surface is a maximum of _____ inches above the floor or grade below.

a. 30

b. 36

c. 48

d. 60

Reference _____

2021 IBC Sections 1010 through 1012 and 1014
Means of Egress II

OBJECTIVE: To obtain an understanding of the general component requirements of a means of egress system, including those regulating doors, gates, stairways, ramps and turnstiles located along the egress path.

REFERENCE: Sections 1010 through 1012 and 1014, 2021 *International Building Code*

KEY POINTS:
- What is the minimum height and width of an egress door?
- What are the limitations on projections into the required clear door width?
- When must doors swing in the direction of egress travel?
- What is the maximum opening force permitted for an interior side-swinging door without a closer? Other side-swinging doors? Sliding and folding doors?
- What are "special" doors? How are they regulated differently than other doors?
- At a door, what change in elevation is permitted for a landing or floor surface?
- How must landings at doors be sized? What is the maximum allowable amount that doors may encroach into the required landing size?
- What is the maximum height of a threshold at a doorway?
- Which types of locks and latches are required on egress doors?
- When is the unlatching of an egress door permitted to take more than a single operation?
- Why do turnstiles create special egress concerns? What are the limitations on their use?
- When is panic hardware required?
- How are gates regulated differently than doors?
- How do interior exit stairways differ from exit access stairways? What code section regulates interior exit stairways? Exit access stairways?
- Under what conditions is an exit access stairway permitted to be unenclosed? Where enclosure is required, what degree of construction is mandated?
- How is the minimum required width of a stairway determined?

KEY POINTS:
(Cont'd)

- At a stairway and its landings, what is the minimum headroom clearance?
- What is the minimum rise of a stair riser? Maximum rise? Minimum tread run?
- What degree of tolerance is permitted between the largest and the smallest tread run within a flight of stairs? Between the greatest and the smallest riser height?
- How are stairway landings regulated for size?
- What is the maximum vertical rise permitted between stairway landings?
- Which special limitations apply to winders? Curved or spiral stairways? Alternate tread devices?
- When is a stairway required to provide access to a roof?
- What is the maximum permissible ramp slope? The maximum permissible rise for a ramp?
- How are ramp landings regulated for width? Length? Construction? Edge protection?
- When are handrails required for ramps?
- What must be the minimum height of a handrail located above the nosing of stairway treads and landings? Maximum height?
- How are handrails to be regulated for graspability?
- What are the exceptions to the general provision that handrails be continuous and without interruption?
- To what extent must handrails extend beyond the top and bottom risers of a stair flight?
- How much clear space is needed between a handrail and a wall or other surface?
- Under which conditions are intermediate handrails required?

Code Text: *Doors, gates and turnstiles provided for egress purposes in numbers greater than required by the IBC shall comply with the requirements of Section 1010. Doors in the means of egress shall be readily distinguishable from the adjacent construction and finishes such that the doors are easily recognizable as doors. Mirrors or similar reflecting materials shall not be used on means of egress doors. Means of egress doors shall not be concealed by curtains, drapes, decorations or similar materials.*

Discussion and Commentary: During a fire or other incident, occupants will attempt to exit through those doors that they believe will eventually lead to the exterior. Accordingly, any doors that would suggest an egress path must meet all of the door requirements. In addition, means of egress doors must be obvious and available for immediate use by the building occupants.

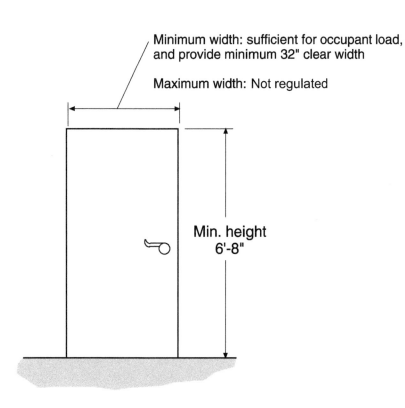

Minimum width: sufficient for occupant load, and provide minimum 32" clear width

Maximum width: Not regulated

Min. height 6'-8"

For SI: 1 inch = 25.4 mm, 1 foot = 304.8 mm.

In accordance with Section 1022.2, any building or structure used for human occupancy must have at least one exterior door opening that complies with the minimum width (32 inches) and height (80 inches) requirements of Section 1010.1.1.

Code Text: *The required capacity of each door opening shall be sufficient for the occupant load thereof and shall provide a minimum clear opening width of 32 inches (813 mm). The clear opening width of doorways with swinging doors shall be measured between the face of the door and the stop, with the door open 90 degrees (1.57 rad). The minimum clear opening height of doors shall not be less than 80 inches (2032 mm). See the exceptions for clear opening width.*

Discussion and Commentary: A clear width of 32 inches is required only to a height of 34 inches above the floor or ground. Beyond this point, projections up to 4 inches into the required width are permitted. Although a single doorway is expected to be used for the egress of one individual at a time, it must also be of adequate width for wheelchair users.

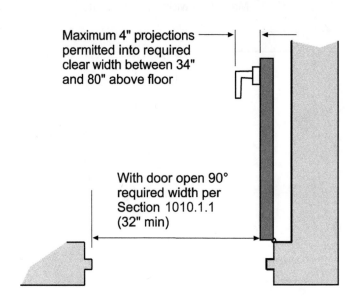

Maximum 4" projections permitted into required clear width between 34" and 80" above floor

With door open 90° required width per Section 1010.1.1 (32" min)

Egress width at doors is net dimension

For SI: 1 inch = 25.4 mm, 1 degree = 0.01745 rad.

The maximum width of a door leaf is not regulated by the code. It is expected that a reasonable door opening effort is addressed in Section 1010.1.3 through the regulation of force levels necessary to unlatch and open a door.

Code Text: *Egress doors shall be of the side-hinged swinging door, pivoted door, or balanced door types.* See the multiple exceptions addressing special conditions. *Side-hinged swinging doors, pivoted doors and balanced doors shall swing in the direction of egress travel where serving a room or area containing an occupant load of 50 or more persons or a Group H occupancy.*

Discussion and Commentary: Numerous fire deaths in buildings have been attributed to improper exit doors, but no single incident is more infamous than the 1942 Coconut Grove fire in Boston. Inward-swinging exterior exit doors were a significant factor in the loss of 492 lives. As a result, doors serving sizable occupant loads or Group H occupancies must swing in the direction of exit flow. For assembly and educational occupancies, the use of panic hardware increases the likelihood that egress doors can be opened easily.

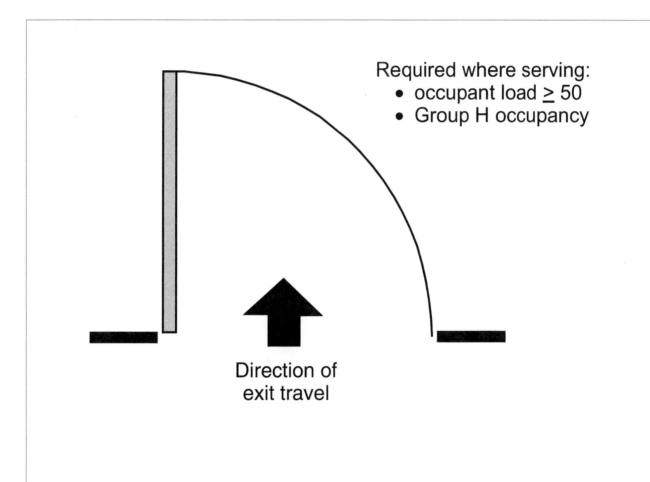

Required where serving:
- occupant load ≥ 50
- Group H occupancy

Direction of exit travel

The maximum force needed to unlatch doors in the means of egress is regulated for two conditions: where door hardware operates by push or pull, and where door hardware operates by rotation. The force required to open the door is regulated based on the specific door type.

Code Text: *There shall be a floor or landing on each side of a door. Such floor or landing shall be at the same elevation on each side of the door.* See the exceptions.

Discussion and Commentary: To avoid a surprise change in the elevation of a walking surface as it passes through a doorway, limitations have been placed on the height differential. The IBC generally requires that no elevation change occur at a door. In many cases, however, such a change in elevation takes place due to a variation in the type or thickness of floor finish materials. Where this occurs, a difference of no more than $^1/_2$ inch is permitted. Otherwise, only those exceptions that apply to certain dwelling units or to exterior doors not on an accessible route may have an elevation change at a doorway.

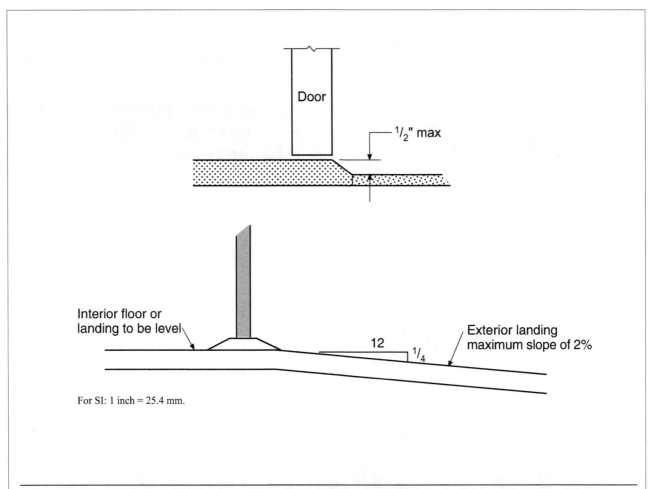

For SI: 1 inch = 25.4 mm.

For interior situations, landings should be level. In exterior applications, landings may have a slope not to exceed $^1/_4$ unit vertical in 12 units horizontal (1:48). This maximum slope of 2 percent provides a relatively flat surface while maintaining adequate drainage.

Code Text: *Landings shall have a width not less than the width of the stairway or the door, whichever is greater. Doors in the fully open position shall not reduce a required dimension by more than 7 inches (178 mm). When a landing serves an occupant load of 50 or more, doors in any position shall not reduce the landing to less than one-half its required width.*

Discussion and Commentary: This provision, which allows a door to project into the path of exit travel on a stairway's landing, comprises two issues. The first issue is that a door is not a fixed obstruction; it swings across the landing when it is used by occupants of the building. The second issue is that a door in any position is allowed to obstruct only one-half of the required width of the landing. The expectation is that the additional width of the landing will be provided for the occupants using the stairway as the door swings toward its fully open or fully closed position.

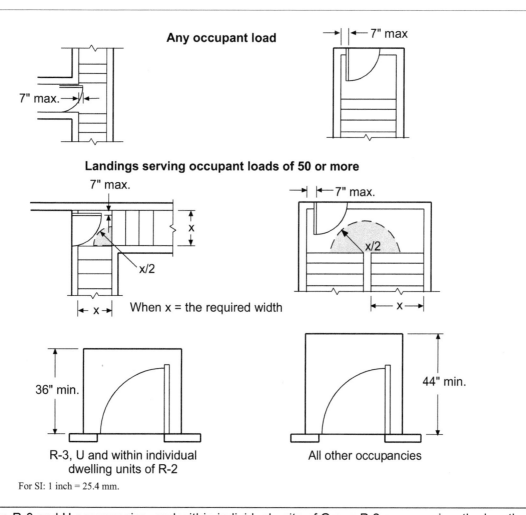

For SI: 1 inch = 25.4 mm.

In Group R-3 and U occupancies, and within individual units of Group R-2 occupancies, the length of a landing can be no less than 36 inches. In all other occupancy groups, the minimum required landing length is 44 inches, measured in the direction of travel.

Code Text: *Space between two doors in series shall be 48 inches (1219 mm) minimum plus the width of a door swinging into the space. Doors in series shall swing either in the same direction or away from the space between doors.* See the exceptions for dwelling units and horizontal sliding power-operated doors.

Discussion and Commentary: Where two doors are installed in a manner to create a vestibule or similar space, they must be located so as to allow building occupants effective and efficient movement through one door prior to continuing through the second door. This is especially true where the person opening the door has limited mobility and is required to make special effort in opening the door and passing through the doorway. The IBC recognizes these concerns by mandating an adequate spatial separation between doors provided in a series.

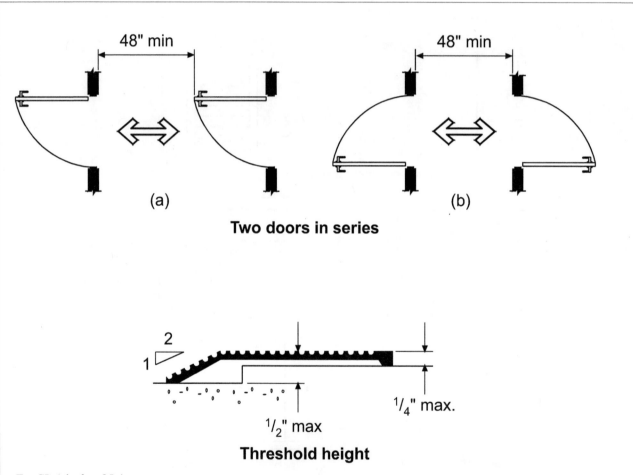

(a)   (b)

Two doors in series

Threshold height

For SI: 1 inch = 25.4 mm.

It is also important that a threshold at a door does not overly restrict safe and efficient passage through the doorway. Where a bevel of 1:2 or less is provided, the maximum threshold height is ¹/₂ inch. Otherwise, an abrupt change in elevation is limited to ¹/₄ inch.

Code Text: *Except as specifically permitted by Section 1010.2, egress doors shall be readily openable from the egress side without the use of a key or special knowledge or effort. Door handles, pulls, latches, locks and other operating devices shall be installed 34 inches (864 mm) minimum and 48 inches (1219 mm) maximum above the finished floor. Locks and latches shall be permitted to prevent operation of doors where any of 10 listed conditions exist. Manually operated flush bolts or surface bolts are not permitted.* See the five exceptions. *The unlatching of any door or leaf for egress shall not require more than one motion in a single linear or rotational direction to release all latching and all locking devices.* See the exceptions identifying four locations that allow for multiple operations.

Discussion and Commentary: Every element along the path of exit travel through a means of egress system, particularly doors, must be under the control of, and operable by, the person seeking egress. The intent is that the hardware installed be of a type familiar to most users, readily recognizable and usable under any emergency conditions.

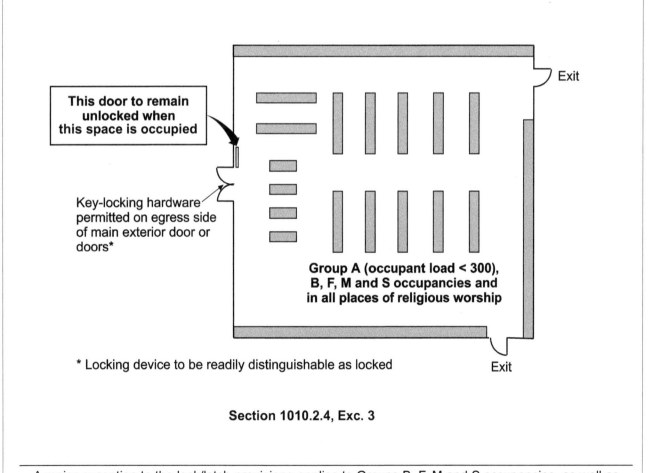

> **This door to remain unlocked when this space is occupied**
>
> Key-locking hardware permitted on egress side of main exterior door or doors*
>
> **Group A (occupant load < 300), B, F, M and S occupancies and in all places of religious worship**
>
> Exit
>
> Exit

* Locking device to be readily distinguishable as locked

Section 1010.2.4, Exc. 3

A major exception to the lock/latch provisions applies to Groups B, F, M and S occupancies, as well as to places of religious worship and smaller assembly uses. Key-operated locking devices from the egress side of doors are permitted under limited conditions, based on compensating safeguards.

Code Text: *Swinging doors serving a Group H occupancy and swinging doors serving rooms or spaces with an occupant load of 50 or more in a Group A or E occupancy shall not be provided with a latch or lock other than panic hardware or fire exit hardware.* See the exceptions for the main exit of a Group A occupancy, electrically locked doors serving Group A or E occupancies, exit access doors serving occupied exterior areas, and doors in courtrooms.

Discussion and Commentary: Panic hardware is a door-latching assembly incorporating a device that releases the latch when force is applied in the direction of exit travel. It is utilized in assembly occupancies because of the hazard that occurs when a large number of occupants reach an exit door at the same instance. In educational occupancies, the same concern is present, along with the need for children to be able to operate the latch of an exit door easily during an emergency. Panic hardware is mandated in all Group H occupancies, regardless of occupant load, on account of the increased hazard level anticipated within the building. Fire exit hardware is merely panic hardware listed for use on a fire door assembly.

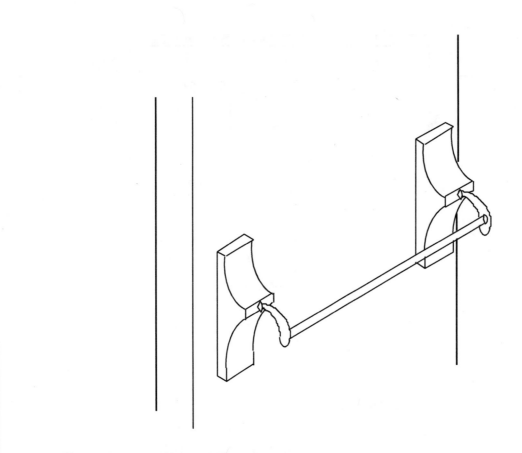

To ensure that contact with the door actuates the releasing device, the code requires that the actuating portion extend for at least one half of the door width. Where balanced or pivoted doors are used, the device width is again limited to one-half of the door width for leverage purposes.

Code Text: *Turnstiles or similar devices that restrict travel to one direction shall not be placed so as to obstruct any required means of egress, except where permitted in accordance with Sections 1010.5.1, 1010.5.2 and 1010.5.3.*

Discussion and Commentary: Turnstiles may serve as an egress component under very specific conditions. Where the listed conditions are met, each turnstile can be assigned a maximum exit capacity of 50 persons. Where permanent turnstiles serve an occupant load greater than 300, additional side-hinged swinging doors must be installed within 50 feet of the permanent turnstiles.

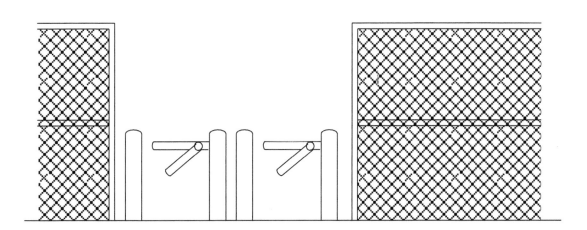

Each turnstile credited for up to 50-person capacity for egress where each turnstile:

- Will turn freely in direction of egress when power is lost, and upon manual release by employee in area

- Only given credit for 50% of required egress capacity (egress other than by turnstiles required)

- Limited to 39 inches in height

- Has minimum of 16$\frac{1}{2}$ inches clear width at and below height of 39 inches

- Has minimum of 22 inches clear width at height above 39 inches

Where the turnstile has a height exceeding 39 inches, the restriction to egress is much like that of a revolving door, and the provisions in Section 1010.3.1 apply to this higher type of turnstile. Compliance as a security access turnstile is also permitted.

Code Text: *Special doors and security grilles shall comply with the requirements of Sections 1010.3.1 through 1010.3.4.*

Discussion and Commentary: In general, doors in means of egress systems must be of the pivoted or side-hinged swinging type. Other doors, identified as special doors, are also addressed in the code. Such doors include revolving doors, power-operated doors, horizontal sliding doors and security grilles. These types of doors are specifically limited in their use because the difficult or unusual operation of such doors increases the likelihood of obstructed travel in an emergency.

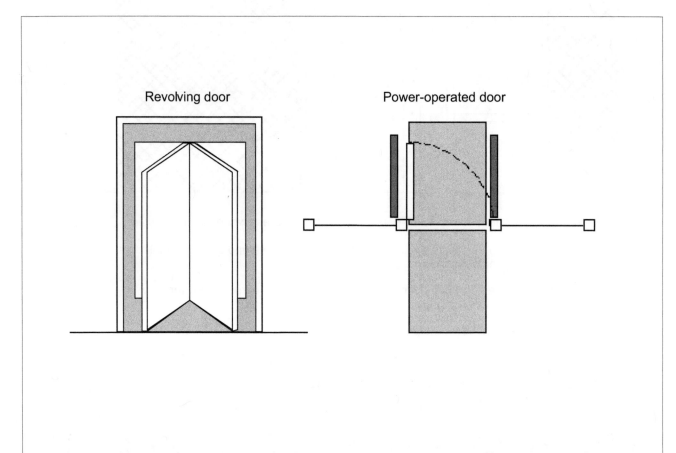

Revolving door   Power-operated door

The various types of special doors are permitted to be used for egress purposes when regulated by occupancy, occupant load, operation, opening force, power supply or other factors that contribute to the effectiveness and reliability of the egress door.

Topic: General Provisions	**Category:** Means of Egress
Reference: IBC 1011.1	**Subject:** Stairways

Code Text: *Stairways serving occupied portions of a building shall comply with the requirements of Sections 1011.2 through 1011.13. Alternating tread devices shall comply with Section 1011.14. Ships ladders shall comply with Section 1011.15. Ladders shall comply with Section 1011.16.* See the exception requiring stepped aisles in assembly spaces to comply with Section 1030.

Discussion and Commentary: In addition to the general design and construction requirements established in Section 1011, provisions regulating stairways used as a required part of the means of egress are also found in Chapter 10. Interior exit stairways, regulated by Section 1023, are considered exits and must always be enclosed with fire-resistance-rated construction. Exit access stairways, regulated in Section 1019, are considered portions of the exit access and are permitted to be unenclosed under a variety of special conditions.

The provisions of Section 1011 regulating the design and construction of stairways are applicable to all stairways, including those that may be considered only "convenience" stairs and not considered a portion of any required means of egress.

Code Text: *The required capacity of stairways shall be determined as specified in Section 1005.1* (calculated based on occupant load) *but the minimum width shall not be less than 44 inches (1118 mm).* See the exceptions for small occupant loads, spiral stairways and where a stairway lift is installed. *Projections into the required width at each side shall not exceed 4¹/₂ inches (114 mm) at or below the handrail height. Projections into the required width shall not be limited above the minimum headroom height required in Section 1011.3.*

Discussion and Commentary: A stairway is considered one or more flights of stairs, each made up of one or more risers and any connecting landings. Any change of elevation along a travel path, unless accomplished by a ramp, must include a stair or stairway. Although stairways are generally required to be at least 44 inches in width, a 36-inch-wide stairway is permitted where serving an occupant load of 49 or less.

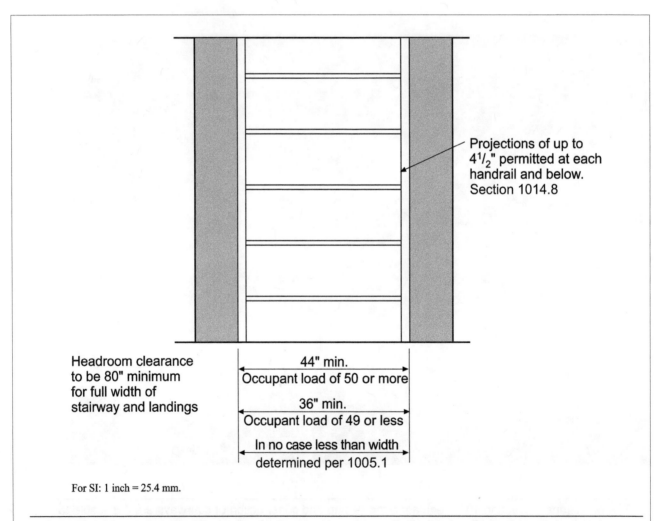

Projections of up to 4¹/₂" permitted at each handrail and below. Section 1014.8

Headroom clearance to be 80" minimum for full width of stairway and landings

44" min.
Occupant load of 50 or more

36" min.
Occupant load of 49 or less

In no case less than width determined per 1005.1

For SI: 1 inch = 25.4 mm.

Stringers, trim and similar decorative features may project a limited amount into the required stairway width unless located above the handrail. Between the rail and the required headroom height of 80 inches, no projection into the required width is permitted.

Code Text: *Stair riser heights shall be 7 inches (178 mm) maximum and 4 inches (102 mm) minimum. Rectangular tread depths shall be 11 inches (279 mm) minimum.* See the exceptions, including the allowance for greater riser heights ($7^3/_4$ inches) and shallower tread depths (10 inches) in Group R-3 and associated Group U occupancies, and within individual dwelling units of Group R-2.

Discussion and Commentary: The stairway 7-11 rule is the result of much research and discussion on stairway design. In addition to the proportional criteria that has been developed, the uniformity of the treads and risers in a flight of stairs is critical. The maximum variation between the highest and lowest risers and between the shallowest and deepest treads is limited to $^3/_8$ inch within any flight, which is intended as a permissible construction tolerance.

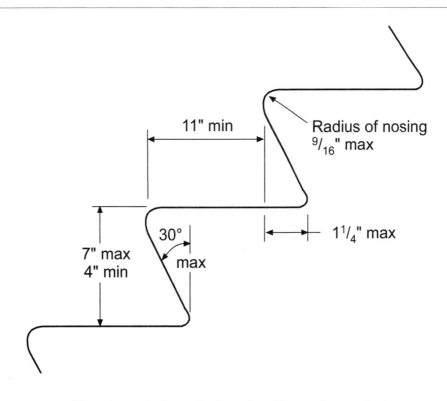

Treads and risers to be of uniform size and shape
($^3/_8$" tolerance permitted between least and greatest within flight)

For SI: 1 inch = 25.4 mm, 1 degree = 0.01745 rad.

Curved stairways, winders, spiral stairways, aisle stairs and alternating tread devices are unique configurations requiring special consideration. The use of these stairways is limited to varying degrees based on occupancy, occupant load, design and use as a required means of egress.

Code Text: *There shall be a floor or landing at the top and bottom of each stairway. The width of landings, measured perpendicular to the direction of travel, shall be not less than the width of stairways served. Every landing shall have a minimum depth measured parallel to the direction of travel, equal to the width of the stairway or 48 inches (1219 mm), whichever is less.* See the exception for stepped aisles.

Discussion and Commentary: A landing that serves a stairway is required to have a length equal to or greater than the stairway width unless the stairway has a straight run. This measurement is based on the actual width of the stairway, not the required width. It is important to ensure that the capacity of the stairway is not reduced as occupants travel between stairway flights. A maximum length of 48 inches is acceptable for straight stairway travel, insofar as the capacity is not reduced for travel through the landing.

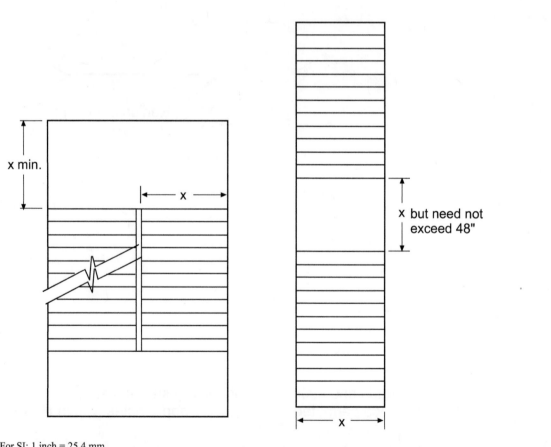

For SI: 1 inch = 25.4 mm.

Because of the difficulty many individuals encounter while negotiating stairs, the code requires a maximum vertical rise between landings of 12 feet. When placed at limited intervals, landings can be used as a resting place for the stair user and can also make stair travel less intimidating.

Topic: Handrail Locations

Category: Means of Egress

Reference: IBC 1011.11, 1014.9

Subject: Stairways and Handrails

Code Text: *Flights of stairways shall have handrails on each side and shall comply with Section 1014. See the four exceptions where a single handrail or no handrail is required. Stairways shall have intermediate handrails located in such a manner so that all portions of the stairway minimum width or required capacity are within 30 inches (762 mm) of a handrail. On monumental stairs, handrails shall be located along the most direct path of egress travel.*

Discussion and Commentary: The handrail, a very important safety element of a stairway, must be located within relatively easy reach of every stair user. Therefore, in most applications, a rail must be provided on both sides of the stairway. In the case of extremely wide stairways, such as monumental stairs, the requirement for additional rails located throughout the width of the stairway is based on the required stairway width, not the actual width.

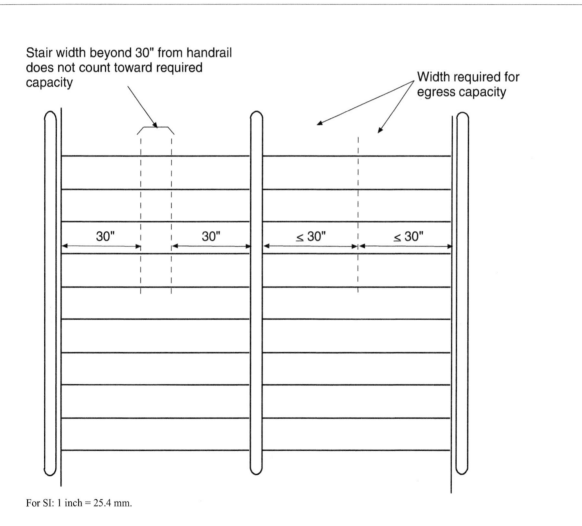

Stair width beyond 30" from handrail does not count toward required capacity

Width required for egress capacity

30" | 30" | ≤ 30" | ≤ 30"

For SI: 1 inch = 25.4 mm.

Various exceptions permit the use of a single handrail, and in some cases no rail, within a dwelling unit. In addition, and applicable to all occupancies, handrails are not required for decks, patios and walkways at any single elevation change where complying landings are provided on each side.

Code Text: *Ramps used as part of a means of egress shall have a running slope not steeper than one unit vertical in 12 units horizontal (8-percent slope). The slope of other pedestrian ramps shall not be steeper than one unit vertical in eight units horizontal (12.5-percent slope). The rise for any ramp run shall be 30 inches (762 mm) maximum. The minimum width and required capacity of a means of egress ramp shall not be less than that required for corridors by Section 1020.3. The clear width of a ramp between handrails, if provided, or other permissible projections shall be 36 inches (914 mm). Ramps with a rise greater than 6 inches (152 mm) shall have handrails on both sides. Handrails shall comply with Section 1014.*

Discussion and Commentary: Although many of the governing ramp provisions are designed for accessibility purposes, egress capabilities must also be considered. Handrails may project into the required ramp width up to $4^{1}/_{2}$ inches at each handrail at or below the handrail height, but in no case shall the clear width between handrails be less than 36 inches. A minimum headroom of 80 inches must be provided at all portions of the ramp.

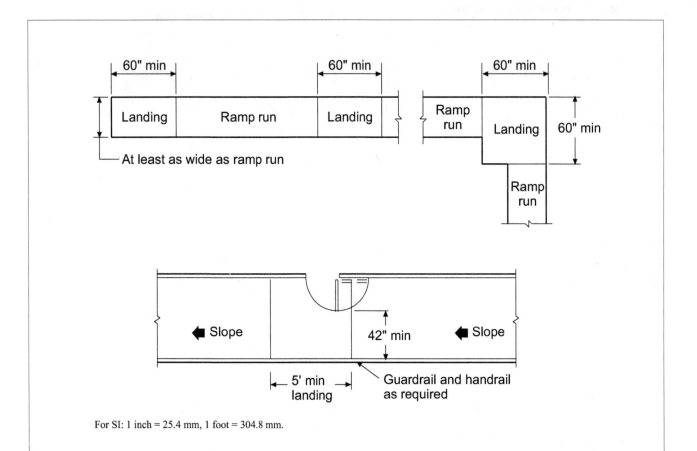

For SI: 1 inch = 25.4 mm, 1 foot = 304.8 mm.

To provide adequate clearance at ramp landings, doors cannot reduce the clear landing width to less than 42 inches. A landing must be at least 60 inches in length and at least as wide as the widest ramp run adjoining the landing.

Topic: Edge Protection

Category: Means of Egress

Reference: IBC 1012.10

Subject: Ramps

Code Text: *Edge protection complying with Sections 1012.10.1 (curb, rail, wall or barrier) or 1012.10.2 (extended floor or ground surface) shall be provided on each side of ramp runs and at each side of ramp landings.* See the exceptions for curb ramps and ramp landings. *A curb must be not less than 4 inches (102 mm) in height. Barriers shall be constructed so that the barrier prevents the passage of a 4-inch-diameter (102 mm) sphere, where any portion of the sphere is within 4 inches (102 mm) of the floor or ground surface, or the floor or ground surface of the ramp run or landing shall extend 12 inches (305 mm) minimum beyond the inside face of a handrail complying with Section 1014.*

Discussion and Commentary: Edge protection at ramps and ramp landings is necessary to prevent the wheels of a wheelchair from leaving the ramp or landing surface, or becoming lodged between the edge of the ramp and any adjacent construction. The protection is also beneficial to those individuals who utilize various forms of walking aids, including canes and crutches.

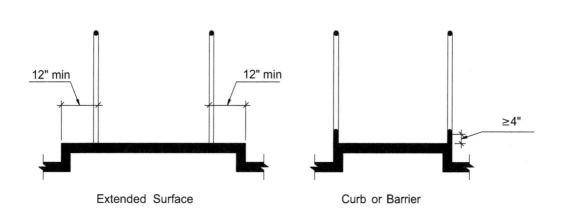

12" min   12" min   ≥4"

Extended Surface   Curb or Barrier

For SI: 1 inch = 25.4 mm

Edge protection is different than that type of protection provided by a guard. The presence of a complying guard does not necessarily provide adequate edge protection, and the presence of adequate edge protection does not typically satisfy the requirements for a guard.

Topic: Handrail Dimensions	**Category:** Means of Egress
Reference: IBC 1014.2, 1014.3	**Subject:** Stairways and Handrails

Code Text: *Handrail height, measured above stair tread nosings, or finish surface of ramp slope, shall be uniform, not less than 34 inches (864 mm) and not more than 38 inches (965 mm).* See lower height range for alternating tread devices and ship ladders. *Handrails with a circular cross section shall have an outside diameter of not less than 1$^1/_4$ inches (32 mm) and not greater than 2 inches (51 mm). Where the handrail is not circular, it shall have a perimeter dimension of not less than 4 inches (102 mm) and not greater than 6$^1/_4$ inches (160 mm) with a maximum cross-section dimension of 2$^1/_4$ inches (57 mm) and a minimum cross-sectional dimension of 1 inch (25 mm).* See allowances for Type II rails and those handrail shapes providing equivalent graspability.

Discussion and Commentary: Handrail height shall be measured from the nosing of the treads to the top of the rail. Handrails located above or below this height range are not easily reached by most individuals. The shape of the rail should allow for easy grasping by most users.

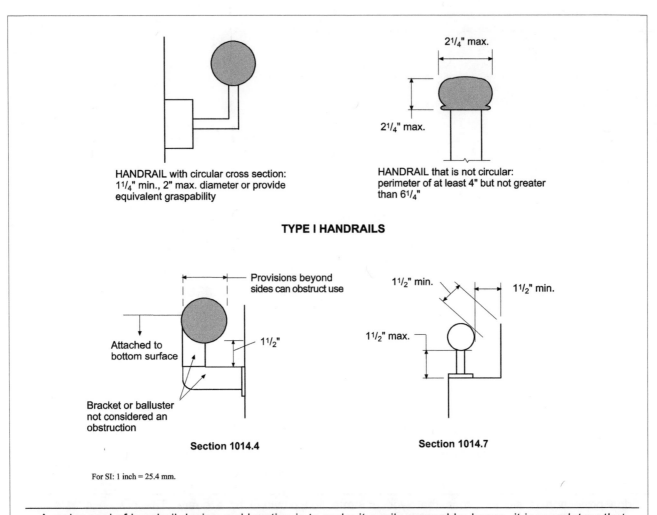

HANDRAIL with circular cross section: 1$^1/_4$" min., 2" max. diameter or provide equivalent graspability

HANDRAIL that is not circular: perimeter of at least 4" but not greater than 6$^1/_4$"

TYPE I HANDRAILS

Provisions beyond sides can obstruct use

Attached to bottom surface

1$^1/_2$"

Bracket or baluster not considered an obstruction

Section 1014.4

1$^1/_2$" min.

1$^1/_2$" min.

1$^1/_2$" max.

Section 1014.7

For SI: 1 inch = 25.4 mm.

A major goal of handrail design and location is to make it easily graspable; hence, it is mandatory that the rail be placed at least 1$^1/_2$ inches from any abutting elements, such as a wall. However, the projection of the rail into the required width is limited to no more than 4$^1/_2$ inches.

Quiz

Study Session 10
IBC Sections 1010 through 1012 and 1014

1. In general, a door opening shall provide a minimum clear width of _____ inches.

    a. 30   b. 32

    c. 34   d. 36

    Reference_____

2. In a Group I-2 occupancy, means of egress doors used for the movement of beds shall have a minimum width of _____ inches.

    a. 32   b. 36

    c. $41^1/_2$ d. 44

    Reference_____

3. The minimum required width for door openings does not apply to storage closets less than _____ square feet in floor area.

    a. 10   b. 25

    c. 50   d. 100

    Reference_____

4. At a door opening, the maximum permitted projection into the required clear width shall be _____ inch(es) at any point between 34 inches and 80 inches above the floor.

    a. 0, no projections are permitted   b. $^1/_2$

    c. 1   d. 4

    Reference_____

5. In which of the following uses must an egress door be a side-hinged swinging door or manually operated horizontal sliding door where serving an occupant load of 10 or less?

   a. office
   b. storage
   c. manufacturing
   d. retail sales

   Reference_____

6. In other than a Group H occupancy, egress doors shall swing in the direction of egress travel where serving a minimum occupant load of _____ persons.

   a. 10
   b. 30
   c. 50
   d. 100

   Reference_____

7. A fire-rated egress door shall move to a full-open position when subjected to a maximum _____ force.

   a. 5-pound
   b. 15-pound
   c. 30-pound
   d. 50-pound

   Reference_____

8. A revolving door shall be provided with a side-hinged swinging door located in the same wall and within _____ feet of the revolving door.

   a. 5
   b. 10
   c. 20
   d. 50

   Reference_____

9. In a Group B occupancy, the minimum length of a landing at a door shall be _____ inches.

   a. 36
   b. 42
   c. 44
   d. 48

   Reference_____

10. Exterior landings at doors shall have a maximum slope of _____ unit vertical in 12 units horizontal.

    a. $\frac{1}{8}$ b. $\frac{1}{4}$

    c. $\frac{1}{2}$ d. 1

    Reference_____

11. Other than at sliding doors serving dwelling units, the maximum height for thresholds at doorways is _____ inch.

    a. $\frac{1}{8}$ b. $\frac{1}{4}$

    c. $\frac{1}{2}$ d. 1

    Reference_____

12. Approved, listed delayed egress locking systems are permitted under specific conditions in all but which one of the following occupancies?

    a. Group H   b. Group I

    c. Group F   d. Group S

    Reference_____

13. In general, door handles, pulls, latches, locks and other operating devices shall be installed a minimum of _____ inches and a maximum of _____ inches above the finished floor.

    a. 32, 48   b. 34, 42

    c. 34, 48   d. 36, 54

    Reference_____

14. Alternating tread devices used as a means of egress shall have a maximum rise between floor levels or landings of _____ feet.

    a. 10   b. 12

    c. 15   d. 20

    Reference_____

15. Stairways, other than spiral stairways, shall have a minimum headroom clearance of _____ inches.

    a. 76   b. 78

    c. 80   d. 84

Reference_____

16. Within an individual dwelling unit of a Group R-2 apartment building, a stair shall have a maximum riser height of_____ inches and a minimum tread depth of _____ inches.

    a. 7, 11   b. $7^3/_4$, 10

    c. 8, 9   d. $8^1/_4$, 9

Reference_____

17. For a 60-inch-wide stairway having a straight run, any intermediate landing shall be a minimum of_____ inches in depth.

    a. 36   b. 44

    c. 48   d. 60

Reference_____

18. There shall be a minimum clear space of _____ inches between a handrail and a wall or other surface.

    a. $1^1/_4$ b. $1^1/_2$

    c. 2   d. $2^1/_4$

Reference_____

19. Where serving a maximum of five occupants, a spiral stairway may be used as a means of egress component from a space having a maximum floor area of _____ square feet.

    a. 200   b. 250

    c. 500   d. 1,000

Reference_____

20. Stairway handrails shall be located a minimum of _____ inches and a maximum of _____ inches above stair tread nosings.

    a. 30, 34   b. 30, 38

    c. 32, 34   d. 34, 38

Reference_____

21. Where handrails are not continuous between stair flights, they shall continue to slope for _____ beyond the bottom riser.

    a. the depth of one tread

    b. a minimum of 12 inches

    c. 12 inches plus one tread depth

    d. one-half the length of the landing

Reference_____

22. Projections into the required width at each stairway handrail shall be limited to a maximum of _____ inches at any point at and below the handrail height.

    a. 0, no projections permitted   b. $1^{1}/_{2}$

    c. $3^{1}/_{2}$ d. $4^{1}/_{2}$

Reference_____

23. The maximum permitted vertical rise of any ramp shall be _____ inches.

    a. 30   b. 44

    c. 48   d. 60

Reference_____

24. Only those ramps having a maximum rise of _____ inches are permitted without complying handrails.

    a. 6   b. 12

    c. 18   d. 24

Reference_____

25. Unless having a maximum height of _____ inches, turnstiles shall be regulated as for revolving doors or security access turnstiles.

    a. 34
               b. 36

    c. 38
               d. 39

Reference_____

26. Where a power-operated door must be opened manually, the maximum force to set the door in motion shall be _____ pounds.

    a. 5
               b. 15

    c. 30
               d. 50

Reference_____

27. The space required between two doors in a series shall be a minimum of _____ inches plus the width of a door swinging into the space.

    a. 30
               b. 44

    c. 48
               d. 60

Reference_____

28. A stairway serving an occupant load of 35 in an office suite shall have a minimum width of _____ inches.

    a. 30
               b. 36

    c. 42
               d. 44

Reference_____

29. Type I stairway handrails having a circular cross section shall have a minimum outside diameter of _____ inches and a maximum outside diameter of _____ inches.

    a. $1^{1}/_{4}$, 2
               b. $1^{1}/_{4}$, $2^{5}/_{8}$

    c. $1^{1}/_{2}$, 2
               d. $1^{1}/_{2}$, $2^{5}/_{8}$

Reference_____

30. Where a railing is used as edge protection along the side of a ramp run, it must have a rail mounted to prevent the passage of a maximum _____-inch sphere, where any portion of the sphere is within 4 inches of the ground.

    a. 4   b. 6

    c. 8   d. 12

    Reference_____

31. Swinging doors serving Group E rooms having a minimum occupant load of _____ must be provided with panic hardware unless not provided with a latch or a lock.

    a. 50   b. 100

    c. 300   d. 500

    Reference _____

32. The minimum required width for a stairway serving 75 occupants in a Group B occupancy shall be _____ inches.

    a. 36   b. 42

    c. 44   d. 48

    Reference _____

33. Where a ramp is not a part of an accessible route, the length of the landing need not be more than _____ inches measured in the direction of travel.

    a. 44   b. 48

    c. 54   d. 60

    Reference _____

34. At ramps where handrails are not continuous between runs, the handrails shall extend horizontally a minimum of _____ inches beyond the top and bottom of the ramp.

    a. 6   b. 8

    c. 12   d. 18

    Reference _____

35. Stairways shall have intermediate handrails located so that all portions of the stairway width required for egress capacity are within _____ inches of a handrail.

    a. 30   b. 32

    c. 35   d. 44

    Reference _____

36. Overhead door stops shall be located a minimum of _____ inches above the floor.

    a. 76   b. 78

    c. 78 $\frac{1}{2}$ d. 80

    Reference _____

37. Where means of egress door hardware operates by rotation, the maximum operational force required to unlatch the door shall be _____ inch-pounds.

    a. 15   b. 22

    c. 28   d. 30

    Reference _____

38. Where an extended floor surface is used to provide the required edge protection for a ramp, the floor shall extend a minimum of _____ inches beyond the inside face of a complying handrail.

    a. 4   b. 8

    c. 12   d. 18

    Reference _____

39. Where a Type II handrail is permitted, it shall have a minimum width of _____ inches above the required recess, with a maximum allowable width of _____ inches.

    a. 1 $\frac{1}{4}$, 2   b. 1 $\frac{1}{4}$, 2 $\frac{3}{4}$

    c. 1 $\frac{1}{2}$, 2   d. 1 $\frac{1}{2}$, 2 $\frac{1}{2}$

    Reference _____

40. Openings in stair walking surfaces shall be of a size that does not permit the passage of a _____ -inch-diameter sphere.

    a. $\frac{1}{8}$ b. $\frac{1}{4}$

    c. $\frac{3}{8}$ d. $\frac{1}{2}$

    Reference _____

2021 IBC Sections 1006, 1007 and 1016 through 1021
Means of Egress III

OBJECTIVE: To obtain an understanding of the system design requirements for the exit access, including number of exits, separation of egress doorways and maximum travel distances, as well as the requirements for the exit access components, including aisles, corridors and egress balconies.

REFERENCE: Sections 1006, 1007 and 1016 through 1021, 2021 *International Building Code*

KEY POINTS:
- What portion of the means of egress system is the exit access?
- Is egress permitted through an adjoining or intervening room? If so, under what conditions?
- How must egress be provided where more than one tenant occupies any single floor of a building or structure?
- What is a common path of egress travel?
- Why is the common path of egress travel so limiting?
- When are at least two exits or exit access doorways required from a room?
- At what point is access required to three or more exits or exit access doorways?
- Why are multiple exit paths required to be separated at a specified minimum distance from each other?
- At what minimum distance must two exits or exit access doorways be separated? Three or more exits or exit access doorways?
- What benefit is derived from exit separation in a sprinklered building?
- Why is travel distance regulated?
- How is the maximum travel distance measured? Where does it start? Where does it end?
- How is travel distance measured where travel involves exit access stairways?
- Which occupancies permit the least travel distance? The most?

- What are the travel distance limitations for low-hazard storage and manufacturing buildings? Which special conditions must be met?
- To what amount can the travel distance be increased on an exterior egress balcony?
- Where must complying aisles be provided?
- What is the minimum permitted aisle width in public areas of Groups B and M? In nonpublic areas?
- What is an aisle accessway? What is the minimum aisle accessway width where the aisle serves merchandise pads?
- What is the purpose of a corridor? When must a corridor be of fire-resistance-rated construction?
- What is the minimum required width of a corridor?
- What is a dead-end condition? When are dead ends limited in length?
- How is the use of corridors for supply, return, exhaust or ventilation air regulated?
- How do the exiting provisions for egress balconies compare with those for corridors?
- When is a fire-resistance-rated separation mandated between the building and an egress balcony?

Topic: Occupant Load and Common Path   **Category:** Means of Egress

Reference: IBC 1006.2.1   **Subject:** Number of Means of Egress

Code Text: *Two exits or exit access doorways from any space shall be provided where the design occupant load or the common path of egress travel distance exceeds the values listed in Table 1006.2.1.*

Discussion and Commentary: A common path of egress travel is defined as that portion of the exit access travel distance measured from the most remote point within a story to that point where the occupants have separate access to two exits or exit access doorways. The concept of limiting the common path of egress travel addresses the concern that multiple egress options must be available to occupants where the expected egress travel distance becomes excessive. Although the overall travel distance in a building may be of considerable length, such travel is greatly limited where only one egress path is available. An additional limitation due to occupant load is also applied to single exit availability.

TABLE 1006.2.1
SPACES WITH ONE EXIT OR EXIT ACCESS DOORWAY

OCCUPANCY	MAXIMUM OCCUPANT LOAD OF SPACE	MAXIMUM COMMON PATH OF EGRESS TRAVEL DISTANCE (feet)		
		Without Sprinkler System (feet) Occupant Load		With Sprinkler System (feet)
		OL ≤ 30	OL > 30	
A[c], E, M	49	75	75	75[a]
B	49	100	75	100[a]
F	49	75	75	100[a]
H-1, H-2, H-3	3	NP	NP	25[b]
H-4, H-5	10	NP	NP	75[b]
I-1, I-2[d], I-4	10	NP	NP	75[a]
I-3	10	NP	NP	100[a]
R-1	10	NP	NP	75[a]
R-2	20	NP	NP	125[a]
R-3[e]	20	NP	NP	125[a, g]
R-4[e]	20	NP	NP	125[a, g]
S[f]	29	100	75	100[a]
U	49	100	75	75[a]

For SI: 1 foot = 304.8 mm.

NP = Not Permitted.

a. Buildings equipped throughout with an *automatic sprinkler system* in accordance with Section 903.3.1.1 or 903.3.1.2. See Section 903 for occupancies where *automatic sprinkler systems* are permitted in accordance with Section 903.3.1.2.

b. Group H occupancies equipped throughout with an *automatic sprinkler system* in accordance with Section 903.2.5.

c. For a room or space used for assembly purposes having *fixed seating*, see Section 1029.8.

d. For the travel distance limitations in Group I-2, see Section 407.4.

e. The *common path of egress travel* distance shall only apply in a Group R-3 occupancy located in a mixed occupancy building.

f. The length of *common path of egress travel* distance in a Group S-2 *open parking garage* shall be not more than 100 feet.

g. For the travel distance limitations in Groups R-3 and R-4 equipped throughout with an *automatic sprinkler system* in accordance with Section 903.3.1.3, see Section 1006.2.2.6.

Two basic criteria establish the point at which it is necessary to provide at least two paths of egress travel from a portion of a building. Both the maximum occupant load and the maximum common path must not be exceeded in spaces having only one exit or exit access doorway.

Code Text: *Each story and occupied roof shall have the minimum number of separate and distinct exits, or access to exits, as specified in Table 1006.3.3. A single exit or access to a single exit shall be permitted in accordance with Section 1006.3.3.* See the five conditions where a single exit or access to a single exit is permitted.

Discussion and Commentary: Although two exits per story is an acceptable minimum for most buildings, those stories with larger occupant loads (greater than 500) must be provided with at least three exits. Four exits are mandated where the occupant load exceeds 1,000. Under no circumstances does the IBC require more than four exits from any story based upon the number of persons present. It must be noted, however, that additional exits will sometimes be required to satisfy other egress requirements of Chapter 10, such as those addressing travel distance. A single exit is permitted in applications where the story is at or near grade level, provided the occupant load is low and the common path of travel is limited.

TABLE 1006.3.3
MINIMUM NUMBER OF EXITS OR
ACCESS TO EXITS PER STORY

OCCUPANT LOAD PER STORY	MINIMUM NUMBER OF EXITS OR ACCESS TO EXITS FROM STORY
1-500	2
501-1,000	3
More than 1,000	4

Total O.L. = 600
3 exits required from story

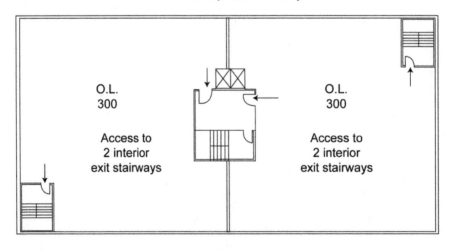

Exits from Stories

Although the use of exit access stairways is permitted to connect stories within a building, the path of egress travel to an exit is limited in a manner such that it cannot pass through more than one adjacent story. There are seven conditions under which such exit access travel to an exit through multiple stories is permitted.

Code Text:　*A single exit or access to a single exit shall be permitted from any story or occupied roof where one of the following conditions exists:* See the five conditions that allow for a single exit.

Discussion and Commentary:　The general provisions call for at least two unique and separate exits from any story of a building. Buildings and stories with one exit are permitted where the configuration and occupancy meet certain characteristics that together do not present an unacceptable fire risk to the buildings' occupants. Those structures that are relatively small in size have a shorter travel distance and fewer occupants; thus, having access to a single exit does not significantly compromise the safety of the occupants.

TABLE 1006.3.4(1)
STORIES WITH ONE EXIT OR ACCESS TO ONE EXIT FOR R-2 OCCUPANCIES

STORY	OCCUPANCY	MAXIMUM NUMBER OF DWELLING UNITS	MAXIMUM EXIT ACCESS TRAVEL DISTANCE
Basement, first, second or third story above grade plane	R-2[a, b]	4 dwelling units	125 feet
Fourth story above grade plane and higher	NP	NA	NA

For SI: 1 foot = 304.8 mm.
NP = Not Permitted.
NA = Not Applicable.
a. Buildings classified as Group R-2 equipped throughout with an automatic sprinkler system in accordance with Section 903.3.1.1 or 903.3.1.2 and provided with emergency escape and rescue openings in accordance with Section 1031.
b. This table is used for R-2 occupancies consisting of dwelling units. For R-2 occupancies consisting of sleeping units, use Table 1006.3.4(2).

TABLE 1006.3.4(2)
STORIES WITH ONE EXIT OR ACCESS TO ONE EXIT FOR OTHER OCCUPANCIES

STORY	OCCUPANCY	MAXIMUM OCCUPANT LOAD PER STORY	MAXIMUM EXIT ACCESS TRAVEL DISTANCE (feet)
First story above or below grade plane	A, B[b], E, F[b], M, U	49	75
	H-2, H-3	3	25
	H-4, H-5, I, R-1, R-2[a, c]	10	75
	S[b, d]	29	75
Second story above grade plane	B, F, M, S[d]	29	75
Third story above grade plane and higher	NP	NA	NA

For SI: 1 foot = 304.8 mm.
NP = Not Permitted.
NA = Not Applicable.
a. Buildings classified as Group R-2 equipped throughout with an automatic sprinkler system in accordance with Section 903.3.1.1 or 903.3.1.2 and provided with emergency escape and rescue openings in accordance with Section 1031.
b. Group B, F and S occupancies in buildings equipped throughout with an automatic sprinkler system in accordance with Section 903.3.1.1 shall have a maximum exit access travel distance of 100 feet.
c. This table is used for R-2 occupancies consisting of sleeping units. For R-2 occupancies consisting of dwelling units, use Table 1006.3.4(1).
d. The length of exit access travel distance in a Group S-2 open parking garage shall be not more than 100 feet.

Table 1006.3.4(1) is only applicable to Group R-2 occupancies containing dwelling units and allows a single exit from the basement, as well as the first, second and third stories under limited conditions. Table 1006.3.4(2) applies to all other occupancy groups and does not permit a single exit from the third story where serving such occupancies.

Code Text: *Where two exits, exit access doorways, exit access stairways or ramps, or any combination thereof, are required from any portion of the exit access, they shall be placed a distance apart equal to not less than one-half of the length of the maximum overall diagonal dimension of the building or area to be served measured in a straight line between them. Interlocking or scissor stairs shall be counted as one exit stairway.* See the exceptions for sprinklered buildings and where a rated corridor connects two interior exit stairways.

Discussion and Commentary: One of the fundamental concepts of exiting is that a single fire incident should not render all means of egress unusable. In this regard, egress doorways and exit access stairways are required to be located so as to minimize the probability of such an occurrence. The required separation in sprinklered buildings is reduced to a distance of one-third of the overall diagonal.

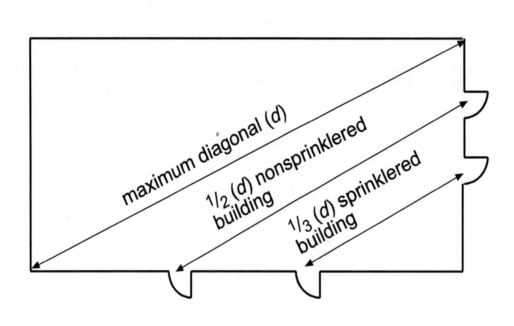

Where more than two exit access doorways are required, they should be situated at reasonable distances from one another so that if one doorway becomes blocked, the others will be available. The use of common sense should dictate the proper separation based on the design and use of the space or room.

Code Text: *Egress from a room or space shall not pass through adjoining or intervening rooms or areas, except where such adjoining rooms or areas are accessory to one or the other; are not a Group H occupancy; and provide a discernible path of egress travel to an exit.* See the exception for Group H, S and F occupancies.

Discussion and Commentary: A workable means of egress system must be direct, obvious and unobstructed. Therefore, egress may only travel through an intervening room, space or area where the exit path is discernable. Travel must be such that it is readily apparent which direction the occupant must go to continue toward the exit. In addition, access through a high-hazard space is prohibited unless traveling from another high-hazard space. It is also expected that any intervening room used for egress will be related to the room from which egress begins.

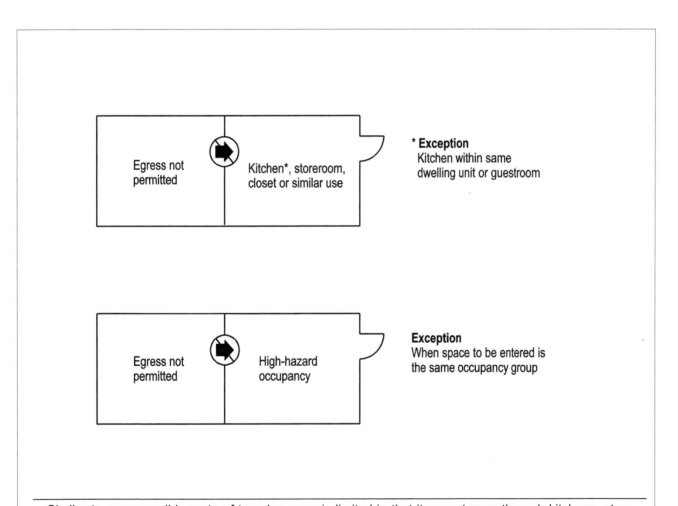

Similar to an accessible route of travel, egress is limited in that it cannot pass through kitchens, store rooms, closets or spaces used for similar purposes. These types of spaces have a high probability of blocked access and egress, due to obstructions created by the use of the space. A dedicated path created by partial or full-height walls is permitted where exiting through a stockroom serving a Group M occupancy.

Code Text: *Exit access travel distance shall not exceed the values given in Table 1017.2. Exit access travel distance shall be measured from the most remote point of each room, area or space along the natural and unobstructed path of horizontal and vertical egress travel to the entrance to an exit. Where more than one exit is required, exit access travel distance shall be measured to the nearest exit.* See the exception for open parking garages.

Discussion and Commentary: Travel distance is considered the portion of egress travel between any occupiable location in a building and the nearest entrance to an exit. Because quick evacuation from a building is the foremost method of protecting the occupants in many fire incidents, the length of travel is limited until the occupant reaches one of the "protected components." Travel should be measured around any obstruction that is considered fixed or permanent, including low-height office partitions, retail shelving, storage racks, fixed seating, etc.

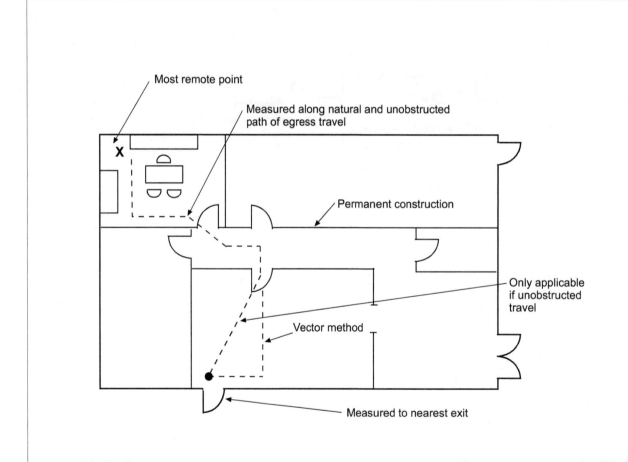

In most sprinklered buildings, the code permits a moderate increase in the permitted travel distance over that permitted in nonsprinklered buildings. An increase of 50 feet is typical of most occupancies; however, a travel distance increase of 100 feet is permitted for Group B occupancies protected by a sprinkler system.

Code Text: *Travel distance on exit access stairways or ramps shall be included in the exit access travel distance measurement. The measurement along stairways shall be made on a plane parallel and tangent to the stair tread nosings in the center of the stair and landings.*

Discussion and Commentary: Travel distance may include travel on an exit access stairway or ramp. In such cases, travel up or down the stairway or ramp would need to be included in the travel distance determination. Exit access stairways are addressed under the provisions of Section 1019.

TABLE 1017.2
EXIT ACCESS TRAVEL DISTANCE[a]

OCCUPANCY	WITHOUT SPRINKLER SYSTEM (feet)	WITH SPRINKLER SYSTEM (feet)
A, E, F-1, M, R, S-1	200[e]	250[b]
I-1	Not Permitted	250[b]
B	200	300[c]
F-2, S-2, U	300	400[c]
H-1	Not Permitted	75[d]
H-2	Not Permitted	100[d]
H-3	Not Permitted	150[d]
H-4	Not Permitted	175[d]
H-5	Not Permitted	200[c]
I-2, I-3	Not Permitted	200[c]
I-4	150	200[c]

For SI: 1 foot = 304.8 mm.

a. See the following sections for modifications to *exit access* travel distance requirements:
   Section 402.8: For the distance limitation in malls.
   Section 407.4: For the distance limitation in Group I-2.
   Sections 408.6.1 and 408.8.1: For the distance limitations in Group I-3.
   Section 411.2: For the distance limitation in special amusement areas.
   Section 412.6: For the distance limitations in aircraft manufacturing facilities.
   Section 1006.2.2.2: For the distance limitation in refrigeration machinery rooms.
   Section 1006.2.2.3: For the distance limitation in refrigerated rooms and spaces.
   Section 1006.3.4: For buildings with one exit.
   Section 1017.2.2: For increased distance limitation in Groups F-1 and S-1.
   Section 1030.7: For increased limitation in assembly seating.
   Section 3103.4: For temporary structures.
   Section 3104.9: For pedestrian walkways.
b. Buildings equipped throughout with an automatic sprinkler system in accordance with Section 903.3.1.1 or 903.3.1.2. See Section 903 for occupancies where automatic sprinkler systems are permitted in accordance with Section 903.3.1.2.
c. Buildings equipped throughout with an automatic sprinkler system in accordance with Section 903.3.1.1.
d. Group H occupancies equipped throughout with an automatic sprinkler system in accordance with Section 903.2.5.1.
e. Group R-3 and R-4 buildings equipped throughout with an automatic sprinkler system in accordance with Section 903.3.1.3. See Section 903.2.8 for occupancies where automatic sprinkler systems are permitted in accordance with Section 903.3.1.3.

As an example, where an exit access stairway is provided as a sole means of egress from a mezzanine, the travel distance would be measured from the most remote point on the mezzanine, down the stairway and continue until reaching the entrance to the nearest exit.

Code Text: *Aisles or aisle accessways shall be provided from all occupied portions of the exit access that contain seats, tables, furnishings, displays and similar fixtures or equipment. The minimum width or required capacity of aisles shall be unobstructed.* See the exception for permissible encroachments. *Aisles and aisle accessways serving a room or space used for assembly purposes shall comply with Section 1030. In Group B and M occupancies, the minimum clear aisle width shall be determined by Section 1005.1 for the occupant load served, but shall not be less than that required for corridors by Section 1020.3.* See the exception for nonpublic aisles.

Discussion and Commentary: Well-defined aisles must be provided throughout office spaces, retail stores and similar facilities. The mandated clear width varies based on the presence of obstructions, such as chairs, clothes racks or other items that can easily interrupt the egress flow to an exit.

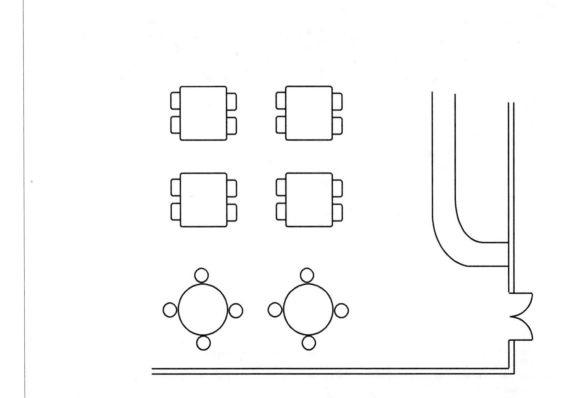

At least 28 inches of egress width are required for nonpublic aisles not required to be accessible, provided they serve less than 50 persons.

Topic: Aisle Accessways in Group M	**Category:** Means of Egress
Reference: IBC 1018.4	**Subject:** Exit Access

Code Text: *An aisle accessway shall be provided on not less than one side of each element within the merchandise pad. The minimum clear width for an aisle accessway not required to be accessible shall be 30 inches (762 mm). The required clear width of the aisle accessway shall be measured perpendicular to the elements and merchandise within the merchandise pad. The 30-inch (762 mm) minimum clear width shall be maintained to provide a path to an adjacent aisle or aisle accessway.*

Discussion and Commentary: A merchandise pad is defined as the merchandise display area that contains multiple counters, shelves, racks and other movable fixtures. Bounded by aisles, permanent fixtures and walls, the merchandise pad also includes aisle accessways utilized to provide both access to an aisle and circulation throughout the pad area.

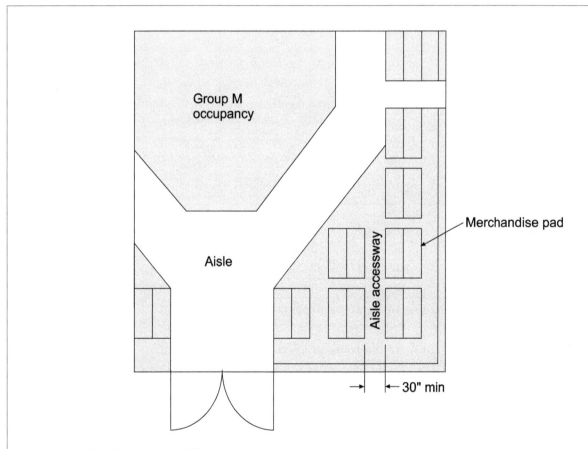

For SI: 1 inch = 25.4 mm

Within a merchandise pad, the common path of travel is limited to 75 feet in length. Where the occupant load of the area served by the common path exceeds 50 persons, the common path cannot exceed 30 feet in length from any point in the merchandise pad.

Code Text: *Corridors shall be fire-resistance rated in accordance with Table 1020.2. The corridor walls required to be fire-resistance rated shall comply with Section 708 for fire partitions. See the five exceptions where a rating is not required.*

Discussion and Commentary: A fire-resistance-rated corridor is intended to protect occupants of the corridor during egress travel from an incident in an enclosed space bordering the corridor. The construction of the corridor provides a minimum level of protection from fire and smoke through the use of fire-resistance-rated walls and ceilings, as well as fire-protected openings. Smoke infiltration is limited also by smoke- and draft-control door assemblies and smoke dampers. Occupancy group, occupant load and presence of a fire sprinkler system are the major factors in determining whether or not a corridor must have a fire-resistance rating.

TABLE 1020.2
CORRIDOR FIRE-RESISTANCE RATING

OCCUPANCY	OCCUPANT LOAD SERVED BY CORRIDOR	REQUIRED FIRE-RESISTANCE RATING (hours)	
		Without sprinkler system	With sprinkler system
H-1, H-2, H-3	All	Not Permitted	1[c]
H-4, H-5	Greater than 30	Not Permitted	1[c]
A, B, E, F, M, S, U	Greater than 30	1	0
R	Greater than 10	Not Permitted	0.5[c]/1[d]
I-2[a]	All	Not Permitted	0
I-1, I-3	All	Not Permitted	1[b, c]
I-4	All	1	0

a. For requirements for occupancies in Group I-2, see Sections 407.2 and 407.3.

b. For a reduction in the fire-resistance rating for occupancies in Group I-3, see Section 408.8.

c. Buildings equipped throughout with an automatic sprinkler system in accordance with Section 903.3.1.1 or 903.3.1.2 where allowed.

d. Group R-3 and R-4 buildings equipped throughout with an automatic sprinkler system in accordance with Section 903.3.1.3. See Section 903.2.8 for occupancies where automatic sprinkler systems are permitted in accordance with Section 903.3.1.3.

Exceptions eliminate the need for a fire-resistance-rated corridor in certain Group E occupancies, in sleeping units or dwelling units of residential occupancies, in open parking garages and in Group B occupancies that are permitted a single means of egress by Section 1006.2.

Code Text: *The required capacity of corridors shall be determined as specified in Section 1005.1, but the minimum width shall be not less than that specified in Table 1020.3.* Table 1020.3 identifies a minimum required width of 44 inches except for: (1) 24 inches for access to building systems or equipment, (2) 36 inches for occupant loads less than 50, (3) 36 inches within a dwelling unit, (4) 72 inches for a Group E corridor with an occupant load of 100 or more, (5) 72 inches in specified areas of ambulatory care facilities, and (6) 96 inches in Group I-2 areas where required for bed movement.

Discussion and Commentary: To allow for adequate circulation throughout a building and, more importantly, for egress purposes, a minimum width requirement is established. In addition, complying routes of travel to accessible spaces must be provided. Only in areas used for access to electrical, mechanical or plumbing systems or equipment is the width permitted to be reduced to less than 36 inches. A minimum 36-inch width is mandated for corridors within dwelling units, or for those corridors serving an occupant load of 50 or less. Only specific projections such as doors are permitted to encroach a limited distance into the required corridor width.

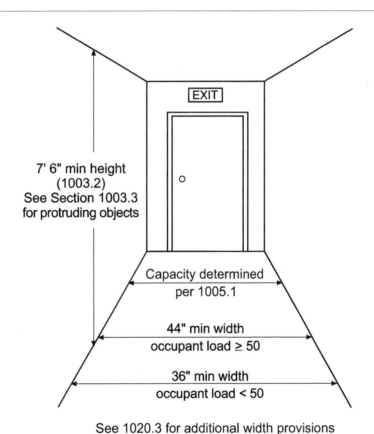

EXIT

7' 6" min height
(1003.2)
See Section 1003.3
for protruding objects

Capacity determined
per 1005.1

44" min width
occupant load ≥ 50

36" min width
occupant load < 50

See 1020.3 for additional width provisions

For SI: 1 inch = 25.4 mm, 1 foot = 304.8 mm.

Certain occupancies require additional corridor widths based on their specialized uses. Corridors serving 100 or more occupants in Group E educational occupancies must be at least 72 inches in width, and healthcare occupancies require increased widths for bed movement.

Code Text: *Where more than one exit or exit access doorway is required, the exit access shall be arranged such that there are no dead ends in corridors more than 20 feet (6096 mm) in length.* See the four exceptions for increased dead-end lengths.

Discussion and Commentary: Limitations on dead-end corridors are established where two or more exit or exit access doorways are required. The intent is to limit the distance building occupants must travel before they determine that there is no way out and that they must retrace steps in order to locate an exit or exit access doorway. Where only a single means of egress is permitted, a dead-end condition is not limited in length; however, the provisions of Section 1006.2.1 for common paths of travel must be considered.

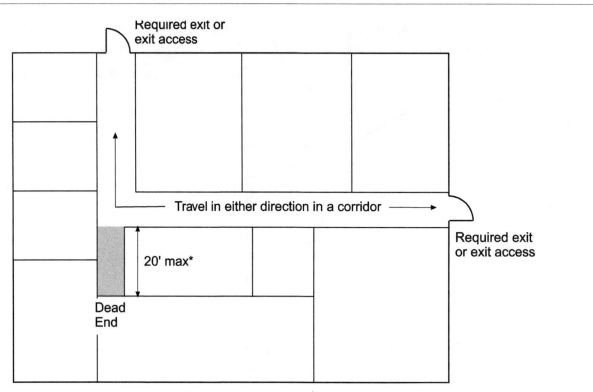

Required exit or exit access

Travel in either direction in a corridor ⟶

Required exit or exit access

20' max*

Dead End

* 50 ft max in sprinklered Group B, E, F, I-1, M, R-1, R-2, R-4, 5 and U occupancies
* Up to 2.5 times the least corridor width
* 50 ft max in I-3 Conditions 2, 3 or 4
* 30 ft max in Group I-2, Condition 2 corridors that do not serve patient rooms or treatment spaces

For SI: 1 inch = 25.4 mm, 1 foot = 304.8 mm.

Once a building occupant enters a corridor during emergency egress conditions, there is an expectation that a direct and obvious exit path is available. Dead-end configurations should be minimal, if not eliminated, to expedite the exiting process.

Code Text: *Corridors shall not serve as supply, return, exhaust, relief or ventilation air ducts or plenums.* See the four exceptions addressing return air, make-up air and incidental air movement. *Use of the space between the corridor ceiling and the floor or roof structure above as a return air plenum is permitted for one or more of the following conditions:* See the five conditions.

Discussion and Commentary: The use of corridors for the movement of air is strictly limited by the code. Because a corridor is intended to be a relatively safe environment for occupants exiting a building, it is not advisable to introduce air movement that might increase the potential for fire, smoke or toxic gases to enter the corridor. It is possible, under specific conditions, to use the space above a corridor ceiling as a return air plenum. For example, where the corridor is not required to be of fire-resistance-rated construction, or where the above-ceiling space is isolated from a rated corridor by fire-resistance-rated construction, the upper area may be used for return air.

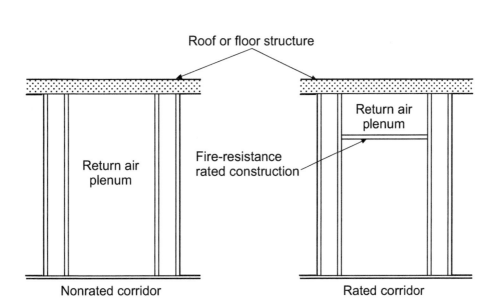

Where a corridor is directly supplied with outdoor air, make-up air for exhaust systems in rooms that open directly into a corridor may be taken from the corridor. The rate at which outdoor air is supplied to the corridor must exceed the rate of makeup air taken from the corridor.

Code Text: *Fire-resistance-rated corridors shall be continuous from the point of entry to an exit, and shall not be interrupted by intervening rooms.* See the exceptions for travel through foyers, lobbies and reception rooms, as well as through enclosed elevator lobbies.

Discussion and Commentary: Once an occupant enters a corridor required to be of fire-resistance-rated construction, he or she expects that travel to an exit will be direct. The level of protection within the corridor must not be reduced at any point along the egress path. Where an intervening room or space interrupts the corridor, it is quite likely that the exitway will be obstructed or confusing. Where corridor travel includes or terminates at a lobby, foyer or reception room, the condition is considered acceptable, insofar as such spaces are usually an extension of the circulation and egress path.

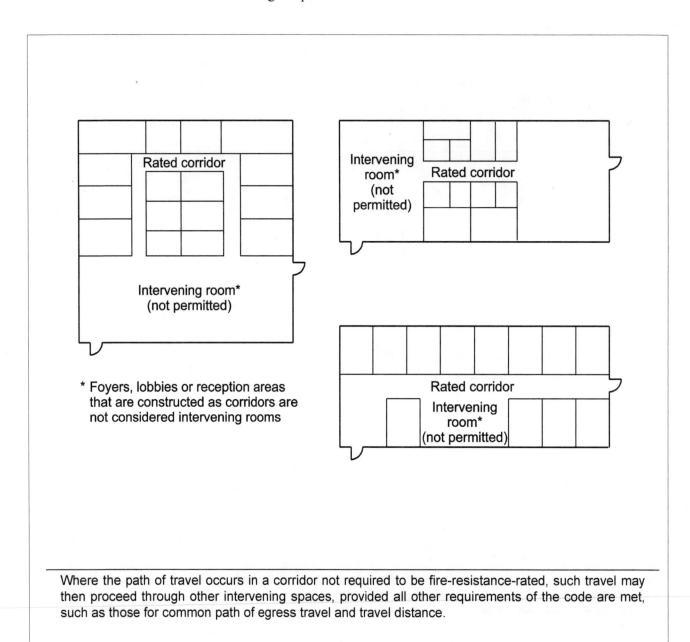

Where the path of travel occurs in a corridor not required to be fire-resistance-rated, such travel may then proceed through other intervening spaces, provided all other requirements of the code are met, such as those for common path of egress travel and travel distance.

Code Text: *Balconies used for egress purposes shall conform to the same requirements as corridors for minimum width, required capacity, headroom, dead ends and projections. Exterior egress balconies shall be separated from the interior of the building by walls and opening protectives as required for corridors.* See the exception for elimination of separation.

Discussion and Commentary: Although the openness of exterior balconies provides some degree of protection from smoke and toxic gases created by a fire, travel along such balconies usually places the occupants at considerable risk. Therefore, the IBC regulates egress balcony travel in a manner consistent with unprotected travel inside the structure. An increase of 100 feet in maximum allowable travel distance is permitted by Section 1017.2.1 for egress balcony travel.

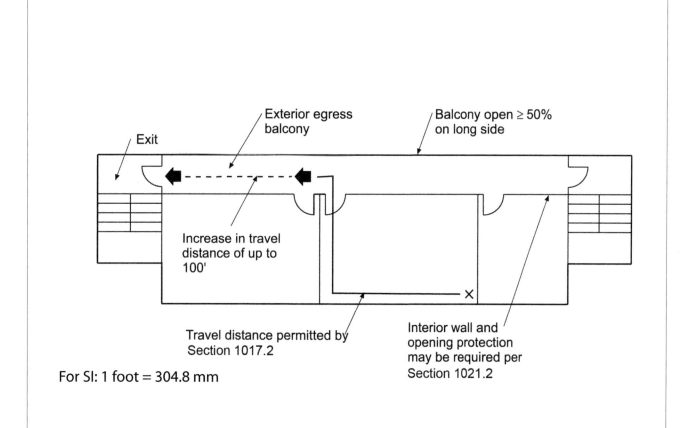

Exit

Exterior egress balcony

Balcony open ≥ 50% on long side

Increase in travel distance of up to 100'

Travel distance permitted by Section 1017.2

Interior wall and opening protection may be required per Section 1021.2

For SI: 1 foot = 304.8 mm

For an exit access element to be considered an egress balcony, it must be sufficiently open to the exterior to minimize the potential for smoke and toxic gases to accumulate. The code considers openings for at least 50 percent of the long side to be adequately open.

Study Session 11
IBC Sections 1006, 1007 and 1016 through 1021

1. Where the common path of travel is within the permitted limits, a Group B occupancy may have a single means of egress where the maximum occupant load is
_____.

    a. 10   b. 20

    c. 29   d. 49

Reference_____

2. In which one of the following occupancies having an occupant load of 40 must at least two exits or exit access doorways always be provided?

    a. A-2   b. B

    c. F-1   d. S-1

Reference_____

3. What is the minimum number of exits or exit access doorways required for a Group M sales floor having an occupant load of 1,200?

    a. 2   b. 3

    c. 4   d. 6

Reference_____

4. Where two means of egress are required from a room in a fully sprinklered building, they shall be separated a minimum of _____ of the length of the maximum overall diagonal dimension of the area served.

    a. one-half   b. one-third

    c. one-fourth   d. one-sixth

Reference_____

5. Which of the following conditions is not specifically required where egress from a room passes through an adjoining room?

    a.   a discernable path of travel must be provided

    b.   the adjoining room and the area served are accessory to one or the other

    c.   no more than one means of egress can pass through the adjoining room

    d.   the adjoining room cannot be classified as Group H

Reference_____

6. In general, through which one of the following spaces is egress not specifically prohibited?

    a.   private offices   b.   storage rooms

    c.   kitchens   d.   closets

Reference_____

7. The means of egress is permitted to pass from a small tenant space through a larger adjoining tenant space, provided the smaller tenant space occupies less than _____ percent of the area of the larger tenant space.

    a.   10   b.   15

    c.   25   d. $33^1/_3$

Reference_____

8. Access to at least two exits or exit access doorways shall be provided in rooms or spaces of Group I-4 facilities having a minimum occupant load of _____.

    a.   6   b.   11

    c.   20   d.   29

Reference_____

9. Three exits or exit access doorways shall be provided from any space with a minimum occupant load of _____ and a maximum occupant load of _____.

    a.   301, 500   b.   301, 600

    c.   501, 800   d.   501, 1000

Reference_____

10. In a nonsprinklered Group A-3 occupancy, what is the maximum permitted exit access travel distance?

    a.   150 feet   b.   200 feet

    c.   250 feet   d.   300 feet

    Reference_____

11. Up to an additional 100 feet of travel distance is available where the last portion of exit access travel occurs _____ .

    a.   within a corridor   b.   within a 1-hour-rated corridor

    c.   on an exterior egress balcony   d.   on an exterior exit stairway

    Reference_____

12. In a Group H-3 occupancy, the common path of egress travel is limited to a maximum of _____ feet.

    a.   25   b.   75

    c.   100   d.   150

    Reference_____

13. In an office tenant space having an occupant load of 24 persons, the maximum length of a common path of egress travel shall be _____ feet.

    a.   25   b.   75

    c.   100   d.   200

    Reference_____

14. In a one-story fully-sprinklered Group F-1 occupancy, the maximum permitted exit access travel distance is 400 feet where the minimum height from the finished floor to the bottom of the ceiling or roof slab is _____ feet.

    a.   20   b.   24

    c.   30   d.   35

    Reference_____

15. Where accessibility is not required, what is the minimum required width of an aisle serving 15 persons in a nonpublic area of a Group B occupancy?

    a. no minimum width required b. 28 inches

    c. 36 inches   d. 44 inches

Reference_____

16. Egress through the stockroom of a Group M occupancy is not permitted where the width of the exit access aisle is less than _____ inches.

    a. 44   b. 48

    c. 60   d. 72

Reference_____

17. A corridor having a required capacity of 125 persons in a Group E occupancy shall be a minimum of _____ inches in width.

    a. 36   b. 44

    c. 60   d. 72

Reference_____

18. A corridor in a Group B occupancy serving an occupant load of 40 persons shall have a minimum width of _____ inches.

    a. 36   b. 44

    c. 48   d. 60

Reference_____

19. In a nonsprinklered Group M retail sales building, a corridor serving a minimum occupant load of _____ persons shall be fire-resistance rated.

    a. any number of   b. 11

    c. 31   d. 51

Reference_____

20. In a fully-sprinklered building, a corridor serving 100 persons in which of the following occupancies must be fire-resistance rated?

    a. Group A-2   b. Group I-2

    c. Group M   d. Group R-1

Reference_____

21. In a Group I-2, Condition 2 occupancy, corridors requiring more than one exit or exit access doorway may have dead ends that do not serve patient rooms or treatment spaces if limited to a maximum of _____ feet in length.

    a. 8   b. 20

    c. 30   d. 50

Reference_____

22. In a fully-sprinklered Group E occupancy, the maximum permitted length of a dead-end condition in a corridor requiring at least two means of egress is

_____ .

    a. 20 feet   b. 50 feet

    c. twice the corridor width   d. four times the corridor width

Reference_____

23. Utilization of corridors as return air plenums is permitted within tenant spaces having a maximum floor area of _____ square feet.

    a. 400   b. 1,000

    c. 3,000   d. 5,000

Reference_____

24. What is the minimum required width of an egress balcony serving an apartment building where the required capacity of the balcony is 55 persons?

    a. 36 inches   b. 42 inches

    c. 44 inches   d. 48 inches

Reference_____

25. The long side of an egress balcony shall be a minimum of _____ percent open.

      a. 25   b. 40

      c. 50   d. $66^2/_3$

Reference_____

26. In a Group A-2 dining room having a single exit access door, the common path of egress travel is limited to a maximum of _____ feet.

      a. 25   b. 75

      c. 100   d. 200

Reference_____

27. At least two exits or exit access doors are required from a refrigeration machinery room where the room has a floor area exceeding _____ square feet.

      a. 0, two exits are always required

      b. 200

      c. 500

      d. 1,000

Reference_____

28. All portions of refrigeration machinery rooms shall be within _____ feet of an exit or exit access doorway.

      a. 25   b. 75

      c. 100   d. 150

Reference_____

29. What is the maximum permitted travel distance for a Group H-1 occupancy protected by an automatic sprinkler system?

      a. 50 feet   b. 75 feet

      c. 100 feet   d. 125 feet

Reference_____

30. A 16-foot-wide dead-end corridor in a nonsprinklered Group E high school is prohibited where the dead end is a minimum of _____ feet in length.

    a. 20   b. 30

    c. 32   d. 40

    Reference_____

31. Where egress is permitted through a stockroom of a Group M occupancy, a maximum of _____ percent of the exit access may pass through the stockroom.

    a. 10   b. 25

    c. $33^{1}/_{3}$ d. 50

    Reference _____

32. An aisle accessway in a merchandise pad of a Group M occupancy shall be a minimum of _____ inches in width on at least one side of each merchandising element.

    a. 30   b. 36

    c. 44   d. 48

    Reference _____

33. A minimum of two exit access doorways are required in boiler rooms with a floor area exceeding a minimum of _____ square feet and any fuel-fired equipment has an input capacity greater than 400,000 Btu.

    a. 100   b. 400

    c. 500   d. 1,000

    Reference _____

34. In a Group M occupancy, the common path of egress travel shall not exceed _____ feet from any point within a merchandise pad with an occupant load of 40.

    a. 20   b. 30

    c. 50   d. 75

    Reference _____

35. What is the minimum required corridor width in areas of Group I-2 occupancies where the movement of beds is required?

      a. 44 inches   b. 60 inches

      c. 72 inches   d. 96 inches

      Reference _____

36. Unoccupied mechanical rooms shall have a common path of travel limitation of _____ feet.

      a. 250   b. 300

      c. 400   d. unlimited (no limit on common path)

      Reference _____

37. Where egress travel in an atrium does not occur at the level of exit discharge, a maximum of _____ feet of exit access travel distance is permitted to occur within the atrium.

      a. 150   b. 200

      c. 250   d. 300

      Reference _____

38. In a Group S occupancy, nonpublic aisles serving less than 50 people and not required to be accessible shall be a minimum of _____ inches in width.

      a. 28   b. 30

      c. 32   d. 34

      Reference _____

39. Within a dwelling unit in a Group R-2 occupancy, exit access stairways are not required to be enclosed with a shaft enclosure where the stairway serves a maximum of _____ stories.

      a. two   b. three

      c. four   d. five

      Reference _____

40. In Group I-2 occupancies, a corridor that does not serve patient rooms or patient treatment spaces shall have a maximum length of _____ feet.

      a. 15   b. 20

      c. 30   d. 50

      Reference _____

2021 IBC Sections 1022 through 1031
Means of Egress IV

OBJECTIVE: To obtain an understanding of the provisions governing the exit and exit discharge portions of the means of egress, the special requirements applicable to egress from assembly occupancies, and the details for emergency escape and rescue openings.

REFERENCE: Sections 1022 through 1031, 2021 *International Building Code*

KEY POINTS:
- What is the definition of an exit? What elements of the building are considered exits?
- For which purposes are exits permitted to be used?
- How many exits from a building are required? From any story within a building?
- What degree of fire resistance is required for interior exit stairways and ramps?
- Where must an interior exit stairway or ramp terminate?
- How are openings in the enclosure for an interior exit stairway or ramp regulated? Elevators? Penetrations? Ventilation?
- How must exterior walls of an interior exit stairway or ramp be protected?
- How is travel in an interior exit stairway or ramp that extends beyond the discharge level addressed?
- Where are stairway floor number signs to be located?
- What is a smokeproof enclosure? When is a smokeproof enclosure required?
- What is an exit passageway?
- How is an exit passageway regulated for width?
- What level of fire-resistance-rated construction is mandated for an exit passageway?
- Which types of openings and penetrations are permitted in an exit passageway or a vertical exit enclosure? How are openings and penetrations to be protected?
- In what manner can an exit passageway be provided with ventilation?
- In what types of buildings are luminous egress path markings required? Where within the building are the markings to be provided?
- What is the function of a horizontal exit? How is it to be constructed?

KEY POINTS: • How is the capacity of a horizontal exit refuge area determined?
(Cont'd) • What is the maximum height permitted for an exterior exit stairway?

• What is the minimum size exterior opening required for an exterior exit stairway?

• Where does the exit discharge begin? Where does it end?

• What is an egress court?

• What is the minimum size of an egress court? When are egress court walls required to be of fire-resistance-rated construction with protected openings?

• What is a safe dispersal area? What conditions must apply where such an area is utilized?

• What is the minimum capacity of the main exit in an assembly occupancy?

• What is smoke-protected assembly seating?

• What minimum aisle widths are required in assembly occupancies without smoke protection? With smoke protection?

• How is the guard height regulated in assembly areas where the guards interfere with occupant sightlines?

• Where are emergency escape and rescue openings required?

• What is the minimum height and width of an emergency escape and rescue opening? Minimum clear opening size? Maximum sill height from floor?

Code Text: An exit is *that portion of a means of egress system between the exit access and the exit discharge or public way. Exit components include exterior exit doors at the level of exit discharge, interior exit stairways and ramps, exit passageways, exterior exit stairways and ramps, and horizontal exits.*

Discussion and Commentary: The path of travel through the exit access portion of the egress system must be designed to lead to one or more exits, which are locations where some degree of protection or safety from fire hazards is provided. Travel distance is no longer regulated once an exit is reached; therefore, travel within an exit component is virtually unlimited.

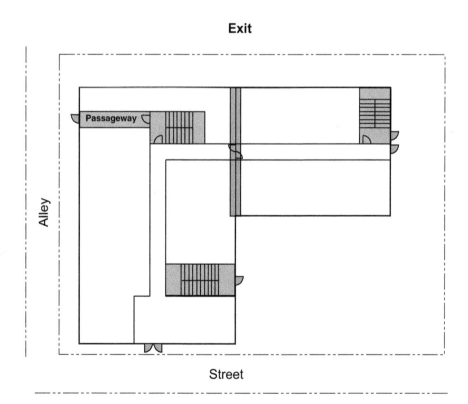

Because an exit must be maintained for egress, it cannot be used for any purpose that interferes with egress. In addition, once a mandated level of protection is provided for occupants reaching an exit, that level cannot be diminished prior to their reaching the exit discharge.

Code Text: *An exit shall not be used for any purpose that interferes with its function as a means of egress. Once a given level of exit protection is achieved, such level of protection shall not be reduced until arrival at the exit discharge. Buildings or structures used for human occupancy shall have at least one exterior door that meets the requirements of Section 1010.1.1 (Size of doors).*

Discussion and Commentary: Exits constitute those portions of the means of egress where the occupant first achieves a significant level of fire protection. An exit is expected to provide a mandated level of protection, and that level cannot be reduced until arrival at the exit discharge. The primary function of an exit component is to provide egress, and any other use cannot interfere with that function. Use of the exit for other purposes can often lead to the egress path being obstructed and possibly unusable. It is not uncommon to find the storage of equipment or furniture occurring within an exit enclosure, creating an unsafe condition.

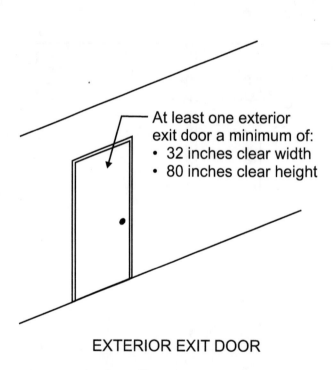

At least one exterior exit door a minimum of:
- 32 inches clear width
- 80 inches clear height

EXTERIOR EXIT DOOR

All buildings, regardless of size, that are intended for human occupancy must have a minimum of one exit door that meets the minimum width and height requirements of Section 1010.1.1. The intent of this provision is to override any exceptions for minimum door width and height that may apply in other locations throughout the building.

Code Text: *Enclosures for interior exit stairways and ramps shall be constructed as fire barriers in accordance with Section 707 or horizontal assemblies constructed in accordance with Section 711, or both. Interior exit stairway and ramp enclosures shall have a fire-resistance rating of not less than 2 hours where connecting four stories or more and not less than 1 hour where connecting less than four stories. Enclosures for interior exit stairways and ramps shall have a fire-resistance rating not less than the floor assembly penetrated, but need not exceed 2 hours.*

Discussion and Commentary: Vertical openings created for stairways must typically be enclosed with fire-resistance-rated construction. The presence of openings into and penetrations through interior exit stairways and ramps is strictly limited due to the high-level nature of the egress elements. Ventilation of an interior stairway or ramp is also highly regulated. The integrity of the means of egress system must be maintained until arrival at the exit discharge or public way.

Interior exit stairways and ramps must always be enclosed with fire-resistance-rated construction. Allowances for unenclosed stairways within the means of egress are established in Section 1019 under the provisions for exit access stairways.

Code Text: *Where nonrated walls or unprotected openings enclose the exterior of the stairway and the walls or openings are exposed to other parts of the building at an angle of less than 180 degrees (3.14 rad), the building exterior walls within 10 feet (3048 mm) horizontally of a nonrated wall or unprotected opening have a fire-resistance rating of not less than 1 hour. Openings within such exterior walls shall be protected by opening protectives having a fire protection rating of not less than $^3/_4$ hour. This construction shall extend vertically from the ground to a point 10 feet (3048 mm) above the topmost landing of the stairway or to the roof line, whichever is lower.*

Discussion and Commentary: Unless regulated according to fire separation distance or type of construction, the exterior wall of an interior exit stairway or ramp usually needs no fire-resistance rating. However, where exposure is possible from other exterior walls of the building in close proximity to the enclosure, a limited degree of fire separation is necessary.

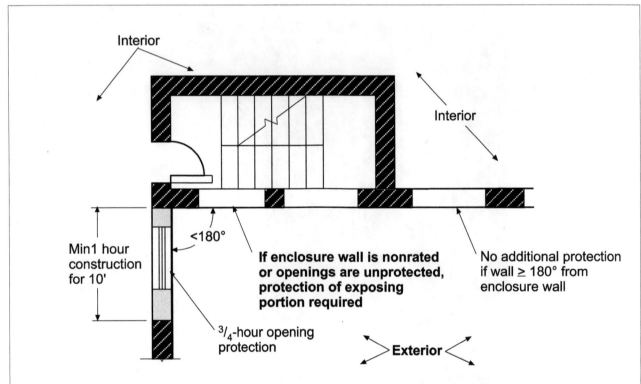

For SI: 1 foot = 304.8 mm, 1 degree = 0.01745 rad.

An alternative to the protection of exterior walls adjacent to an interior exit stairway or ramp is the protection of the exterior wall of the enclosure itself. Should a fire breach an adjacent exterior wall, its penetration of the stairway or ramp enclosure would be halted for an acceptable time period.

Topic: Smokeproof Enclosures	**Category:** Means of Egress
Reference: IBC 1023.12, 1023.12.2	**Subject:** Interior Exit Stairways and Ramps

Code Text: *Where required by Section 403.5.4* (high-rise buildings)*, 405.7.2* (underground buildings) *or 412.2.2.1* (airport traffic control towers) *interior exit stairways and ramps shall be smokeproof enclosures in accordance with Section 909.20. Access to the stairway within a smokeproof enclosure shall be by way of a vestibule or an open exterior balcony.* See the exception for stairways using the pressurization alternative complying with Section 909.20.5.

Discussion and Commentary: In those buildings where vertical egress travel is extensive, an additional level of protection is mandated, primarily to address the hazard of smoke and toxic gases that are produced in a fire. Through ventilation or pressurization, the potential for smoke and gases to enter the enclosure is dramatically reduced.

Smokeproof enclosures

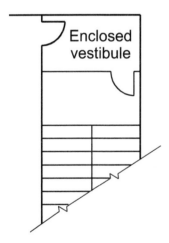

Mechanical ventilation
alternative

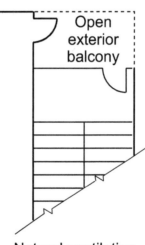

Natural ventilation
alternative

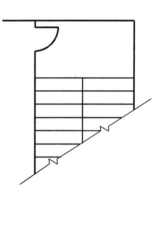

Stair pressurization
alternative

If a smokeproof enclosure does not exit directly to a yard, court or public way, then an exit passageway must be provided to extend protected travel to the exterior. The exit passageway may have no other openings unless it is protected in the same manner as the vertical enclosure.

Code Text: *Except as permitted in Section 402.8.7 (exit passageways in covered mall buildings), openings in interior exit stairways and ramps (and exit passageways) other than unprotected exterior openings shall be limited to those necessary for exit access to the enclosure from normally occupied spaces and for egress from the enclosure (or exit passageway). Penetrations into and openings through interior exit stairways and ramps are prohibited except for: See seven different conditions under which penetrations are acceptable.*

Discussion and Commentary: Given the importance of an exit enclosure in the means of egress system, no unnecessary openings or penetrations are permitted to breach the fire-resistant separation. The provisions are essentially the same for both interior exit stairways and exit passageways.

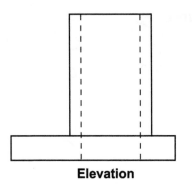

Elevation

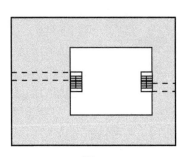

Plan

Enclosure construction:

- Four or more stories—2-hour fire resistance
- Less than four stories—1-hour fire resistance

Openings and penetrations:

- Permitted exterior openings (705)
- Egress from normally occupied spaces
- Egress from enclosure
- Fire protection systems
- Ductwork for independent pressurization
- Limited electrical conduit
- Security systems
- Two-way communication systems
- Structural elements supporting stairway or enclosure

Doors: (716)

- Self-closing or automatic closing
- 1-hour rating in 1-hour construction
- $1^1/_2$-hour rating in 2-hour construction
- Temperature rise limit of 450°F above ambient

Several methods are set forth in the code to provide for ventilation of an exit enclosure. In general, penetrations for ductwork must enter directly from the building's exterior or from an interior space separated from the remainder of the building by a shaft enclosure.

Code Text: *An exit passageway shall not be used for any purpose other than a means of egress and a circulation path. Exit passageway enclosures shall have walls, floors and ceilings of not less than 1-hour fire-resistance rating, and not less than that required for any connecting interior exit stairway or ramp. Exit passageways shall be constructed as fire barriers in accordance with Section 707, or horizontal assemblies constructed in accordance with Section 711, or both.*

Discussion and Commentary: An exit passageway is defined as an exit component that is separated from all other interior spaces of a building or structure by fire-resistance-rated construction and opening protectives, and provides for a protected path of egress travel in a horizontal direction to an exit or to the exit discharge. It is an egress component of a higher level than a fire-resistance-rated corridor, based primarily on limited openings and penetrations, and increased fire ratings.

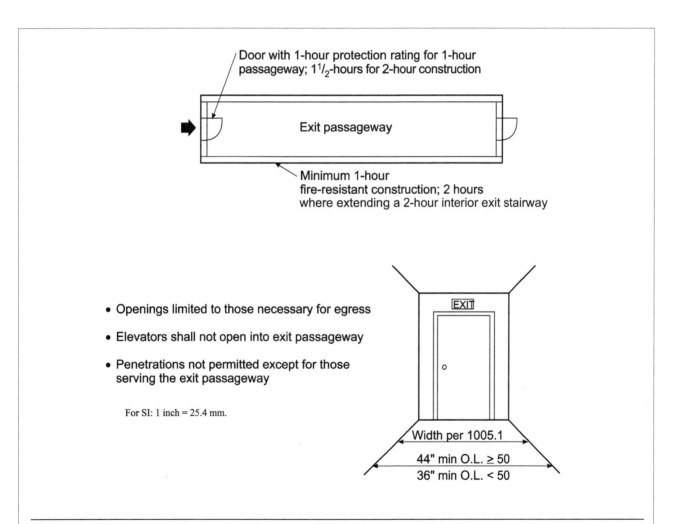

Once in an exit passageway, the building occupant is considered to be in a relatively safe location; thus, travel distances within the exit passageway are unregulated. Simply put, an exit passageway is a horizontal exit enclosure, with conditions and limitations similar to those required for an interior exit stairway.

Code Text: *Approved luminous egress path markings delineating the exit path shall be provided in high-rise buildings of Groups A, B, E, I-1, M and R-1 occupancies in accordance with Sections 1025.1 through 1025.5. See the exception for lobbies on the level of exit discharge.*

Discussion and Commentary: Photoluminescent or self-luminous materials are required in interior exit stairways and exit passageways of certain high-rise buildings in order to delineate the exit path. Improved safety for individuals negotiating stairs during the extended egress required in a high-rise building is provided by improving the visibility of stair treads and handrails under normal and emergency conditions.

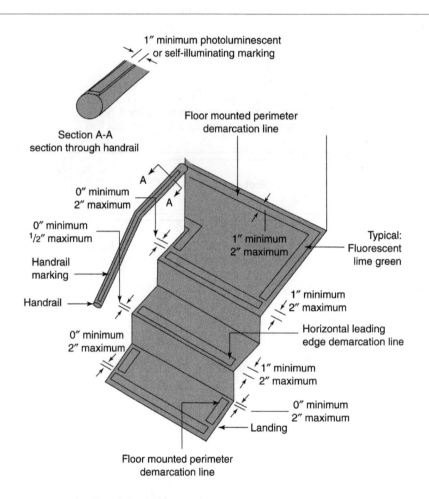

1″ minimum photoluminescent or self-illuminating marking

Section A-A
section through handrail

Floor mounted perimeter demarcation line

0″ minimum
2″ maximum

0″ minimum
1/2″ maximum

Handrail marking

Handrail

1″ minimum
2″ maximum

Typical:
Fluorescent
lime green

1″ minimum
2″ maximum

Horizontal leading
edge demarcation line

0″ minimum
2″ maximum

1″ minimum
2″ maximum

0″ minimum
2″ maximum

Landing

Floor mounted perimeter
demarcation line

Note: The width of demarcation lines at horizontal leading edges of stairs,
perimeter demarcation line and handrails may be less than 1″ width
when listed in accordance UL 1944.

Analogous to rechargeable batteries, many photoluminescent and self-illuminating egress path markings require exposure to light to perform properly. Thus, such markings must be exposed to a minimum of 1 foot-candle of light energy at the walking surface for at least 60 minutes prior to the building being occupied.

Code Text: *A horizontal exit shall not serve as the only exit from a portion of a building, and where two or more exits are required, not more than one-half of the total number of exits or total exit minimum width or required capacity shall be horizontal exits.* See the exceptions for Group I-2 and I-3 occupancies. *The refuge area of a horizontal exit shall be a space occupied by the same tenant or public areas and each such area of refuge shall be adequate to house the original occupant load of the refuge area plus the occupant load anticipated from the adjoining compartment.*

Discussion and Commentary: A horizontal exit is defined as a path of egress travel from one building to an area in another building on approximately the same level, or a path of egress travel through or around a wall or partition to an area on approximately the same level in the same building, which affords safety from fire and smoke from the area of incidence and areas communicating therewith. Constructed as a minimum 2-hour fire wall or fire barrier, a horizontal exit is an exit component of the means of egress system.

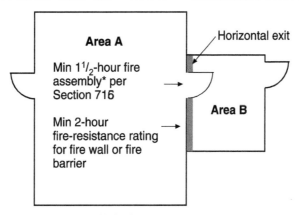

* must be self-closing or automatic closing upon activation of a smoke detector

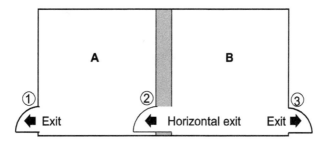

NOTE: Exit for "A" adequate to meet the provisions of Chapter 10 but need not include added capacity imposed by occupants entering through horizontal exit from "B."

Horizontal exits must extend vertically through all levels of the building, unless minimum 2-hour floor assemblies with no unprotected openings are provided. The horizontal exit walls are to extend continuously from exterior wall to exterior wall in order to completely divide the floor.

Code Text: *Exterior exit stairways and ramps serving as an element of a required means of egress shall be open on not less than one side. An open side shall have not less than 35 square feet (3.3 m²) of aggregate open area adjacent to each floor level and the level of each intermediate landing. The required open area shall be located not less than 42 inches (1067 mm) above the adjacent floor or landing level.*

Discussion and Commentary: For a stairway or ramp to be considered exterior, it must be open enough to the outside so that smoke and toxic gases will not tend to corrupt the exit route. An exterior exit ramp or exterior exit stairway is considered an exit component and is permitted as an egress element in all occupancies except Group I-2. Where permitted as an element of a required means of egress, an exterior exit stairway is limited to buildings with a maximum of 6 stories and no more than 75 feet in height above the lowest level of fire department vehicle access.

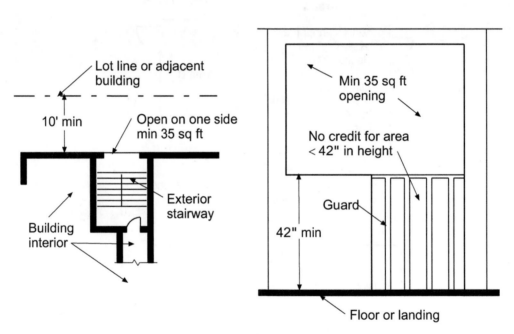

For SI: 1 inch = 25.4 mm, 1 foot = 304.8 mm, 1 square foot = 0.093 m².

Consistent with the requirements for other exit components, an exterior exit ramp or stairway must be separated from the remainder of the building by fire-resistance-rated construction and protected openings. The IBC provides four exceptions where separation is not warranted.

Code Text: The exit discharge is *that portion of a means of egress system between the termination of an exit and a public way. Exits shall discharge directly to the exterior of the building.* See the exceptions for discharge level spaces, vestibules and horizontal exits. *The exit discharge shall be at grade or shall provide direct access to grade. The exit discharge shall not reenter a building. Exit discharge components shall be sufficiently open to the exterior so as to minimize the accumulation of smoke and toxic gases.*

Discussion and Commentary: Exit discharge travel typically takes place outside of the building, where hazards to the occupants are greatly reduced. Although concern over the accumulation of smoke and toxic gases is eliminated, there is still a risk to the occupants, which is eliminated only at a point of considerable distance from the structure, generally the public way.

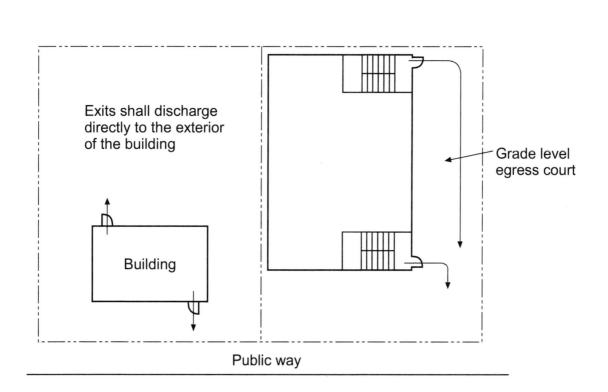

Exits shall discharge directly to the exterior of the building

Grade level egress court

Building

Public way

Number of exits maintained until arrival at grade or public way

When specific conditions are met, up to 50 percent of the number and capacity of interior exit stairways may exit through a vestibule or an area on the discharge level, provided all the stated conditions have been met.

Code Text: *The exit discharge shall provide a direct and unobstructed access to a public way.* See the exception for designation of a safe dispersal area where access to a public way cannot be provided.

Discussion and Commentary: The means of egress is not complete until the occupants of the building have reached a safe place. Such a place is typically a public way, in that it is relatively unobstructed, and more importantly, continuous. It is always possible to continue egress travel along a public way until the necessary level of safety is achieved. The path to reach the public way, as for all other components of the means of egress, must be free of obstructions and other concerns that would cause the occupants' egress travel to be delayed, restricted or unavailable. It is important that the travel path outside of the building be continuously maintained in order to keep the means of egress in a complying condition.

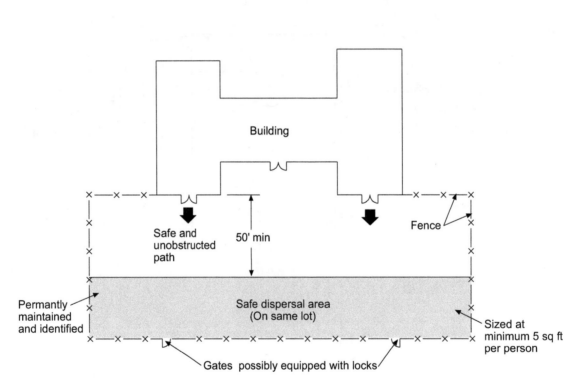

For SI: 1 foot = 304.8 mm, 1 square foot = 0.0929 m².

Safe dispersal areas

Occasionally it is impractical, and at times impossible, to provide a fully complying means of egress the entire distance to the public way. A safe dispersal area can be utilized where such conditions exist, such as on large industrial or educational campus sites.

Code Text: *Where an egress court serving a building or portion thereof is less than 10 feet (3048 mm) in width, the egress court walls shall be not less than 1-hour fire-resistance-rated construction for a distance of 10 feet (3048 mm) above the floor of the court. Openings within such walls shall be protected by opening protectives having a fire protection rating of not less than $^3/_4$ hour. See the exceptions for small occupant loads and Group R-3 occupancies.*

Discussion and Commentary: An egress court is defined as a court or yard which provides access to a public way for one or more exits. Because an egress court is an element of the exit discharge, occupants must be afforded sufficient protection from a fire within the structure to be reasonably sure that once outside they will reach the safety of a public way. Therefore, fire-resistance-rated exterior walls and openings must be provided where such occupants must travel adjacent to an exterior wall in order to reach the public way.

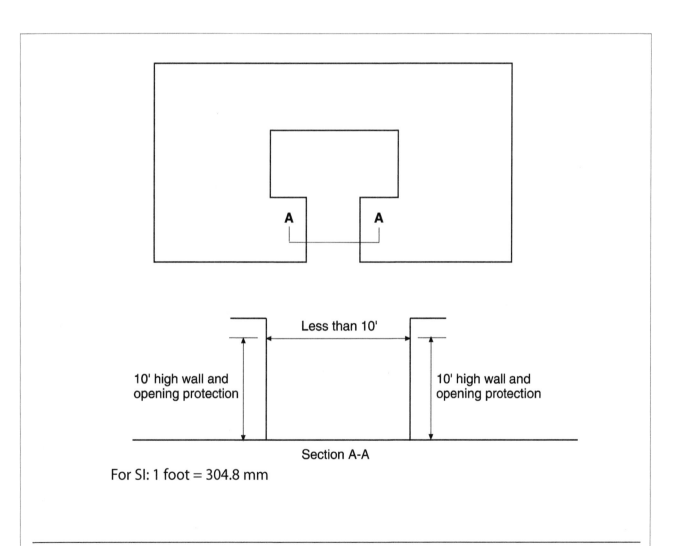

Section A-A

For SI: 1 foot = 304.8 mm

The minimum required width of an egress court is addressed in a manner similar to that of aisles, corridors and stairways. The width must accommodate the calculated capacity, based on occupant load served; however, in no case may it be less than a specified width of 44" (36" in Group R-3).

Code Text: *A building, room or space used for assembly purposes that has an occupant load of greater than 300 and is provided with a main exit, that main exit shall be of sufficient capacity to accommodate not less than one-half of the occupant load, but such capacity shall not be less than the total required capacity of all means of egress leading to the exit.*

Discussion and Commentary: In most assembly-type uses, the occupants tend to enter the room or space at a single location. It is expected that under emergency conditions, most of the occupants will attempt to exit at the same point. Therefore, the main entrance/exit must be wide enough to handle a sizeable percentage of the occupants. If there is no well-defined main exit or where multiple main entrance/exits are provided, the required exit width can be distributed among the exits around the perimeter of the building.

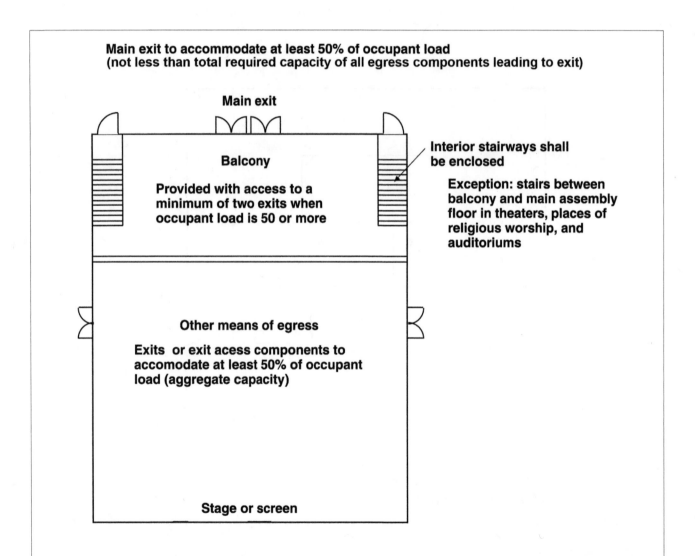

Main exit to accommodate at least 50% of occupant load
(not less than total required capacity of all egress components leading to exit)

Main exit

Balcony

Provided with access to a minimum of two exits when occupant load is 50 or more

Interior stairways shall be enclosed

Exception: stairs between balcony and main assembly floor in theaters, places of religious worship, and auditoriums

Other means of egress

Exits or exit acess components to accomodate at least 50% of occupant load (aggregate capacity)

Stage or screen

To better define and maintain the egress path through a lobby or foyer to the main entrance/exit in a Group A-1 occupancy, the code mandates that the waiting area not encroach upon the required clear egress width.

Code Text: *Aisle accessways serving arrangements of seating at tables or counters shall have suffi-cient clear width to conform to the capacity requirements of Section 1005.1, but shall not have less than 12 inches (305 mm) plus $^1/_2$ inch (12.7 mm) of width for each additional 1 foot (305 mm), or fraction thereof, beyond 12 feet (3658 mm) of aisle accessway length measured from the center of the seat farthest from an aisle. See the exception for aisle accessways of limited lengths and occupant loads. The length of travel along the aisle accessway shall not exceed 30 feet (9144 mm) from any seat to the point where a person has a choice of two or more paths of egress travel to separate exits.*

Discussion and Commentary: To facilitate progress toward an established aisle, it is important that a minimum degree of egress width be established within areas furnished with tables and chairs. An aisle accessway, defined as that portion of an exit access that leads to an aisle, is thus regulated.

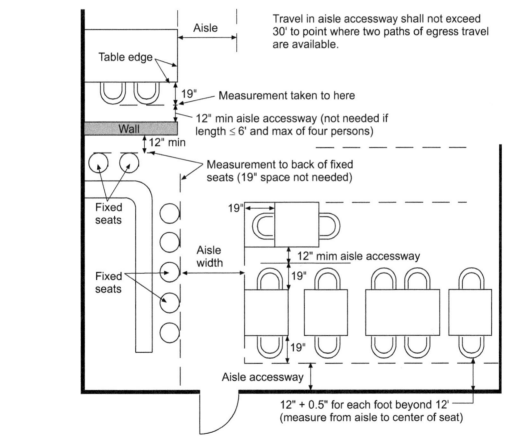

For SI: 1 inch = 25.4 mm.

The method of determining the clear width differs based on the type of seating that is provided. For fixed seats, the measurement is made from the back of the seats. Otherwise, the clear width is measured to a line 19 inches from the edge of the table or counter.

Code Text: *Ramped aisles having a slope exceeding one unit vertical in 15 units horizontal (6.7-percent slope) and stepped aisles shall be provided with handrails in compliance with Section 1014 located either at one or both sides of the aisle or within the aisle width.* See the exceptions for (1) ramped aisles with a slope no greater than 1:8 with seating on both sides, (2) guards that comply with the graspability requirements of handrails and (3) where crossovers are permitted within the aisles. *Where there is seating on both sides of the aisle, the mid-aisle handrails shall be discontinuous with gaps or breaks at intervals not exceeding five rows to facilitate access to seating and to permit crossing from one side of the aisle to the other.*

Discussion and Commentary: Where seating is located on both sides of an aisle, the required handrails may be placed either on both sides of, or down the center of, the aisle served. Where seating is located on only one side of the aisle, a handrail is only required on one of the sides.

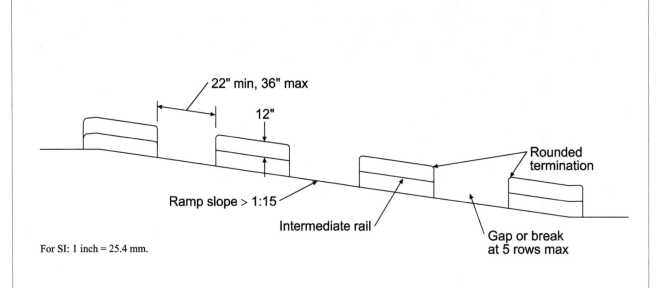

22" min, 36" max

12"

Rounded termination

Ramp slope > 1:15

Intermediate rail

Gap or break at 5 rows max

For SI: 1 inch = 25.4 mm.

Where discontinuous handrails are provided, an intermediate handrail located 12 inches below the main handrail is required to prevent users from ducking under the handrail and hindering flow. It also provides a handrail for toddlers who may be using the aisle.

Code Text: *In addition to the means of egress required by* Chapter 10, *emergency escape and rescue openings shall be provided in the following occupancies: (1) Group R-2 occupancies located in stories with only one exit or access to only one exit as permitted by Tables 1006.3.4(1) and 1006.3.4(2), and (2) Group R-3 and R-4 occupancies. Basements and sleeping rooms below the fourth story above grade plane shall have not fewer than one emergency escape and rescue opening in accordance with Section 1031.* See the four exceptions, including one for basements with a ceiling height of less than 80 inches and one for small basements without habitable spaces. *Such openings shall open directly into a public way or a yard or court that opens to a public way.*

Discussion and Commentary: In those occupancies where persons are sometimes sleeping, a fire will often spread quickly and block the normal egress routes. By requiring a sizeable opening directly from the sleeping room to the exterior, rescue can be more easily accomplished, or alternatively, the occupants may escape without having to travel through the building.

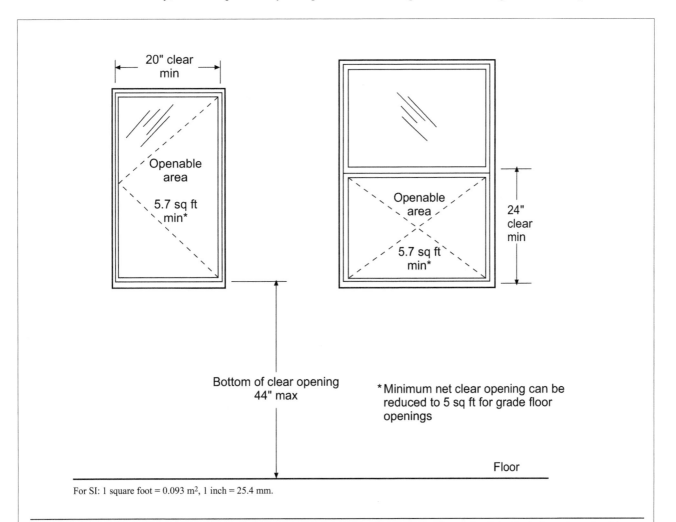

For SI: 1 square foot = 0.093 m², 1 inch = 25.4 mm.

When operable windows are used for egress or rescue purposes, the intent is that they be double-hung, horizontal sliding or casement styles operated by a simple operation. Special types other than those listed must be evaluated for compliance with the operational constraint limitations.

Code Text: *An emergency escape and rescue opening with a finished sill height below the adjacent ground level shall be provided with a window well in accordance with Sections 1030.4.1 and 1030.4.2. The minimum horizontal area of the window well shall be 9 square feet (0.84 m²), with a minimum dimension of 36 inches (914 mm). The area of the window well shall allow the emergency escape and rescue opening to be fully opened. Window wells with a vertical depth of more than 44 inches (1118 mm) shall be equipped with an approved permanently affixed ladder or steps.*

Discussion and Commentary: It is important that persons who travel through an emergency escape and rescue opening located below grade be provided with adequate space in the window well to allow for escape or rescue from the area. Therefore, a complying window well is mandated that provides an adequate cross-sectional area for escape and rescue operations.

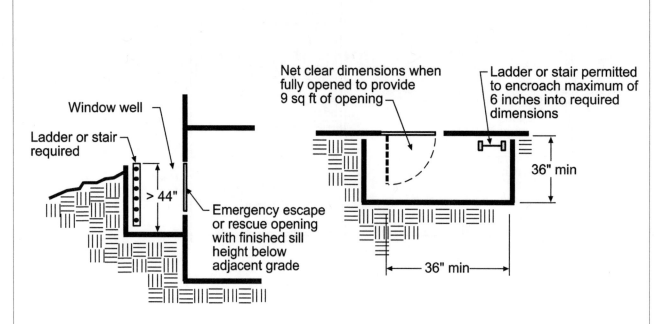

For SI: 1 inch = 25.4 mm, 1 square foot = 0.093 m².

Window well ladders must have a minimum clear rung width of 12 inches with the rungs spaced at maximum 18-inch intervals vertically. The ladder or steps cannot encroach into the required dimensions of the window well more than 6 inches.

Study Session 12
IBC Sections 1022 through 1031

1. Required stairway identification signs shall be a minimum size of _____.
    a. 12 inches by 8 inches   b. 12 inches by 12 inches
    c. 18 inches by 12 inches   d. 18 inches by 18 inches

    Reference_____

2. In which one of the following high-rise buildings is the installation of luminous egress path markings not required?
    a. Group B   b. Group M
    c. Group R-1   d. Group R-2

    Reference_____

3. Where photoluminescent exit path markings are required in specified high-rise buildings, they shall be provided with not less than 1 footcandle of illumination for a minimum time period of _____ minutes prior to periods when the building is occupied and continuous during occupancy.
    a. 15   b. 30
    c. 45   d. 60

    Reference_____

4. Enclosures for interior exit stairways connecting a minimum of _____ stories shall be 2-hour fire-resistance rated.
    a. three   b. four
    c. five   d. six

    Reference_____

5. Exterior exit stairways shall be provided with a minimum fire separation distance of _____ feet from the exterior edge of the stairway to adjacent lot lines.

    a. 5   b. 10

    c. 15   d. 20

Reference_____

6. Where a smokeproof enclosure is extended by an exit passageway, the exit passageway shall be separated from the remainder of the building by minimum _____ -hour fire barriers and/or horizontal assemblies.

    a. $^3/_4$ b. 1

    c. 2   d. 3

Reference _____

7. Stairway floor number signs shall be provided in interior exit stairways and ramps connecting a minimum of _____ stories.

    a. 2   b. 3

    c. 4   d. 6

Reference_____

8. Smokeproof enclosures or pressurized stairways or ramps are only required in aircraft traffic control towers, _____ buildings and _____ buildings.

    a. high-rise, underground   b. high-rise, Group I-2

    c. Group I-2, Group I-3   d. atrium, underground

Reference_____

9. Exit passageways shall be constructed as minimum _____ .

    a. 1-hour fire partitions   b. 1-hour fire barriers

    c. 2-hour fire barriers   d. 2-hour fire walls

Reference_____

10. In other than Group I-1, I-2 and I-3 occupancies and ambulatory care facilities, a refuge area serving a horizontal exit shall be sized for capacity based on _____ square feet for each occupant to be accommodated.

    a. 3   b. 6

    c. 15   d. 30

Reference_____

11. Where serving as a required means of egress for other than a Group I-2 occupancy, exterior exit stairways are permitted as means of egress elements for non-high-rise buildings a maximum of _____ stories above grade plane.

    a. three   b. four

    c. five   d. six

Reference_____

12. An exterior exit stairway serving as an element of a required means of egress must be open on at least one side, with such open area a minimum of _____ square feet and located a minimum of _____ inches above the adjacent floor or landing level.

    a. 9, 36   b. 16, 42

    c. 20, 36   d. 35, 42

Reference_____

13. Where a safe dispersal area is provided in lieu of access to a public way, the area shall be of a size to accommodate a minimum of _____ square feet for each person.

    a. 3   b. 5

    c. 7   d. 15

Reference_____

14. What is the minimum required width of an egress court serving 40 occupants from an office building?

    a. 36 inches   b. 44 inches

    c. 48 inches   d. 60 inches

Reference_____

15. Where seating is located at a table and is adjacent to an aisle, the measurement of required clear width of the aisle shall be made to a line _____ inches away from and parallel to the edge of the table.

   a. 15   b. 19

   c. 21   d. 24

   Reference_____

16. Where an assembly space with a main exit has a minimum occupant load of _____ persons, the main exit shall be of sufficient width to accommodate at least one-half of the occupant load.

   a. 51   b. 301

   c. 501   d. 1,001

   Reference_____

17. At least two means of egress shall be provided from assembly seating areas in balconies having a minimum seating capacity of _____ persons.

   a. 10   b. 30

   c. 50   d. 100

   Reference_____

18. In assembly areas not provided with smoke protection, the minimum width for stairs having 8-inch risers is based on a minimum of _____ inch of width for each occupant served.

   a. 0.2   b. 0.22

   c. 0.3   d. 0.35

   Reference_____

19. In a 15,000-seat arena provided with smoke-protected assembly seating, the minimum width for a 1:12 ramped aisle is based on a minimum of _____ inch of width for each occupant served.

   a. 0.300   b. 0.200

   c. 0.120   d. 0.070

   Reference_____

20. The smoke level in a means of egress serving a smoke-protected assembly seating area is intended to be maintained a minimum of _____ feet above the floor of the means of egress.

      a. 6   b. 8

      c. 12   d. 15

Reference_____

21. What is the maximum travel distance for seating in open-air assembly structures of Type I or II construction?

      a. 200 feet   b. 300 feet

      c. 400 feet   d. unlimited

Reference_____

22. Where serving more than 5 rows, what is the minimum required clear width for stepped aisles having seating on only one side?

      a. 32 inches   b. 36 inches

      c. 42 inches   d. 44 inches

Reference_____

23. In stepped aisles of assembly seating areas, the maximum tolerance permitted between adjacent treads is _____ inch.

      a. $^1/_8$ b. $^3/_{16}$

      c. $^1/_4$ d. $^3/_8$

Reference_____

24. Where the foot of the aisle is more than 30 inches above the floor or grade below, a railing or fascia system at the foot of aisles in an assembly occupancy shall be a minimum of _____ in height.

      a. 26 inches   b. 32 inches

      c. 36 inches   d. 42 inches

Reference_____

25. What is the minimum net clear opening required for emergency escape and rescue grade floor openings?

    a.   20 inches by 22 inches   b.   20 inches by 24 inches

    c.   5.0 square feet   d.   5.7 square feet

Reference_____

26. Where horizontal exits are used in the means of egress in a Group I-2 hospital, the horizontal exits can be used for a maximum of _____ of the required exits.

    a.   one   b.   two

    c.   one-half   d.   two-thirds

Reference_____

27. Along with other limitations, the exit discharge may occur through a vestibule, provided the vestibule has a maximum depth from the exterior of the building of _____ feet and a maximum length of _____ feet.

    a.   8, 15   b.   10, 20

    c.   10, 30   d.   15, 30

Reference_____

28. Egress need not extend to a public way where a safe dispersal area is provided a minimum of _____ feet from the building.

    a.   30   b.   50

    c.   75   d.   100

Reference_____

29. An emergency escape and rescue opening shall be located so that the bottom of the clear opening is a maximum of _____ inches above the floor surface.

    a.   36   b.   42

    c.   44   d.   48

Reference_____

30. Where a window well is provided to serve an emergency escape and rescue opening, it shall have a minimum horizontal area of _____ square feet.

    a.   5.0   b.   5.7

    c.   9.0   d.   10.0

    Reference_____

31. The separation between refuge areas connected by a horizontal exit will be provided by a fire wall or fire barrier having a minimum fire-resistance rating of _____ hour(s).

    a.   1   b.   2

    c.   3   d.   4

    Reference _____

32. Where seating rows in an assembly seating area have 14 or fewer seats, the clear aisle accessway width shall be a minimum of _____ inches measured horizontally from the back of the row ahead to the nearest projection of the row behind.

    a.   12   b.   16

    c.   19   d.   22

    Reference _____

33. Where there is assembly seating on both sides of an aisle, the handrails shall be discontinuous with gaps or breaks a minimum of _____ inches and a maximum of _____ inches in width, measured horizontally.

    a.   16, 32   b.   20, 34

    c.   22, 36   d.   27, 42

    Reference _____

34. An emergency escape and rescue opening is not required from a basement without habitable spaces, provided the floor area of the basement is a maximum of _____ square feet.

    a.   120   b.   200

    c.   240   d.   400

    Reference _____

35. An emergency escape and rescue opening shall be a minimum of _____ inches in net clear opening height and a minimum of _____ inches in net clear opening width.

    a. 24, 20   b. 24, 22

    c. 20, 26   d. 20, 28

Reference _____

36. What door openings are not permitted in interior exit stairways?

    a. Unprotected exterior openings

    b. Those required for exit access to the enclosure from normally occupied spaces

    c. Egress doors used for egress from the enclosure

    d. Elevator doors

Reference _____

37. An exit passageway serving an occupant load of less than 50 shall have a minimum width of _____ inches.

    a. 36   b. 42

    c. 44   d. 48

Reference _____

38. Where luminous egress path markings are required in interior exit stairways, handrails shall be marked with a solid and continuous stripe having a minimum width of _____ inch.

    a. $\frac{1}{4}$ b. $\frac{1}{2}$

    c. $\frac{3}{4}$ d. 1

Reference _____

39. Open-ended corridors that lead to exterior exit stairways shall be provided with complying openings at any location where a change of direction exceeding _____ degrees occurs.

    a. 15   b. $22\frac{1}{2}$

    c. 30   d. 45

Reference _____

40. For open-air assembly seating areas, the common path of egress travel shall be a maximum of _____ feet.

    a. 20   b. 30

    c. 50   d. 75

    Reference _____

2021 IBC Chapter 11
Accessibility

OBJECTIVE: To become familiar with the scoping provisions relating to the design and construction of accessible buildings, facilities and elements.

REFERENCE: Chapter 11, 2021 *International Building Code*

KEY POINTS:
- What is the scope of the provisions regulating accessibility and usability?
- How does ICC A117.1 relate to the IBC?
- Are temporary buildings regulated for accessibility?
- How are employee work areas viewed for accessibility?
- Which types of uses are not required to be accessible?
- Where within employee work areas is an accessible route not required?
- What is an accessible route? Which site elements must be connected by an accessible route to an accessible building entrance?
- Which areas within a building must be connected by an accessible route?
- Under which conditions is a vertical accessible route not required?
- How should the accessible route be provided in relationship to the general circulation path?
- How many entrances to a building must be accessible? To a tenant space within a building?
- What percentage of parking spaces must be designed as accessible?
- When is a van-accessible space required?
- Where must accessible parking spaces be located?
- When is an accessible loading zone required?
- What is a Type A dwelling unit? Type B unit? In which types of buildings are such units located?

- Where dwelling units and sleeping units are required to be accessible, what accessible features are required in each Accessible unit, Type A unit and Type B unit?
- In a theater, auditorium or similar assembly area, how is the minimum number of required wheelchair spaces determined?
- How shall wheelchair spaces be distributed throughout a multilevel assembly facility?
- What is the function of an assistive listening system? Under which conditions are assistive listening systems required?
- Under what conditions must prerecorded or real-time captions of audible public announcements be provided?
- Which types of dining areas must be accessible?
- What specific areas of a judicial facility must be accessible?
- What percentage of toilet rooms are required to be accessible? Bathing facilities?
- What are family or assisted-use toilet rooms and bathing rooms? When are such rooms required?
- What are the features required in a family or assisted-use toilet room? Bathing room?
- What are water closet and shower compartments designed for assisted use? Where are such facilities permitted?
- Where drinking fountains are provided, how many must be accessible? Storage lockers? Fitting rooms? Check-out aisles? Saunas and steam rooms?
- Under what conditions is a platform (wheelchair) lift permitted to be a part of a required accessible route?
- Where are detectable warnings required?
- What type of operating mechanisms or controls are regulated for usability?
- When must a stairway be considered an accessible element?
- How are recreational facilities serving residential occupancies regulated for accessibility?
- What is the *International Symbol of Accessibility*? Where are such signs required?
- What types of recreational facilities require some degree of access and usability?
- Where is directional signage mandated?

Code Text: *The provisions of* Chapter 11 *shall control the design and construction of facilities for accessibility for individuals with disabilities. Buildings and facilities shall be designed and constructed to be accessible in accordance with* the IBC *and ICC A117.1.*

Discussion and Commentary: Chapter 11 of the *International Building Code* sets forth the scoping provisions that identify where and to what degree access must be provided. Once it has been determined that accessible elements are required, the ICC design standard *Accessible and Usable Buildings and Facilities* sets forth the specific technical criteria. As with any other provision of the code, alternative designs, products or technologies that provide equivalent or superior compliance may be accepted by the building official.

Scope
The provisions of Chapter 11 shall control the design and construction of facilities for accessibility for individuals with disabilities.

Design
Buildings and facilities shall be designed and constructed to be accessible in accordance with the IBC and ICC A117.1.

Although space requirements can vary greatly depending on the nature of the disability and the physical functions of the individual, it is generally accepted that spaces designed to accommodate persons using wheelchairs will be functional for most people.

Code Text: *Sites, buildings, structures, facilities, elements and spaces, temporary or permanent, shall be accessible to individuals with disabilities.* See the fourteen general exceptions.

Discussion and Commentary: In general, all portions of all buildings are to be provided with elements that will make them fully accessible to individuals with disabilities. There are, however, a number of general exceptions that reduce or eliminate accessibility requirements. Specific areas that are not required to be accessible include: individual employee work areas; detached dwellings and their accessory structures; construction sites; raised security or safety areas, such as observation galleries or fire towers; nonoccupiable spaces and equipment spaces, including elevator pits and transformer vaults; and single-occupant structures accessed at other than grade, such as toll booths.

Specific requirements. Where not required per Sections 1104 through 1111.

Employee work areas. Need only comply with fire alarm, accessible means of egress and common use circulation path provisions. Must be able to approach, enter and exit the work area (small raised work areas totally exempted).

Detached dwellings. Detached one- and two-family dwellings and accessory structures, and their associated sites and facilities.

Utility buildings. Group U are exempt except:

1. In agricultural buildings, access is required to paved work areas and areas open to the general public.

2. Private garages or carports that contain required accessible parking.

Construction sites. Structures, sites and equipment directly associated with the actual processes of construction.

Raised areas. Raised areas used primarily for purpose of security, life safety or fire safety.

Limited access spaces. Nonoccupiable spaces accessed only by ladders, catwalks, crawl spaces, freight elevators, very narrow passageways or tunnels.

Areas in places of religious worship. Raised or lowered areas in places of religious worship of limited size where used primarily for the performance of religious ceremonies.

Equipment spaces. Spaces frequented only by personnel for maintenance, repair or monitoring of equipment.

Highway toll booths. Where accessed only by passageways below grade or elevated above grade.

Residential Group R-1. Buildings of Group R-1 containing not more than five sleeping units for rent or hire which are also occupied as the residence of the proprietor.

Day care facilities. Where part of a dwelling unit.

Detention and correctional facilities. Common use areas not serving accessible cells.

Walk-in coolers and freezers. Cooler and freezer equipment accessed only from employee work areas.

Other than those residential occupancies exempt from the accessibility provisions, most buildings will require some level of accessibility. Only those specific areas identified by the code are exempt, whereas the remainder of the structure is regulated for complying accessibility and usability.

Code Text: *When a building or portion of a building is required to be accessible, at least one accessible route shall be provided to each portion of the building, to accessible building entrances connecting accessible pedestrian walkways and the public way.* See the exceptions for (1) stories and mezzanines exempted by Section 1104.4, (2) fixed-seating assembly areas, (3) elevated work stations within a courtroom and (4) recreational facilities.

Discussion and Commentary: An accessible route is defined as a continuous, unobstructed path that complies with Chapter 11. It potentially includes corridors, aisles, ramps, elevators, platform (wheelchair) lifts and clear floor space at fixtures. The general requirement for the connection of accessible spaces is modified for common use circulation paths within employee work areas and for access to press boxes. Chapter 4 of ICC A117.1 addresses the design and construction specifications for the elements of an accessible route.

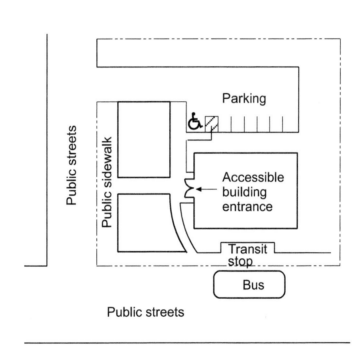

Site arrival points and exterior elements on the site must also be provided with an accessible route to an accessible building entrance. The elements addressed may include public transportation stops, accessible passenger loading zones and accessible parking spaces.

Code Text: *At least one accessible route shall connect each accessible story, mezzanine and occupied roofs in multilevel buildings and facilities.* See the exceptions for specific occupancies with small floor areas, areas without accessible elements, air traffic control towers and two-story buildings with a small occupant load on one story.

Discussion and Commentary: Access must be provided both horizontally and vertically throughout a building. Under most conditions, multilevel facilities will contain an accessible elevator to extend an accessible route to the other levels. Ramps also can be used where the elevation change is not excessive. In some occupancies, an accessible route is not required for levels above or below an accessible level, provided that the aggregate size of the inaccessible levels does not exceed 3,000 square feet. It has been determined that it is not feasible to require elevator service for such small spaces.

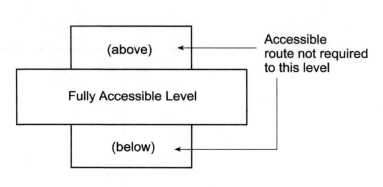

Exception 1:
Accessible route not required to floors above and below if aggregate area ≤ 3,000 sq ft and does not contain offices of health care providers, passenger transportation facilities and airports, or multiple tenant (≥ 5) facilities of Group M. Also not applicable to government buildings and structures with ≥4 dwelling units.

(above)

Fully Accessible Level

(below)

Accessible route not required to this level

Exception 2:
Levels that do not contain accessible elements or other spaces as determined by Section 1108 or 1109 need not be served by an accessible route from an accessible level.

Level without accessible elements, or space not required by Section 1108 or 1109 to be served by accessible route

Accessible Level

Accessible route between levels is not required per Section 1108 or 1109.

Where a multilevel building is provided with an interior circulation path between levels, the required accessible route must also be interior. In such situations, it is inappropriate to use an exterior route, such as a series of ramps, as the only accessible means between floor levels.

Code Text: *In addition to accessible entrances required by Sections 1105.1.1 through 1105.1.8* (parking garage entrances, entrances from tunnels or elevated walkways, restricted entrances, entrances for inmates or detainees, service entrances and entrances to tenant spaces, dwelling units and sleeping units), *at least 60 percent of all public entrances shall be accessible.* See the exceptions for entrances to areas not required to be accessible and loading/service entrances that are not the only tenant space entrance.

Discussion and Commentary: To provide accessibility to all buildings and tenant spaces, a minimum of one accessible entrance is required. Where additional entrances are provided, often for convenience purposes, at least 60 percent of the total number of entrances must be accessible. Elements to be considered at entrances include the slope of exterior surfaces, door hardware and clear floor space for maneuvering clearances.

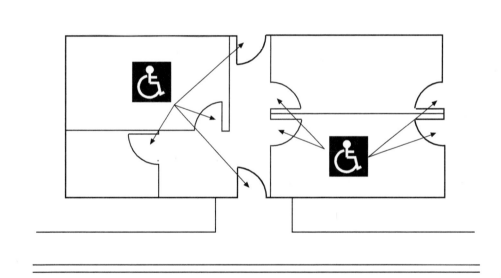

When a building has entrances that normally serve accessible parking facilities, passenger loading zones, public sidewalks and other site elements, then at least one of the entrances serving each of the functions shall comply with the accessible route provisions.

Code Text: *Where parking is provided, accessible parking spaces shall be provided in compliance with Table 1106.2 except as required by Sections 1106.3 (Groups R-2 and R-3), 1106.4, (hospital outpatient facilities) and 1106.5 (rehabilitation facilities). For every six or fraction of six accessible parking spaces, at least one shall be a van-accessible parking space. See the exception for private garages serving Groups R-2 and R-3. Accessible parking spaces shall be located on the shortest accessible route of travel from adjacent parking to an accessible building entrance.*

Discussion and Commentary: The number of required accessible parking spaces is based on the total number of spaces in the lot or garage. In hospital outpatient facilities where it is anticipated that more accessible spaces will be needed, at least one in ten parking spaces must be accessible. All accessible parking spaces shall be located as close as possible to an accessible building entrance to reduce the distance of travel for those individuals with mobility limitations.

Where parking is provided, accessible parking spaces shall be provided in compliance with Table 1106.2.

Exceptions:

1. Where Group R-2, R-3 and R-4 occupancies are required to have accessible dwelling units, 2% of the parking spaces shall be accessible. (Sec. 1106.3)

2. Where parking is provided within or beneath a building, accessible parking spaces shall also be provided within or beneath the building.

3. Where care recipient and visitor parking spaces serve hospital outpatient facilities, 10% of the spaces shall be accessible. (Sec. 1106.4)

4. At rehabilitation facilities and outpatient physical therapy facilities, 20% of care recipient and visitor parking spaces shall be accessible.

TABLE 1106.2
ACCESSIBLE PARKING SPACES

TOTAL PARKING SPACES PROVIDED IN PARKING FACILITIES	REQUIRED MINIMUM NUMBER OF ACCESSIBLE SPACES
1 to 25	1
26 to 50	2
51 to 75	3
76 to 100	4
101 to 150	5
151 to 200	6
201 to 300	7
301 to 400	8
401 to 500	9
501 to 1,000	2% of total
1,001 and over	20, plus one for each 100, or fraction thereof, over 1,000

Every parking facility with at least one accessible parking space must provide for accessible van parking. Based on a percentage of the total number of accessible spaces, the van space or spaces must have a vertical clearance of at least 98 inches and a minimum 8-foot access aisle.

Code Text: *In Group I-1, Condition 1, at least 4 percent, but not less than one, of the dwelling units and sleeping units shall be Accessible units. In Group I-1, Condition 2, at least 10 percent, but not less than one, of the dwelling units and sleeping units shall be Accessible units. In nursing homes of Group I-2 occupancies, at least 50 percent but not less than one of each type of the dwelling units and sleeping units shall be Accessible units. In general-purpose hospitals, psychiatric facilities, detoxification facilities and residential care/ assisted living facilities of Group I-2 occupancies, at least 10 percent, but not less than one, of the dwelling units and sleeping units shall be Accessible units. In hospitals and rehabilitation facilities of Group I-2 occupancies which specialize in treating conditions that affect mobility, or units within either which specialize in treating conditions that affect mobility, 100 percent of the dwelling and sleeping units shall be Accessible units. In Group I-3 occupancies, at least 3 percent of the total number of sleeping units in the facility, but not less than one unit in each classification, shall be Accessible units.*

Discussion and Commentary: In Groups I-1, I-2 and I-3, a percentage of dwelling and sleeping units must be Accessible units as regulated by Section 1102 of ICC A117.1. The percentage of required Accessible units varies based on the anticipated need for such units because of the specifics of the institutional use.

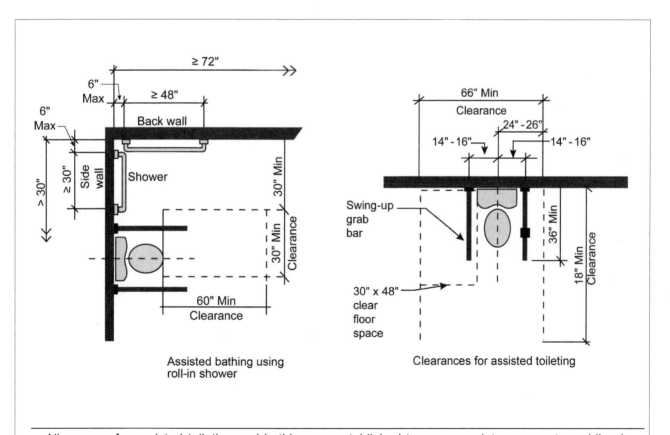

Assisted bathing using roll-in shower

Clearances for assisted toileting

Allowances for assisted toileting and bathing are established to accommodate occupants residing in accessible housing units in Group I-1 and I-2 assisted living facilities, nursing homes and rehabilitation facilities.

Code Text: In Group R-1 occupancies, *Accessible dwelling units and sleeping units shall be provided in accordance with Table 1108.6.1.1. In Group R-2 occupancies* (limited to apartment houses, monasteries and convents) *containing more than 20 dwelling units or sleeping units, at least 2 percent but not less than one of the units shall be a Type A unit. Where there are four or more dwelling units or sleeping units intended to be occupied as a residence in a single structure, every dwelling and sleeping unit intended to be occupied as a residence shall be a Type B unit.* See the general exceptions in Section 1108.7.

Discussion and Commentary: Accessible, Type A and Type B dwelling units and sleeping units are defined in IBC Section 202 and described in Chapter 10 of ICC A117.1. Accessible units are generally regarded as fully accessible. Type A units provide a considerable degree of accessibility, whereas Type B units are only required to have specific accessible elements. A dwelling unit designed and constructed as a Type B unit is intended to comply with the technical requirements for Fair Housing required by federal law.

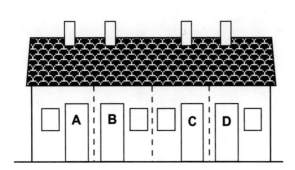

In R-2 and R-3 occupancies where there are ≥ 4 dwelling units in a single structure, every unit shall be a Type B dwelling unit. (Type A units may be substituted for Type B.)

In R-2 occupancies containing > 20 dwelling units, at least 2 percent but not less than 1 shall be a Type A dwelling unit.

The general exceptions of Section 1108.7 selectively permit the required number of Type A units and Type B units to be reduced.

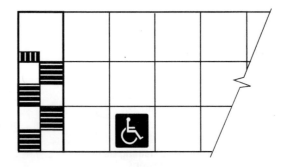

Where Group R-2 and R-3 occupancies contain public or common-use areas, such areas must be accessible if they serve accessible dwelling units. Any recreational facilities serving these occupancies must also must be accessible to a limited degree.

Topic: Assembly Area Seating   **Category:** Accessibility

Reference: IBC 1109.2   **Subject:** Special Occupancies

Code Text: *In rooms and spaces used for assembly purposes with fixed seating, accessible wheelchair spaces complying with ICC A117.1 shall be provided in accordance with Sections 1109.2.2.1 through 1109.2.2.3. Wheelchair spaces shall be provided in accordance with Table 1109.2.2.1. In multilevel assembly seating areas, wheelchair spaces shall be provided on the main floor level and on one of each two additional floor or mezzanine levels. See the two exceptions where all wheelchair spaces may be located on the main level.*

Discussion and Commentary: The unique features of assembly occupancies dictate special accessibility features. In addition to the requirements for wheelchair spaces and assistive listening devices, the code requires accessible seating throughout all dining areas. Specific provisions address fixed seating at booths and tables, as well as at counters.

In dining areas, the total floor area allotted for seating and tables shall be accessible.

Exception: An accessible route to a mezzanine seating area is not required, provided that the mezzanine contains less than 25 percent of the total area and the same services are provided in the accessible area.

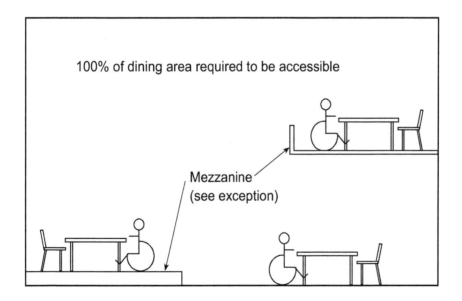

100% of dining area required to be accessible

Mezzanine
(see exception)

Under limited conditions, a dining area may have a mezzanine level that is not served by an accessible route. The mezzanine must be limited in size to 25 percent of the total floor area, and the services provided on the mezzanine must be available on the accessible level.

Code Text: *Each building, room or space used for assembly purposes where audible communications are integral to the use of the space shall have an assistive listening system.* See the exception for spaces, other than courtrooms, where no audio amplification system is installed. *The number and type of receivers shall be provided for assistive listening systems in accordance with Table 1109.2.7.1.* See the exceptions for (1) buildings with multiple assembly areas, and (2) assembly areas where all seats are served by an induction loop system.

Discussion and Commentary: These provisions are intended to accommodate people with a hearing impairment. In these assembly areas, audible communication is often integral to the use and full enjoyment of the space. This requirement offers the possibility for individuals with hearing impairments to attend functions in these facilities without having to give advance notice and without disrupting the event in order to have a portable assistive listening system set up and made ready for use.

International symbol of access for
hearing loss

TABLE 1109.2.7.1
RECEIVERS FOR ASSISTIVE LISTENING SYSTEMS

CAPACITY OF SEATING IN ASSEMBLY AREAS	MINIMUM REQUIRED NUMBER OF RECEIVERS	MINIMUM NUMBER OF RECEIVERS TO BE HEARING-AID COMPATIBLE
50 or less	2	2
51 to 200	2, plus 1 per 25 seats over 50 seats*	2
201 to 500	2, plus 1 per 25 seats over 50 seats*	1 per 4 receivers*
501 to 1,000	20, plus 1 per 33 seats over 500 seats*	1 per 4 receivers*
1,001 to 2,000	35, plus 1 per 50 seats over 1,000 seats*	1 per 4 receivers*
Over 2,000	55, plus 1 per 100 seats over 2,000 seats*	1 per 4 receivers*

Note: * = or fraction thereof

There are four primary types of listening systems available: induction loop, FM, sound field and infrared. Each type of system has certain advantages and disadvantages that should be taken into consideration when choosing the system that is most appropriate for the intended application.

Topic: General Provisions	Category: Accessibility
Reference: IBC 1110	Subject: Features and Facilities

Code Text: *Accessible building features and facilities shall be provided in accordance with Sections 1110.2 through 1110.16.* See the exception for Type A and Type B dwelling and sleeping units.

Discussion and Commentary: Where elements such as sinks, drinking fountains, storage lockers, fitting rooms and check-out aisles are provided, a portion, but not less than one of each type of element, must be accessible. In general, all toilet rooms must be accessible. Within each toilet room, at least one water closet and lavatory must be accessible. When other elements are provided, such as mirrors and towel fixtures, at least one must be accessible. Operating mechanisms intended for occupant operation, such as light switches and convenience outlets, must also be usable by persons with physical disabilities.

In other than Type A and Type B dwelling units, accessible building features and facilities shall be provided as required in Section 1110. This includes:

- Toilet and bathing facilities

- Sinks

- Kitchens and kitchenettes

- Drinking fountains

- Bottle-filling stations

- Saunas and steam rooms

- Elevators

- Lifts

- Storage

- Detectable warnings

- Seating at tables, counters and work surfaces

- Service facilities

- Controls, operating mechanisms and hardware

- Fuel-dispensing systems

- Gaming machines and gaming tables

Certain elements addressed in ICC A117.1, including telephones and automatic teller machines, have not been included in the scoping provisions of Chapter 11. However, scoping requirements for such features are set forth in Appendix E of the IBC.

Code Text: *Each toilet room and bathing room shall be accessible. Where a floor level is not required to be connected by an accessible route, the only toilet rooms or bathing rooms provided within the facility shall not be located on the inaccessible floor. Except as provided for in Sections 1110.2.4 through 1110.2.5, at least one of each type of fixture, element, control or dispenser in each accessible toilet room and bathing room shall be accessible.* See the exceptions for toilet rooms and bathing rooms (1) accessed through a private office and intended for use by a single occupant, (2) that serve a dwelling unit or sleeping unit not required to be accessible, (3) clustered in a single location, (4) part of critical care or intensive care patient sleeping rooms, (5) designed for bariatrics patients, and (6) primarily for children's use. An additional exception provides that where only one urinal is provided in a toilet room or bathing facility, it need not be accessible. Two exceptions also address allowances for water closets designed for assisted toileting and showers designed for assisted bathing.

Discussion and Commentary: As a general rule, all toilet rooms and bathing facilities must provide for accessibility. There are limited conditions under which some facilities need not be made accessible.

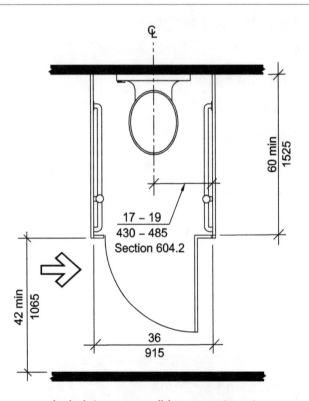

Ambulatory accessible compartment

In those toilet rooms and bathing facilities where water closet compartments are provided, a minimum of 5 percent of the compartments must be wheelchair-accessible. If the total number of water closet compartments and urinals provided is six or more, a minimum of 5 percent of compartments must also be ambulatory-accessible water closet compartments.

Code Text: *In assembly and mercantile occupancies, an accessible family or assisted-use toilet room shall be provided where an aggregate of six or more male and female water closets is required. In recreational facilities where separate-sex bathing rooms are provided, an accessible family or assisted-use bathing room shall be provided.* See the exception for single-fixture bathing rooms. *Fixtures located within family or assisted-use toilet and bathing rooms shall be included in determining the number of fixtures provided in an occupancy.*

Discussion and Commentary: The primary issue relative to family or assisted-use toilet/bathing facilities is that some people with disabilities require assistance to utilize them. If the attendant is of the opposite sex, a facility that can accommodate both persons is required. The provisions are applicable only to those types of transient uses where it is expected such facilities are frequently required.

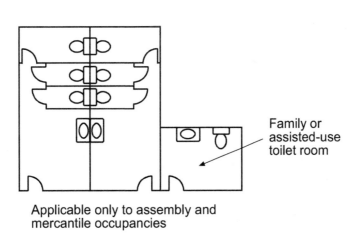

Family or
assisted-use
toilet room

Applicable only to assembly and
mercantile occupancies

Family or assisted-use toilet rooms shall include only one water closet and one lavatory. A urinal is also permitted but not required. Doors to family or assisted-use toilet and bathing rooms must be securable from within the room.

Code Text: *Recreational facilities shall be provided with accessible features in accordance with Sections 1111.2 through 1111.4.*

Discussion and Commentary: Some degree of accessibility and usability is required for a wide variety of recreational facilities. Although full accessibility is typically not required, some degree of access is mandated in order to provide recreational opportunities to a wide spectrum of individuals. Facilities that are specifically addressed include (1) team or player seating; (2) bowling lanes; (3) court sports; (4) raised boxing or wrestling rings; (5) raised refereeing, judging and scoring areas; (6) animal containment areas; (7) amusement rides; (8) recreational boating facilities; (9) exercise machines and equipment; (10) fishing piers and platforms; (11) miniature golf facilities; (12) play areas; (13) swimming pools, wading pools, hot tubs and spas; and (14) shooting facilities with firing positions.

Specific provisions are established for recreational facilities that serve residential Group R-2, R-3 and R-4 occupancies. The required number of accessible facilities varies based upon the type of accessible units provided (Accessible, Type A, Type B), as well as the number of residential buildings on the site.

| **Topic:** Signs | **Category:** Accessibility |
| **Reference:** IBC 1112 | **Subject:** Signage |

Code Text: *Required accessible elements shall be identified by the* International Symbol of Accessibility *at the following locations: (1) accessible parking spaces required by Section 1106.2 except where the total number of parking spaces provided is four or less; (2) accessible parking spaces required by Section 1106.3 (not required where dwelling and sleeping units have assigned spaces); (3) accessible passenger loading zones; (4) accessible toilet or bathing rooms where not all toilet or bathing rooms are accessible; (5) accessible entrances where not all entrances are accessible; (6) accessible check-out aisles where not all aisles are accessible; (7) accessible dressing, fitting, and locker rooms where not all such rooms are accessible; (8) accessible areas of refuge in accordance with Section 1009.9; (9) exterior areas for assisted rescue in accordance with Section 1110.10 and (10) in recreational facilities, lockers that are required to be accessible.*

Discussion and Commentary: Those site or building elements that need to be identified as accessible for convenience, clarification or life safety purposes are specified in the code. Special signage is also required for assistive listening capabilities and at every exit stairway door.

International Symbol of Accessibility

Where building entrances are not accessible, directional signage must be installed indicating the travel route to the nearest accessible entrance. Signs must also be provided at inaccessible public toilets directing occupants to the nearest accessible toilet facilities.

Study Session 13

IBC Chapter 11

1. For the purpose of accessibility, which of the following areas in a bank is considered an employee work area?

    a. vault

    b. toilet room

    c. corridor

    d. break room

    Reference_____

2. A continuous, unobstructed path complying with the provisions of *IBC Chapter 11* is considered a(n) _____ .

    a. accessible route

    b. accessible means of egress

    c. circulation path

    d. public entrance

    Reference_____

3. Raised or lowered areas in places of religious worship are not required to be accessible where less than _____ square feet, where a minimum of _____ inches above or below the finished floor, and where used primarily for the performance of religious ceremonies.

    a. 100, 4

    b. 200, 6

    c. 300, 7

    d. 500, 12

    Reference_____

4. When occupied as the residence for the proprietor, Group R-1 occupancies containing a maximum of _____ sleeping units for rent or hire are not required to comply with Chapter 11.

    a. 5

    b. 6

    c. 10

    d. 15

    Reference_____

5. In other than an Accessible, Type A or Type B dwelling unit, where only one accessible route is provided, the route is permitted to pass through a _____ .

    a. kitchen   b. break room

    c. storage room   d. restroom

    Reference_____

6. Where four public entrances are provided to a building, a minimum of _____ entrance(s) shall be accessible.

    a. one   b. two

    c. three   d. four

    Reference_____

7. Where a 1,625-space parking garage serves a covered mall building, a minimum of _____ accessible parking spaces must be provided.

    a. 20   b. 27

    c. 33   d. 42

    Reference_____

8. Where a 282-space parking lot serves a cluster of Group R-2 apartment buildings required to have Type A dwelling units, a minimum of _____ accessible parking spaces must be provided.

    a. 3   b. 6

    c. 7   d. 14

    Reference_____

9. A minimum of _____ van-accessible parking space(s) shall be provided for a parking facility containing 16 accessible parking spaces.

    a. one   b. two

    c. three   d. six

    Reference_____

10. Where stadiums, arenas and grandstands have a minimum of _____ fixed seats and provide audible public announcements, pre-recorded or real-time captions of those audible public announcements shall be provided.

    a. 3,000   b. 5,000

    c. 10,000   d. 15,000

Reference_____

11. Where cubicles are provided in the visiting area of a judicial facility, a minimum of _____ of the cubicles shall be accessible.

    a. 5 percent   b. 10 percent

    c. 25 percent   d. 50 percent

Reference_____

12. At least one ambulatory-accessible water closet compartment is required in a toilet room where the total number of water closet compartments and urinals provided in the room is a minimum of _____ fixtures.

    a. 4   b. 6

    c. 10   d. 12

Reference_____

13. In a Group R-2 fraternity house having a minimum of _____ sleeping units, every unit intended to be occupied as a residence shall be a Type B unit unless a reduction is permitted.

    a. 4   b. 10

    c. 16   d. 20

Reference_____

14. In a 250-seat motion picture theater, a minimum of _____ receivers shall be provided for the assistive listening system.

    a. 2   b. 6

    c. 10   d. 14

Reference_____

15. In a Group I-1, Condition 2 occupancy, a minimum of _____ percent of the dwelling units and sleeping units shall be Accessible units.

    a. 4   b. 10

    c. 20   d. 50

Reference_____

16. In a 185-room Group R-1 hotel, a minimum of _____ sleeping units shall be Accessible units.

    a. two   b. four

    c. seven   d. eight

Reference_____

17. A minimum of _____ Accessible units in a 410-room hotel shall be provided with bathing facilities other than roll-in showers.

    a. 4   b. 9

    c. 12   d. 13

Reference_____

18. A Group R-2 apartment building having 16 dwelling units shall be provided with a minimum of _____ Type A dwelling units.

    a. zero (no Type A units are required)

    b. one

    c. two

    d. four

Reference_____

19. A self-storage facility containing 160 storage spaces shall be provided with a minimum of _____ accessible individual self-storage spaces.

    a. one   b. two

    c. five   d. eight

Reference_____

20. Based on the number of required water closets, an accessible family or assisted-use toilet room may be required in which of the following occupancies?

    a. assembly and educational   b. assembly and mercantile

    c. business and mercantile   d. factory and storage

Reference_____

21. The maximum distance of the accessible route from any separate-sex toilet room to a family or assisted-use toilet room shall be _____.

    a. 200 feet   b. 300 feet

    c. 500 feet   d. unlimited

Reference_____

22. In a large manufacturing plant, a minimum of how many of the 24 drinking fountains shall be accessible to standing persons?

    a. 0   b. 4

    c. 12   d. 24

Reference_____

23. A minimum of _____ percent of seating at fixed tables in an accessible space shall be accessible.

    a. 5   b. 10

    c. 20   d. 50

Reference_____

24. A 4,000-square-foot retail sales room with six check-out aisles requires a minimum of _____ accessible check-out aisle(s).

    a. one   b. two

    c. three   d. four

Reference_____

25. An *International Symbol of Accessibility* sign is not required at an accessible parking space in parking facilities having a maximum of _____ total parking spaces.

    a.   one, the sign is always required

    b.   two

    c.   four

    d.   five

Reference_____

26. Permanently defined common use circulation paths that are located within an employee work area are not required to be regulated as accessible routes, provided the work area is less than _____ square feet in floor area.

    a.   300   b.   500

    c.   1,000   d.   1,500

Reference_____

27. A press box serving bleachers is not required to be served by an accessible route where it is a maximum of _____ square feet in floor area and has its points of entry at only one level.

    a.   500   b.   1,000

    c.   1,500   d.   3,000

Reference_____

28. What is the minimum number of accessible parking spaces required to be provided in a 40-space parking lot serving an outpatient physical therapy facility?

    a.   one   b.   two

    c.   four   d.   eight

Reference_____

29. Where a dining surface is provided at a counter for the consumption of food or drink, a minimum of _____ seating and standing space(s) shall be accessible.

    a.   zero   b.   one

    c.   two   d.   four

Reference_____

30. At which of the following locations is directional signage not required to indicate the route to the nearest like accessible element?

    a.   inaccessible building entrances

    b.   elevators not serving an accessible route

    c.   inaccessible dressing rooms

    d.   inaccessible public toilet facilities

Reference_____

31. Where passenger loading zones are provided, at least one accessible passenger loading zone is required in every continuous _____ linear feet maximum of loading zone space.

    a.   100   b.   150

    c.   200   d.   300

Reference _____

32. All required wheelchair spaces are permitted to be located on the main level in multi-level assembly spaces used for religious worship where the mezzanine level contains a maximum of _____ percent of the total seating capacity.

    a.   10   b.   20

    c.   25   d. $33^1/_3$

Reference _____

33. Where multiple single-user toilet rooms are clustered at a single location, a minimum of _____ percent, but not less than one room, shall be accessible.

    a.   5   b.   10

    c.   25   d.   50

Reference _____

34. Where a total of eight accessible drinking fountains are provided, _____ drinking fountain(s) shall comply with the requirements for persons who use a wheelchair.

    a.   one   b.   two

    c.   four   d.   five

Reference _____

35. In a 40-lane bowling facility, an accessible route shall be provided to a minimum of _____ bowling lane(s).

    a. one   b. two

    c. four   d. ten

Reference _____

36. At least one public entrance to a Group M occupancy shall be either a full power-operated door or a low-energy power-operated door unless the maximum occupant load is _____.

    a. 100   b. 300

    c. 500   d. 1,000

Reference _____

37. Where electrical vehicle charging stations are provided on a site, a minimum of _____ percent, but not less than one, of each type of charging system shall be accessible.

    a. 5   b. 10

    c. 20   d. 25

Reference _____

38. In Group I-2 nursing homes, roll-in showers are not required to meet ICC A117.1 in a maximum of _____ percent of the Accessible units where assisted bathing facilities are provided.

    a. 10   b. 20

    c. 50   d. 90

Reference _____

39. Standard roll-in-type shower compartments designed for assisted bathing shall have minimum inside clear dimensions of _____ inches in width and _____ inches in depth.

    a. 48, 30   b. 48, 36

    c. 60, 30   d. 60, 36

Reference _____

40. At miniature golf courses, a minimum of _____ percent of the holes are required to be accessible.

      a.   0 (no holes are required to be accessible)

      b. $33^{1}/_{3}$

      c.   50

      d.   100

Reference _____

2021 IBC Chapter 4

Special Detailed Requirements Based on Use and Occupancy

OBJECTIVE: To obtain an understanding of special building types, features and uses, including covered mall and open mall buildings, high-rise buildings, atriums, underground buildings, storm shelters, motor-vehicle-related occupancies, stages and platforms, concealed combustible storage areas, hazardous materials, dwelling unit and sleeping unit separations, live/work units, ambulatory care facilities, and Group I-2, I-3 and H occupancies.

REFERENCE: Chapter 4, 2021 *International Building Code*

KEY POINTS:
- How are covered mall and open mall buildings, anchor buildings and food courts defined?
- In a covered mall building, which special conditions relate to the automatic sprinkler system, standpipe system and smoke-control system?
- How is the occupant load determined for a covered mall building?
- Which specific provisions relate to covered mall and open mall buildings in determining the number and arrangement of means of egress?
- What qualifies a structure as a high-rise building?
- In a high-rise building, how are the type-of-construction provisions modified?
- What are the specific provisions relating to smoke detection, fire alarms and communication systems in high-rise buildings?
- What additional provisions are applicable to high-rise buildings more than 420 feet in height?
- What are the various required elements in a fire command center?
- In a high-rise structure, which types of standby power, light and emergency systems are required?
- What defines an atrium? What are the limits of an atrium's use? What fire protection features must be provided in a building containing an atrium?
- How must adjacent spaces be separated from an atrium?
- What is the maximum travel distance when a required exit path enters the atrium space?
- What are the conditions that create an underground building?
- In an underground building, when is compartmentalization required?

- What is the maximum floor area permitted for a private garage?

- How must exterior openings be sized and distributed for a garage to qualify as open?

- How do the provisions differ for an open parking garage in either a single-use or multiple-occupancy building?

- What are the benefits of an open parking garage as opposed to an enclosed garage?

- Which special criteria must be applied to motor vehicle service stations? Repair garages?

- How does a platform differ from a stage?

- What are the minimum construction requirements for stages and platforms?

- What is a technical production area? What special provisions apply to such areas?

- When must a stage area be provided with a means for emergency ventilation?

- How shall the proscenium opening between a stage and an auditorium be protected?

- What is a special amusement area? What special provisions apply to such areas?

- How are airport traffic control towers regulated?

- What specific requirements are applicable to aircraft hangars? What type of fire suppression is required? What unique requirements apply to residential aircraft hangars? Aircraft paint hangars?

- What type of fire separation is required for combustible storage in concealed spaces?

- When are smoke compartments required in Group I-2 occupancies?

- Which special considerations are given to detention facilities because of their unique characteristics?

- How are Group I-3 occupancies classified according to their occupancy condition?

- What is the function of a control area? How many control areas are permitted in a building?

- How must control areas be separated from other portions of the building?

- At what distance must Group H occupancies be set back from lot lines?

- Where the spraying of flammable finishes occurs, what special conditions must be met?

- What type of use is regulated as a live/work unit? What are its limitations? What special provisions are applicable?

- How must dwelling units or sleeping units be separated from other such units in Group I-1, R-1, R-2 and R-3 occupancies?

- Under what conditions are smoke barriers required in ambulatory care facilities? Automatic sprinkler system protection? Fire alarm system protection?

- What referenced standard is applicable to storm shelters?

- In which occupancies are children's play structures regulated? What special requirements are applicable?

- What types of building uses are required to be provided with a storm shelter? What technical requirements are to be used in the design and construction?

- What referenced standard is required to be applied to hyperbaric facilities?

- How are buildings to be regulated in which materials that produce combustible dusts are stored or used?

- What are the two types of medical gas rooms? How do the construction requirements differ between the room types?

- What is a laboratory suite in a college or university building? How is a laboratory suite to be classified for occupancy purposes?

Code Text: *A covered mall building* (or open mall building) *and attached anchor buildings and parking garages shall be surrounded on all sides by a permanent open space or not less than 60 feet (18 288 mm). The building area of any covered mall or open mall building shall not be limited provided the covered mall or open mall building does not exceed three floor levels at any point nor three stories above grade plane, and is of Type I, II, III or IV construction.* See the allowance for anchor buildings. *Fire-resistance-rated separation is not required between tenant spaces and the mall.*

Discussion and Commentary: A covered mall building is defined as a single building enclosing a number of tenants and occupants, such as retail stores, drinking and dining establishments, entertainment and amusement facilities, passenger transportation terminals, offices, and other similar uses wherein two or more tenants have a main entrance into one or more malls. Because of its character, a covered mall building is uniquely regulated for fire protection and egress. An open mall building, where the pedestrian ways are unroofed, is regulated in a similar manner.

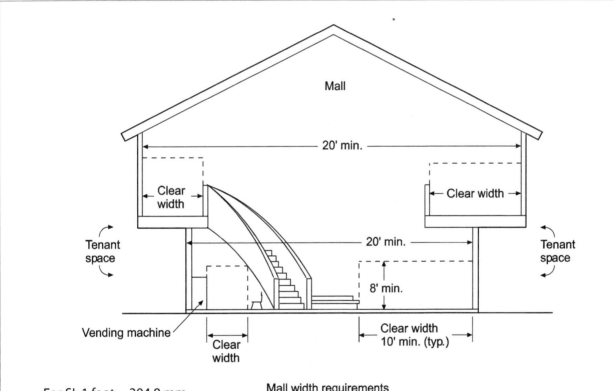

For SI: 1 foot = 304.8 mm

Mall width requirements

The provisions for covered mall and open mall buildings and their associated anchor buildings and parking structures allow for an alternative method of design for structures that have these specific features. Where compliant with the provisions of Section 402, similar requirements found elsewhere in the code can be superseded.

Code Text: A high-rise building *is a building with an occupied floor located more than 75 feet (22 860 mm) above the lowest level of fire department vehicle access.* See the five exceptions where high-rise provisions are not applicable. *Buildings and structures shall be equipped throughout with an automatic sprinkler system in accordance with Section 903.3.1.1 and a secondary water supply where required by Section 403.3.3.*

Discussion and Commentary: A high-rise building is characterized by several features: (1) it is impractical to completely evacuate the building in a timely manner, (2) prompt rescue and fire fighting operations are difficult, (3) the occupant load is relatively high and (4) a potential exists for stack effect. The special provisions of Section 403 are designed to address these concerns. Additional provisions are applicable for those buildings more than 420 feet in height, sometimes referred to as super high-rises. Prohibited reductions in fire-resistance rating, additional criteria for structural integrity and bond strength of SFRM, and an additional required exit stairway are a few of the extra requirements for these super high-rise buildings.

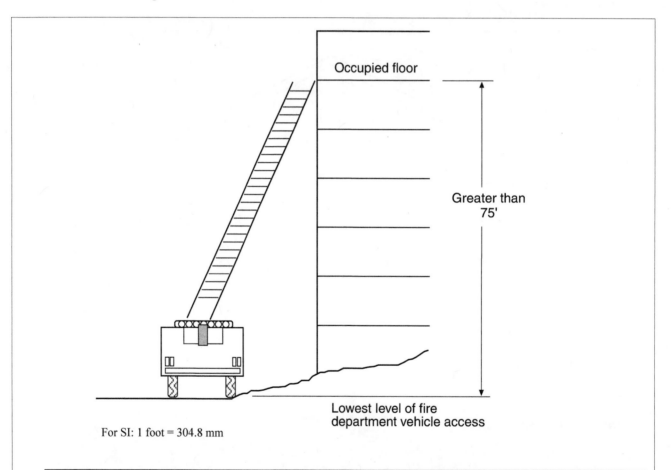

Occupied floor

Greater than 75'

Lowest level of fire department vehicle access

For SI: 1 foot = 304.8 mm

Additional provisions for a high-rise building include the installation of a smoke detection system, emergency voice/alarm and fire department communications systems, a fire command center for use by fire department personnel, smokeproof exit stairway enclosures, luminous egress path markings, and standby power, light and emergency systems.

Code Text: *An atrium is a vertical space that is closed at the top, connecting two or more stories in Group I-2 and I-3 occupancies or three or more stories in all other occupancies. An approved automatic sprinkler system shall be installed throughout the entire building. A smoke-control system shall be installed in accordance with Section 909. Atrium spaces shall be separated from adjacent spaces by a 1-hour fire barrier.* See the exceptions to the sprinkler system, smoke-control system and fire barrier separation requirements.

Discussion and Commentary: The concept of developing atriums is to maintain equivalence in safety to that of an open court, as well as to provide protection of a shaft enclosure. The provisions for atriums are only applicable where Section 712.1.7 is utilized to address vertical openings. Where another method established in Section 712.1 is used, such as Section 712.1.3 applicable to escalator openings, the atrium provisions of Section 404 are not to be applied.

Sprinkler system throughout—prevents spread of fire.

Smoke-control system—keeps building and atrium clear of smoke so that safe exiting may be accomplished through the atrium.

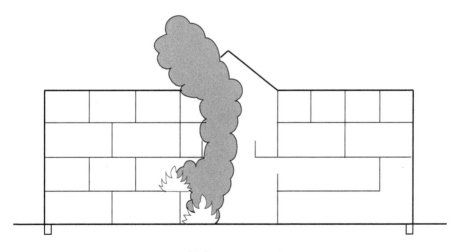

Atrium concept

Atriums are permitted based on alternative methods of protecting the building from vertical spread of fire, smoke and toxic gases. Additional protection is provided through (1) limited travel distance, (2) standby power, (3) smoke detection and (4) interior finish regulation.

Code Text: *The provisions of Sections 405.2 through 405.9 apply to building spaces having a floor level used for human occupancy more than 30 feet (9144 mm) below the finished floor of the lowest level of exit discharge.* See the six exceptions for uses not regulated as underground buildings. *The underground portion of the building shall be of Type I construction. The highest level of exit discharge serving the underground portions of the building and all levels below shall be equipped with an automatic sprinkler system installed in accordance with Section 903.3.1.1.*

Discussion and Commentary: An underground building is highly regulated for many of the same reasons as is a high-rise building. In the case of a structure substantially below ground level, fire department access and fire-fighting operations are often even more difficult. Therefore, the code mandates the installation of multiple fire protection systems, including a smoke-control system.

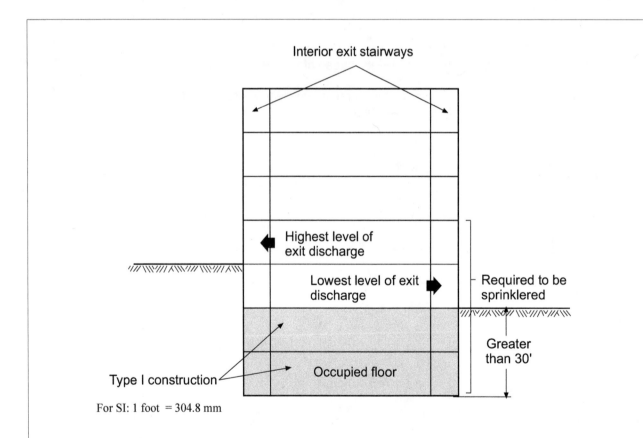

Interior exit stairways

Highest level of exit discharge

Lowest level of exit discharge

Required to be sprinklered

Greater than 30'

Type I construction

Occupied floor

For SI: 1 foot = 304.8 mm

Additional protection must be provided where an underground building has a floor level more than 60 feet below the finished floor of the lowest level of exit discharge. The required creation of multiple compartments assists in both occupant egress and fire department operations.

Code Text: *All motor-vehicle-related occupancies shall comply with Section 406.2. Private garages and carports shall also comply with Section 406.3. Open public parking garages shall also comply with Sections 406.4 and 406.5. Enclosed public parking garages shall also comply with Sections 406.4 and 406.6. Motor fuel-dispensing facilities shall also comply with Section 406.7. Repair garages shall also comply with Section 406.8.*

Discussion and Commentary: Where motor vehicles are located within a structure, varying degrees of hazard are involved. In a small, private garage or carport, the hazard is relatively low. A moderate level of hazard exists in open parking garages, increasing where the parking garage is enclosed. In structures where vehicles are being fueled or repaired, a relatively high hazard exists. Specific provisions of the IBC address each type of motor-vehicle-related use.

Exterior walls must have uniformly distributed openings on two or more sides.

Interior wall and column lines shall be at least 20 percent open (area) with uniformly distributed openings.

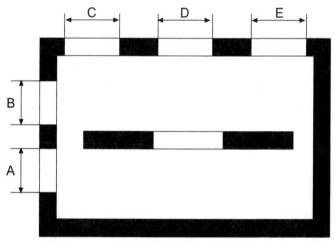

General case

1. Area: A + B + C + D + E ≥ 20% total perimeter area of each tier
2. Length: A + B + C + D + E ≥ 40% total perimeter area of each tier

Open parking garages

Private garages classified as Group U occupancies are limited to 1,000 square feet in floor area. However, such structures are permitted to be increased in floor area to that allowed by Section 506 provided the garages are separated from each other by minimum 1-hour fire barriers.

Code Text: *Smoke barriers shall be provided to subdivide every story used by persons receiving care, treatment or sleeping and to divide other stories with an occupant load of 50 or more persons, into no fewer than two smoke compartments. Stories shall be divided into smoke compartments with an area of not more than 22,500 square feet (2092 m²) in Group I-2 occupancies.* See two exceptions where the maximum smoke compartment size can be extended to 40,000 square feet. *The distance of travel from any point in a smoke compartment to a smoke barrier door shall be not greater than 200 feet (60 960 mm).*

Discussion and Commentary: Hospitals, nursing homes and similar uses must have unique life-safety characteristics due to the immobility or limited mobility of most of the care recipients. By providing multiple refuge areas on each story of the building, occupants can be moved horizontally into an adjoining smoke compartment that provides protection from adjacent areas. In multistory buildings, smoke compartments are further enclosed through the use of horizontal assemblies that must be designed to resist the movement of smoke.

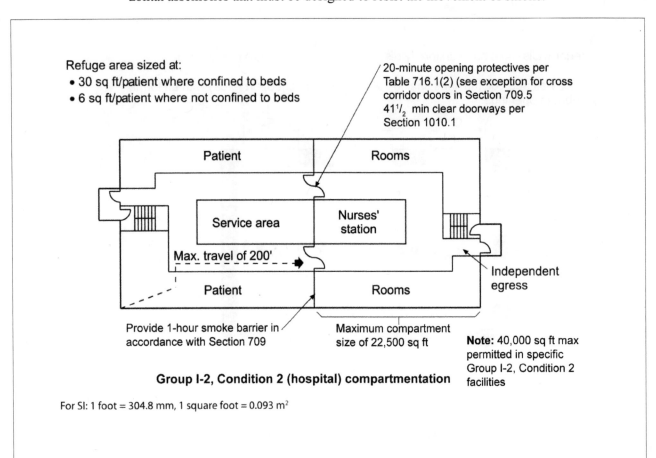

Refuge area sized at:
- 30 sq ft/patient where confined to beds
- 6 sq ft/patient where not confined to beds

20-minute opening protectives per Table 716.1(2) (see exception for cross corridor doors in Section 709.5 41½ min clear doorways per Section 1010.1

Patient Rooms

Service area

Nurses' station

Max. travel of 200'

Independent egress

Patient Rooms

Provide 1-hour smoke barrier in accordance with Section 709

Maximum compartment size of 22,500 sq ft

Note: 40,000 sq ft max permitted in specific Group I-2, Condition 2 facilities

Group I-2, Condition 2 (hospital) compartmentation

For SI: 1 foot = 304.8 mm, 1 square foot = 0.093 m²

An automatic sprinkler system is required throughout all smoke compartments containing sleeping rooms. To provide for a more immediate response, the use of approved quick-response or residential sprinklers is mandated throughout the smoke compartments containing care recipient sleeping units.

Code Text: In Group I-3 occupancies, *egress doors are permitted to be locked in accordance with the applicable use condition. Doors from a refuge area to the outside are permitted to be locked with a key in lieu of locking methods described in Section 408.4.1 (remote release). The keys to unlock the exterior doors shall be available at all times and the locks shall be operable from both sides of the door. Remote release of locks on doors in a means of egress shall be provided with reliable means of operation, remote from the resident living areas, to release locks on all required doors.*

Discussion and Commentary: The need for restraint or security in specific types of uses such as jails, prisons and detention centers makes it necessary to install locking devices that are usually unacceptable for a means of egress. The code recognizes such a need and provides alternative design methods to balance the desire for both safety and security.

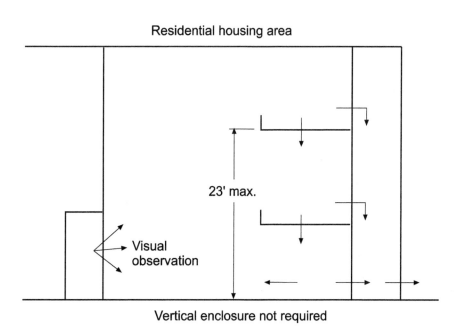

Residential housing area

23' max.

Visual observation

Vertical enclosure not required

For SI: 1 foot = 304.8 mm

It is often important to ensure that several resident detention areas can be observed from a single location. The code permits the design of a vertical arrangement where several tiers of resident housing areas can be open to each other and to the supervisory area.

Code Text: A stage is *a space within a building utilized for entertainment or presentations, which includes overhead hanging curtains, drops, scenery or stage effects other than lighting or sound. Stages shall be constructed of materials as required for floors for the type of construction of the building in which such stages are located.* See the three exceptions. *Where the stage height is greater than 50 feet (15 240 mm), all portions of the stage shall be completely separated from the seating area by a proscenium wall with not less than a 2-hour fire-resistance rating extending continuously from the foundation to the roof.*

Discussion and Commentary: Given the increased potential for fire hazards in an assembly occupancy with a stage, such a use is regulated for certain elements. The stage must be separated from accessory spaces by fire barriers; ventilation of the stage must be accomplished through smoke control or roof vents; and the proscenium opening must be protected with a curtain of approved materials or an approved water curtain.

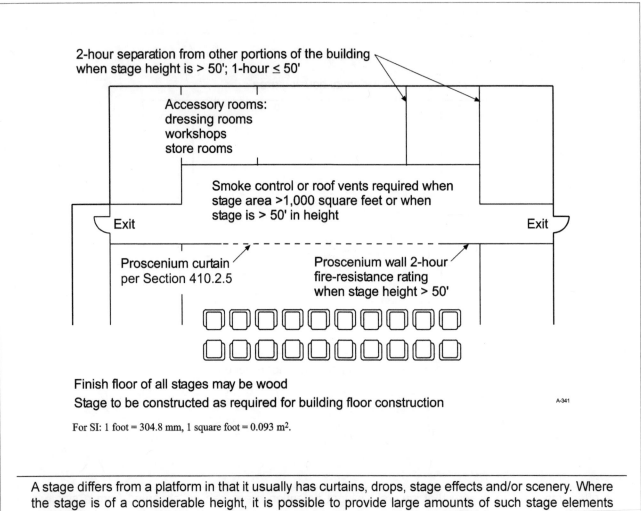

2-hour separation from other portions of the building when stage height is > 50'; 1-hour ≤ 50'

Accessory rooms:
dressing rooms
workshops
store rooms

Smoke control or roof vents required when stage area >1,000 square feet or when stage is > 50' in height

Exit

Exit

Proscenium curtain per Section 410.2.5

Proscenium wall 2-hour fire-resistance rating when stage height > 50'

Finish floor of all stages may be wood

Stage to be constructed as required for building floor construction

A-341

For SI: 1 foot = 304.8 mm, 1 square foot = 0.093 m².

A stage differs from a platform in that it usually has curtains, drops, stage effects and/or scenery. Where the stage is of a considerable height, it is possible to provide large amounts of such stage elements overhead and out of sight. This condition creates the potential for a high fire load.

Code Text: A platform is *a raised area within a building used for worship, the presentation of music, plays or other entertainment; the head table for special guests; the raised area for lecturers and speakers; boxing and wresting rings; theater-in-the-round stages; and similar purposes wherein, other than horizontal sliding curtains, there are no overhead hanging curtains, drops, scenery or stage effects other than lighting and sound. Permanent platforms shall be constructed of materials as required for the type of construction of the building in which the permanent platform is located.* See allowances for use of fire-retardant-treated wood in Types I, II or IV construction.

Discussion and Commentary: Few requirements are placed on platforms. However, a minimum 1-hour fire-resistant platform floor construction is required when the area below the platform is used for storage or a similar purpose, because of concern about combustibles being stored within a concealed space below a raised area.

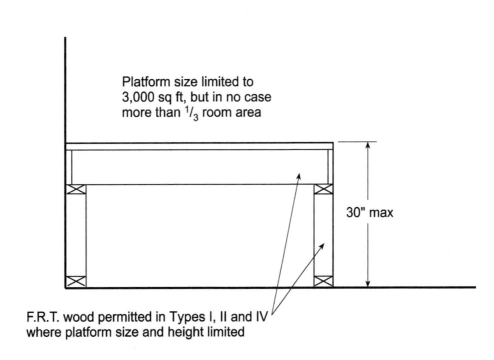

Platform size limited to 3,000 sq ft, but in no case more than $\frac{1}{3}$ room area

30" max

F.R.T. wood permitted in Types I, II and IV where platform size and height limited

For SI: 1 inch = 25.4 mm, 1 square foot = 0.093 m²

Temporary platforms are those platforms used within an area for a period not to exceed 30 days. They may be constructed of any materials; however, the space between the floor and the platform cannot be used for any purpose other than wiring or plumbing for platform equipment.

Code Text: A special amusement area *is any temporary or permanent building or portion thereof that is occupied for amusement, entertainment or educational purposes and is arranged in a manner that: (1) makes the means of egress path not readily apparent due to visual or audio distractions, (2) intentionally confounds identification of the means of egress path, or (3) otherwise makes the means of egress path not readily available because of the nature of the attraction or mode of conveyance through the building or structure.*

Discussion and Commentary: In most cases, an amusement building will be classified as a Group A occupancy. The hazards associated with such a unique use are addressed through provisions for the detection of fire, the illumination of the exit path, the presence of an alarm and emergency voice/alarm communications system and the sprinklering of the structure. Sprinklers are not required for small temporary buildings with limited exit access travel distance.

Rapid detection and notification of a fire condition, as well as the discernment of the exit path, are critical in an amusement building. Actuation of either the sprinkler system or the fire detection system shall automatically activate the approved egress directional markings.

Topic: Aircraft Hangars

Category: Detailed Use Requirements

Reference: IBC 412.3

Subject: Aircraft-Related Occupancies

Code Text: Aircraft hangar *exterior walls located less than 30 feet (9144 mm) from lot lines or a public way shall have a fire-resistance rating not less than 2 hours. Heating equipment shall be placed in another room separated by 2-hour fire barriers, or horizontal assemblies, or both. Aircraft hangars shall be provided with a fire suppression system designed in accordance with NFPA 409, based upon the classification for the hangar given in Table 412.3.6.*

Discussion and Commentary: Although most commercial aircraft hangars will not be limited in height (Section 504.1) or in area (Section 507) based on the presence of an automatic sprinkler system, they must be regulated in regards to exterior-wall fire-resistance ratings, basement limitations, floor surfaces, heating equipment separation and finishing restrictions. All of these provisions serve to abate the hazards associated with large aircraft and their integral fuel tanks to acceptable fire safety levels.

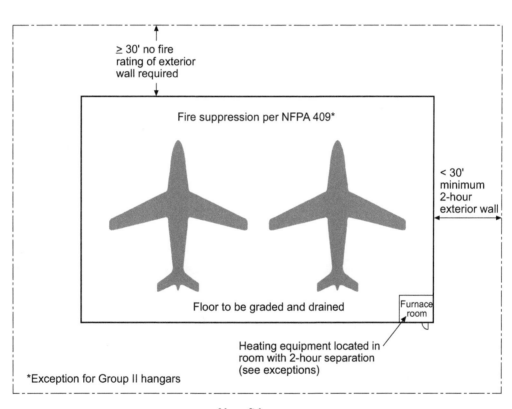

Aircraft hangars

Table 412.3.6 provides the fire suppression requirements for aircraft hangars based upon the fire area size and construction type. Maximum single fire areas are to be separated by minimum 2-hour fire walls.

Code Text: *Attic, under-floor and concealed spaces used for storage of combustible materials shall be protected on the storage side as required for 1-hour fire-resistant-rated construction. Openings shall be protected by assemblies that are self-closing and are of noncombustible construction or solid wood core not less than 1³/₄ inch (45 mm) in thickness. See the exceptions for (1) areas protected by an automatic sprinkler system, and (2) Group R-3 and U occupancies.*

Discussion and Commentary: Those areas in a building that tend to be unoccupied present a potential fire hazard where combustible goods are being stored. The presence of a considerable fire load, coupled with the probable delay in recognition of the fire, makes it necessary to provide some degree of protection. A sprinkler system or a fire-resistant separation are considered acceptable methods to address any potential hazards.

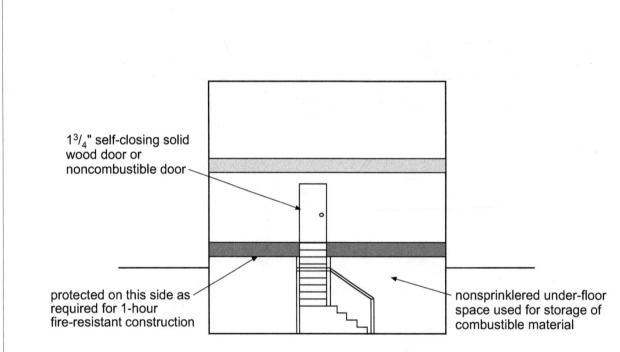

1³/₄" self-closing solid wood door or noncombustible door

protected on this side as required for 1-hour fire-resistant construction

nonsprinklered under-floor space used for storage of combustible material

For SI: 1 inch = 25.4 mm.

The code does not mandate a full 1-hour fire-resistance-rated assembly to isolate the combustible storage area from the unoccupied space. Because the hazard presumably exists only on the inside of the storage space, that is the only side where the protection is required.

Topic: Control Areas

Reference: IBC 414.2.1, 202

Category: Detailed Use Requirements

Subject: Hazardous Materials

Code Text: Control areas are *spaces within a building where quantities of hazardous materials not exceeding the maximum allowable quantities per control area are stored, dispensed, used or handled. Control areas shall be separated from each other by fire barriers constructed in accordance with Section 707 or horizontal assemblies constructed in accordance with Section 711, or both.*

Discussion and Commentary: The use of control areas provides an alternative method for the use and storage of hazardous materials without classifying the building or structure as a high-hazard (Group H) occupancy. This concept is based on regulating the allowable quantities of hazardous materials per control area rather than per building area by giving credit for further compartmentation through the use of fire-resistance-rated fire barrier walls and horizontal assemblies.

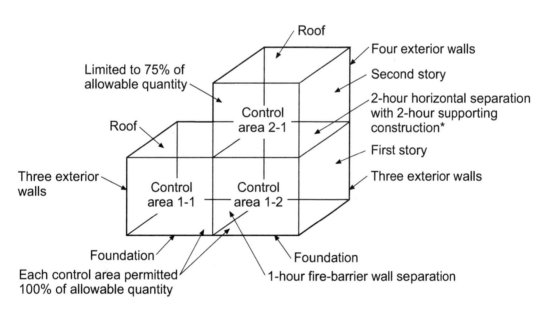

*Exception allows for 1-hour in fully sprinklered Type IIA, IIIA and VA buildings no more than three stories in height.

Multistory control areas

The maximum quantities of hazardous materials within a given control area cannot exceed the quantities for a given material listed in either Table 307.1(1) for physical hazards and Table 307.1(2) for health hazards, as modified by Table 414.2.2 for location within the building.

Topic: Control Areas
Reference: IBC 414.2.2–414.2.4

Category: Detailed Use Requirements
Subject: Hazardous Materials

Code Text: *The percentage of maximum allowable quantities of hazardous materials per control area permitted at each floor level within a building shall be in accordance with Table 414.2.2. The maximum number of control areas within a building shall be in accordance with Table 414.2.2. The required fire-resistance rating for fire barriers shall be in accordance with Table 414.2.2. The floor assembly of the control area and the construction supporting the floor of the control area shall have a fire-resistance rating of not less than 2 hours. See the exception permitting a 1-hour floor separation in fully-sprinklered Type IIA, IIIA and VA buildings not exceeding three stories in height above grade.*

Discussion and Commentary: By distributing hazardous materials in multiple fire-resistant compartments throughout a structure, the amount of material exposed to an immediate fire event is limited. The code allows such limited quantities in buildings of other than Group H occupancy; hence, the use of control areas is an effective method for reducing the occupancy classification by reducing the hazard.

[F] TABLE 414.2.2
DESIGN AND NUMBER OF CONTROL AREAS

STORY		PERCENTAGE OF THE MAXIMUM ALLOWABLE QUANTITY PER CONTROL AREA[a]	NUMBER OF CONTROL AREAS PER STORY	FIRE-RESISTANCE RATING FOR FIRE BARRIERS IN HOURS[b]
Above grade plane	Higher than 9	5	1	2
	7–9	5	2	2
	6	12.5	2	2
	5	12.5	2	2
	4	12.5	2	2
	3	50	2	1
	2	75	3	1
	1	100	4	1
Below grade plane	1	75	3	1
	2	50	2	1
	Lower than 2	Not Allowed	Not Allowed	Not Allowed

a. Percentages shall be of the maximum allowable quantity per control area shown in Tables 307.1(1) and 307.1(2), with all increases allowed in the notes to those tables.

b. Separation shall include fire barriers and horizontal assemblies as necessary to provide separation from other portions of the building.

The purpose of a control area is to allow the building to be classified according to its general occupancy instead of being classified as a Group H occupancy. A building may comprise a single control area where the amount of hazardous materials in the entire structure is compliant.

Topic: Distance to Lot Lines

Reference: IBC 415.6.4

Category: Detailed Use Requirements

Subject: Group H Occupancies

Code Text: *Regardless of any other provisions, buildings containing Group H occupancies shall be set back to the minimum fire separation distance as set forth in Sections 415.6.4.1 through 415.6.4.4. Distances shall be measured from the walls enclosing the occupancy to lot lines, including those on a public way.*

Discussion and Commentary: Because of the potentially volatile nature of hazardous materials, specific setback requirements are necessary for Group H occupancies. These provisions take precedence over Table 705.5 regarding the minimum fire separation distance based on building construction type and exposure. The listed conditions are dependent on the type of materials that are indicative of the specified Group H occupancies, the size of the hazardous material storage area and whether or not a detached building is required.

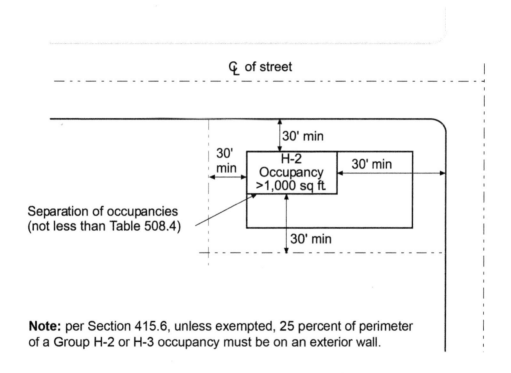

Location on lot for mixed occupancies that include a Group H-2 Occupancy

For SI: 1 foot = 304.8 mm, 1 square foot = 0.093 m²

Note that the measurement is made to the lot line adjacent to a public way, not the centerline as utilized in Table 705.5. In addition, the distance is measured from the walls enclosing the Group H occupancy, which may not necessarily be the exterior wall lines.

Topic: Detached Buildings

Category: Detailed Use Requirements

Reference: IBC 415.7, 415.8

Subject: Group H Occupancies

Code Text: *Group H-1 occupancies shall be in detached buildings used for no other purpose. Group H-2 and H-3 occupancies containing quantities of hazardous materials in excess of those set forth in Table 415.6.5 shall be in detached buildings used for manufacturing, processing, dispensing, use or storage of hazardous materials. Materials listed for Group H-1 occupancies in Section 307.3 are permitted to be located within Group H-2 or H-3 detached buildings provided the amount of materials per control area do not exceed the maximum allowed quantity specified in Table 307.1(1).*

Discussion and Commentary: Because of the explosion hazard potential associated with Group H-1 materials, Group H-1 occupancies are required to be in separate detached structures. Higher-level Group H-2 and Group H-3 occupancies where the quantities of hazardous materials pose an extremely high risk must also be located in buildings with no other uses.

[F] TABLE 415.6.5
DETACHED BUILDING REQUIRED

A DETACHED BUILDING IS REQUIRED WHERE THE QUANTITY OF MATERIAL EXCEEDS THAT SPECIFIED HEREIN			
Material	**Class**	**Solids and Liquids (tons)[a, b]**	**Gases (cubic feet)[a, b]**
Explosives	Division 1.1	Maximum Allowable Quantity	Not Applicable
	Division 1.2	Maximum Allowable Quantity	
	Division 1.3	Maximum Allowable Quantity	
	Division 1.4	Maximum Allowable Quantity	
	Division 1.4[c]	1	
	Division 1.5	Maximum Allowable Quantity	
	Division 1.6	Maximum Allowable Quantity	
Oxidizers	Class 4	Maximum Allowable Quantity	Maximum Allowable Quantity
Unstable (reactives) detonable	Class 3 or 4	Maximum Allowable Quantity	Maximum Allowable Quantity
Oxidizer, liquids and solids	Class 3	1,200	Not Applicable
	Class 2	2,000	Not Applicable
Organic peroxides	Detonable	Maximum Allowable Quantity	Not Applicable
	Class I	Maximum Allowable Quantity	Not Applicable
	Class II	25	Not Applicable
	Class III	50	Not Applicable
Unstable (reactives) nondetonable	Class 3	1	2,000
	Class 2	25	10,000
Water reactives	Class 3	1	Not Applicable
	Class 2	25	Not Applicable
Pyrophoric gases[d]	Not Applicable	Not Applicable	2,000

For SI: 1 ton = 906 kg, 1 cubic foot = 0.02832 m³, 1 pound = 0.454 kg.

a. For materials that are detonable, the distance to other buildings or lot lines shall be in accordance with Section 415.6 of this code or Chapter 56 of the *International Fire Code* based on trinitrotoluene (TNT) equivalence of the material, whichever is greater.

b. "Maximum Allowable Quantity" means the maximum allowable quantity per control area set forth in Table 307.1(1).

c. Limited to Division 1.4 materials and articles, including articles packaged for shipment, that are not regulated as an explosive under Bureau of Alcohol, Tobacco, Firearms and Explosives (BATF) regulations or unpackaged articles used in process operations that do not propagate a detonation or deflagration between articles, provided that the net explosive weight of individual articles does not exceed 1 pound.

d. Detached buildings are not required, for gases in gas rooms that support H-5 fabrication facilities where the gas room is separated from other areas by a fire barrier with a fire-resistance rating of not less than 2 hours and the gas is located in a gas cabinet that is internally sprinklered, equipped with continuous leak detection, automatic shutdown and is not manifolded upstream of pressure controls. Additionally, the gas supply is limited to cylinders that do not exceed 125 pounds (57 kg) water capacity in accordance with 49 CFR 173.192 for Hazard Zone A toxic gases.

The need for detached storage is a function of the type, physical state and quantity of material. Because such a single-use structure must be located an adequate distance from surrounding lot lines and other buildings, exterior walls and exterior openings need not be protected for exposure.

Code Text: *The provisions of* Section 416 *shall apply to the construction, installation and use of buildings and structures, or parts thereof, for the spray application of flammable finishes. Operations and equipment shall comply with the* International Fire Code. *Spray rooms shall be enclosed with not less than 1-hour fire barriers constructed in accordance with Section 707 or horizontal assemblies constructed in accordance with Section 711, or both. Floors shall be waterproofed and drained in an approved manner. Mechanical ventilation and interlocks with the spraying operation shall be in accordance with the* International Fire Code *and* International Mechanical Code.

Discussion and Commentary: The primary hazards associated with paint spraying and spray booths originate from the presence of flammable liquids or powders and their vapors or mists. The requirements address such issues as the ventilation, sprinkler protection and interior surfaces of spray rooms and spraying spaces.

Spray rooms	**Spray booths**	**Limited spray space**
• Designed and constructed per IBC Section 416 • Separated from remainder of building by 1-hour fire barriers • Automatic fire-extinguishing system required	• Designed and constructed per IFC Section 2404.3.3 • Constructed of approved noncombustible materials • Limited in size and location • Automatic fire-extinguishing system required	• Aggregate surface area to be sprayed limited to 9 sq ft • Spraying operations not to be continuous in nature • Mechanical ventilation and hazardous location wiring regulated

Chapter 24 of the *International Fire Code* provides comprehensive requirements for the application of flammable finishes, including detailed provisions for spray booths. Spray finishing operations in Group A, E, I or R occupancies shall be located in a spray room. In other occupancies, such operations may occur in a spray room, spray booth or spraying space approved for such use.

Code Text: *Occupancies in Groups I-1, R-1, R-2, R-3 and R-4 shall comply with the provisions of Sections 420.1 through 420.11 and other applicable provisions of the IBC. Walls separating dwelling units in the same building, walls separating sleeping units in the same building and walls separating dwelling or sleeping units from other occupancies contiguous to them in the same building shall be constructed as fire partitions in accordance with Section 708. Floor assemblies separating dwelling units in the same buildings, floor assemblies separating sleeping units in the same building and floor assemblies separating dwelling or sleeping units from other occupancies contiguous to them in the same building shall be constructed as horizontal assemblies in accordance with Section 711. See appliable exceptions.*

Discussion and Commentary: In residential-type occupancies, it is important that some degree of fire-resistive separation be provided to isolate each individual living unit from all others in the building. It is intended that should a fire initiate within one of the dwelling units or sleeping units, the occupants and contents of the other units would be adequately protected.

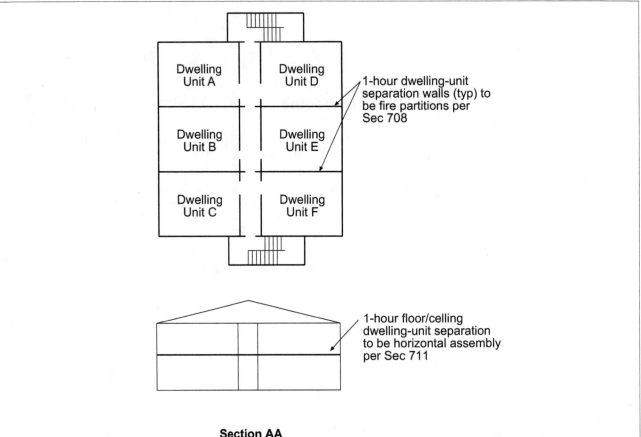

Section AA

All vertical (fire partitions) and horizontal (horizontal assemblies) separation elements are required to be of minimum one-hour fire-resistance-rated construction and provided with protected openings. Where the building is sprinklered throughout with an NFPA 13 system, the required separation may be reduced to $^1/_2$ hour.

Topic: Smoke Barriers	Category: Detailed Use Requirements
Reference: IBC 422.2	Subject: Ambulatory Care Facilities

Code Text: *Ambulatory care facilities where the potential for four or more care recipients are to be incapable of self preservation at any time shall be separated from adjacent spaces, corridors or tenants with a fire partition installed in accordance with Section 708. Where the aggregate area of one or more ambulatory care facilities is greater than 10,000 square feet (929 m²) on one story, the story shall be provided with a smoke barrier to subdivide the story into no fewer than two smoke compartments. The area of any one such smoke compartment shall be not greater than 22,500 square feet (2092 m²).*

Discussion and Commentary: A building used to provide medical, surgical, psychiatric, nursing or similar care on a less than 24-hour basis to individuals who are rendered incapable of self-preservation by the services provided is considered an ambulatory care facility. Although classified as a Group B occupancy in the same manner as an outpatient clinic or other health care office, such facilities pose distinctly different hazards to life and fire safety because of the presence of individuals who are temporarily rendered incapable of self-preservation that is due to the application of nerve blocks, sedation or anesthesia.

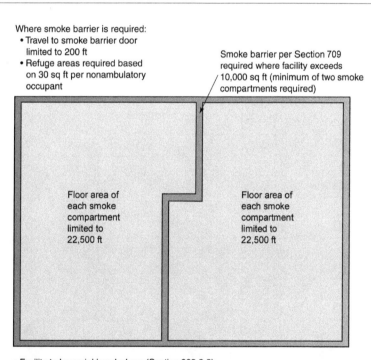

Where smoke barrier is required:
- Travel to smoke barrier door limited to 200 ft
- Refuge areas required based on 30 sq ft per nonambulatory occupant

Smoke barrier per Section 709 required where facility exceeds 10,000 sq ft (minimum of two smoke compartments required)

Floor area of each smoke compartment limited to 22,500 ft

Floor area of each smoke compartment limited to 22,500 ft

- Facility to be sprinklered where (Section 903.2.2):
  - Four or more persons incapable of self-preservation, or
  - Any persons incapable of self-preservation located at other than level of exit discharge
- Manual fire alarm system required (Section 907.2.2.1)
  - Alarm boxes not required where building is fully sprinklered and notification appliances activate upon sprinkler water flow

For SI: 1 foot = 304.8 mm, 1 square foot = 0.093 m²   **Ambulatory health care facility**

In addition to the requirement for smoke compartments in those ambulatory care facilities over 10,000 square feet in floor area, the installation of fire protection systems is often mandated. A manual fire alarm system is required in all ambulatory care facilities, and an automatic sprinkler system is required where there are four or more care recipients incapable of self-preservation, or if one or more such recipients is located on other than the level of exit discharge.

Topic: Required Shelters
Reference: IBC 423.4, 423.5

Category: Detailed Use Requirements
Subject: Storm Shelters

Code Text: *In areas where the shelter design wind speed for tornados in accordance with Figure 304.2(1) of ICC 500 is 250 MPH, 911 call stations, emergency operation centers and fire, rescue, ambulance and police stations shall be provided with a storm shelter constructed in accordance with ICC 500. In areas where the shelter design wind speed for tornados in accordance with Figure 304.2(1) of ICC 500 is 250 MPH, all Group E occupancies with an aggregate occupant load of 50 or more shall have a storm shelter constructed in accordance with ICC 500. See the exceptions for day care centers, areas accessory to places of worship, and where an entire building is designed as storm shelter.*

Discussion and Commentary: Critical emergency operations facilities are essential for the delivery of vital services or the protection of a community. Due to the unpredictability and often very short tornado warning time, there are many high-wind events where it is unfeasible to evacuate school buildings. Therefore, the IBC mandates that storm shelters be provided in these types of structures where the tornado risk is high.

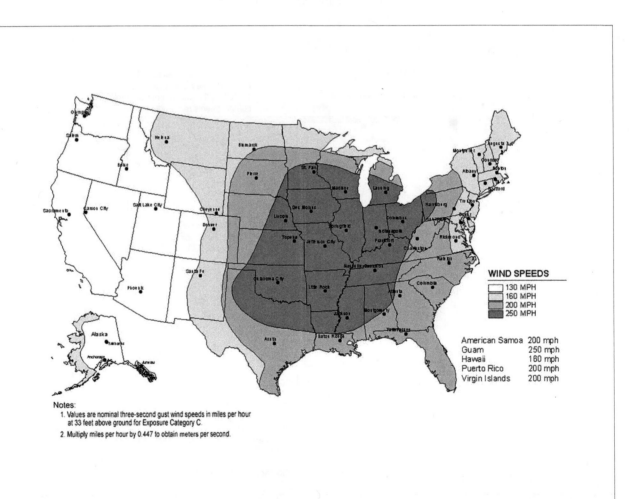

WIND SPEEDS
- 130 MPH
- 160 MPH
- 200 MPH
- 250 MPH

American Samoa 200 mph
Guam 250 mph
Hawaii 160 mph
Puerto Rico 200 mph
Virgin Islands 200 mph

Notes:
1. Values are nominal three-second gust wind speeds in miles per hour at 33 feet above ground for Exposure Category C.
2. Multiply miles per hour by 0.447 to obtain meters per second.

In addition to the necessary administrative and application provisions established in Chapter 1 and definitions in Chapter 2, ICC 500, *ICC/NSSA Standard for the Design and Construction of Storm Shelters,* includes criteria for structural design, siting, occupancy, means of egress, access, accessibility and fire safety.

Quiz

Study Session 14
IBC Chapter 4

1. In a covered mall building, the maximum distance from any point within a mall to an exit shall be _____ feet.

    a. 75   b. 200

    c. 250   d. 300

    Reference_____

2. In a covered mall building, groupings of kiosks shall be separated a minimum of _____ feet from other structures within the mall.

    a. 6   b. 10

    c. 20   d. 30

    Reference_____

3. A high-rise building is defined as a building having an occupied floor located more than _____ feet above the lowest level of fire department vehicle access.

    a. 55   b. 75

    c. 120   d. 160

    Reference_____

4. In a high-rise building, if standby power is a generator within the building, it shall be located in a separate room enclosed by minimum _____ fire-resistance-rated assemblies or horizontal assemblies, or both.

    a. 1-hour fire barrier   b. 1 hour fire-partition

    c. 2-hour fire wall   d. 2- hour fire barrier

    Reference_____

5. What is the minimum required classification for the interior finish of atrium walls and ceilings?

    a. A   b. B

    c. C   d. DOC FF-1

Reference_____

6. At other than the level of exit discharge from the atrium, the maximum permitted travel distance within an atrium space is _____ feet.

    a. 75   b. 100

    c. 150   d. 200

Reference_____

7. An underground building need not be divided into at least two compartments when a floor level is located a maximum of _____ feet below the lowest level of exit discharge.

    a. 30   b. 60

    c. 75   d. 120

Reference_____

8. In parking facilities, vehicle barriers need not be provided where the vertical difference from the floor to the ground or surface directly below is a maximum of _____ inches.

    a. 12   b. 30

    c. 48   d. 60

Reference_____

9. Canopies under which fuels are dispensed shall have a minimum clearance of _____ above the surface of the drive-through area.

    a. 12 feet, 0 inches   b. 13 feet, 6 inches

    c. 14 feet, 6 inches   d. 16 feet, 0 inches

Reference_____

10. Unless a permitted increase is applied, what is the maximum number of tiers permitted in a ramp-accessed single-use open parking garage of Type IIA construction?

    a. 8   b. 10

    c. 12   d. 15

Reference_____

11. Smoke compartments in a Group I-2, Condition 1 occupancy shall have a maximum floor area of _____ square feet.

    a. 5,000   b. 10,000

    c. 12,000   d. 22,500

Reference_____

12. On floors housing patients confined to beds, a minimum of _____ net square feet per care recipient shall be provided in refuge areas of Group I-2 occupancies.

    a. 3   b. 6

    c. 15   d. 30

Reference_____

13. Doors to resident sleeping units in Group I-3 occupancies shall have a minimum clear width of _____ inches.

    a. 22   b. 26

    c. 28   d. 32

Reference_____

14. In a Group I-3 occupancy, what is the maximum permitted number of residents in any single smoke compartment?

    a. 30   b. 50

    c. 100   d. 200

Reference_____

15. The minimum permitted size of a regulated motion picture projection room containing eight projecting machines shall be _____ square feet.

    a. 320   b. 360

    c. 600   d. 640

Reference_____

16. An approved fire curtain or water curtain need not be provided at the proscenium opening of stages having a maximum height of _____ feet.

    a. 35   b. 50

    c. 55   d. 75

Reference_____

17. Stages exceeding _____ square feet in floor area shall be provided with emergency ventilation.

    a. 200   b. 400

    c. 500   d. 1,000

Reference_____

18. What is the minimum required interior finish classification for walls and ceilings in a special amusement area?

    a. A   b. B

    c. C   d. DOC FF-1

Reference_____

19. An aircraft hangar of Type IIB construction may be classified as Group III for fire suppression purposes, provided the hangar has a maximum single fire area size of _____ square feet.

    a. 5,000   b. 12,000

    c. 20,000   d. 40,000

Reference _____

20. What is the maximum number of control areas permitted on the sixth floor above grade plane of a research and development building?

   a. zero

   b. one

   c. two

   d. four

   Reference_____

21. A Group H-2 liquid use, dispensing and mixing room need not be located on the outer perimeter of a building when limited to a maximum floor area of _____ square feet.

   a. 100

   b. 200

   c. 500

   d. 1,000

   Reference_____

22. An ambulatory care facility shall be separated from adjacent spaces, corridors and tenants with a fire partition where a minimum of _____ care recipients are to be incapable of self-preservation at any time.

   a. 4

   b. 10

   c. 20

   d. 30

   Reference_____

23. Dead ends in service corridors of Group H-5 occupancies shall be a maximum of _____ feet in length.

   a. 4

   b. 15

   c. 20

   d. 30

   Reference_____

24. In a drying room, all overhead heating piping shall be located a minimum of _____ inches from combustible contents in the dryer.

   a. 1

   b. 2

   c. 4

   d. 6

   Reference_____

25. Nitrocellulose storage located in a building where organic coatings are manufactured shall be stored in a room enclosed with minimum _____ fire barriers and/or horizontal assemblies.

    a. 1-hour   b. 2-hour

    c. 3-hour   d. 4-hour

Reference_____

26. Where a stage height exceeds 50 feet, workshops and storerooms serving the stage shall be separated from the stage by minimum _____ and/or horizontal assemblies.

    a. 1-hour fire partitions   b. 1-hour fire barriers

    c. 2-hour fire barriers   d. 2-hour fire walls

Reference_____

27. In a nonsprinklered office building, an attic space used for the storage of combustible material shall be protected on the storage side _____ .

    a. with $^1/_2$-inch gypsum board

    b. with $^1/_2$-inch Type X gypsum board

    c. with $^5/_8$-inch gypsum board

    d. as required for one-hour fire-resistance-rated construction

Reference_____

28. A minimum _____ fire-resistance rating is required for the floor construction separating multiple control areas within a Type IIIB building.

    a. $^1/_2$-hour   b. 1-hour

    c. 2-hour   d. 3-hour

Reference_____

29. Where weather protection shelters an outdoor hazardous material storage area, the sheltered area can only be considered outdoor storage for purposes of the code where the overhead structure is of noncombustible construction and the maximum allowable area of the structure is _____ square feet, plus any permitted increases.

    a. 1,000   b. 1,500

    c. 2,000   d. 3,000

Reference_____

30. What is the minimum level of wall construction required to enclose spray rooms used for the application of flammable paints?

    a. noncombustible, nonrated   b. 1-hour fire partitions

    c. 1-hour fire barriers   d. 2-hour fire barriers

Reference_____

31. In a Type IIB 600,000-square-foot building used for the manufacturing of aircraft, the maximum travel distance is _____ feet where the minimum height from the finished floor to the bottom of the ceiling or roof slab or deck is 65 feet.

    a. 400   b. 500

    c. 600   d. 700

Reference _____

32. A temporary platform shall be installed for a maximum of _____ days.

    a. 10   b. 30

    c. 90   d. 180

Reference _____

33. Unless located a minimum of _____ feet from lot lines or a public way, exterior walls of an aircraft hangar shall have a minimum 2-hour fire-resistance rating.

    a. 20   b. 30

    c. 40   d. 60

Reference _____

34. Walls separating sleeping units in the same buildings shall comply with the provisions for _____ .

    a. fire partitions   b. fire barriers

    c. smoke partitions   d. smoke barriers

Reference _____

35. Storm shelters are required in critical emergency operation facilities and most Group E occupancies where the shelter design wind speed for tornados is _____ mph.

    a. 150   b. 200

    c. 225   d. 250

Reference _____

36. In a Group I-2 care suite, a maximum of _____ feet of egress travel is permitted within the suite to a door leading to a corridor or horizontal exit.

    a. 75   b. 100

    c. 125   d. 150

Reference _____

37. The path of egress travel within and from a technical support area serving a stage shall be a minimum of _____ inches in width.

    a. 22   b. 28

    c. 30   d. 32

Reference _____

38. Where intended as other than a dedicated residential storm shelter, a facility designed solely as a storm shelter and having an occupant load of 90 shall be classified as a Group _____ occupancy.

    a. A-1   b. A-3

    c. B   d. U

Reference _____

39. Unless a special investigation acceptable to the building official has demonstrated adequate fire safety play structures shall be a maximum of _____ square feet in area.

    a. 150   b. 300

    c. 600   d. 1,000

Reference _____

40. A maximum of _____ laboratory suites is permitted on the second story above grade plane in a higher education facility.

a. 2

b. 3

c. 4

d. 6

Reference _____

2021 IBC Chapters 14, 15 and 18

Exterior Wall Coverings, Roofs and Foundations

OBJECTIVE: To obtain an understanding of the requirements for exterior wall coverings, including weather-resistant coverings and veneer; roofing assemblies, roof coverings and rooftop structures; and footings and foundations.

REFERENCE: Chapters 14, 15 and 18, 2021 *International Building Code*

KEY POINTS:
- What are the components of a weather-resistant wall envelope?
- What material is considered acceptable as a water-resistive barrier?
- In what geographical areas are Class I or II vapor retarders required on the interior side of framed walls? Under what conditions are Class III vapor retarders permitted?
- Where is flashing to be installed?
- What is the minimum required thickness of wood veneers on exterior walls of Type I, II, III and IV buildings?
- What is anchored masonry veneer? Adhered masonry veneer?
- How must metal veneers be attached? Glass veneer? Stone veneer?
- What limitations are placed on the sill height of operable windows?
- Under what conditions is vinyl siding permitted?
- How is fiber cement siding to be applied?
- How are combustible exterior wall coverings regulated for ignition resistance? Fire-blocking?
- How shall bay windows and oriel windows be constructed?
- What is a roof assembly? Roof covering?
- What is the purpose of a roof assembly?
- How are roof assemblies classified?
- What is the effectiveness of a Class A roof assembly? Class B? Class C?
- What is a nonclassified roof? A special purpose roof? Where are such roofs permitted?
- How must roof covering materials be identified?

- How shall asphalt shingles be installed? Clay and concrete tile? Wood shakes and shingles? Metal roof panels and roof shingles?

- What is considered a penthouse? When is a penthouse considered an additional story? How must a penthouse be constructed?

- What is the maximum permitted height of a penthouse? Tower or spire?

- How is reroofing addressed?

- What is the minimum depth of a footing below the undisturbed ground surface?

- How shall backfill in the excavated area adjacent to the foundation be placed?

- What special considerations are applicable to footings adjacent to ascending slopes? Descending slopes?

- If not specifically designed, how must footings supporting walls of light-frame construction be constructed?

- Where is dampproofing required? Waterproofing?

- What are deep foundations? Shallow foundations? How are such foundations regulated?

Topic: Weather Protection

Category: Exterior Walls

Reference: IBC 1402.2

Subject: Performance Requirements

Code Text: *Exterior walls shall provide the building with a weather-resistant exterior wall envelope. The exterior wall envelope shall include flashing, as described in Section 1404.4. The exterior wall envelope shall be designed and constructed in such a manner as to prevent the accumulation of water within the wall assembly by providing a water-resistive barrier behind the exterior veneer, as described in Section 1403.2, and a means for draining water that enters the assembly to the exterior.* See the three exceptions.

Discussion and Commentary: The code considers it necessary to apply at least one layer of water-resistive barrier material attached to the *studs or sheathing in order to provide a continuous water-resistive-barrier behind the exterior wall veneer.* The use of flashing in conjunction with the felt provides a continuous barrier against water penetration.

TABLE 1404.2
MINIMUM THICKNESS OF WEATHER COVERINGS

COVERING TYPE	MINIMUM THICKNESS (inches)
Adhered masonry veneer	0.25
Aluminum siding	0.019
Anchored masonry veneer	
Stone (natural)	2.0
Architectural cast stone	2.5
Other	2.0
Asbestos-cement boards	0.125
Asbestos shingles	0.156
Cold-rolled copper[d]	0.0216 nominal
Copper shingles[d]	0.0162 nominal
Exterior plywood (with sheathing)	0.313
Exterior plywood (without sheathing)	See Section 2304.6
Fiber cement lap siding	0.25[c]
Fiber cement panel siding	0.25[c]
Fiberboard siding	0.5
Glass-fiber reinforced concrete panels	0.375
Hardboard siding[c]	0.25
High-yield copper[d]	0.0162 nominal
Lead-coated copper[d]	0.0216 nominal
Lead-coated high-yield copper	0.0162 nominal
Marble slabs	1
Particleboard (with sheathing)	See Section 2304.6
Particleboard (without sheathing)	See Section 2304.6
Porcelain tile	0.125 nominal
Steel (approved corrosion resistant)	0.0149

(Continued)

For all exterior walls other than those constructed of concrete or masonry, the IBC requires the installation of a weather-resistant exterior wall envelope. Any other approved method to resist condensation and moisture leakage is also acceptable.

Code Text: *Vapor retarder materials shall be classified in accordance with Table 1404.3(1). A vapor retarder shall be provided on the interior side of frame walls in accordance with Tables 1404.3(2) and 1404.3(3), or an approved design using accepted engineering practice for hydrothermal analysis. Only Class III vapor retarders shall be used on the interior side of frame walls where foam plastic insulating sheathing with a perm rating of less than 1 is applied in accordance with Table 1404.3(3) on the exterior side of the frame wall.*

Discussion and Commentary: Prescriptive methods are provided in Section 1404.3 to address moisture control. The code prescribes three different vapor retarder classes, based on the vapor permeability of the material as defined in Chapter 2.

TABLE 1404.3(1)
VAPOR RETARDER MATERIALS AND CLASSES

VAPOR RETARDER CLASS	ACCEPTABLE MATERIALS
I	Sheet polyethylene, nonperforated aluminum foil, or other approved materials with a perm rating of less than or equal to 0.1
II	Kraft-faced fiberglass batts or vapor retarder paint or other approved materials, applied in accordance with the manufacturer's instructions for a perm rating greater than 0.1 and less than or equal to 1.0
III	Latex paint, enamel paint, or other approved materials, applied in accordance with the manufacturer's instructions for a perm rating of greater than 1.0 and less than or equal to 10

Wall assemblies can be designed and constructed to dry inward, outward and to both sides in all climate zones. The provisions allow more flexibility in the design and construction of moisture-forgiving wall systems. The requirements recognize that many common materials function to various degrees to slow the passage of moisture.

Code Text: *Flashing shall be installed in such a manner so as to prevent moisture from entering the wall or to redirect that moisture to the surface of the exterior wall finish or to a water-resistive barrier that is part of a means of drainage complying with Section 1402.2. Flashing shall be installed at the perimeters of exterior door and window assemblies, penetrations and terminations of exterior wall assemblies, exterior wall intersections with roofs, chimneys, porches, decks, balconies and similar projections and at built-in gutters and similar locations where moisture could enter the wall. Flashing with projecting flanges shall be installed on both sides and the ends of copings, under sills and continuously above projecting trim.*

Discussion and Commentary: In general, the code requires that all intersections of exterior surfaces and/or components be flashed to prevent water intrusion. Roof and wall intersections and parapets are especially troublesome, as are exterior wall openings exposed to weather and, in particular, wind-driven rain.

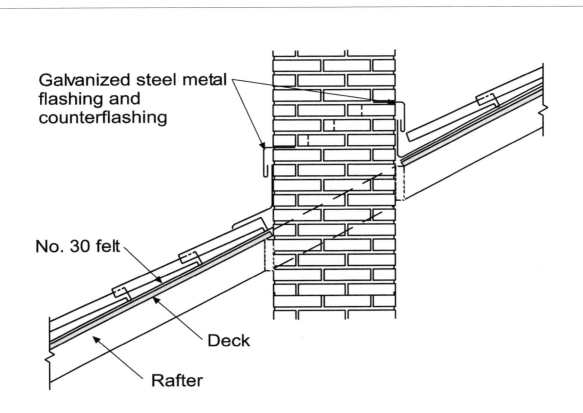

Galvanized steel metal flashing and counterflashing

No. 30 felt

Deck

Rafter

For SI: 1 inch = 25.4 mm.

Chimney flashing detail

Where anchored masonry veneer is installed, the masonry must be provided with flashing and weepholes in the first course above finished ground level above the foundation wall or slab, as well as at other points of support.

Code Text: Veneer is *a facing attached to a wall for the purpose of providing ornamentation, protection, or insulation, but not counted as adding strength to the wall.* Adhered masonry veneer is *veneer secured and supported through the adhesion of an approved bonding material applied to an approved backing.* Anchored masonry veneer is *veneer secured with approved mechanical fasteners to an approved backing. Wood veneers on exterior walls of buildings of Type I, II, III and IV construction shall be not less than 1 inch (25 mm) nominal thickness, 0.438-inch (11.1 mm) exterior hardboard siding or 0.375-inch (9.5 mm) exterior-type wood structural panels or particleboard. Metal veneers shall not be less than 0.0149-inch (0.378 mm) nominal thickness sheet steel mounted on wood or metal furring strips or approved sheathing on light-frame construction.*

Discussion and Commentary: Years ago, veneer was considered an ornamental facing for a masonry wall. Today, the IBC regulates a variety of veneer materials: wood, anchored masonry, stone, slab-type, terra cotta, adhered masonry, metal, glass and, in Chapter 26, plastic. The code regulates material size, type and attachment, as well as other concerns that would cause the veneer to fail.

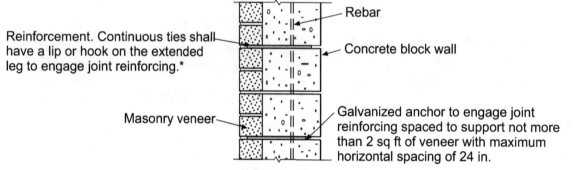

Reinforcement. Continuous ties shall have a lip or hook on the extended leg to engage joint reinforcing.*

Masonry veneer

Rebar

Concrete block wall

Galvanized anchor to engage joint reinforcing spaced to support not more than 2 sq ft of veneer with maximum horizontal spacing of 24 in.

A. To concrete block wall

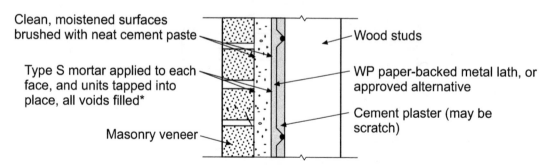

Clean, moistened surfaces brushed with neat cement paste

Type S mortar applied to each face, and units tapped into place, all voids filled*

Masonry veneer

Wood studs

WP paper-backed metal lath, or approved alternative

Cement plaster (may be scratch)

B. To wood studs and paper-backed metal lath

Generic application of anchored masonry veneer (5 in. max thickness)

For SI: 1 inch = 25.4 mm, 1 square foot = 0.093 m².

As they are constantly subjected to alternate cycles of wetting and drying, the anchors, ties or supports used in the attachment of veneer must be corrosion resistant. These materials, when used on the exterior of a building, must support the veneer properly for the life of the building.

Code Text: *The provisions of Chapter 15 shall govern the design, materials, construction and quality of roof assemblies and rooftop structures. A roof assembly is a system designed to provide weather protection and resistance to design loads. The system consists of a roof covering and roof deck or a single component serving as both the roof covering and the roof deck. A roof assembly can include an underlayment, a thermal barrier, insulation or vapor retarder. Roof covering is the covering applied to the roof deck for weather resistance, fire classification or appearance.*

Discussion and Commentary: There are many components of a roof assembly. Viewed as a unit, a roof assembly is regulated for its resistance to wind, weathering, impact and fire. In addition, roof coverings must be designed, installed and maintained to protect the building from the weather.

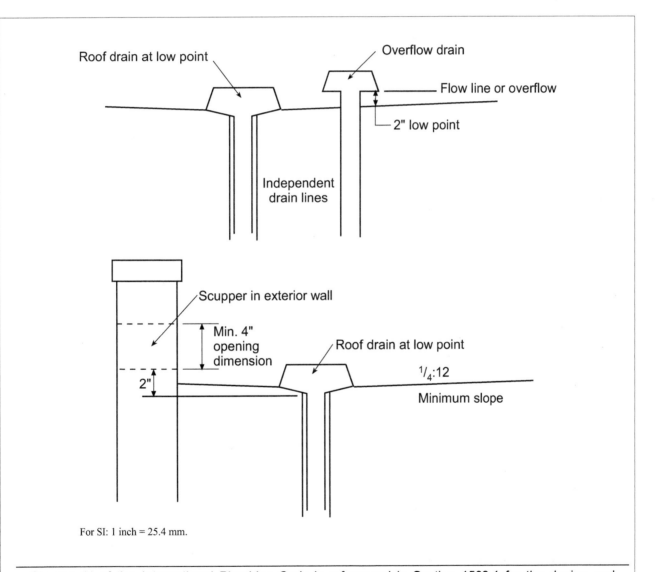

For SI: 1 inch = 25.4 mm.

Chapter 11 of the *International Plumbing Code* is referenced in Section 1502.1 for the design and installation of roof drainage systems. Where water on the roof is not intended to flow over the roof edge, provisions for roof drainage will include primary roof drains supplemented by overflow drains.

Code Text: *Roof decks shall be covered with approved roof coverings secured to the building or structure in accordance with the provisions of Chapter 15. Roof coverings shall be designed in accordance with the IBC, and installed in accordance with the IBC and the manufacturer's approved instructions. Roof coverings shall be applied in accordance with the applicable provisions of Section 1507 and the manufacturer's installation instructions.*

Discussion and Commentary: The IBC contains installation requirements for a number of types of roof covering materials and systems. Selectively included in the provisions are deck requirements, limitations on roof slope, underlayment, materials, fasteners and attachment, flashings and application methods.

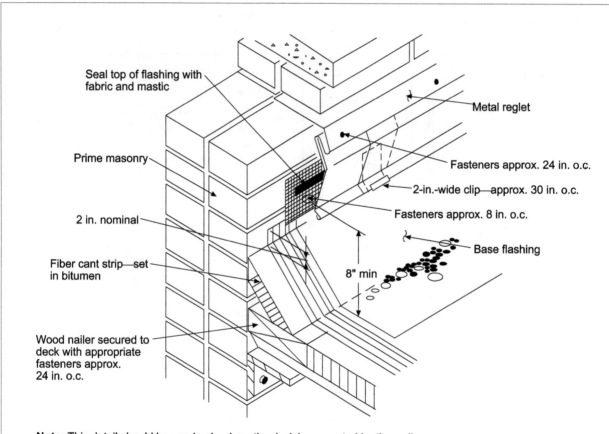

Note: This detail should be used only where the deck is supported by the wall.

Base flashing at bearing wall

For SI: 1 inch = 25.4 mm.

Flashing is essential to a weatherproof roofing assembly. It is required at wall and roof intersections, at gutters, around roof openings such as chimneys and vents, and wherever there is a change in roof slope or direction. Metal flashing shall be minimum No. 26 galvanized sheet.

Code Text: *Parapets shall be provided for aggregate surfaced roofs and shall comply with Table 1504.9.*

Discussion and Commentary: Field assessments of damage to buildings caused by high-wind events have shown that aggregate, gravel or stone blown from the roofs of buildings has increased the damage to other buildings due to the breakage of glass. Once the glass is broken, higher internal pressures are created within the building, often resulting in substantial structural damage. In addition, breakage of windows will generally result in considerable wind and water damage to the building's interior and contents. Table 1504.9 considers aggregate size, roof height and wind speed to determine the minimum required parapet height for aggregate-surfaced roofs.

TABLE 1504.9
MINIMUM REQUIRED PARAPET HEIGHT (INCHES) FOR AGGREGATE SURFACED ROOFS[a, b, c]

| AGGREGATE SIZE | MEAN ROOF HEIGHT (ft) | WIND EXPOSURE AND BASIC DESIGN WIND SPEED (MPH) | | | | | | | | | | | | | | | | | |
| | | Exposure B | | | | | | | | | Exposure C[d] | | | | | | | | |
		≤ 95	100	105	110	115	120	130	140	150	≤ 95	100	105	110	115	120	130	140	150
ASTM D1863 (No. 7 or No. 67)	15	2	2	2	2	12	12	16	20	24	2	13	15	18	20	23	27	32	37
	20	2	2	2	2	12	14	18	22	26	12	15	17	19	22	24	29	34	39
	30	2	2	2	13	15	17	21	25	30	14	17	19	22	24	27	32	37	42
	50	12	12	14	16	18	21	25	30	35	17	19	22	25	28	30	36	41	47
	100	14	16	19	21	24	27	32	37	42	21	24	26	29	32	35	41	47	53
	150	17	19	22	25	27	30	36	41	46	23	26	29	32	35	38	44	50	56
ASTM D1863 (No. 6)	15	2	2	2	2	12	12	12	15	18	2	2	2	13	15	17	22	26	30
	20	2	2	2	2	12	12	13	17	21	2	2	12	15	17	19	23	28	32
	30	2	2	2	2	12	12	16	20	24	2	12	14	17	19	21	26	31	35
	50	12	12	12	12	14	16	20	24	28	12	15	17	19	22	24	29	34	39
	100	12	12	14	16	19	21	26	30	35	16	18	21	24	26	29	34	39	45
	150	12	14	17	19	22	24	29	34	39	18	21	23	26	29	32	37	43	48

For SI: 1 inch = 25.4 mm; 1 foot = 304.8 mm; 1 mile per hour = 0.447 m/s.
a. Interpolation shall be permitted for mean roof height and parapet height.
b. Basic design wind speed, *V*, and wind exposure shall be determined in accordance with Section 1609.
c. Where the minimum required parapet height is indicated to be 2 inches (51 mm), a gravel stop shall be permitted and shall extend not less than 2 inches (51 mm) from the roof surface and not less than the height of the aggregate.
d. For Exposure D, add 8 inches (203 mm) to the parapet height required for Exposure C and the parapet height shall not be less than 12 inches (305 mm).

Critical parameters established in Table 1504.9 govern performance. The use of aggregate-surfaced roofing systems is a viable option in high-wind areas with appropriate aggregate sizing and parapet height.

Code Text: *Roof assemblies shall be divided into the classes defined below. Class A, B and C roof assemblies and roof coverings required to be listed by* Section 1505 *shall be tested in accordance with ASTM E108 or UL 790. The minimum roof coverings installed on buildings shall comply with Table 1505.1 based on the type of construction of the building.* See the exception for skylights and sloped glazing.

Discussion and Commentary: The various required roof covering classifications are related directly to the type of construction of the building. Based on Table 1505.1, a minimum level of fire protection is assigned to address external fire exposures. The exposures are generally created by fires in adjoining structures, wild fires and fire from the subject building that may extend up the exterior wall and onto the top surface of the roof.

TABLE 1505.1[a, b]
MINIMUM ROOF COVERING CLASSIFICATION
FOR TYPES OF CONSTRUCTION

IA	IB	IIA	IIB	IIIA	IIIB	IV	VA	VB
B	B	B	C[c]	B	C[c]	B	B	C[c]

For SI: 1 foot = 304.8 mm, 1 square foot = 0.0929 m^2.

a. Unless otherwise required in accordance with the *International Wildland-Urban Interface Code* or due to the location of the building within a fire district in accordance with Appendix D.

b. Nonclassified roof coverings shall be permitted on buildings of Group R-3 and Group U occupancies, where there is a minimum fire-separation distance of 6 feet measured from the leading edge of the roof.

c. Buildings that are not more than two stories above grade plane and having not more than 6,000 square feet of projected roof area and where there is a minimum 10-foot fire-separation distance from the leading edge of the roof to a lot line on all sides of the building, except for street fronts or public ways, shall be permitted to have roofs of No. 1 cedar or redwood shakes and No. 1 shingles.

In addition to the Class A, B and C listed roof assemblies, the IBC permits the use of nonclassified roofing and special purpose roofs under limited conditions. These types of roof coverings are limited, respectively, to Group R-3 occupancies and small nonfire-rated buildings.

Code Text: *Class A roof assemblies are those that are effective against severe fire-test exposure. Class B roof assemblies are those that are effective against moderate fire-test exposure. Class C roof assemblies are those that are effective against light fire-test exposure. Non-classified roofing is approved material that is not listed as a Class A, B or C roof covering.*

Discussion and Commentary: Class A roof coverings include masonry, concrete, slate, tile and cement-asbestos, as well as ferrous or copper shingles or sheets, metal sheets and metal shingles. Additionally, any assembly that is tested as Class A in accordance with ASTM E108 or UL 790 by an approved testing agency and is listed and identified by that agency is included. There are no specific materials that qualify as Class B or C; therefore all Class B and C roof covering are listed as such.

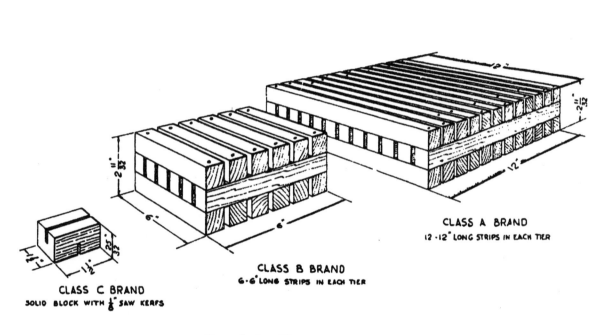

CLASS C BRAND
SOLID BLOCK WITH 1/8" SAW KERFS

CLASS B BRAND
6·6" LONG STRIPS IN EACH TIER

CLASS A BRAND
12·12" LONG STRIPS IN EACH TIER

Brands for Classes A, B, and C Tests

Several test methods are included as parts of the fire-test-response standards ASTM E108 and UL 790, including the intermittent flame exposure test, spread of flame test, burning brand test, flying brand test and rain test. It also is critical that the roof coverings do not slip from position.

Code Text: *Roof covering materials shall be delivered in packages bearing the manufacturer's identifying marks and approved testing agency labels required in accordance with Section 1505. Bulk shipments of materials shall be accompanied with the same information issued in the form of a certificate or on a bill of lading by the manufacturer.*

Discussion and Commentary: Roof covering materials must comply with the appropriate quality standards set forth in Section 1507 for each different type of material. The materials must be compatible with the building or structure to which they are applied. In addition, identification of the roof covering materials is mandatory to verify that they comply with the quality standard. Gardens and other landscaping installed on a roof are specifically regulated in regard to roof construction and structural integrity. For structural purposes, the provisions of Sections 1607.13.3 and 1607.13.3.1 addressing occupiable and landscaped roofs, respectively, are applicable.

Asphalt Shingles	**Section 1507.2**
Clay and Concrete Tile	**Section 1507.3**
Metal Roof Panels	**Section 1507.4**
Metal Roof Shingles	**Section 1507.5**
Mineral-surfaced Roll Roofing	**Section 1507.6**
Slate Shingles	**Section 1507.7**
Wood Shingles	**Section 1507.8**
Wood Shakes	**Section 1507.9**
Built-up Roofs	**Section 1507.10**
Modified Bitumen Roofing	**Section 1507.11**
Single-ply Roofing	**Section 1507.12**
Sprayed Polyurethane Foam Roofing	**Section 1507.13**
Liquid-applied Roofing	**Section 1507.14**
Vegetative Roofs and Roof Gardens	**Section 1507.15**
Photovoltaic Shingles	**Section 1507.16**
BIPV Roof Panels	**Section 1507.17**

Where there are not applicable standards for a specific roof covering material, or where the materials are of questionable suitability, the building official must ask for testing by an approved agency to determine the material's character, quality and limitations of application.

Topic: Asphalt Shingles	**Category:** Roof Assemblies and Rooftop Structures
Reference: IBC 1507.2	**Subject:** Roof Coverings

Code Text: *Asphalt shingles shall be fastened to solidly sheathed decks. Asphalt shingles shall only be used on roof slopes of two units vertical in 12 units horizontal (17-percent slope) or greater. For roof slopes from two units vertical in 12 units horizontal (17-percent slope), up to four units vertical in 12 units horizontal (33-percent slope), double underlayment application is required in accordance with Section 1507.2.8. Asphalt shingles shall have the minimum number of fasteners required by the manufacturer, but not less than four fasteners per strip shingle or two fasteners per individual shingle. A drip edge shall be provided at eaves and rake edges of shingle roofs.*

Discussion and Commentary: There are two fundamental types of asphalt shingles: strip shingles (the most common type) such as three-tab shingles, and individual interlocking shingles such as t-lock shingles. In addition to three-tab, other strip shingles include random or multi-tab, no-cut-out and laminated architectural.

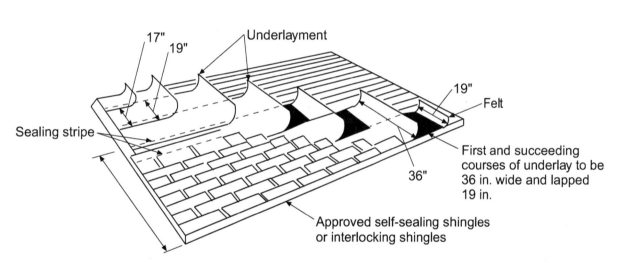

Note: In areas where there has been a history of ice forming along the eaves causing a backup of water, felt plies of underlayment should be cemented up from eaves far enough to overlie a point 24 in. inside the wall line of the building.

source NRCA

For SI: 1 inch = 25.4 mm, °C = [(°F)-32/1.8].

Application of asphalt shingle on slopes between 2:12 and 4:12

Asphalt shingles are typically classified in two types, either cellulose felt reinforced (i.e., organic shingles) and fiberglass mat reinforced (i.e., fiberglass shingles). Consistent with the requirements of Section 1203.2, the roofing industry recommends the attic space below asphalt shingle roofs be properly ventilated.

Code Text: *Wood shakes shall only be used on solid or spaced sheathing. Wood shakes shall only be used on slopes of not less than four units vertical in 12 units horizontal (33-percent slope). Interlayment shall comply with ASTM D226, Type I. Fasteners for wood shakes shall be corrosion resistant with a minimum penetration of $^3/_4$ inch (19.1 mm) into the sheathing. Wood shakes shall be laid with a side lap not less than $1^1/_2$ inches (38 mm) between joints in adjacent courses. Spacing between shakes in the same course shall be $^3/_8$ to $^5/_8$ (9.5 to 15.9 mm) inches for shakes and taper sawn shakes of naturally durable wood and shall be $^1/_4$ to $^3/_8$ inch (6.4 to 9.5 mm) for preservative taper sawn shakes. Weather exposure for wood shakes shall not exceed those set in Table 1507.9.8.*

Discussion and Commentary: Wood shakes, which are defined as roofing products split from logs and then shaped as required by the individual manufacturers, differ from wood shingles in that shingles are defined as sawed wood products featuring a uniform butt thickness per individual length.

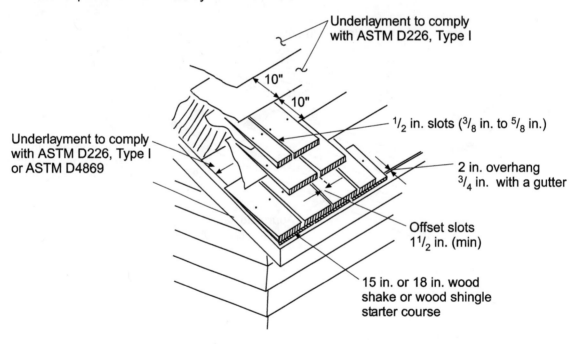

Weather exposure to be limited by Table 1507.9.8

Underlayment to comply with ASTM D226, Type I

10"

10"

$^1/_2$ in. slots ($^3/_8$ in. to $^5/_8$ in.)

Underlayment to comply with ASTM D226, Type I or ASTM D4869

2 in. overhang $^3/_4$ in. with a gutter

Offset slots $1^1/_2$ in. (min)

15 in. or 18 in. wood shake or wood shingle starter course

Wood shake application

For SI: 1 inch = 25.4 mm.

Both wood shakes and wood shingles are required to be labeled by an approved third-party inspection agency. The applicable set of grading rules, required of the quality control program, is typically prescribed by the Cedar Shake and Shingle Bureau.

Topic: Penthouses	**Category:** Roof Assemblies and Rooftop Structures
Reference: IBC 1511.2, 202	**Subject:** Rooftop Structures

Code Text: A penthouse is *an enclosed, unoccupied rooftop structure used for sheltering mechanical and electrical equipment, tanks, elevators and related machinery, stairways and vertical shaft openings. Penthouses in compliance with Sections 1511.2.1 through 1511.2.4 shall be considered as a portion of the story directly below the roof deck on which such penthouses are located. Other penthouses shall be considered as an additional story of the building. Penthouses shall not be used for purposes other than the shelter of mechanical or electrical equipment, tanks, elevators and related machinery, stairways or vertical shaft openings in the roof assembly, including ancillary spaces used to access elevators and stairways.*

Discussion and Commentary: The general premise is that a penthouse be treated no differently than any other portion of the building. However, the reductions in the general requirements for a story recognize the lack of occupant load or fire loading, as well as the reduced exposure of penthouses when the exterior wall is recessed from the exterior wall of the building. Penthouses do not contribute to the building area, number of stories or fire area of the buildings on which they are located.

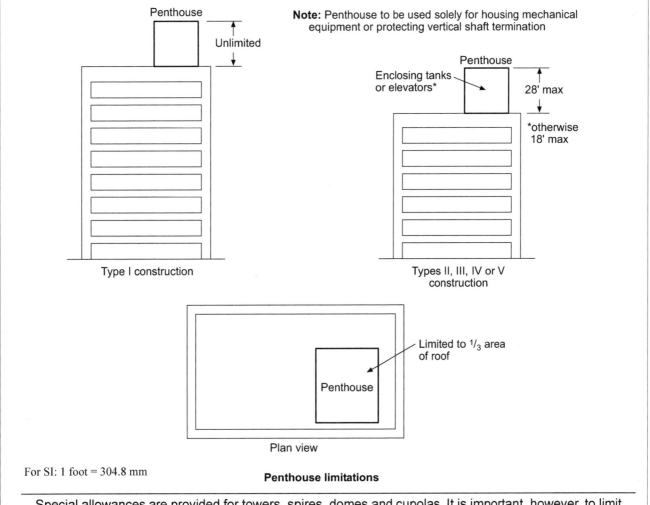

Penthouse limitations

For SI: 1 foot = 304.8 mm

Special allowances are provided for towers, spires, domes and cupolas. It is important, however, to limit the height of such structures where constructed of combustible materials. Limited provisions also regulate the installation of tanks and cooling towers on buildings.

Code Text: *On graded sites, the top of any exterior foundation shall extend above the elevation of the street gutter at point of discharge or the inlet of an approved drainage device a minimum of 12 inches (305 mm) plus 2 percent. Alternate elevations are permitted subject to the approval of the building official, provided it can be demonstrated that required drainage to the point of discharge and away from the structure is provided at all locations on the site.*

Discussion and Commentary: Where natural drainage away from a building is not available, the site must be graded so that water will not drain toward, or accumulate at, the exterior foundation wall. A prescriptive elevation is set forth that will ensure positive drainage to a street gutter or other drainage point; however, any other method that moves water away from the building can be accepted by the building official.

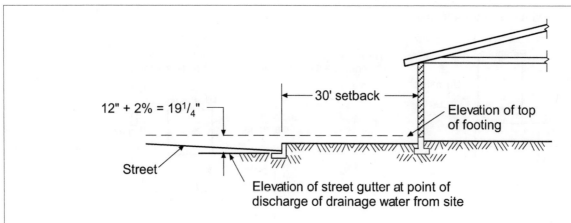

Footing elevation on graded sites

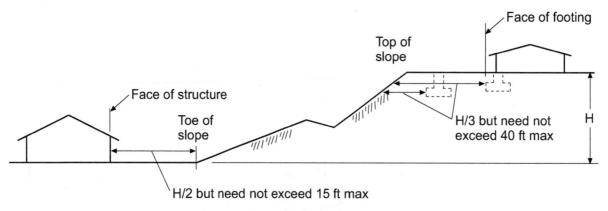

Foundation clearances from slopes

For SI: 1 foot = 304.8 mm, 1 inch = 25.4 mm.

Where footings are located adjacent to a slope steeper than 1:3 (1 vertical to 3 horizontal), either at the top or the bottom, special clearances between the building and the sloping surfaces are required to protect against slope drainage, erosion and shallow failures.

Code Text: *Shallow foundations shall be built on undisturbed soil, compacted fill material, or controlled low-strength material (CLSM). The top surface of footings shall be level. The bottom surface of footings are permitted to have a slope not exceeding 1 unit vertical in 10 units horizontal (10-percent slope). Footings shall be stepped where it is necessary to change the elevation of the top surface of the footing or where the surface of the ground slopes more than 1 unit vertical in 10 units horizontal (10-percent slope).*

Discussion and Commentary: If compacted fill material is used to support a footing, the material must be in compliance with the provisions of an approved report. The code identifies a number of issues that must be addressed in the report, including specifications for both the site preparation and the material to be used as fill.

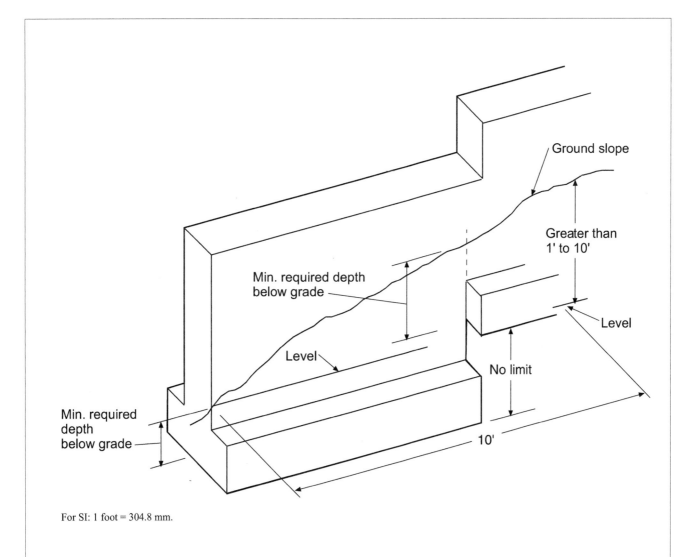

For SI: 1 foot = 304.8 mm.

Footings must be placed at least 12 inches below the undisturbed ground surface. Where the site is recognized to contain shifting or moving soils, the footings must be extended to a sufficient depth to ensure stability.

Code Text: *The minimum depth of footings below the undisturbed ground surface shall be 12 inches (305 mm). Except where otherwise protected from frost, foundations and other permanent supports of buildings and structures shall be protected from frost by one or more of the following methods: (1) extending below the frost line of the locality, (2) construction in accordance with ASCE 32 (Design and Construction of Frost Protected Shallow Foundations), or (3) erecting on solid rock. See the exception for small free-standing structures. Shallow footings shall not bear on frozen soil unless such frozen condition is of a permanent character.*

Discussion and Commentary: In winter, frost action can raise the ground level (frost heave), whereas in springtime, the same area will soften and settle back. If foundations are constructed on soils that can freeze, then the heave or vertical movement of the ground, which is rarely uniform, can cause serious damage to buildings and other structures.

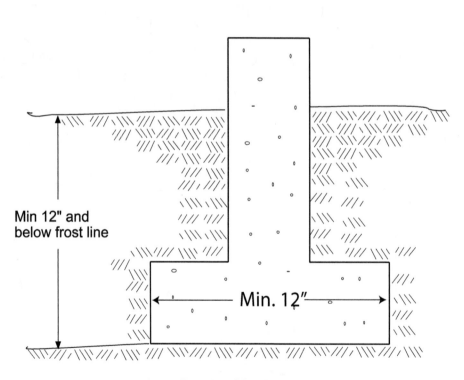

Min 12" and below frost line

Min. 12"

Depth of footing

For SI: 1 inch = 25.4 mm.

The frost line is set for the particular locality of construction. The factors determining the depth of the frost line are air temperature and the length of time it remains below freezing, as well as the soil's level of thermal conductivity and its ability to conduct heat.

Code Text: *Where a specific design is not provided, concrete or masonry-unit footings supporting walls of light frame construction are permitted to be designed in accordance with Table 1809.7.*

Discussion and Commentary: In lieu of an engineered design, Table 1809.7 provides a prescriptive method for determining footing size criteria that can be used in conjunction with conventional light-framed construction. The minimum thickness of the foundation wall, as well as the minimum width and thickness of the footing, are specified based on the number of floors supported. The minimum depth below undisturbed ground surface is also addressed. Unless protected from frost or erected on solid rock, the footings must also extend below the frost line. The table is based on anticipated loads on the footings and foundations due to wall, floor and roof systems.

TABLE 1809.7
PRESCRIPTIVE FOOTINGS SUPPORTING WALLS OF
LIGHT-FRAME CONSTRUCTION[a, b, c, d, e]

NUMBER OF FLOORS SUPPORTED BY THE FOOTING[f]	WIDTH OF FOOTING (inches)	THICKNESS OF FOOTING (inches)
1	12	6
2	15	6
3	18	8[g]

For SI: 1 inch = 25.4 mm, 1 foot = 304.8 mm.

a. Depth of footings shall be in accordance with Section 1809.4.

b. The ground under the floor shall be permitted to be excavated to the elevation of the top of the footing.

c. Interior stud-bearing walls shall be permitted to be supported by isolated footings. The footing width and length shall be twice the width shown in this table, and footings shall be spaced not more than 6 feet on center.

d. See Section 1908 for additional requirements for concrete footings of structures assigned to Seismic Design Category C, D, E or F.

e. For thickness of foundation walls, see Section 1807.1.6.

f. Footings shall be permitted to support a roof in addition to the stipulated number of floors. Footings supporting roof only shall be as required for supporting one floor.

g. Plain concrete footings for Group R-3 occupancies shall be permitted to be 6 inches thick.

Although Table 1809.7 is normally used for continuous footings, it can also be used for isolated footings that support interior-stud bearing walls. The footings shall be spaced a maximum of 6 feet on center, with their widths and lengths being twice that shown in the table.

Study Session 15
IBC Chapters 14, 15 and 18

1. An exterior wall is defined as a building enclosing wall that has a minimum slope of _____ degrees with the horizontal plane.

    a. 45   b. 60

    c. 75   d. 90

Reference_____

2. Veneer secured and supported through the adhesion of an approved bonding material applied to an approved backing is considered _____ masonry veneer.

    a. adhered   b. anchored

    c. attached   d. spandrel

Reference_____

3. The minimum required fire separation distance between a building with polypropylene siding and an adjacent building shall be _____ feet.

    a. 5   b. 10

    c. 20   d. 30

Reference _____

4. Anchored masonry veneer of natural stone shall be a minimum of _____ inch(es) in thickness in order to be acceptable as an approved weather covering.

    a. 0.50   b. 1.00

    c. 1.50   d. 2.00

Reference_____

5. Where thin exterior structural glass veneer is located no more than 15 feet above grade, the area of a single veneer section is limited to a maximum of _____ square feet.

    a. 6   b. 8

    c. 10   d. 12

Reference_____

6. As a general requirement, exterior walls of a Type IIB building exceeding a minimum height of _____ feet above grade plane shall comply with the acceptance criteria of NFPA 285 where the walls contain a combustible water-resistive barrier.

    a. 25   b. 30

    c. 40   d. 60

Reference_____

7. Combustible exterior wall coverings are permitted on Type II buildings if located a maximum height of _____ feet above grade plane.

    a. 25   b. 30

    c. 35   d. 40

Reference_____

8. Roofing interlayment shall have a minimum width of _____ inches.

    a. 12   b. 18

    c. 34   d. 36

Reference_____

9. What is the minimum required roof covering classification for a roof assembly on a building of Type IA construction?

    a. Class A   b. Class B

    c. Class C   d. nonclassified

Reference_____

10. Roof assemblies consisting of metal sheets or shingles installed on noncombustible decks are considered _____ roof assemblies.

    a. Class A   b. Class B

    c. Class C   d. special purpose

Reference_____

11. Double underlayment application is required beneath asphalt shingles on roofs having a slope of 2:12 up to _____ .

    a. $2^1/_2$:12   b. 3:12

    c. 4:12   d. 5:12

Reference_____

12. In areas where the maximum basic design wind speed is over 140 mph, all laps of underlayment for asphalt shingles shall be a minimum of _____ inches.

    a. 3   b. 4

    c. 6   d. 9

Reference_____

13. Fasteners for concrete or clay roof tiles shall penetrate the deck a minimum of _____ inch or through the thickness of the deck, whichever is less.

    a. $^1/_2$ b. $^5/_8$

    c. $^3/_4$ d. 1

Reference_____

14. What is the minimum permitted roof slope for the installation of metal roof shingles?

    a. 2:12   b. 3:12

    c. 4:12   d. 5:12

Reference_____

15. Wood shakes shall be applied to a roof with a minimum side lap of _____ inch(es) between joints in adjacent courses.

    a. $^3/_8$ b. $^1/_2$

    c. $^3/_4$ d. $1^1/_2$

Reference_____

16. Where 18-inch-long No. 1 wood shingles are installed on a roof of 12:12 pitch, the maximum weather exposure shall be _____ inches.

    a. $3^3/_4$ b. $4^1/_4$

    c. $4^1/_2$ d. $5^1/_2$

Reference_____

17. Sprayed polyurethane foam roofs shall have a minimum design slope of _____ for drainage purposes.

    a. $^1/_8$:12   b. $^1/_4$:12

    c. 1:12   d. 2:12

Reference_____

18. In other than Type I construction, a penthouse shall extend a maximum of _____ feet above the roof deck when used for the protection of rooftop mechanical equipment.

    a. 8   b. 12

    c. 18   d. 28

Reference_____

19. The bottom surface of footings shall have a maximum slope of _____ .

    a. $^1/_2$:12   b. 1:12

    c. 1:10   d. 1:20

Reference_____

20. The bottom of a footing shall be located a minimum of _____ inches below the undisturbed ground surface.

    a. 6   b. 12

    c. 15   d. 18

Reference_____

21. Unless data is submitted that substantiates the use of a higher value, the presumptive vertical foundation pressure for sandy gravel supporting soil shall be _____ pounds per square foot.

    a. 12,000   b. 4,000

    c. 3,000   d. 2,000

    Reference_____

22. Where a swimming pool is located adjacent to a slope, any pool wall located a maximum distance of _____ feet from the top of a slope shall be capable of supporting the water in the pool without soil support.

    a. 5   b. 7

    c. 10   d. 15

    Reference _____

23. Concrete foundations shall be protected from freezing during depositing and for a minimum time period of _____ thereafter.

    a. 12 hours   b. 24 hours

    c. 3 days   d. 5 days

    Reference_____

24. The minimum concrete cover for reinforcement in precast nonprestressed deep foundation elements not manufactured under plant conditions shall be _____ inch(es).

    a. 1   b. 2

    c. 2.5   d. 3

    Reference_____

25. At the girder supports at the top of hollow masonry foundation walls, a minimum of _____ inches of solid masonry shall be provided.

    a. 3   b. 4

    c. 6   d. 8

    Reference_____

26. Where glass veneer extends to the surface of a sidewalk, each section shall be set a minimum of _____ inch above the highest point of the sidewalk.

     a. $^1/_4$ b. $^1/_2$

     c. $^5/_8$ d. $^3/_4$

     Reference _____

27. The construction of a special purpose wood shake roof mandates a minimum underlayment of _____ placed under the roof sheathing.

     a. $^5/_8$-inch wood structural panel

     b. $^1/_2$-inch gypsum wallboard

     c. $^5/_8$-inch Type X water resistant gypsum backer board or sheathing

     d. $^1/_2$-inch water-resistant gypsum backing board

     Reference _____

28. Slate shingles shall be installed only on roof decks having a slope of _____ or greater.

     a. 2:12   b. $2^1/_2$:12

     c. 3:12   d. 4:12

     Reference _____

29. A cupola located on the top of a building with a minimum building height of _____ feet shall be supported by noncombustible materials.

     a. 45   b. 50

     c. 60   d. 85

     Reference _____

30. Unless warranted by climatic or soil conditions, a minimum ground slope of _____ is required away from a building's foundation wall for a minimum distance of _____ feet.

     a. 1:48, 10   b. 1:20, 10

     c. 1:15, 5   d. 1:12, 5

     Reference _____

31. Sheet polyethylene and nonperforated aluminum foil with a perm rating no more than 0.1 are considered to be Class _____ vapor retarders.

    a. 0   b. I

    c. II   d. III

Reference _____

32. Fiber cement horizontal lap siding shall be installed with a minimum lap of _____ inch(es).

    a. $^3/_4$ b. 1

    c. $1^1/_4$ d. $1^1/_2$

Reference _____

33. On other than buildings of Type IA construction, mechanical equipment screens located on the roof are limited to a maximum height of _____ feet above the roof deck

    a. 12   b. 15

    c. 16   d. 18

Reference _____

34. Where a roof of a building with a mean roof height of 30 feet is surfaced with No. 7 aggregate, what is the minimum required parapet height for Exposure B and a basic design wind speed of 110 mph?

    a. 13 inches   b. 22 inches

    c. 24 inches   d. 30 inches

Reference _____

35. The steel pipe or tube used for a micropile shall have a minimum wall thickness of _____ inch.

    a. $^1/_8$ b. $^3/_{16}$

    c. $^1/_4$ d. $^5/_{16}$

Reference _____

36. Where architectural cast stone is used as the weather protection for the exterior walls of a building, the stone must have a minimum thickness of _____ inch(es).

    a. 0.875   b. 1.0

    c. 2.0   d. 2.5

Reference _____

37. A cricket or saddle is not required to be installed on the ridge side of any chimney that is a maximum of _____ inches in width as measured perpendicular to the roof slope.

    a. 18   b. 24

    c. 30   d. 36

Reference _____

38. Single-ply membrane roofs shall have a minimum design slope of _____ unit vertical in 12 units horizontal.

    a. $^1/_8$ b. $^1/_4$

    c. $^3/_8$ d. $^1/_2$

Reference _____

39. Where a specific design is not provided for concrete footings supporting walls of light-frame construction, what is the minimum required footing width where supporting two floors and a roof?

    a. 12 inches   b. 15 inches

    c. 18 inches   d. 21 inches

Reference _____

40. Unless otherwise approved by the building official, deep foundation elements that stand unbraced in water are considered to be laterally supported at a minimum point of _____ feet into soft soil.

    a. 18   b. 15

    c. 10   d. 5

Reference _____

Study Session

16

2021 IBC Chapters 16, 17, 19, 21, 22 and 23
Special Inspections, Concrete, Masonry and Wood

OBJECTIVE: To identify the provisions relating to general structural forces and engineered design; applicable structural tests; special inspections and structural observation; and specific materials of construction, including concrete, masonry, steel and wood.

REFERENCE: Chapters 16, 17, 19, 21, 22 and 23, 2021 *International Building Code*

KEY POINTS:
- In structural design, what is considered a live load? A dead load?
- How is the minimum design live load for a floor system determined? Concentrated loads? Partition loads?
- How shall design roof loads be determined? When should snow loads be considered?
- What is the design criteria for wind loads? Seismic loads? Flood loads?
- What is special inspection? What are the duties and responsibilities of a special inspector?
- Which types of work shall be inspected by a special inspector?
- What is structural observation? When is structural observation required?
- What information is required in the statement of special inspections?
- How does Chapter 19 (Concrete) relate to the provisions of ACI 318?
- How shall concrete be evaluated and accepted?
- Where are the general requirements for concrete mixing, conveying, depositing and curing located?
- What are the minimum requirements for concrete floor slabs supported directly on the ground?
- How must a masonry chimney be designed, anchored, supported and reinforced?
- What are the minimum required thicknesses of masonry fireplace walls and firebox walls?
- What is the minimum clearance required between combustible materials and fireplace or chimney walls? Between combustible materials and the fireplace opening?
- How must the hearth be constructed for a masonry fireplace?
- Hearth extensions must be of what minimum size?

- At what minimum height must a masonry chimney terminate?
- How can the minimum capacity of structural wood-framing members be established?
- For decay and termite protection, what manner of under-floor clearance is required between exposed ground and wood girders, joists or structural floors?
- How must structural floor and roof sheathing be designed?
- What is considered "conventional light-frame construction"?
- How shall girders be supported?
- What are the limitations on the notching and boring of holes in floor joists, ceiling joists and roof rafters?
- What are braced wall panels? Where are such panels required?
- How shall rafters be framed at the ridge?
- What is a purlin? How shall a purlin system be constructed?

Topic: Uniform and Concentrated Loads

Category: Structural Design

Reference: IBC 1607.3, 1607.4

Subject: Live Loads

Code Text: *The live loads used in the design of buildings and other structures shall be the maximum loads expected by the intended use or occupancy but shall in no case be less than the minimum uniformly distributed live loads given in Table 1607.1. Floors, roofs and other similar surfaces shall be designed to support the uniformly distributed live loads prescribed in Section 1607.3 or the concentrated live loads, in pounds (kilonewtons), given in Table 1607.1, whichever produces the greater load effects.*

Discussion and Commentary: The anticipated live loads are based on the daily use of the building, as well as any temporary loading conditions such as remodeling activities, large group gatherings and short-term storage. They also reflect that, within the general use category, changes will likely occur in furniture layout, traffic patterns, etc. Concentrated loads take into account more specific types of loading consistent with the use of the building.

TABLE 1607.1
MINIMUM UNIFORMLY DISTRIBUTED LIVE LOADS, L_o, AND MINIMUM CONCENTRATED LIVE LOADS

	OCCUPANCY OR USE		UNIFORM (psf)	CONCENTRATED (pounds)	ALSO SEE SECTION
1.	Apartments (see residential)		—	—	—
2.	Access floor systems	Office use	50	2,000	—
		Computer use	100	2,000	—
3.	Armories and drill rooms		150[b]	—	—
4.	Assembly areas	Fixed seats (fastened to floor)	60[a]		
		Follow spot, projections and control rooms	50		
		Lobbies	100[a]		
		Movable seats	100[a]		
		Stage floors	150[b]		
		Platforms (assembly)	100[a]		
		Bleachers, folding and telescopic seating and grandstands	100[a] (See Section 1607.19)	—	—
		Stadiums and arenas with fixed seats (fastened to the floor)	60[a] (See Section 1607.19)		
		Other assembly areas	100[a]		
5.	Balconies and decks		1.5 times the live load for the area served, not required to exceed 100	—	—
6.	Catwalks for maintenance and service access		40	300	—
7.	Cornices		60	—	—
8.	Corridors	First floor	100		
		Other floors	Same as occupancy served except as indicated	—	—
9.	Dining rooms and restaurants		100[a]	—	—
10.	Dwellings (see residential)		—	—	—
11.	Elevator machine room and control room grating (on area of 2 inches by 2 inches)		—	300	—
12.	Finish light floor plate construction (on area of 1 inch by 1 inch)		—	200	—
13.	Fire escapes		100		
		On single-family dwellings only	40	—	—
14.	Fixed ladders		See Section 1607.17		—
15.	Garages	Passenger vehicles only	40[c]	See Section 1607.7	—
		Trucks and buses	See Section 1607.8		
16.	Handrails, guards and grab bars		See Section 1607.9		—
17.	Helipads		See Section 1607.6		—

(Continued)

The code does not require the concurrent application of uniform live load and concentrated live load. The load to be utilized in the structural design of the building would be of the type that produces the greater stress in the structural elements.

Topic: General Requirements

Category: Structural Design

Reference: IBC 1610.1

Subject: Soil Lateral Loads

Code Text: *Foundation walls and retaining walls shall be designed to resist lateral soil loads from adjacent soil. Soil loads specified in Table 1610.1 shall be used as the minimum design lateral soil loads unless determined otherwise by a geotechnical investigation in accordance with Section 1803. Lateral pressure from surcharge loads shall be added to the lateral soil load. Lateral pressure shall be increased if expansive soils are present at the site.*

Discussion and Commentary: Lateral soil loads are established in Table 1610.1 for various soil types. The indicated loads address both at-rest pressure and active pressure conditions. It is noted that expansive soils are not to be used as backfill, as such materials can exert very high pressures against walls. Special soil testing is required to determine the magnitude of these pressures.

TABLE 1610.1
LATERAL SOIL LOAD

DESCRIPTION OF BACKFILL MATERIAL[c]	UNIFIED SOIL CLASSIFICATION	DESIGN LATERAL SOIL LOAD[a] (pound per square foot per foot of depth)	
		Active pressure	At-rest pressure
Well-graded, clean gravels; gravel-sand mixes	GW	30	60
Poorly graded clean gravels; gravel-sand mixes	GP	30	60
Silty gravels, poorly graded gravel-sand mixes	GM	40	60
Clayey gravels, poorly graded gravel-and-clay mixes	GC	45	60
Well-graded, clean sands; gravelly sand mixes	SW	30	60
Poorly graded clean sands; sand-gravel mixes	SP	30	60
Silty sands, poorly graded sand-silt mixes	SM	45	60
Sand-silt clay mix with plastic fines	SM-SC	45	100
Clayey sands, poorly graded sand-clay mixes	SC	60	100
Inorganic silts and clayey silts	ML	45	100
Mixture of inorganic silt and clay	ML-CL	60	100
Inorganic clays of low to medium plasticity	CL	60	100
Organic silts and silt clays, low plasticity	OL	Note b	Note b
Inorganic clayey silts, elastic silts	MH	Note b	Note b
Inorganic clays of high plasticity	CH	Note b	Note b
Organic clays and silty clays	OH	Note b	Note b

For SI: 1 pound per square foot per foot of depth = 0.157 kPa/m, 1 foot = 304.8 mm.

a. Design lateral soil loads are given for moist conditions for the specified soils at their optimum densities. Actual field conditions shall govern. Submerged or saturated soil pressures shall include the weight of the buoyant soil plus the hydrostatic loads.

b. Unsuitable as backfill material.

c. The definition and classification of soil materials shall be in accordance with ASTM D 2487.

Basement and foundation walls that have restricted horizontal movement at the top shall be designed for at-rest pressure. Retaining walls free to move and rotate at the top are permitted to be designed for active pressure. Where basement walls extend a maximum of 8 feet below grade and support a flexible floor system, they also may be designed for active pressure.

Topic: Scope and Definitions	Category: Structural Tests and Special Inspections
Reference: IBC 1701.1, 1704.6, 202	Subject: Inspections and Observations

Code Text: *The provisions of* Chapter 17 *shall govern the quality, workmanship and requirements for materials covered.* Special inspection (continuous and periodic) is *the inspection of construction requiring the expertise of an approved special inspector in order to ensure compliance with* the IBC *and the approved construction documents.* Structural observation is *the visual observation of the structural system by a registered design professional for general conformance to the approved construction documents. Structural observation does not include or waive the responsibility for the inspection required by Section 110, Section 1705 or other sections of* the IBC.

Discussion and Commentary: In addition to the general inspections called for in Section 110 (footings, frame, final, etc.), it is often necessary to call for a more exacting review of the construction process. Through special inspections and structural observation, the work can be evaluated more closely for compliance with the approved construction documents.

Special Cases	**Section 1705.1.1**
Steel Construction	**Section 1705.2**
Concrete Construction	**Section 1705.3**
Masonry Construction	**Section 1705.4**
Wood Construction	**Section 1705.5**
Soils	**Section 1705.6**
Driven Deep Foundations	**Section 1705.7**
Cast-in-Place Deep Foundations	**Section 1705.8**
Helical Pile Foundations	**Section 1705.9**
Deep Foundation Elements	**Section 1705.10**
Fabricated Items	**Section 1705.11**
Wind Resistance	**Section 1705.12**
Seismic Resistance	**Section 1705.13**
Testing for Seismic Resistance	**Section 1704.14**
Sprayed Fire-resistant Materials	**Section 1705.15**
Mastic and Intumescent Fire-Resistant Coatings	**Section 1705.16**
Exterior Insulation and Finish Systems (EIFS)	**Section 1705.17**
Fire-Resistant Penetrations and Joints	**Section 1705.18**
Testing for Smoke Control	**Section 1705.19**
Sealing of Mass Timber	**Section 1705.20**

A statement of special inspections must be prepared by the registered design professional in responsible charge where special inspection or testing is required. The code specifies the content required to be provide in the statement. The code also sets forth unique provisions for special inspections and structural testing for seismic-resistance and wind-resistance considerations.

Topic: General Requirements

Category: Structural Tests and Special Inspections

Reference: IBC 1704.2

Subject: Special Inspections

Code Text: *Where application is made to the building official for construction as specified in Section 105, the owner or the owner's authorized agent, other than the contractor, shall employ one or more approved agencies to perform special inspections and tests during construction on the types of work specified in Section 1705 and identify the approved agencies to the building official.* See the exceptions for work, components or occupancies where special inspection is not required. *These special inspections and tests are in addition to the inspections by the building official that are identified in Section 110.*

Discussion and Commentary: Most building departments do not have the staff of inspectors to provide detailed inspections on large and complex projects. There are also projects where the nature of construction is such that extra care in quality control must be exercised to assure compliance. For these reasons, the code mandates continuous or periodic inspection by special inspectors for certain types of work.

TABLE 1705.5.3
REQUIRED SPECIAL INSPECTIONS OF MASS TIMBER CONSTRUCTION

	TYPE		CONTINUOUS SPECIAL INSPECTION	PERIODIC SPECIAL INSPECTION
1.	Inspection of anchorage and connections of mass timber construction to timber deep foundation systems.		—	X
2.	Inspect erection of mass timber construction.		—	X
3.	Inspection of connections where installation methods are required to meet design loads.			
	Threaded fasteners	Verify use of proper installation equipment.	—	X
		Verify use of pre-drilled holes where required.	—	X
		Inspect screws, including diameter, length, head type, spacing, installation angle and depth.	—	X
	Adhesive anchors installed in horizontal or upwardly inclined orientation to resist sustained tension loads.		X	—
	Adhesive anchors not defined in preceding cell.		—	X
	Bolted connections.		—	X
	Concealed connections.		—	X

TABLE 1705.6
REQUIRED SPECIAL INSPECTIONS AND TESTS OF SOILS

	TYPE	CONTINUOUS SPECIAL INSPECTION	PERIODIC SPECIAL INSPECTION
1.	Verify materials below *shallow foundations* are adequate to achieve the design bearing capacity.	—	X
2.	Verify excavations are extended to proper depth and have reached proper material.	—	X
3.	Perform classification and testing of compacted fill materials.	—	X
4.	During fill placement, verify use of proper materials and procedures in accordance with the provisions of the approved geotechnical report. Verify densities and lift thicknesses during placement and compaction of compacted fill.	X	—
5.	Prior to placement of compacted fill, inspect subgrade and verify that site has been prepared properly.	—	X

A statement of special inspections containing the work requiring special inspection, the specific inspections to be performed, and the individuals or firms to be retained for conducting special inspections must be submitted by the permit applicant prior to issuance of the building permit.

Code Text: *Prior to the start of the construction, the approved agencies shall provide written documentation to the building official demonstrating the competence and relevant experience or training of the special inspectors who will perform the special inspections and tests during construction. Experience or training shall be considered relevant when the documented experience or training is related in complexity to the same type of special inspection or testing activities for projects of similar complexity and material qualities. The approved agency shall submit reports of special inspections and tests to the building official, and to the registered design professional in responsible charge.*

Discussion and Commentary: It is the duty of the special inspector not only to observe the work, but also to furnish inspection reports indicating that the work inspected was done in accordance with the approved construction documents. If discrepancies are found in the work, the inspector should bring them to the immediate attention of the contractor for correction. If the discrepancies are not corrected, the building official and registered design professional in responsible charge should be notified.

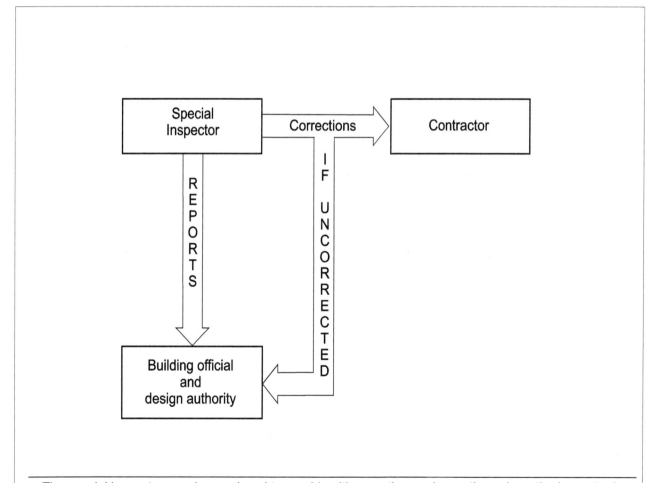

The special inspector may be employed to provide either continuous inspection, where the inspector is present for full-time observation of the work, or periodic inspection, where he or she only intermittently observes the work.

Code Text: *Where required by the provisions of Section 1704.6.1, the owner or owner's authorized agent shall employ a registered design professional to perform structural observations. At the conclusion of the work included in the permit, the structural observer shall submit to the building official a written statement that the site visits have been made and identify any reported deficiencies that, to the best of the structural observer's knowledge, have not been resolved.*

Discussion and Commentary: Structural observations are mandated for those structures assigned to Seismic Category E that are more than two stories in height. The building official or registered design professional in responsible charge can also mandate such observation. Structural observation is also mandated for high-rise buildings as well as those structures classified as Risk Category III or IV. The role of the structural observer is to visually observe representative locations of structural systems, details and load paths for general conformance to the approved construction documents.

Structural observation is not to be confused with the mandated inspections specified in Section 110, or with the special inspections listed in Section 1705. This activity is intended to provide an additional level of expertise in the review of structures posing a very high level of complexity.

Topic: Scope

Category: Concrete

Reference: IBC 1901

Subject: Plain and Reinforced Concrete

Code Text: *The provisions of* Chapter 19 *shall govern the materials, quality control, design and construction of concrete used in structures. Structural concrete shall be designed and constructed in accordance with the requirements of* Chapter 19 *and ACI 318 as amended in Section 1905 of the IBC. Special inspections and tests of concrete elements of buildings and structures and concreting operations shall be as required by Chapter 17.*

Discussion and Commentary: Requirements for the design, testing, mixing, placing and protection of concrete construction are located in ACI 318, *Building Code Requirements for Structural Concrete*, a publication published and copyrighted by the American Concrete Institute. Section 1905 contains the primary modifications to the provisions of ACI 318.

Construction Requirements
for Concrete Work

Specifications for Tests and Materials (Chapter 3)	Section 1903
Durability Requirements (Chapter 4)	Section 1904

Where modifications have been made to the text of ACI 318, the section designations of *IBC Section 1905* are followed by those found in ACI 318. Italics are used to indicate where the IBC differs substantially from the ACI standard.

Code Text: *The thickness of concrete floor slabs supported directly on the ground shall not be less than $3^1/_2$ inches (89 mm). A 6-mil (0.006 inch; 0.15 mm) polyethylene vapor retarder with joints lapped not less than 6 inches (152 mm) shall be placed between the base course or subgrade and the concrete floor slab, or other approved equivalent methods or materials shall be used to retard vapor transmission through the floor slab. See the five exceptions that identify conditions where a vapor retarder is not required.*

Discussion and Commentary: Concrete slabs on grade must be a minimum thickness so superimposed loads are transmitted to the subgrade without causing structural distress to the slab. As a matter of experience, a minimum $3^1/_2$-inch minimum slab thickness is needed to support typical concentrated loads without damage to the concrete. Additionally, slabs must be protected on the underside so moisture levels are not excessive due to migration through the slab into the space above.

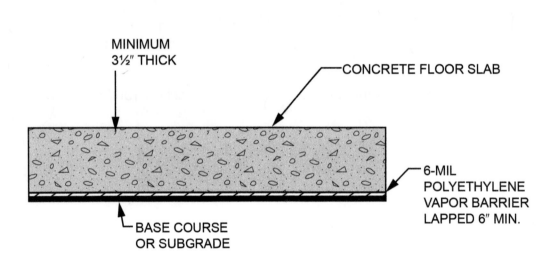

MINIMUM
3½″ THICK

CONCRETE FLOOR SLAB

6-MIL
POLYETHYLENE
VAPOR BARRIER
LAPPED 6″ MIN.

BASE COURSE
OR SUBGRADE

For SI: 1 inch = 25.4 mm

Five exceptions to the use of a vapor retarder below a concrete floor slab acknowledge conditions where the migration of limited moisture through the slab will not adversely affect the occupancy of the structure. Exceptions vary, with two allowances related to Group R-3 occupancies.

Code Text: *Masonry fireboxes shall be constructed of solid masonry units, hollow masonry units grouted solid, stone, or concrete. When a lining of firebrick at least 2 inches (51 mm) in thickness or other approved lining is provided, the minimum thickness of back and sidewalls shall each be 8 inches (203 mm) of solid masonry, including the lining. The width of joints between firebricks shall not be greater than $^3/_4$ inch (6.4 mm). When no lining is provided, the total minimum thickness of back and sidewalls shall be 10 inches (254 mm) of solid masonry.*

Discussion and Commentary: Firebox thickness is regulated in order to insulate surrounding construction, both exposed and concealed, from excessive temperature levels. It is important that the walls be constructed in such a fashion that they are solid throughout.

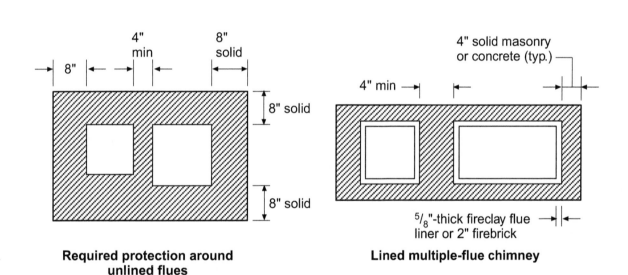

Required protection around unlined flues

For SI: 1 inch = 25.4 mm.

Lined multiple-flue chimney

**Lined and unlined masonry chimneys - residential
Greater thicknesses are required for unburned clay units and stone**

The use of steel fireplace units is permitted under specific conditions. The unit must have a minimum $^1/_4$-inch steel firebox liner and an air chamber. The total thickness at the back and sides must be at least 8 inches, with no less than 4 inches of solid masonry.

Code Text: *Hearth extensions shall extend at least 16 inches (406 mm) in front of, and at least 8 inches (203 mm) beyond, each side of the fireplace opening. Where the fireplace opening is 6 square feet (0.557 m²) or larger, the hearth extension shall extend at least 20 inches (508 mm) in front of, and at least 12 inches (305 mm) beyond, each side of the fireplace opening. The minimum thickness of hearth extensions shall be 2 inches (51 mm).* See the exception for raised firebox openings.

Discussion and Commentary: Hearth extensions are necessary to keep sparks and embers that fly from the firebox from igniting combustible material, such as carpet, on the floor. Radiated heat from the fireplace can also ignite combustible flooring materials located adjacent to the fireplace opening and adjacent fireplace walls.

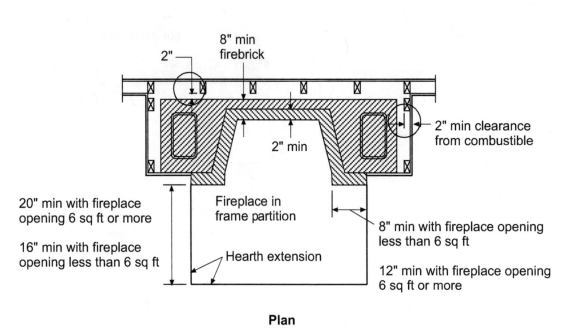

Plan

For SI: 1 inch = 25.4 mm, 1 square foot = 0.093 m².

The hearth and the hearth extension must be constructed of, and supported by, noncombustible materials. Hearths must be specifically constructed of either concrete or masonry. The minimum required thickness of fireplace hearths is 4 inches.

Topic: Clearance to Combustible Material	**Category:** Masonry
Reference: IBC 2111.12	**Subject:** Fireplaces

Code Text: *Any portion of a masonry fireplace located in the interior of a building or within the exterior wall of a building shall have a clearance to combustibles of not less than 2 inches (51 mm) from the front faces and sides of masonry fireplaces and not less than 4 inches (102 mm) from the back faces of masonry fireplaces. The airspace shall not be filled, except to provide fireblocking in accordance with Section 2111.13. See the four exceptions for* alternate methods to the required clearances.

Discussion and Commentary: The radiant heat transfer through the materials used to construct a masonry fireplace and/ or chimney necessitates a minimum separation between the masonry and combustible materials, such as wood floor, wall or ceiling framing. The depth of the noncombustible fireblocking, placed on metal strips or lath, is to be 1 inch.

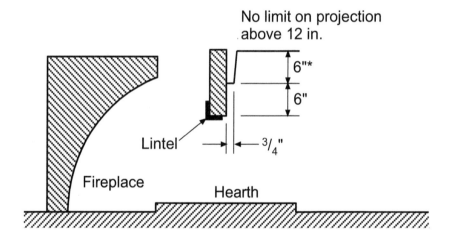

No limit on projection above 12 in.

6"*

6"

Lintel

³/₄"

Fireplace

Hearth

* Combustible materials may project ¹/₈ in. for each 1 in. clearance.
No combustible materials permitted within 6 in. of opening.

For SI: 1 inch = 25.4 mm.

Combustible materials projection from fireplace

No combustible materials, such as trim and ornamentation, are permitted within 6 inches directly above the opening at the face of the fireplace. Combustibles placed less than 12 inches from the opening, while permitted, are very limited in their projection from the fireplace opening.

Code Text: *Sawn lumber used for load-supporting purposes, including end-jointed or edge-glued lumber, machine stress-rated or machine-evaluated lumber, shall be identified by the grade mark of a lumber grading or inspection agency that has been approved by an accreditation body that complies with DOC PS 20 or equivalent procedures. Wood structural panels, when used structurally (including those used for siding, roof and wall sheathing, subflooring, diaphragms and built-up members), shall conform to the requirements for its type in DOC PS 1, DOC PS 2 or ANSI/APA PRP 210.*

Discussion and Commentary: The proper use of a wood structural member cannot be determined unless it has been identified. Grade marks, identification marks, certificates of inspection and quality marks are various methods of indicating the type and quality of wood members.

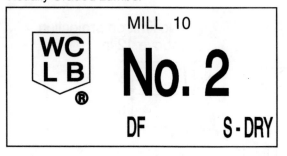

Visually Graded Lumber

Machine Stress-rated lumber

Lumber and, particularly, wood structural panels are highly variable in strengths and other mechanical properties; hence, such materials must conform to the applicable standards or grading rules specified in the code.

Code Text: *Wood used above ground in the locations specified in Sections 2304.12.1.1 through 2304.12.1.5, 2304.12.3 and 2304.12.5 shall be naturally durable wood or preservative-treated wood using water-borne preservatives, in accordance with AWPA U1 for above-ground use.*

Discussion and Commentary: To protect against decay and termite infestation, the code addresses those members for which care must be taken, including: joists, girders and subfloor adjacent to exposed ground in crawl spaces; framing members and wall sheathing that rest on exterior foundation walls; sleepers and sills on a concrete slab in direct contact with earth; girder ends in masonry or concrete walls; wood siding adjacent to the ground; and posts and columns supported by a concrete slab.

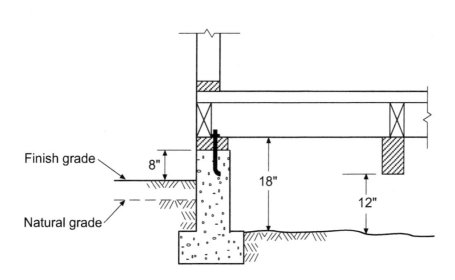

Finish grade

8"

Natural grade

18"

12"

For SI: 1 inch = 25.4 mm.

Under-floor clearance

The term "naturally durable wood" describes the heartwood of a select group of wood species that provide a natural resistance to decay (redwood, cedar, black locust and black walnut) and/or termites (redwood, Alaska yellow cedar, Eastern red cedar and Western red cedar).

Code Text: *The requirements of Section 2308 are intended for conventional light-frame construction. Other methods are permitted to be used provided a satisfactory design is submitted showing compliance with other provisions of the IBC. Interior nonload-bearing partitions, ceilings and curtain walls of conventional light-frame construction are not subject to the limitations of Section 2308.2.*

Discussion and Commentary: Conventional light-frame wood construction is considered a type of construction whose primary structural elements are formed by a system of repetitive wood-framing members. The provisions of Section 2308 are based on experience gained over the last several decades. This experience has resulted in the prescriptive requirements contained in this section.

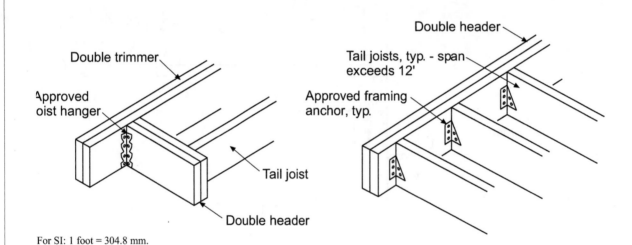

For SI: 1 foot = 304.8 mm.

Framing around openings - header span > 6'

Floor framing at openings

The limitations placed on buildings of conventional light-frame construction are based on limits to: number of stories; floor-to-floor height of bearing walls; live, dead and snow loads; wind speeds; rafter span; and seismic design categories.

Topic: Foundation Plates or Sills	**Category:** Wood
Reference: IBC 2308.3.1	**Subject:** Conventional Light-Frame Construction

Code Text: *Foundation plates or sills shall be bolted or anchored to the foundation with not less than $^{1}/_{2}$-inch (12.7 mm) diameter steel bolts or approved anchors spaced to provide equivalent anchorage as the steel bolts. Bolts shall be embedded at least 7 inches (178 mm) into concrete or masonry. The bolts shall be located in the middle third of the width of the plate. Bolts shall be spaced not more than 6 feet (1829 mm) on center and there shall be not less than two bolts or anchor straps per piece with one bolt or anchor strap located not more than 12 inches (305 mm) or less than 4 inches (102 mm) from each end of each piece. A properly sized nut and washer shall be tightened on each bolt to the plate.*

Discussion and Commentary: The prescriptive requirements for the installation of anchor bolts are applicable to all buildings of conventional light-frame wood construction. The provisions set forth the necessary criteria to adequately tie the framing system to the foundation.

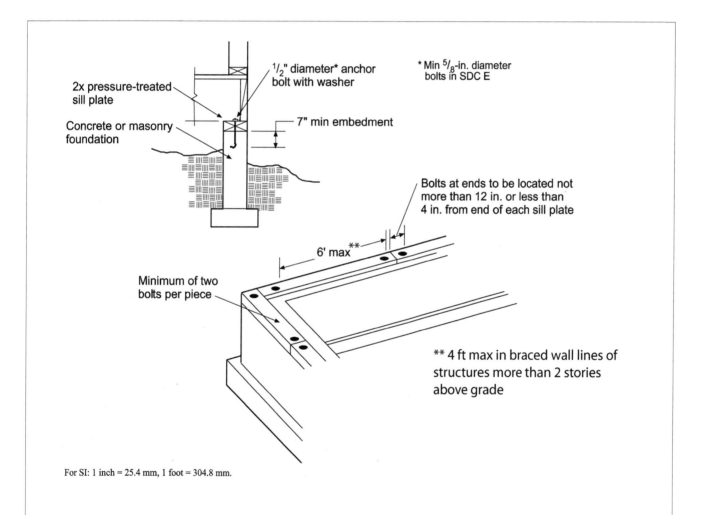

For SI: 1 inch = 25.4 mm, 1 foot = 304.8 mm.

In Seismic Design Categories D and E, it has been shown that additional anchorage methods are necessary to resist the lateral forces being applied at the foundation connection. Thus, minimum 0.229-inch by 3-inch by 3-inch steel plate washers are mandated between the sill plate and the nut, in accordance with Section 2308.3.1.1 or 2308.3.1.2.

Study Session 16
IBC Chapters 16, 17, 19, 21, 22 and 23

1. Construction documents shall indicate the flat-roof snow load, snow exposure factor, snow load importance factor, thermal factor, drift surcharge load and width of snow drift unless the ground snow load in the area is a maximum of _____ pounds per square foot.

    a. 5   b. 10

    c. 20   d. 30

Reference_____

2. The minimum uniformly distributed live load used in the design of the seating area of a fixed-seat arena is determined to be _____ pounds per square foot.

    a. 50   b. 60

    c. 100   d. 125

Reference_____

3. Buildings used for fire, rescue, ambulance and police stations and emergency vehicle garages shall be designated as Risk Category _____ .

    a. I   b. II

    c. III   d. IV

Reference_____

4. Roof areas not intended for occupancy on landscaped roofs shall be designed for a minimum uniform live load of _____ pounds per square foot.

    a. 20   b. 40

    c. 60   d. 100

Reference_____

5. For wind design purposes, Surface Roughness Category_____ includes flat open country and grasslands.

    a. A   b. B

    c. C   d. D

Reference_____

6. Foundation walls in which horizontal movement is restricted at the top shall be designed for _____ pressure.

    a. at-rest   b. controlled

    c. flexible   d. active

Reference_____

7. Special inspection thickness testing for sprayed fire-resistant material applied to structural framing members shall be performed on a minimum of _____ percent of the structural members on each floor.

    a. 10   b. 25

    c. 50   d. 100

Reference_____

8. Structures a minimum of _____ stories in height above grade plane shall be provided with structural observation assigned to Seismic Design Category E.

    a. two   b. three

    c. four   d. five

Reference_____

9. A structural plain concrete footing is permitted to be 6 inches in thickness in a building of other than Group R-3 occupancy, provided the building is a maximum of _____ above grade plane.

    a. 0 stories, structural plain concrete footings are only permitted in Group R-3 occupancies

    b. 1 story

    c. 2 stories

    d. 3 stories

Reference_____

10. In general, an interior partition with a plaster finish shall have a deflection limit of
_____.

    a. $l/120$ b. $l/180$

    c. $l/240$ d. $l/360$

Reference _____

11. The maximum allowable deflection of framing members supporting glass subject to 0.6 times the component and cladding wind loads shall be _____ inch(es) for framing members having a length of 20 feet.

    a. $1^{1}/_{4}$ b. 1

    c. $^{7}/_{8}$ d. $^{3}/_{4}$

Reference _____

12. The minimum thickness of a concrete floor slab supported directly on the ground shall be _____ inches.

    a. $3^{1}/_{2}$ b. 4

    c. 5   d. 6

Reference_____

13. What is the term used to describe masonry in which the tensile resistance of the masonry is taken into consideration and the effects of stresses in reinforcement are neglected?

    a. ashlar masonry   b. plain masonry

    c. reinforced masonry   d. solid masonry

Reference_____

14. In order to meet the structural stability requirements of Section 706.2 where the structure on either side of the wall has collapsed, fire walls and their supports shall be designed to withstand a minimum horizontal allowable stress load of _____ pounds per square foot.

    a. 5   b. 10

    c. 15   d. 20

Reference _____

15. A vapor retarder is required between a base course and a concrete floor slab for any unheated storage rooms having a minimum floor area of _____ square feet where attached to a Group R-3 occupancy.

    a. 50   b. 70

    c. 100   d. 120

Reference _____

16. A hearth extension for a masonry fireplace with a 24-inch by 42-inch opening shall extend a minimum of _____ inches in front of, and a minimum of _____ inches beyond, each side of the fireplace opening.

    a. 16, 8   b. 16, 10

    c. 20, 12   d. 24, 12

Reference_____

17. Combustible materials located 10 inches directly above the opening of a masonry fireplace shall have a maximum projection of _____ inch(es).

    a. 0, no projection is permitted   b. $^3/_4$

    c. 1   d. $1^1/_4$

Reference_____

18. Masonry chimneys shall extend at least 2 feet higher than any portion of the building within 10 feet, with a minimum height of _____ feet above the point where the chimney passes through the roof.

    a. 2   b. $2^1/_2$

    c. 3   d. 4

Reference_____

19. Unless naturally durable or preservative-treated wood is used, what is the minimum air space required on the top, sides and end of wood girders entering exterior concrete walls?

    a. $^1/_2$ inch   b. 1 inch

    c. $1^1/_2$ inch   d. 2 inches

Reference_____

20. Which of the following types of naturally durable wood cannot qualify as decay resistant?

    a. redwood   b. cedar

    c. black walnut   d. red oak

    Reference_____

21. What is the minimum number and size of common nails required to connect a wood roof rafter to a hip rafter?

    a. two 10d, face nail   b. three 10d, toenail

    c. two 16d, toenail   d. three 16d, face nail

    Reference_____

22. In conventional light-frame construction of structures of a maximum plan dimension of _____ feet, continuous foundations supporting braced wall lines need only be provided at exterior walls.

    a. 20   b. 25

    c. 35   d. 50

    Reference_____

23. In conventional light-frame construction, trimmer and header joists in framing around openings shall be doubled, or lumber of equivalent cross section shall be provided, where the span of the header exceeds a minimum of _____ feet.

    a. 4   b. 6

    c. 10   d. 12

    Reference_____

24. In conventional light-frame wall construction, the edge of a bored hole shall be a minimum of _____ inch(es) from the edge of the stud.

    a. $\frac{5}{8}$ b. $\frac{3}{4}$

    c. 1   d. $1\frac{1}{4}$

    Reference_____

25. In conventional light-frame roof construction, the maximum span of a 2-inch by 6-inch purlin shall be _____ feet.

      a. 4   b. 6

      c. 8   d. 12

Reference_____

26. In the design of stairway treads, a minimum concentrated live load of _____ pounds must be used, determined on an area of 2 inches by 2 inches.

      a. 40   b. 100

      c. 200   d. 300

Reference_____

27. Where it is necessary to convert wind speed, a basic design wind speed of 130 mph converts to an allowable stress design wind speed of _____ mph.

      a. 85   b. 101

      c. 117   d. 124

Reference_____

28. In the construction of foundations for adobe construction, stabilized adobe units shall be used in adobe walls for the first _____ inches above the finished first-floor elevation.

      a. 4   b. 6

      c. 8   d. 12

Reference_____

29. Masonry nonstructural floor surfacing a maximum of _____ inches in thickness is permitted to be supported by wood members without checking for the effects of long-term loading.

      a. 2   b. 4

      c. 6   d. 8

Reference_____

30. In conventional light-frame construction, foundation cripple walls exceeding
_____ in height shall be framed of wood studs having the size required
for an additional story.

  a. 14 inches   b. 20 inches

  c. 30 inches   d. 48 inches

  Reference_____

31. Unless the specified live load is 80 psf or greater, the partition load in an office building shall be a minimum uniformly distributed live load of _____ pounds.

  a. 5   b. 10

  c. 15   d. 20

  Reference _____

32. Grab bars shall be designed to resist a single minimum concentrated load of
_____ pounds applied in any direction at any point.

  a. 160   b. 225

  c. 250   d. 300

  Reference _____

33. Areas along the U.S. Gulf of Mexico coast are not considered hurricane-prone
regions where the maximum ultimate design wind speed is _____ miles
per hour.

  a. 100   b. 110

  c. 115   d. 130

  Reference _____

34. Where a cold-formed steel truss has a minimum clear span of _____ feet,
a special inspector shall verify that the temporary installation restraint bracing is
installed in accordance with the approved truss submittal package.

  a. 40   b. 50

  c. 60   d. 80

  Reference _____

35. Combustible framing shall be located a minimum of _____ inch(es) away from flue openings.

    a. 1   b. 2

    c. 4   d. 6

Reference _____

36. Unless determined otherwise by a geotechnical investigation, a minimum design lateral soil load under active pressure of _____ psf per foot of depth shall be used in the design of retaining walls to resist lateral soil loads from adjacent Class ML soil.

    a. 30   b. 45

    c. 60   d. 100

Reference _____

37. The periodic inspection of the erection of mass timber construction is not required for which one of the following types of construction?

    a. Type IV-A   b. Type IV-B

    c. Type IV-C   d. Type IV-HT

Reference _____

38. The special inspection of penetration firestops and fire-resistant joint systems is required in fire areas containing Group R occupancies with a minimum fire area occupant load of _____.

    a. 101   b. 201

    c. 251   d. 301

Reference _____

39. In heavy timber construction, what are the minimum required dimensions of structural composite lumber beams supporting floor and roof loads?

    a. 6″ by 10″   b. 5″ by 10″

    c. $5\frac{1}{4}$″ by $9\frac{1}{2}$″   d. 8″ by 10″

Reference _____

40. Enclosed wood framing in exterior balconies that have weather-exposed surfaces shall be provided with ventilation openings that provide a minimum net free cross-ventilation area of _____ of the area of each separate space.

a. $^1/_{100}$ b. $^1/_{150}$

c. $^1/_{300}$ d. $^1/_{600}$

Reference _____

2021 IBC Chapters 8, 12, 25 and 30

Interior Finishes, Interior Environment, Gypsum Board and Elevators

OBJECTIVE: To gain an understanding of the limitations on interior wall and ceiling finishes; the installation requirements for gypsum board, lath and plaster; the important issues concerning the interior environment, including light, ventilation and sound transmission; and the provisions for elevators and their hoistways.

REFERENCE: Chapters 8, 12, 25 and 30, 2021 *International Building Code*

KEY POINTS:
- Which building elements are considered to be interior wall and ceiling finishes?
- Which types of materials are not regulated as wall or ceiling finishes?
- What is the standard of quality that addresses interior wall and ceiling finishes?
- Based on flame-spread index, what are the various classes of finish materials?
- When tested in a manner consistent with their use, what is the maximum smoke density index permitted for finish materials?
- In general, what is the maximum thickness of an interior wall or ceiling finish that must be applied directly against a noncombustible backing?
- Under what conditions are interior wall and ceiling finishes tested to NFPA 286 permitted?
- How is Table 803.13 used to regulate the finish materials on ceilings and walls?
- Under which conditions are textile wall coverings permitted as wall and ceiling finishes?
- In what portions of a building are the interior floor finishes regulated? In which specific occupancies?
- What are the limitations on combustible trim and decorative materials?
- How must the occupiable portions of buildings be illuminated? Ventilated?
- When yards and courts are adjacent to exterior openings providing natural light and ventilation, how shall the openings be located?
- In which type of occupancy is the transmission of sound regulated?
- How is air-borne sound to be controlled? Structure-borne sound?
- What are the minimum room widths of habitable spaces? Minimum ceiling heights of occupiable spaces?

- How are efficiency dwelling units regulated for interior environment?
- What minimum size access opening is required for a crawl space? An attic?
- How must walls and floors in toilet rooms and bathing rooms be surfaced?
- What are the limitations for gypsum wallboard in regard to exterior installation and weather protection?
- How shall fasteners for gypsum wallboard be applied?
- What type of gypsum board assembly requires treated joints and fasteners?
- Where is water-resistant gypsum backing board required?
- Water-resistant gypsum backing board is not permitted for use in which three locations?
- Where used to provide a horizontal diaphragm, how shall gypsum board be installed in a ceiling application?
- What level of fire resistance is required for elevator shaft enclosures?
- What is the maximum number of elevator cars that may be located in a single elevator hoistway? At what point are two hoistways required?
- What types of doors are prohibited at the point of access to an elevator car?
- In what buildings are elevator lobbies required to protect the hoistway openings? How are the lobbies to be constructed?
- What is a fire service access elevator? In what buildings is such an elevator required? What special features are provided?
- Where are occupant evacuation elevators required? Can such elevators be used as a portion of the means of egress? What special features are provided?

Topic: Definition and Classifications   **Category:** Interior Finishes
Reference: IBC 802.1, 202   **Subject:** Wall and Ceiling Finishes

Code Text: *The provisions of Section 803 shall limit the allowable fire performance and smoke development of interior wall and ceiling finish materials based upon occupancy classification. Interior wall and ceiling finish includes the exposed interior surfaces of buildings including, but not limited to: fixed or movable walls and partitions; toilet room privacy partitions; columns; ceilings; and interior wainscotting, paneling, or other finish applied structurally or for decoration, acoustical correction, surface insulation, structural fire resistance or similar purposes, but not including trim.*

Discussion and Commentary: It is the intent of the IBC to govern those materials applied to walls or ceilings that could contribute to the spread of flame or the development of smoke. Floor finishes are regulated in a different manner as set forth in Section 804.

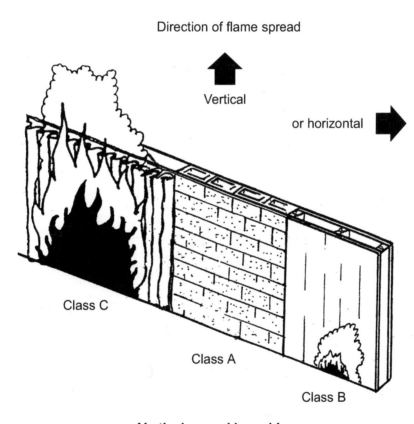

The classification of interior wall and ceiling finishes is based primarily on their flame spread index. Class A has an index of 0 to 25, Class B of 26 to 75, and Class C of 76 to 200. The smoke-developed index for all three classifications is limited to 450.

Code Text: *Interior wall and ceiling finish shall have a flame spread index not greater than that specified in Table 803.13 for the group and location designated.*

Discussion and Commentary: Based on fire statistics, the rapid spread of fire across an interior finish material has been second only to vertical fire spread through openings between floors as a cause of life loss during building fires. Therefore, limitations are placed on the materials that are used to cover the walls and ceilings of rooms and other enclosed spaces, corridors, and vertical exits and exit passageways. The rapid spread of fire and the increased contribution of fuel to the fire are the major reasons why finish materials must meet stringent criteria to gain acceptance.

TABLE 803.13
INTERIOR WALL AND CEILING FINISH REQUIREMENTS BY OCCUPANCY[k]

GROUP	SPRINKLERED[l]			NONSPRINKLERED		
	Interior exit stairways and ramps and exit passageways[a, b]	Corridors and enclosure for exit access stairways and ramps	Rooms and enclosed spaces[c]	Interior exit stairways and ramps and exit passageways[a, b]	Corridors and enclosure for exit access stairways and ramps	Rooms and enclosed spaces[c]
A-1 & A-2	B	B	C	A	A[d]	B[e]
A-3[f], A-4, A-5	B	B	C	A	A[d]	C
B, E, M, R-1	B	C[m]	C	A	B	C
R-4	B	C	C	A	B	B
F	C	C	C	B	C	C
H	B	B	C[g]	A	A	B
I-1	B	C	C	A	B	B
I-2	B	B	B[h, i]	A	A	B
I-3	A	A[j]	C	A	A	B
I-4	B	B	B[h, i]	A	A	B
R-2	C	C	C	B	B	C
R-3	C	C	C	C	C	C
S	C	C	C	B	B	C
U	No restrictions			No restrictions		

For SI: 1 inch = 25.4 mm, 1 square foot = 0.0929 m².

a. Class C interior finish materials shall be permitted for wainscotting or paneling of not more than 1,000 square feet of applied surface area in the grade lobby where applied directly to a noncombustible base or over furring strips applied to a noncombustible base and fireblocked as required by Section 803.15.1.

b. In other than Group I-3 occupancies in buildings less than three stories above grade plane, Class B interior finish for nonsprinklered buildings and Class C interior finish for sprinklered buildings shall be permitted in interior exit stairways and ramps.

c. Requirements for rooms and enclosed spaces shall be based on spaces enclosed by partitions. Where a fire-resistance rating is required for structural elements, the enclosing partitions shall extend from the floor to the ceiling. Partitions that do not comply with this shall be considered to be enclosing spaces and the rooms or spaces on both sides shall be considered to be one room or space. In determining the applicable requirements for rooms and enclosed spaces, the specific occupancy thereof shall be the governing factor regardless of the group classification of the building or structure.

d. Lobby areas in Group A-1, A-2 and A-3 occupancies shall be not less than Class B materials.

e. Class C interior finish materials shall be permitted in places of assembly with an occupant load of 300 persons or less.

f. For places of religious worship, wood used for ornamental purposes, trusses, paneling or chancel furnishing shall be permitted.

g. Class B material is required where the building exceeds two stories.

h. Class C interior finish materials shall be permitted in administrative spaces.

i. Class C interior finish materials shall be permitted in rooms with a capacity of four persons or less.

j. Class B materials shall be permitted as wainscotting extending not more than 48 inches above the finished floor in corridors and exit access stairways and ramps.

k. Finish materials as provided for in other sections of this code.

l. Applies when protected by an automatic sprinkler system installed in accordance with Section 903.3.1.1 or 903.3.1.2.

m. Corridors in ambulatory care facilities shall be provided with Class A or B materials.

Textile materials, where applied to walls or ceilings, must meet additional criteria prior to approval. Finishes that have napped, tufted, looped, nonwoven, woven or similar surface characteristics present a unique hazard on account of their contribution to extremely rapid fire spread.

Topic: Floor Finish Requirements   **Category:** Interior Finishes
Reference: IBC 804.4.2   **Subject:** Interior Floor Finish

Code Text: *In all occupancies, interior floor finish and floor covering materials in enclosures for stairways and ramps, exit passageways, corridors and rooms or spaces not separated from corridors by partitions extending from the floor to the underside of the ceiling shall withstand a minimum critical radiant flux not less than Class I in Groups I-1, I-2 and I-3 and not less than Class II in Groups A, B, E, H, I-4, M, R-1, R-2 and S.* See the exception for the permitted reduction of classification in fully sprinklered buildings.

Discussion and Commentary: Although there are many different types of floor finishes and floor coverings, only those flooring materials composed of fibers are regulated by Section 804. Where required to be classified as Class I or Class II materials, the floor covering materials must be tested by an approved agency in accordance with NFPA 253 or ASTM E648. In order to verify compliance, the materials must be identified by a hang tag or other suitable method that identifies the manufacturer or supplier, style and finish classification.

Types of classifications: (in terms of heat flux, Sec. 804.2)

- Class I: Minimum 0.45 watts/cm^2 per NFPA 253 or ASTM E648
- Class II: Minimum 0.22 watts/cm^2 per NFPA 253 or ASTM E648
- DOC FF-1: Minimum 0.04 watts/cm^2

Required classifications: (Sec. 804.4)

	Nonsprinklered[a]		Sprinklered (NFPA 13 only)	
	Exit/Corr.[b]	Other Areas	Exit/Corr.[b]	Other Areas
Groups I-1, I-2 and I-3	Class I	DOC FF-1[c]	Class II	DOC FF-1[c]
Groups F, R-3, R-4 and U	DOC FF-1[c]	DOC FF-1[c]	DOC FF-1[c]	DOC FF-1[c]
Other Groups	Class II	DOC FF-1[c]	DOC FF-1[c]	DOC FF-1[c]

Note: [a]Section 903.2 requires sprinklers in various occupancies

[b]Includes enclosures for stairways and ramps, exit passageways, corridors and rooms or spaces not separated from corridors by full-height partitions.

[c]Compliance with ASTM D2859 also permitted

DOC FF-1, often referred to as the Methenamine Pill Test, essentially evaluates the floor covering when subjected to a cigarette-type ignition by using a small methenamine tablet. All carpeting sold in the United States is required by federal law to pass this test procedure.

Code Text: *Buildings shall be provided with natural ventilation in accordance with Section 1202.5 or mechanical ventilation in accordance with the* International Mechanical Code. *Natural ventilation of an occupied space shall be through windows, doors, louvers or other openings to the outdoors. The minimum openable area to the outdoors shall be 4 percent of the floor area being ventilated.*

Discussion and Commentary: To obtain a minimum level of environmental comfort, as well as to maintain sanitary conditions, some form of ventilation must be provided to portions of a building that are normally occupied. The *International Mechanical Code* will usually be used to determine the minimum acceptable ventilation methods and quantities.

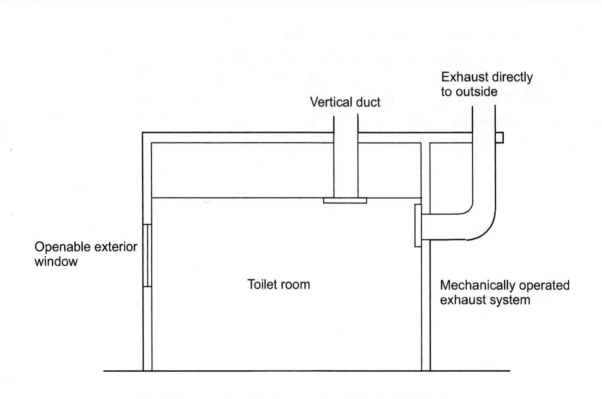

Ventilation regulated by *International Mechanical Code*

The *International Mechanical Code* regulates ventilation of bathrooms, toilet rooms, shower rooms and similar spaces containing bathtubs, showers and spas. The *International Fire Code*, in addition to the IMC, addresses ventilation and exhaust systems where flammable and combustible hazards are present.

Code Text: *Enclosed attics and enclosed rafter spaces formed where ceilings are applied directly to the underside of roof framing members shall have cross ventilation for each separate space by ventilating openings protected against the entrance of rain and snow. The space between the bottom of the floor joists and the earth under any building except spaces occupied by a basement or cellar shall be provided with ventilation in accordance with one of three methods. The openings shall be placed so as to provide cross-ventilation of the under-floor space.*

Discussion and Commentary: Ventilation of the attic and under-floor spaces prevents moisture condensation, which can have adverse effects on the materials of construction located in those spaces. Various exceptions are available that provide equivalent results.

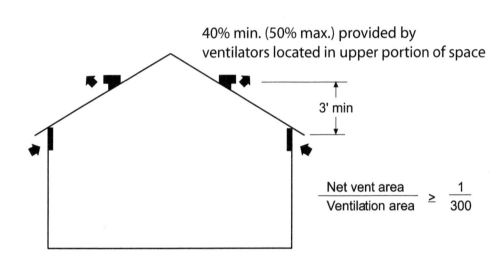

40% min. (50% max.) provided by ventilators located in upper portion of space

3' min

$$\frac{\text{Net vent area}}{\text{Ventilation area}} \geq \frac{1}{300}$$

Attic ventilation - calculations

For SI: 1 foot = 304.8 mm.

The general requirement for under-floor ventilation mandates a minimum net area of ventilation openings of $1/_{150}$ of the area of the space ventilated. In addition, all openings to the exterior must be screened to prevent the entry of birds, rodents and similar creatures.

Code Text: *Every space intended for human occupancy shall be provided with natural light by means of exterior glazed openings in accordance with Section 1204.2 or shall be provided with artificial light in accordance with Section 1204.3. Exterior glazed openings shall open directly onto a public way or onto a yard or court in accordance with Section 1205. The minimum net glazed area shall not be less than 8 percent of the floor area of the room served. Artificial light shall be provided that is adequate to provide an average illumination of 10 foot-candles (107 lux) over the area of the room at a height of 30 inches (762 mm) above the floor level.*

Discussion and Commentary: It is fundamental that all occupiable areas of a building be provided with adequate illumination. The use of artificial light to satisfy the code is acceptable because it can produce the light necessary for occupancy at any time of the day or night.

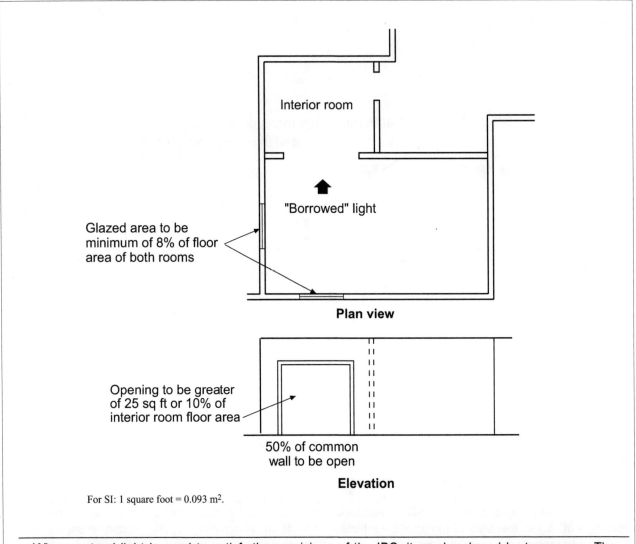

Plan view

Elevation

Glazed area to be minimum of 8% of floor area of both rooms

Interior room

"Borrowed" light

Opening to be greater of 25 sq ft or 10% of interior room floor area

50% of common wall to be open

For SI: 1 square foot = 0.093 m².

Where natural light is used to satisfy the provisions of the IBC, it can be shared by two rooms. The common wall between the rooms must be adequately open, and the total floor area of both rooms shall be used to calculate the minimum glazed area.

Code Text: *Walls, partitions and floor/ceiling assemblies separating dwelling units and sleeping units from each other or from public or service areas shall have a sound transmission class of not less than 50 where tested in accordance with ASTM E90, or have a Normalized Noise Isolation Class (NNIC) rating of not less than 45 if field tested, in accordance with ASTM E336 for airborne noise. Floor/ceiling assemblies between dwelling units and sleeping units or between a dwelling unit or sleeping unit and a public or service area within the structure shall have an impact insulation class rating of not less than 50 where tested in accordance with ASTM E492, or have a Normalized Impact Sound Rating (NISR) of not less than 45 if field tested in accordance with ASTM E1007.*

Discussion and Commentary: To control sound transmission between areas of a residential building, insulated walls and floor/ceiling assemblies are necessary. The regulations address air-borne sound that may be carried throughout the structure, as well as impact noise created on the floor of a floor/ceiling assembly.

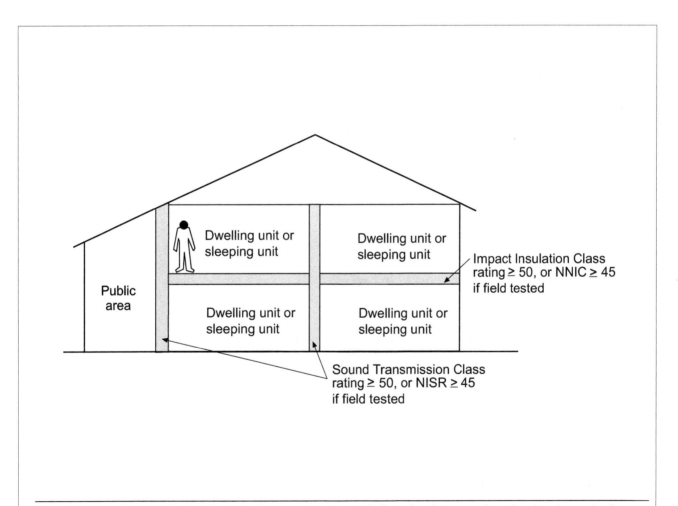

To maintain the required ratings, it is necessary to seal, line, insulate or otherwise treat penetrations through the sound transmission assemblies. The code exempts unit entrance doors from sound transmission limits, provided that they are tight fitting to the frame and sill.

Code Text: *Habitable spaces, other than a kitchen, shall not be less than 7 feet (2134 mm) in any plan dimension. Kitchens shall have a clear passageway of not less than 3 feet (914 mm) between counter fronts and appliances or counter fronts and walls. Occupiable spaces, habitable spaces and corridors shall have a ceiling height of not less than 7 feet 6 inches (2286 mm) above the finished floor. Bathrooms, toilet rooms, kitchens, storage rooms and laundry rooms shall have a ceiling height of not less than 7 feet (2134 mm) above the finished floor.* See the exceptions for ceilings with exposed beams, sloped ceilings, mezzanines and corridors. *Every dwelling unit shall have not less than one room that shall have not less than 120 square feet (13.9 m²) of net floor area. Other habitable rooms shall have a net floor area of not less than 70 square feet (6.5 m²).* See the exception for kitchens.

Discussion and Commentary: For fundamental usability and environmental purposes, it is necessary to mandate minimum requirements for the size and height of occupiable spaces.

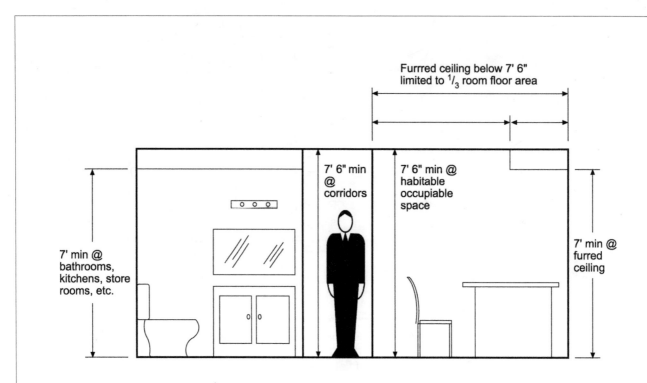

For SI: 1 inch = 25.4 mm, 1 foot = 304.8 mm.

Efficiency dwelling units, often referred to as studio apartments, typically consist of a single room used as a combination living/sleeping/dining/cooking area, and a bathroom. The code regulates living room size at a minimum of 190 square feet, and also addresses the closet, bathroom and kitchen spaces.

Code Text: *Crawl spaces shall be provided with no fewer than one access opening that shall be not less than 18 inches by 24 inches (457 mm by 610 mm). An opening not less than 20 inches by 30 inches (559 mm by 762 mm) shall be provided to any attic area having a clear height of over 30 inches (762 mm). A 30-inch (762 mm) minimum clear headroom in the attic space shall be provided at or above the access opening.*

Discussion and Commentary: Items such as plumbing and wiring installations pass through crawl space at times. Required initial and periodic inspections and maintenance and repairs cannot be carried out without access to such crawl spaces. Attic access is also required for similar reasons. Although uncommon, access to the attic for fire department purposes can also be accomplished through such openings. The required openings are a convenient and nondestructive means for any user to access such concealed spaces.

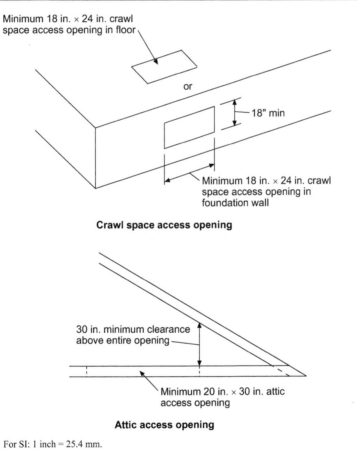

Minimum 18 in. × 24 in. crawl space access opening in floor

or

18" min

Minimum 18 in. × 24 in. crawl space access opening in foundation wall

Crawl space access opening

30 in. minimum clearance above entire opening

Minimum 20 in. × 30 in. attic access opening

Attic access opening

For SI: 1 inch = 25.4 mm.

The *International Mechanical Code* regulates access to both underfloor and attic spaces for the inspection, service, repair or replacement of any mechanical equipment. In addition to the access opening, the passageway and service area sizes are also addressed.

Code Text: *In other than dwelling units, toilet, bathing and shower room floor finish materials shall have a smooth, hard, nonabsorbent surface. The intersections of such floors with walls shall have a smooth, hard, nonabsorbent vertical base that extends upward onto the walls not less than 4 inches (102 mm). Walls and partitions within 2 feet (610 mm) of urinals and water closets shall have a smooth, hard, nonabsorbent surface, to a height of not less than 4 feet (1219 mm) above the floor, and except for structural elements, the materials used in such walls shall be of a type that is not adversely affected by moisture. See the exceptions for dwelling units, sleeping units and private toilet rooms. Accessories such as grab bars, towel bars, paper dispensers and soap dishes, provided on or within walls, shall be installed and sealed to protect structural elements from moisture.*

Discussion and Commentary: For sanitary reasons, it is necessary to provide surfaces in bath and toilet areas that are easily cleaned and maintained.

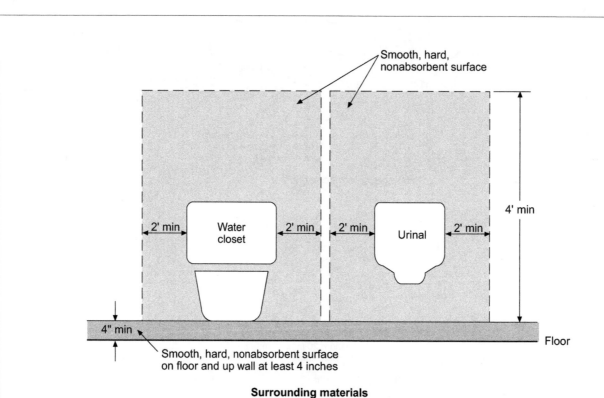

Surrounding materials

For SI: 1 inch = 25.4 mm, 1 foot = 304.8 mm.

Shower stalls and compartments must be enclosed with smooth, hard, nonabsorbent surfaces to a minimum height of 72 inches above the drain inlet. This requirement is also applicable to those bathtubs that are provided with shower heads.

Topic: Installation	**Category:** Gypsum Board and Plaster
Reference: IBC 2508.2, 2508.3	**Subject:** Gypsum Construction

Code Text: *Gypsum wallboard or gypsum plaster shall not be used in any exterior surface where such gypsum construction will be exposed directly to the weather. Gypsum wallboard, gypsum lath or gypsum plaster shall not be installed until weather protection for the installation is provided. Edges and ends of gypsum board and gypsum panel products shall occur on the framing members, except those edges and ends that are perpendicular to the framing members.*

Discussion and Commentary: Gypsum wallboard and gypsum panel products, like gypsum plaster, are subject to deterioration from moisture. Accordingly, the code does not permit such gypsum materials to be installed on weather-exposed surfaces, as defined in Section 202. Gypsum materials shall not be installed on interior surfaces until adequate protection from the weather has been provided.

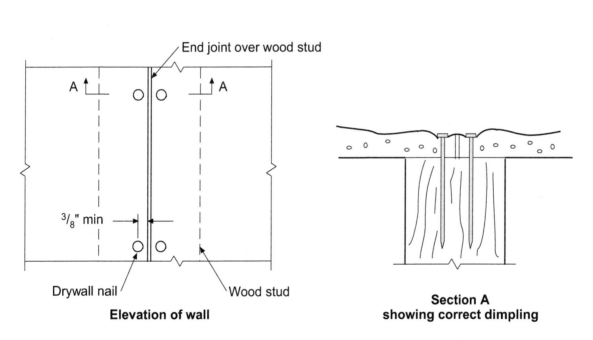

Gypsum wallboard nailing

For SI: 1 inch = 25.4 mm.

For appearance purposes in exposed locations, edges and ends of gypsum wallboard and gypsum panel products must be in moderate contact. In concealed areas, such contact is not necessary unless fire-resistance-rated construction, shear resistance or diaphragm action is required.

Code Text: *Materials used as a base for wall tile in tub and shower areas and wall and ceiling panels in shower areas shall be of materials listed in Table 2509.2 and installed in accordance with manufacturer recommendations. Water-resistant gypsum backing board shall be used as a base for tile in water closet compartment walls when installed in accordance with GA-216 or ASTM C840 and manufacturer recommendations. Regular gypsum wallboard is permitted under tile or wall panels in other wall and ceiling areas when installed in accordance with GA-216 or ASTM C840.*

Discussion and Commentary: Because of their moisture-resistant qualities, special types of panels or sheets are required when used as a backing material for tile in high-moisture areas. Although water-resistant gypsum backing board is required as a base for tile on public water closet compartment walls, such gypsum board is prohibited for use in three locations: (1) over a vapor retarder in tub or shower compartments, (2) in areas subject to continuous high humidity or where there will be direct exposure to water, and (3) on ceilings with excessive spacing between framing members.

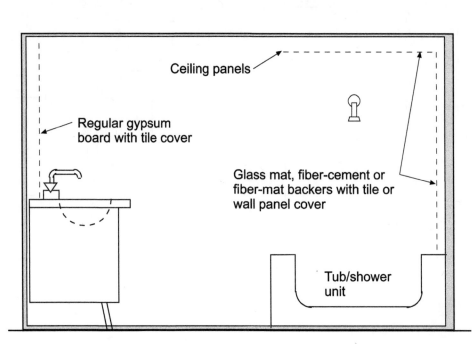

Ceiling panels

Regular gypsum board with tile cover

Glass mat, fiber-cement or fiber-mat backers with tile or wall panel cover

Tub/shower unit

For SI: 1 inch = 25.4 mm.

Water-resistant gypsum backing board is prohibited where either one of two general conditions exist: (1) over a vapor retarder in shower or bathtub compartments, or (2) where there will be direct exposure to water or in areas subject to continuous high humidity.

Topic: Weep Screeds   **Category:** Gypsum Board and Plaster
Reference: IBC 2512.1.2   **Subject:** Exterior Plaster

Code Text: *A minimum 0.019-inch (0.48 mm) (No. 26 galvanized sheet gage), corrosion-resistant weep screed with a minimum vertical attachment flange of 3^1/$_2$ inches (89 mm) shall be provided at or below the foundation plate line on exterior stud walls in accordance with ASTM C926. The weep screed shall be placed a minimum of 4 inches (102 mm) above the earth or 2 inches (51 mm) above paved areas and be of a type that will allow trapped water to drain to the exterior of the building.*

Discussion and Commentary: Water can penetrate exterior plaster walls for a variety of reasons. Once it penetrates the plaster, the water will run down the exterior face of the weather-resistive barrier until it reaches the sill plate or mudsill. At this point, the water will seek exit from the wall and, if the exterior plaster is not applied to allow the water to escape, it will exit through the inside of the wall and into the interior of the building. Therefore, a weep screed, when properly installed, will permit the water's escape to the exterior of the building.

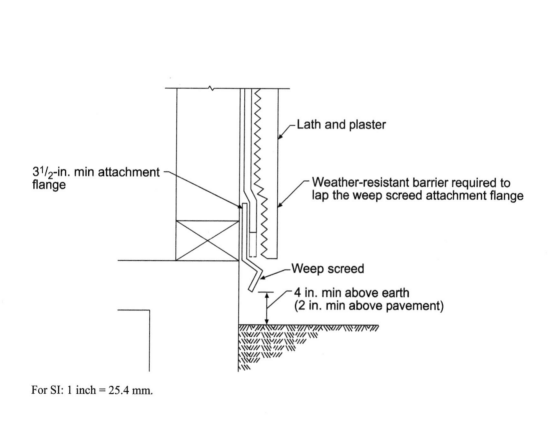

3^1/$_2$-in. min attachment flange

Lath and plaster

Weather-resistant barrier required to lap the weep screed attachment flange

Weep screed

4 in. min above earth (2 in. min above pavement)

For SI: 1 inch = 25.4 mm.

To allow the water to escape away from the building, the required water-resistive barrier in the wall assembly must lap the attachment flange of the weep screed. In addition, the exterior lath shall cover and terminate on the attachment flange.

Code Text: *Elevator, dumbwaiter and other hoistway enclosures shall be shaft enclosures complying with Sections 712 and 713. Openings in hoistway enclosures shall be protected as required in Chapter 7. Doors, other than hoistway doors and the elevator car door, shall be prohibited at the point of access to an elevator car unless such doors are readily openable from the car side without a key, tool, special knowledge or effort.*

Discussion and Commentary: An elevator shaft is regulated under the shaft enclosure provisions of Section 713. Generally, an elevator enclosure must be of 2-hour fire-resistance-rated construction in Type I buildings or where four or more stories are connected. A 1-hour rating is permitted where the shaft enclosure connects three stories or less.

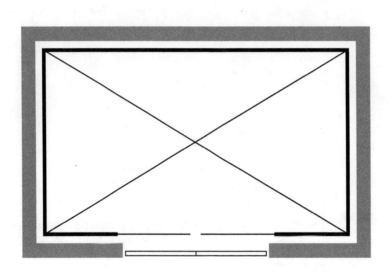

Number of stories connected	Minimum rating of elevator enclosure
Four or more	2 hours
Three or less	1 hour

In many buildings, an elevator lobby is provided adjacent to the elevator. To help ensure that an individual does not become trapped within such a lobby, the lobby door must be openable without the use of a key.

Code Text: *Where four or more elevator cars serve all or the same portion of a building, the elevators shall be located in at least two separate hoistways. Not more than four elevator cars shall be located in any single hoistway enclosure. Elevators shall not be in a common shaft enclosure with a stairway.* See the exception for open parking garages.

Discussion and Commentary: The basis for limiting the number of elevator cars in a single hoistway is to provide a reasonable level of assurance that a multilevel building served by several elevators would not have all of its elevator cars disabled by a single fire incident. The provisions increase the chance that some of the elevators would remain operational during an emergency situation.

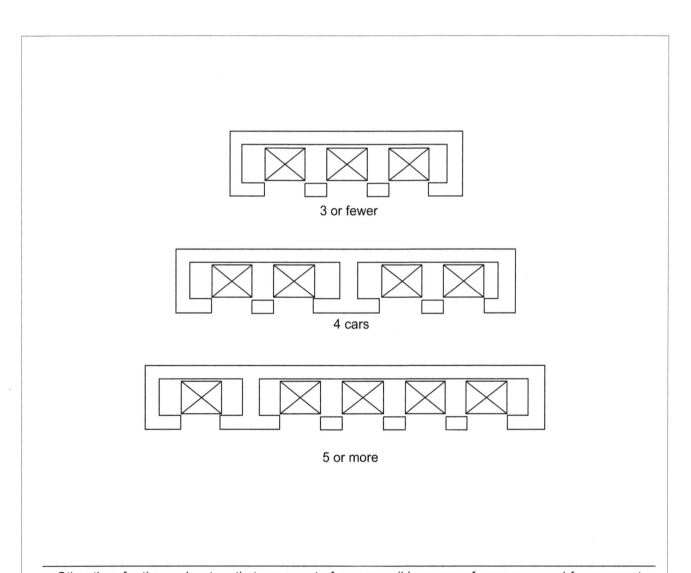

3 or fewer

4 cars

5 or more

Other than for those elevators that are a part of an accessible means of egress or used for occupant self-evacuation in accordance with Section 3008, an approved pictorial sign must be provided adjacent to each elevator call station on all floors.

Code Text: *Where elevators are provided in buildings four or more stories above, or four or more stories below, grade plane, at least one elevator shall be provided for fire department emergency access to all floors. The elevator car shall be of such a size and arrangement to accommodate an ambulance stretcher 24 inches by 84 inches (610 mm by 2134 mm) with not less than 5-inch (127 mm) radius corners, in the horizontal, open position.*

Discussion and Commentary: In those buildings over three stories in height with one or more elevators, it is necessary that a minimum of one elevator car be of sufficient size to hold an ambulance stretcher. The elevator car must access all floor levels within the building or additional complying cars must be provided to provide such access. The minimum size requirement is based on the stretchers now commonly in use by medical service personnel and emergency responders.

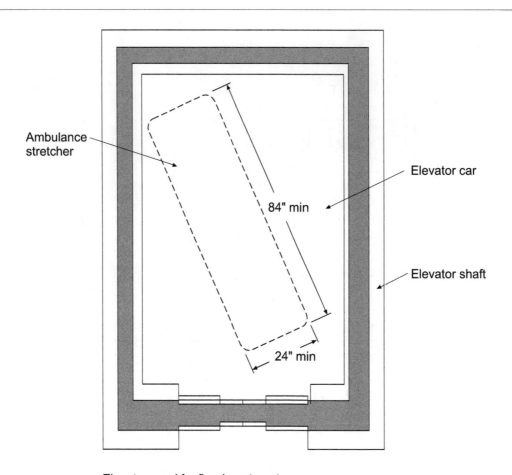

Ambulance stretcher

Elevator car

Elevator shaft

84" min

24" min

Elevator used for fire department emergency access

For SI: 1 inch = 24.5 mm.

The elevator car sized in a manner to accommodate the required size ambulance stretcher must be identified by the international symbol for emergency medical services (star of life). The symbol is required to be a minimum of 3 inches in height and is to be placed on both sides of the hoistway door frame.

Code Text: *Elevator hoistway door openings shall be protected in accordance with Section 3006.3 where an elevator hoistway connects more than three stories, is required to be enclosed within a shaft enclosure in accordance with Section 712.1.1 and any of the following conditions apply:* See the five conditions including nonsprinklered buildings; Group I-1, Condition 2, I-2 and I-3 occupancies; and high-rise buildings. Also see the three exceptions.

Discussion and Commentary: The purpose of an elevator lobby under this provision is to reduce the potential for smoke to travel from the floor of fire origin to any other floor of the building by way of an elevator shaft enclosure. An allowance is provided for those low-rise buildings where the elevator shaft connects only two or three stories.

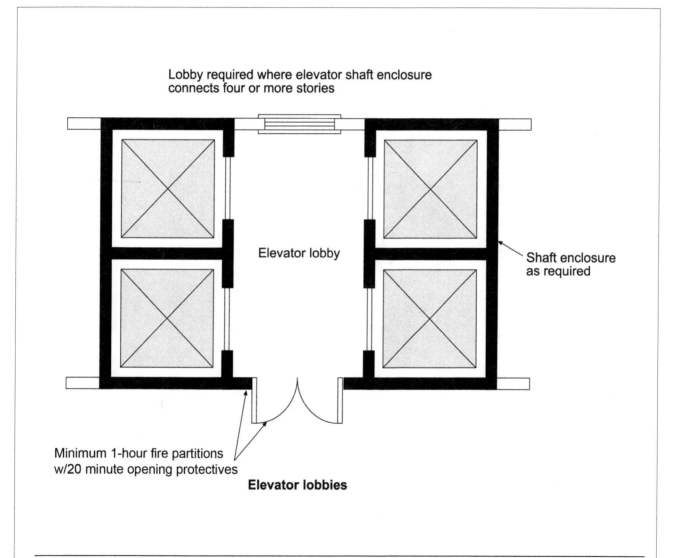

Lobby required where elevator shaft enclosure connects four or more stories

Elevator lobby

Shaft enclosure as required

Minimum 1-hour fire partitions w/20 minute opening protectives

Elevator lobbies

In those cases where a fire-resistance-rated corridor is required by Section 1020.2 and an elevator hoistway opening opens directly into the corridor, the opening must be protected by either an elevator lobby, an additional door or hoistway pressurization.

Code Text: *Where required by Section 403.6.1* (high-rise buildings with an occupied floor more than 120 feet above the lowest level of fire department vehicle access), *every floor above and including the lowest level of fire department vehicle access of the building shall be served by fire service access elevators complying with Sections 3007.1 through 3007.9. The fire service access elevator shall open into a fire service access elevator lobby in accordance with Sections 3007.6.1 through 3007.6.5. The enclosed fire service access elevator lobby shall have direct access from the enclosed elevator lobby to an enclosure for an interior exit stairway or ramp.* See the exception where equivalent protection is provided.

Discussion and Commentary: To facilitate the rapid deployment of firefighters, fire service access elevators are required in all high-rise buildings that have at least one floor level more than 120 feet above the lowest level of fire department vehicle access. This type of elevator has a number of key features that will allow firefighters to safely access an area of a building that may be involved in a fire or to facilitate the rescue of building occupants.

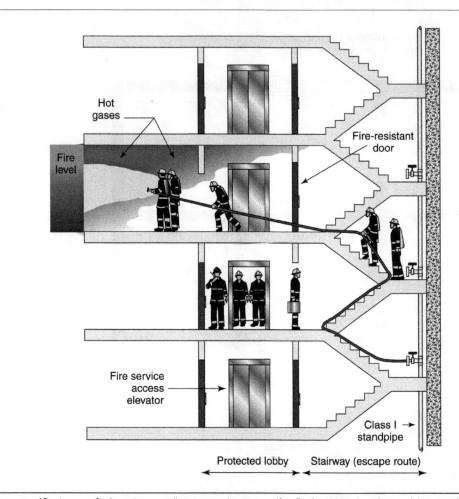

Hot gases

Fire-resistant door

Fire level

Fire service access elevator

Class I standpipe

Protected lobby Stairway (escape route)

Another specific type of elevator, an "occupant evacuation" elevator, is also addressed in Chapter 30. Public-use passenger elevators are specifically allowed to be used for the self-evacuation of occupants in high-rise buildings. The installation of such elevators is voluntary; however, they can be installed as an alternative to the additional exit stairway mandated by Section 403.5.2.

Quiz

Study Session 17
IBC Chapters 8, 12, 25 and 30

1. Where classified in accordance with ASTM E84, Class B interior wall and ceiling finishes have a flame spread index of _____ and a smoke-developed index of 0-450.

    a. 0-25

    b. 26-75

    c. 76-200

    d. 201 and greater

Reference_____

2. Unless a noncombustible material or qualified by tests, an interior wall or ceiling finish that is a maximum of _____ -inch thick shall be applied directly against a noncombustible backing.

    a. $^1/_{16}$

    b. $^1/_8$

    c. $^1/_4$

    d. $^1/_2$

Reference_____

3. Where regulated by testing to ASTM E84, the wall finish in a dining room classified as Group A-2 in a sprinklered building shall have a minimum flame spread index classification of Class _____.

    a. A

    b. B

    c. C

    d. no restrictions

Reference_____

4. The wall finish in an interior exit stairway of a four-story nonsprinklered Group B office building shall have a minimum flame spread index classification of Class _____ when regulated by ASTM E84.

    a. A

    b. B

    c. C

    d. no restrictions

Reference_____

5. In a patient room of a fully-sprinklered Group I-2 occupancy, the interior finish materials are permitted to be a maximum of Class C when the room has a maximum capacity of _____ persons.

    a. 1   b. 2

    c. 3   d. 4

Reference_____

6. Unless in compliance with the Method B test protocol of NFPA 265, textile wall coverings shall have a minimum Class _____ flame spread index where installed in a fully-sprinklered art gallery.

    a. A   b. B

    c. C   d. not permitted

Reference_____

7. In a fully sprinklered Group I-1 occupancy, carpet installed as an interior floor finish in an exit passageway shall be a minimum _____ .

    a. Class I   b. Class II

    c. Class A   d. DOC FF-1 "pill test"

Reference_____

8. Combustible trim, excluding handrails and guardrails, shall be limited to a maximum of _____ percent of the aggregate wall or ceiling area in which it is attached.

    a. 5   b. 10

    c. 25   d. 50

Reference_____

9. In a fully sprinklered Group A auditorium, complying flame-resistant decorative material shall be limited to a maximum of _____ percent of the aggregate area of walls and ceilings.

    a. 10   b. 25

    c. 50   d. 75

Reference_____

10. What is the minimum required flame spread and smoke-developed index for materials, other than foam plastic, used as interior trim?

    a. Class A
    b. Class B
    c. Class C
    d. unlimited

Reference_____

11. Within a sleeping unit of a Group R-1 hotel, a space-heating system shall be provided that is capable of maintaining a minimum indoor temperature of_____ at a point 3 feet above the floor on the design heating day.

    a. 65 °F
    b. 68 °F
    c. 70 °F
    d. 72 °F

Reference_____

12. Where natural light by means of exterior glazed openings is utilized as the required lighting for an occupied space, the minimum net glazed area shall not be less than _____ percent of the floor area of the room served.

    a. 4
    b. 5
    c. 8
    d. 10

Reference_____

13. A stairway within a dwelling unit in a Group R-2 apartment building shall be provided with a minimum illumination level on tread runs of _____ foot-candle(s).

    a. 1
    b. 2
    c. 5
    d. 10

Reference_____

14. A floor/ceiling assembly between a dwelling unit and a public area within the same building shall have a minimum Normalized Impact Sound Rating (NISR) of _____ when field tested.

    a. 40
    b. 45
    c. 50
    d. not regulated

Reference_____

15. Occupiable spaces in an office building shall have a minimum ceiling height of
_____ .

    a. 6 feet, 8 inches   b. 7 feet, 0 inches

    c. 7 feet, 6 inches   d. 8 feet, 0 inches

    Reference_____

16. Every dwelling unit shall have at least one room with a minimum floor area of
_____ square feet.

    a. 70   b. 120

    c. 150   d. 220

    Reference_____

17. The minimum size of the required access opening to a crawl space shall be
_____ .

    a. 18 inches by 24 inches   b. 20 inches by 24 inches

    c. 20 inches by 30 inches   d. 22 inches by 30 inches

    Reference_____

18. The minimum size of the required access opening to an attic area over 30 inches in clear height shall be _____ .

    a. 18 inches by 24 inches   b. 20 inches by 24 inches

    c. 20 inches by 30 inches   d. 22 inches by 30 inches

    Reference_____

19. Where urinal partitions are required, the partitions shall begin at a maximum height of _____ inches above the finished floor surface and extend to a minimum height of _____ inches above the floor surface.

    a. 12, 54   b. 12, 60

    c. 15, 54   d. 15, 60

    Reference_____

20. Roof soffits are considered weather-exposed surfaces except for those portions located a minimum horizontal distance of _____ feet from the outer edges of the soffit.

    a. 3   b. 5

    c. 8   d. 10

Reference_____

21. In which of the following locations is the use of water-resistant gypsum backing board permitted?

    a.   as a base for tile in water closet compartment walls

    b.   over a vapor retarder in shower compartment

    c.   where there is direct exposure to water

    d.   areas subject to continuous high humidity

Reference_____

22. For exterior plastering, the second coat shall have a maximum variation of _____ inch in any direction under a 5-foot straight edge.

    a. $^1/_8$ b. $^3/_{16}$

    c. $^1/_4$ d. $^3/_8$

Reference_____

23. A maximum of _____ elevator car(s) shall be located in any single hoist-way enclosure.

    a. 1   b. 2

    c. 3   d. 4

Reference_____

24. A fire service access elevator shall be provided with an enclosed lobby a minimum of _____ square feet in floor area.

    a. 100   b. 120

    c. 150   d. 200

Reference_____

25. Where elevators are provided in buildings with four or more stories above grade plane, at least one elevator car shall be of such a size to accommodate a minimum _____ ambulance stretcher in the horizontal, open position.

    a. 24-inch by 76-inch   b. 24-inch by 84-inch

    c. 28-inch by 78-inch   d. 30-inch by 78-inch

Reference_____

26. A fibrous floor covering installed in the dining area of a Group A-2 sprinklered meeting room shall comply with the requirements of _____ or ASTM D2859.

    a. DOC FF-1 "pill test"   b. Class I

    c. Class II   d. Class A

Reference_____

27. Where a crawl space has an open earth floor, the minimum net area of ventilation openings for under-floor ventilation shall be based on 1 square foot for each _____ square feet of crawl-space area.

    a. 100   b. 120

    c. 150   d. 300

Reference_____

28. Where a court is adjacent to window openings on both sides of the court that provide for the required natural ventilation, the minimum court width shall be_____ feet if the building is five stories in height.

    a. 3   b. 6

    c. 9   d. 10

Reference_____

29. In the construction of a gypsum board fire-resistance-rated assembly, for which of the following applications is joint and fastener treatment required on single-layer systems?

    a. walls that extend above a fire-rated ceiling

    b. where joints occur over wood framing

    c. assemblies tested without joint treatment

    d. tongue-and-groove edge gypsum board

Reference_____

30. In a single-elevator building where standby power is provided to operate the elevator, the transfer to standby power shall occur automatically within a maximum of _____ seconds after failure of normal power.

      a.   10   b.   15

      c.   30   d.   60

Reference_____

31. In a Group E occupancy, combustible decorative materials suspended from walls and ceilings are limited to a maximum of _____ percent of the specific area to which such materials are attached.

      a.   0, no materials are permitted   b.   10

      c.   25   d.   50

Reference _____

32. Where ceilings are applied directly to the underside of roof framing members to form enclosed rafter spaces, such spaces shall be provided with cross ventilation with a minimum of _____ inch(es) of airspace provided between the insulation and the roof sheathing.

      a.   1   b.   2

      c.   3   d.   4

Reference _____

33. In other than dwelling units, sleeping units and toilet rooms not accessible to the public with a single water closet, walls within 2 feet of urinals and water closets shall have a smooth, hard, nonabsorbent surface to a minimum height of _____ feet above the floor.

      a.   3   b.   4

      c.   5   d.   6

Reference _____

34. Fasteners used to attach gypsum board to a horizontal diaphragm ceiling shall be spaced at a maximum of _____ inches on center at all supports and located a maximum of _____ inch from the edges and ends of the gypsum board.

      a.   7, $^3/_8$ b.   8, $^3/_8$

      c.   7, $^1/_2$ d.   8, $^1/_2$

Reference _____

35. Unless special provisions are made, exterior cement plaster shall not be applied when the ambient temperature is a maximum of_____ .

    a. 32°F   b. 35°F

    c. 40°F   d. 45°F

Reference _____

36. Exposed portions of heavy timber building elements are not subject to interior finish requirements where located in _____.

    a. exit passageways

    b. smoke compartments

    c. Group I-2 occupancies

    d. Group R fire areas

Reference _____

37. In Group E occupancies, enhanced classroom acoustics shall be provided in all classrooms with a maximum volume of _____ cubic feet.

    a. 10,000   b. 12,000

    c. 20,000   d. 32,000

Reference _____

38. Efficiency dwelling units shall have a living room with a minimum floor area of _____ square feet.

    a. 120   b. 150

    c. 190   d. 220

Reference _____

39. Where openings below grade provide required natural ventilation, the outside horizontal clear space measured perpendicular shall be a minimum of _____ times the depth of the opening.

    a. $1^1/_2$

    b. 2

    c. 3

    d. 5

Reference _____

40. In the application of exterior plaster, the weep screed shall be placed a minimum of _____ inches above paved areas.

    a. $1^1/_2$ b. 2

    c. 3   d. 4

Reference _____

2021 IBC Chapters 24 and 26
Glazing, Skylights and Plastics

OBJECTIVE: To gain an understanding of the installation requirements for glass and glazing, glazing support and framing, safety glazing, skylights, foam plastics, light-transmitting plastics and plastic veneers.

REFERENCE: Chapters 24 and 26, 2021 *International Building Code*

KEY POINTS:
- How is the installation of replacement glass regulated?
- How must a pane of glass be identified? Tempered glass?
- How must glazing be supported?
- What are the limitations for louvered windows and jalousies?
- Sloped glazing provisions for skylights, roofs and sloped walls apply when the glazing material is installed at what minimum slope from the vertical plane?
- Which materials are permitted for sloped glazing? What limitations are placed on these materials?
- For which sloped glazing installations are screens mandated?
- Skylight frames must be constructed of noncombustible materials in which types of construction?
- When are curbs required for the mounting of skylights?
- How are unit skylights regulated?
- What is safety glazing? What are the standards that regulate safety glazing?
- How shall safety glazing be identified? What information must be included as a part of the identifying mark?
- Which types of doors are exempt from the glazing requirements for hazardous locations?
- When glazing is located adjacent to a door, how is it determined if safety glazing is required?
- Which areas of tub and shower enclosures are considered hazardous locations for glazing?

- Individual fixed or operable glazed panels exceeding nine square feet in area must be safety glazed where which three conditions exist?

- How is glazing adjacent to stairways and landings to be addressed?

- What are the three types of glass permitted to be used as structural balustrade panels in rails?

- What is the maximum flame spread index for foam plastic insulation used in building construction? What is the maximum smoke-developed index?

- When is a thermal barrier necessary to separate the interior of a building from foam plastic insulation?

- Under which conditions may foam plastic insulation be incorporated as a part of a roof covering assembly?

- What are the limitations for the use of plastic veneer within a building? On the exterior wall of a building?

- How are light-transmitting plastics used as wall or roof panels regulated?

- Which specific provisions apply to plastic used as exterior wall panels? As roof panels? In skylights? In light-diffusing systems?

Code Text: Section 2405 *applies to the installation of glass and other transparent, translucent or opaque glazing material installed at a slope more than 15 degrees (0.26 rad) from the vertical plane, including glazing materials in skylights, roofs and sloped walls. For monolithic glazing systems, the glazing material of the single light or layer shall be laminated glass with a minimum 30-mil (0.76 mm) polyvinyl butyral (or equivalent) interlayer, wired glass, light-transmitting plastic materials meeting the requirements of Section 2607, heat-strengthened glass or fully tempered glass.*

Discussion and Commentary: The provisions for skylights are intended to protect such glazed openings from flying firebrands, to provide adequate strength to carry the load normally attributed to roofs, and to protect the occupants of a building from falling glazing materials.

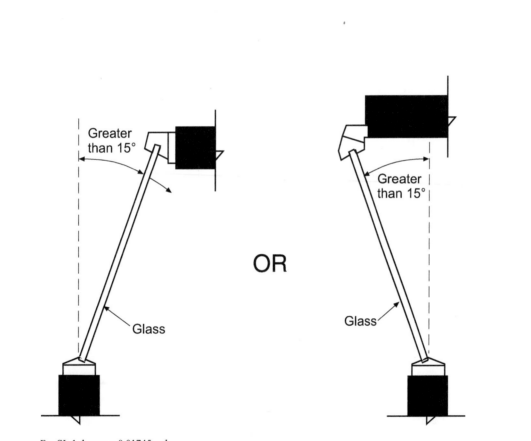

For SI: 1 degree = 0.01745 rad.

Annealed glass is limited to those areas where the walking surface below is isolated or protected from the risk of falling glass, or to specified greenhouses. Multiple-layer glazing systems must be glazed with only those materials permitted for single-layer glazing systems.

Topic: Screening	**Category:** Glass and Glazing
Reference: IBC 2405.3	**Subject:** Sloped Glazing and Skylights

Code Text: *Where used in monolithic glazing systems, annealed, heat-strengthened, fully tempered and wired glass shall have broken glass retention screens installed below the glazing material.* See the exceptions. *The screens and their fastenings shall: (1) be capable of supporting twice the weight of the glazing, (2) be firmly and substantially fastened to the framing members, and (3) be installed within 4 inches (102 mm) of the glass.*

Discussion and Commentary: Heat-strengthened glass has the undesirable characteristic of breaking into shards, whereas tempered glass has been shown to break spontaneously such that large chunks of glass may fall unexpectedly. Thus, these two types of glass require screen protection below the skylight to protect the occupants below.

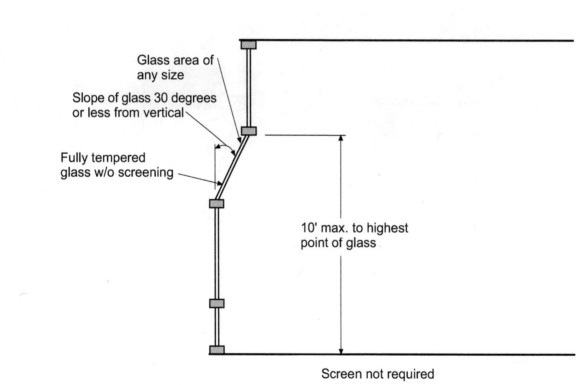

For SI: 1 foot = 304.8 mm, 1 degree = 0.01745 rad.

A commonly used exception allows fully tempered glass without screening where two conditions are met: (1) the slope of the skylight is limited to 30 degrees from the vertical plane, and (2) the highest point of the glass is no more than 10 feet above the walking surface.

Code Text: *Where required by other sections of the IBC, glazing shall be tested in accordance with CPSC 16 CFR 1201. Glazing shall comply with the test criteria for Category II unless otherwise indicated in Table 2406.2(1).* See the exception permitting the use of Class A or B glazing material tested in accordance with ANSI Z97.1 in locations other than entrance/exit doors, storm doors, combination doors, patio doors, closet doors, and shower and tub doors and enclosures.

Discussion and Commentary: The only test standard recognized for the acceptance of safety glazing materials in all hazardous locations identified by the IBC is CPSC 16 CFR 1201. Developed by the Consumer Product Safety Commission in 1977, in cooperation with building officials and the glass industry, the standard sets forth the criteria for glazing that is required in areas subject to human impact.

TABLE 2406.2(1)
MINIMUM CATEGORY CLASSIFICATION OF GLAZING USING CPSC 16 CFR 1201

EXPOSED SURFACE AREA OF ONE SIDE OF ONE LITE	GLAZING IN STORM OR COMBINATION DOORS (Category class)	GLAZING IN DOORS (Category class)	GLAZED PANELS REGULATED BY ITEM 7 OF SECTION 2406.4 (Category class)	GLAZED PANELS REGULATED BY ITEM 6 OF SECTION 2406.4 (Category class)	DOORS AND ENCLOSURES REGULATED BY ITEM 5 OF SECTION 2406.4 (Category class)	SLIDING GLASS DOORS PATIO TYPE (Category class)
9 square feet or less	I	I	No requirement	I	II	II
More than 9 square feet	II	II	II	II	II	II

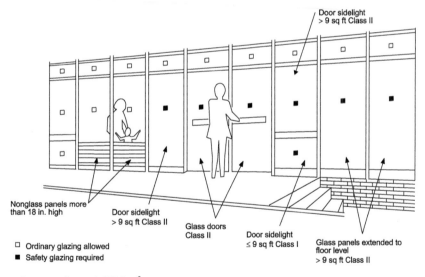

Nonglass panels more than 18 in. high
Door sidelight > 9 sq ft Class II
Glass doors Class II
Door sidelight ≤ 9 sq ft Class I
Glass panels extended to floor level > 9 sq ft Class II
Door sidelight > 9 sq ft Class II

☐ Ordinary glazing allowed
■ Safety glazing required

For SI: 1 inch = 25.4 mm, 1 square foot = 0.0929 m²

The tests established in CPSC 16 CFR Part 1201 vary with the category classification. As a part of the test, Category I glazing is impacted from a drop height of 18 inches. Limitations are placed on the damage that can occur due to the impact. Category II glazing is impacted from a drop height of 48 inches, resulting in a more severe test of compliance. Category II glazing is permitted in all safety glazing locations, whereas glazing only recognized as Category I materials are limited to specific locations.

Code Text: *Except as indicated in Section 2406.3.1, each pane of safety glazing installed in hazardous locations shall be identified by a manufacturer's designation specifying who applied the designation, the manufacturer or installer and the safety glazing standard with which it complies, as well as the information specified in Section 2403.1 (general glazing identification). The designation shall be acid etched, sand blasted, ceramic fired, laser etched, embossed or of a type that once applied, cannot be removed without being destroyed.* See the exceptions for certifications of compliance and tempered spandrel glass.

Discussion and Commentary: Improper glazing installed in areas subject to human impact can create a serious hazard. Accordingly, it is critical that glazing in such locations be appropriately identified to ensure that the proper glazing is in place.

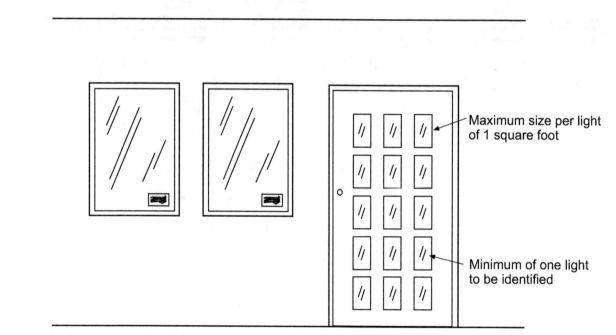

For SI: 1 square foot = 0.093 m².

In multi-pane assemblies, such as french doors, where the individual lights do not exceed 1 square foot in exposed area, Section 2406.3.1 provides for a reduction in the required information on all but one pane. At least one pane must be fully identified.

Code Text: *The following locations shall be considered specific hazardous locations requiring safety glazing materials: Glazing in all fixed and operable panels of swinging, sliding, and bifold doors.* See the four exceptions where safety glazing is not required.

Discussion and Commentary: As a general rule, any door containing glazing must be glazed with safety glass or other safety glazing material recognized by the code for that intended purpose. Glazing in doors is of particular concern due to the increased likelihood of accidental impact by individuals operating or opening the doors. In addition, a person may push against a glazed portion of the door to gain leverage in pushing it open. Therefore, it is important that only safety glazing materials be used for glazing in doors.

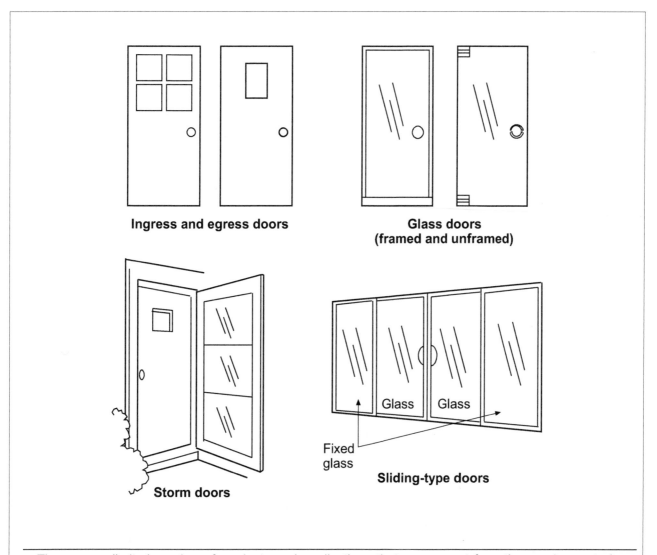

Ingress and egress doors

Glass doors (framed and unframed)

Storm doors

Fixed glass

Glass | Glass

Sliding-type doors

There are a limited number of products and applications that are exempt from the requirements for hazardous locations, including small openings in doors through which a 3-inch-diameter sphere will not pass, and specific decorative assemblies, such as leaded, faceted or carved glass.

Code Text: *The following locations shall be considered specific hazardous locations requiring safety glazing materials: Glazing in an individual fixed or operable panel adjacent to a door where the nearest vertical edge of the glazing is within a 24-inch (610 mm) arc of either vertical edge of the door in a closed position and where the bottom exposed edge of the glazing is less than 60 inches (1524 mm) above the walking surface. See the four exceptions where safety glazing is not mandated.*

Discussion and Commentary: When an individual approaches a doorway, areas adjacent to the door pose a risk when glazing is within 60 inches vertically of the walking surface. A person may slip or mistake the glass panel adjacent to a door for a passageway and walk into the glass, or a person may push against the sidelight with one hand for support while opening the door with the other hand. Therefore, safety glazing is required for any glazed opening located within 24 inches horizontally of the vertical edge of the door.

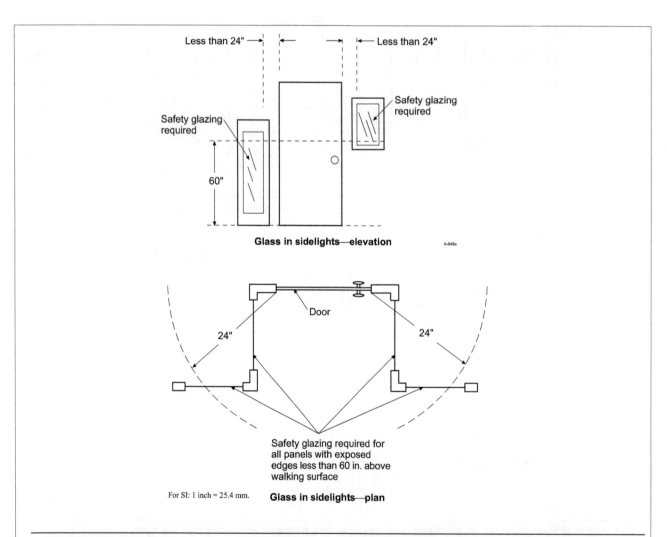

Glass in sidelights—elevation

Glass in sidelights—plan

For SI: 1 inch = 25.4 mm.

Where there is an intervening wall or similar permanent barrier between the door and the glazing, or where access through the door is to a closet or similar storage area of limited depth, safety glazing is not required, as the potential for contact is greatly reduced.

Code Text: *The following locations shall be considered specific hazardous locations requiring safety glazing materials: Glazing in a fixed or operable panel that meets all of the following conditions: (1) exposed area of an individual pane greater than 9 square feet (0.84 m²), (2) exposed bottom edge less than 18 inches (457 mm) above the floor, (3) exposed top edge greater than 36 inches (914 mm) above the floor, and (4) one or more walking surface(s) within 36 inches (914 mm) horizontally of the plane of the glazing.* See the exceptions for decorative glazing, where complying protective bar is installed or where multiple glazed units are located at least 25 feet above the surface below.

Discussion and Commentary: Large pieces of glass create a hazard where located close to a travel path because it is possible to impact glazing where no obstacle or barrier is provided as an alternative impact area. Expansive glazing may also be mistaken for a clear opening in the wall.

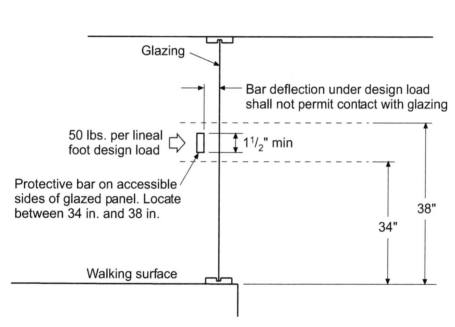

For SI: 1 inch = 25.4 mm.

Protective bar alternative

Where a minimum 1¹/₂-inch protective bar is installed on the accessible sides of a large glazed panel, it is not necessary to provide the opening with safety glazing. Located between 34 inches and 38 inches above the floor, the bar must be capable of withstanding a 50 plf horizontal load.

Topic: Glazing in Guards and Railings	**Category:** Glass and Glazing
Reference: IBC 2406.4.4	**Subject:** Hazardous Locations

Code Text: *The following locations shall be considered specific hazardous locations requiring safety glazing materials: Glazing in guards and railings, including structural baluster panels and nonstructural in-fill panels, regardless of area or height above a walking surface.*

Discussion and Commentary: Both intentional and unintentional contact with guards and railings are expected to occur; therefore, the IBC mandates that glazing used in such applications always be safety glazing. Safety glazing is required when the glazed infill panel is nonstructural and is supported by a structural frame system. Occasionally, glazing is used as a structural guard rail system without any other means of support. In this case, the glazing is required to be safety glazing.

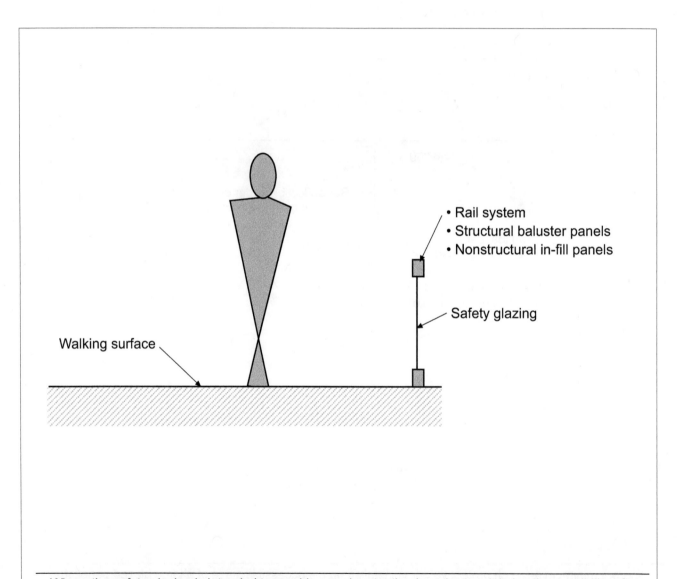

Where the safety glazing is intended to provide guard protection in order to minimize the possibility of a fall from a walking surface to a lower level, it must also meet the strength and attachment requirements prescribed in Section 1607.9.1 for live loads.

Code Text: *The following locations shall be considered specific hazardous locations requiring safety glazing materials: Glazing in walls, enclosures or fences containing or facing hot tubs, spas, whirlpools, saunas, steam rooms, bathtubs, showers and indoor or outdoor swimming pools where the bottom exposed edge of the glazing is less than 60 inches (1524 mm) measured vertically above any standing or walking surface.* See the exception for glazing located at least 60 inches horizontally from the water's edge.

Discussion and Commentary: Because the standing surfaces in or adjacent to bathtubs, showers, hot tubs, swimming pools, spas and similar elements are wet and slippery, glazing adjacent to these elements must be regulated due to the potential for human impact. It is not uncommon for the user to slip while trying to enter or exit. Safety glazing is mandated where any of the glazing within the enclosed area extends to within 60 inches vertically of the standing surface.

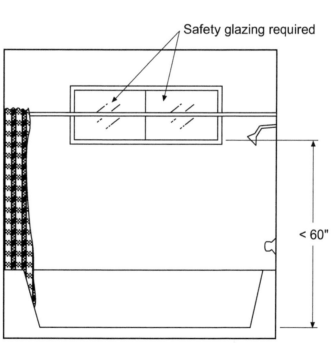

For SI: 1 inch = 25.4 mm.

Glazing within a shower enclosure

Where a "garden tub" or similar element is installed within an alcove or similar recessed area having windows or other glazed openings, the glazing in the walls of the alcove are considered a portion of the enclosure and are thus regulated.

Code Text: *The following locations shall be considered specific hazardous locations requiring safety glazing materials: Glazing where the bottom exposed edge of the glazing is less than 60 inches (1524 mm) above the plane of the adjacent walking surface of stairways, landings between flights of stairs, and ramps.* See the two exceptions where safety glazing is not required.

Discussion and Commentary: Stairways and ramps present users with a greater risk for injury caused by falling than does a flat surface. Not only is the risk of falling greater when using a stair, but the injuries are generally more severe. Unlike falling on a flat surface where the floor will break a person's fall, there is nothing to stop someone from continuing to fall until he or she reaches the bottom of the stair.

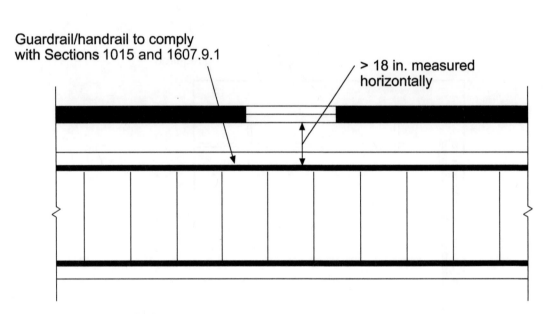

Safety glazing not required adjacent to stairway

For SI: 1 inch = 25.4 mm.

Guards and railings that comply with the means of egress provisions of Section 1015 and the structural requirements of Section 1607.9.1, and that are located more than 18 inches from the glazing measured horizontally, will prevent human impact to the point that safety glazing is not required.

Topic: Glazing at Bottom of Stairways	**Category:** Glass and Glazing
Reference: IBC 2406.4.7	**Subject:** Hazardous Locations

Code Text: *The following locations shall be considered specific hazardous locations requiring safety glazing materials: Glazing adjacent to the landing at the bottom of a stairway where the glazing is less than 60 inches (1524 mm) above the landing and within 60 inches (1524 mm) horizontally of the bottom tread.* See the exception where safety glazing is not required.

Discussion and Commentary: Historically, stairways have been considered one of the most dangerous elements of a building. Missteps and falls on stairways are quite common; therefore, it is important that any glazing that may be impacted is made of safety glazing materials. Where a complying guard rail or handrail is provided and the glazing is located a sufficient distance from the railing, safety glazing is not mandated.

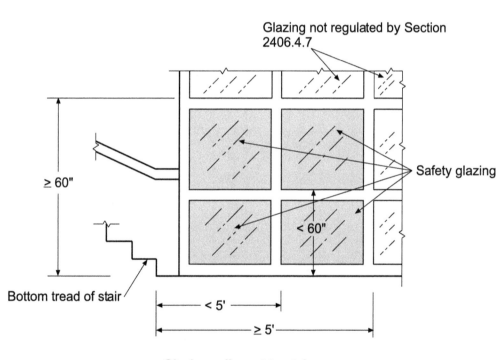

Glazing adjacent to stairways

For SI: 1 inch = 25.4 mm, 1 foot = 304.8 mm.

The IBC limits the area of concern in this item to the bottom of a stair flight and its adjacent landing. Glazing that is located at least 60 inches vertically above the walking surface is not considered an impact risk.

Code Text: Foam plastic insulation is *a plastic that is intentionally expanded by the use of a foaming agent to produce a reduced-density plastic containing voids consisting of open or closed cells distributed throughout the plastic for thermal insulating or acoustical purposes and that has a density less than 20 pounds per cubic foot. The provisions of* Section 2603 *shall govern the requirements and uses of foam plastic insulation in buildings and structures.*

Discussion and Commentary: Foam plastic is a general term given to insulating products that have been manufactured by intentionally expanding plastic by the use of a foaming agent. Two basic concepts address the hazards created when foam plastic is exposed to fire conditions: (1) limitation of flame spread and smoke development, and (2) separation from the interior of the building by an approved thermal barrier.

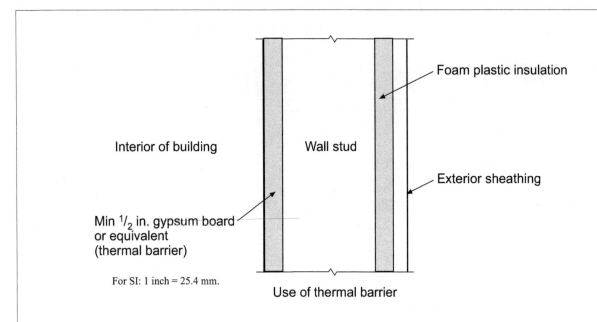

Interior of building

Wall stud

Foam plastic insulation

Exterior sheathing

Min $^1/_2$ in. gypsum board or equivalent (thermal barrier)

For SI: 1 inch = 25.4 mm.

Use of thermal barrier

To ensure that the proper materials are utilized in building construction, all packages and containers of foam plastic insulation must be properly identified. Such identification must include information to show that the final use of the product complies with the code requirements.

| **Topic:** Thermal Barrier | **Category:** Plastic |
| **Reference:** IBC 2603.4 | **Subject:** Foam Plastic Insulation |

Code Text: *Except as provided for in Sections 2603.4.1 and 2603.9, foam plastic shall be separated from the interior of a building by an approved thermal barrier of ¹/₂ inch (12.7 mm) gypsum wallboard, heavy timber in accordance with Section 602.4 or a material that is tested in accordance with and meets the acceptance criteria of both the Temperature Transmission Fire Test and the Integrity Fire Test of NFPA 275. Combustible concealed spaces shall comply with Section 718.*

Discussion and Commentary: A barrier is mandated to provide a minimum degree of protection between foam plastic materials and a building's occupants. Any type of separation equivalent to that provided by ¹/₂-inch gypsum board is considered acceptable. Where one of the fourteen conditions established by Section 2603.4.1 is met, a thermal barrier as described in Section 2603.4 is not required.

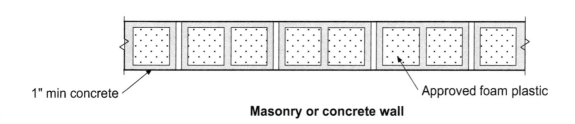

1" min concrete — Approved foam plastic

Masonry or concrete wall

1" min concrete — Foam

Roof or floor sandwich panel

Encapsulated foam plastic

For SI: 1 inch = 25.4 mm.

In addition to the required thermal barrier, foam plastic insulation must be limited in its surface-burning characteristics. Unless exempted, the flame spread index is limited to 75 and the smoke-developed index is not to exceed 450.

Code Text: *Within an attic or crawl space where entry is made only for service of utilities, foam plastic insulation shall be protected against ignition by 1¹/₂-inch-thick (38 mm) mineral fiber insulation; ¹/₄-inch-thick (6.4 mm) wood structural panel, particleboard, or hardboard; ³/₈-inch (9.5 mm) gypsum wallboard, corrosion-resistant steel having a base metal thickness of 0.016 inch (0.4 mm); 1 ¹/₂-inch-thick (38 mm) self-supported spray-applied cellulose insulation in attic spaces only or other approved material installed in such a manner that the foam plastic insulation is not exposed.*

Discussion and Commentary: Although the general requirements of Section 2603.4 mandate a thermal barrier to isolate foam plastic from the interior of the building, Section 2603.4.1 reduces or eliminates the protective membrane requirements. One such reduction involves attic spaces and crawl spaces. Where access to the concealed attic or crawl space is only necessary to allow for the service of above-ceiling or under-floor utilities, such as plumbing, mechanical, electrical or communication elements, a reduced level of foam plastic protection is permitted.

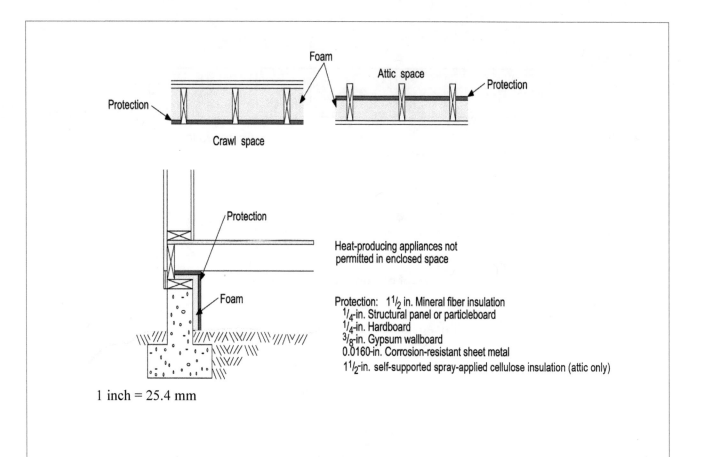

1 inch = 25.4 mm

If there are no utilities within the attic space or crawl space that require service, the reduced level of separation set forth in Section 2603.4.1.6 must still be provided. Where the attic or crawl space provides a usable area that exists for a purpose other than access to utilities, such as storage, a thermal barrier complying with Section 2603.4 is required.

Topic: Interior Finish and Trim	**Category:** Plastic
Reference: IBC 2604.2	**Subject:** Foam Plastic

Code Text: *For foam plastics used as interior trim: (1) the minimum density of the interior trim shall be 20 pcf (320 kg/m³), (2) the maximum thickness of the interior trim shall be ¹/₂ inch (12.7 mm) and the maximum width shall be 8 inches (204 mm), (3) the interior trim shall not constitute more than 10 percent of the specific wall or ceiling area of any room or space, and (4) the flame spread index shall not exceed 75 where tested in accordance with ASTM E84 or UL 723. The smoke-developed index shall not be limited.* See the exception to the required flame spread index.

Discussion and Commentary: The general provisions regulating the use of decorations and trim in buildings are found in Section 806. They include plastics materials, other than foam plastics, used as interior trim. All foam plastic trim must comply with the provisions of Section 2604.2.

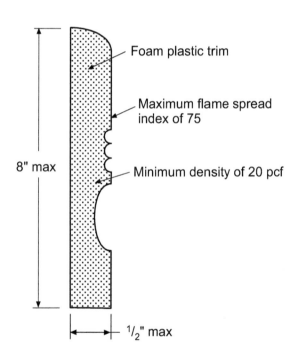

8" max

Foam plastic trim

Maximum flame spread index of 75

Minimum density of 20 pcf

¹/₂" max

For SI: 1 inch = 25.4 mm.

The use of foam plastics as interior finish is limited to applications that comply with Section 2603.9. This provision allows special approval based on the use of large-scale tests. Foam plastic finishes accepted by testing must also conform to Chapter 8 flame spread requirements.

Quiz

Study Session 18
IBC Chapters 24 and 26

1. Patterned glass in louvered windows shall have a maximum length of
_____ inches.

    a. 36   b. 42

    c. 48   d. 60

Reference_____

2. Where screening is required below the glazing material in a skylight, the screen shall be installed a maximum of _____ inch(es) below the glass.

    a. 1   b. 3

    c. 4   d. 6

Reference_____

3. When used as the bottom glass layer in a multiple-layer glazing system installed above a walking surface, which of the following glazing materials never needs to be equipped with complying screening?

    a. fully tempered glass   b. laminated glass

    c. heat-strengthened glass   d. wired glass

Reference_____

4. When set at an angle less than 45 degrees from the horizontal plane, a skylight shall be mounted on a curb a minimum of _____ inch(es) above the plane of the roof of other than a Group R-3 occupancy.

    a. 1   b. 2

    c. 3   d. 4

Reference_____

5. Class I safety glazing with a maximum size of _____ per light is permitted in doors.

    a. 0 square inches (not permitted of any size)

    b. 100 square inches

    c. 144 square inches

    d. 9 square feet

    Reference_____

6. Which one of the following types of safety glazing materials shall not be solely identified by a certificate or affidavit?

    a. tempered glass   b. wired glass

    c. laminated glass   d. plastic glazing

    Reference_____

7. Glazing within a shower enclosure shall be safety glazing where the bottom exposed edge of the glazing is less than _____ inches above a standing surface.

    a. 60   b. 66

    c. 72   d. 78

    Reference_____

8. In general, where located less than 60 inches above the walking surface, glazing adjacent to a door within what maximum horizontal distance of either vertical door edge must be safety glazing?

    a. 12 inches   b. 18 inches

    c. 24 inches   d. 36 inches

    Reference_____

9. Where a protective bar is permitted as protection in lieu of safety glazing in a fixed or operable panel, the bar must be capable of withstanding a minimum horizontal load of _____ pounds per linear foot without contacting the glass.

    a. 15   b. 20

    c. 40   d. 50

    Reference_____

10. Unless located at least 60 inches measured vertically above any standing or walking surface, glazing in walls enclosing a swimming pool is required to be safety glazing where located a maximum of _____ feet horizontally from the water's edge.

  a. 5   b. 6

  c. 8   d. 10

  Reference_____

11. At other than the bottom tread, glazing adjacent to stairways does not need to be safety glazing where the plane of the glass is a minimum of_____inches horizontally from the walking surface.

  a. 12   b. 18

  c. 24   d. 36

  Reference_____

12. Glazed openings in doors are not considered hazardous locations for safety glazing purposes, provided the openings will not allow passage of a _____ -inch sphere.

  a. 3   b. 4

  c. 6   d. 9

  Reference_____

13. Where glass vision panels are provided in elevator hoistway doors, the area of any single panel shall be a minimum of _____ square inches.

  a. 24   b. 36

  c. 100   d. 144

  Reference_____

14. Where structural glass baluster panels support a handrail or the top rail of a guard, the handrail or top rail shall be supported by a minimum of _____ glass baluster panels.

  a. 2   b. 3

  c. 4   d. 6

  Reference_____

15. By definition, foam plastic insulation shall have a density less than
_____ pounds per cubic foot.

    a. 2   b. 4

    c. 10   d. 20

Reference_____

16. _____ is considered to be a plastic material that is capable of being changed into a substantially nonreformable product when cured.

    a. Approved plastic   b. Glass fiber reinforced plastic

    c. Thermoplastic material   d. Thermosetting material

Reference_____

17. Unless otherwise specified, foam plastic shall have a maximum flame spread index of _____ and a maximum smoke-developed index of _____ where tested in the maximum thickness intended for use.

    a. 25, 200   b. 25, 450

    c. 50, 200   d. 75, 450

Reference_____

18. What material is specifically identified as an approved thermal barrier for separating foam plastic from the interior of a building?

    a. $1/2$-inch gypsum wallboard   b. $3/8$-inch Type x gypsum wallboard

    c. $3/8$-inch gypsum sheathing   d. $1/2$-inch wood structural panel

Reference_____

19. Within a concrete floor system, all foam plastic insulation shall be covered on each face by a minimum of a _____ -inch thickness of concrete.

    a. $1/2$ b. 1

    c. $1\,1/2$ d. 2

Reference_____

20. The maximum allowable thickness of foam plastic interior trim shall be
_____ inch(es), with a maximum permitted width of _____
inches.

    a. 4, 12   b. 2, 12

    c. 1, 8   d. $1/_2$, 8

Reference_____

21. Exterior plastic veneer, other than plastic siding, may be installed on the exterior
walls of buildings of any type of construction to a maximum height of
_____ feet above grade.

    a. 25   b. 35

    c. 50   d. 75

Reference_____

22. In a nonsprinklered Group B building, Class CC2 light-transmitting wall panels used
in an exterior wall with a fire separation distance of 18 feet are limited to a maximum
of _____ percent of the exterior wall.

    a. 10   b. 15

    c. 25   d. 50

Reference_____

23. In a fully sprinklered building, what is the maximum height light-transmitting plastic
glazing is permitted to be installed above grade level?

    a. 35 feet   b. 55 feet

    c. 75 feet   d. unlimited

Reference_____

24. In which one of the following occupancies may light-transmitting plastic roof panels
be installed?

    a. Group A-1   b. Group H-1

    c. Group I-2   d. Group I-3

Reference_____

25. An interior wall sign of Class CC2 light-transmitting plastic is limited in size to _____ square feet.

    a. 16   b. 24

    c. 48   d. 100

Reference_____

26. Glass in window walls sloped a maximum of _____ degrees from the vertical shall be designed to resist the required wind loads for components and cladding.

    a. 15   b. 30

    c. 45   d. 60

Reference_____

27. For which of the following applications is the use of a removable paper label specifically permitted for identifying tempered glass for safety glazing purposes?

    a. storm doors   b. spandrel panels

    c. unframed swinging doors   d. structural balustrade panels

Reference_____

28. Only one individual pane in a multipane glazed door assembly requires safety glazing identification, provided each pane is a maximum of _____ in size.

    a. 64 square inches   b. 100 square inches

    c. 1 square foot   d. $1^1/_2$ square feet

Reference_____

29. All glazing subject to human impact located in a(n) _____ shall comply with Category II of CPSC 16 CFR 1201 or Class A of ANSI Z97.1.

    a. school classroom   b. detention facility

    c. multipurpose gymnasium   d. manufacturing building

Reference_____

30. Foam plastic spray applied to a sill plate in Type V construction shall have a maximum thickness of _____ .

    a. 1 inch   b. $1^1/_2$ inches

    c. 3 inches   d. $3^1/_4$ inches

Reference_____

31. Any glazing material is permitted to be installed without screens in the sloped glazing system of commercial noncombustible greenhouses, provided the maximum ridge height is _____ feet above grade.

    a. 16   b. 20

    c. 25   d. 30

Reference _____

32. Glazing installed in sliding glass patio doors shall have a minimum category classification of Class _____ .

    a. A   b. B

    c. I   d. II

Reference _____

33. For all glazing types, the minimum required thickness for glass used as a handrail assembly or guard section shall be _____ inch nominal.

    a. $^1/_4$ b. $^3/_8$

    c. $^1/_2$ d. $^9/_{16}$

Reference _____

34. Individual panels or units of light-transmitting plastic used in a light-diffusing system shall have a maximum size of _____ square feet and be a maximum of _____ feet in length.

    a. 10, 5   b. 15, 10

    c. 30, 10   d. 36, 12

Reference _____

35. In a nonsprinklered building with no smoke and heat vents, light-transmitting plastic skylight assemblies shall each have a maximum glazed area of _____ square feet within the curb.

    a. 16   b. 36

    c. 64   d. 100

Reference _____

36. To be considered firmly supported, the framing members for each individual pane of glass shall be designed so that the maximum allowable deflection of the edge of the glass perpendicular to the glass pane is _____ of the glass edge length for an edge having a length of 12 feet.

    a. $1/_{120}$ b. $1/_{150}$

    c. $1/_{175}$ d. $1/_{240}$

Reference _____

37. Where glazing is located in an individual fixed panel adjacent to a closet door, the glazing is not considered to be located in a hazardous location where the maximum depth of the closet is _____ inches.

    a. 30   b. 36

    c. 48   d. 60

Reference _____

38. Glass guards shall be designed with a safety factor of _____.

    a. 1.5   b. 2

    c. 3   d. 4

Reference _____

39. Unless protected by an approved means, a minimum clearance of _____ inch(es) shall be provided between foam plastics installed above grade and exposed earth.

    a. 1   b. 2

    c. 4   d. 6

Reference _____

40. Plastic materials installed as interior trim shall constitute a maximum of _____ percent of the specific wall to which it is attached.

    a. 10   b. 20

    c. 25   d. 40

Reference _____

Answer Keys

Study Session 1

2021 *International Building Code*

1.	c	Sec. 101.2, Exc.
2.	c	Sec. 101.2.1
3.	b	Sec. 102.1
4.	a	Sec. 103.1
5.	d	Sec. 104.1
6.	a	Sec. 104.9.1
7.	b	Sec. 104.10
8.	b	Sec. 104.11
9.	c	Sec. 104.11.2
10.	b	Sec. 105.2, #B1
11.	c	Sec. 105.2, #B13
12.	c	Sec. 110.3.12.1
13.	a	Sec. 105.7
14.	d	Sec. 107.3.1
15.	b	Sec. 107.5
16.	c	Sec. 110.3
17.	a	Sec. 110.5
18.	d	Sec. 111.2
19.	d	Sec. 111.3
20.	b	Sec. 113.2
21.	c	Sec. 101.2, Exc.
22.	c	Sec. 101.4.7
23.	a	Sec. 102.4.1
24.	b	Sec. 105.2, #B2
25.	d	Chapter 35
26.	b	Sec. 105.2, #B9
27.	d	Sec. 105.2, #B12
28.	d	Sec. 105.6
29.	b	Sec. 108.1
30.	d	Sec. 110.3.6, Exc.

31.	b	Sec. 105.2, #M7
32.	a	Sec. 107.2.3
33.	b	Sec. 109.3
34.	a	Sec. 110.1
35.	c	Sec. 115.2
36.	d	Sec. 104.7
37.	a	Sec. 106.1
38.	d	Sec. 110.3.5
39.	c	Chapter 35
40.	c	Sec. 102.4.2

Study Session 2

2021 *International Building Code*

1.	c	Sec. 302.1, #6
2.	d	Sec. 302.1, #10
3.	a	Sec. 303.1.4
4.	c	Sec. 303.1.2, #2
5.	a	Sec. 303.1.3
6.	d	Sec. 303.5
7.	a	Sec. 304.1, 309.1
8.	a	Sec. 303.3
9.	b	Sec. 307.4
10.	a	Sec. 307.3
11.	c	Sec. 308.3
12.	d	Table 307.1(1)
13.	a	Sec. 308.2
14.	c	Sec. 309.1, 304.1
15.	b	Sec. 310.3
16.	d	Sec. 310.5, 308.3
17.	d	Sec. 311.3, 312.1
18.	d	Sec. 304.1
19.	d	Sec. 307.6
20.	c	Sec. 307.1.1, # 12
21.	a	Sec. 310.4.2
22.	b	Sec. 304.1
23.	c	Sec. 310.4
24.	b	Sec. 202
25.	c	Table 509.1, Sec. 509.4.1
26.	d	Table 509.1
27.	d	Table 509.1, Sec. 509.4.1
28.	d	Sec. 509.4.2
29.	a	Sec. 508.2.3
30.	c	Sec. 508.2.4, Exc. 1

31.	a	Sec. 508.3.1
32.	c	Table 508.4
33.	c	Table 508.4
34.	b	Table 508.4
35.	a	Table 508.4
36.	c	Sec. 311.2; 307.1.1 #19
37.	d	Sec. 312.1
38.	a	Sec. 509.4.1.1
39.	d	Sec. 508.4.2
40.	b	Sec. 508.5.2

Study Session 3

2021 *International Building Code*

1.	a	Sec. 602.2
2.	c	Sec. 602.3
3.	d	Sec. 602.4
4.	a	Sec. 602.3
5.	d	Sec. 602.4.4, Table 2304.11
6.	c	Sec. 602.4.4, Table 2304.11
7.	c	Sec. 602.4
8.	d	Sec. 602.5
9.	b	Table 601
10.	d	Sec. 202
11.	a	Table 601
12.	c	Table 601
13.	b	Table 601, Note a
14.	d	Sec. 603.1, #1.3
15.	b	Table 601, Note b
16.	a	Table 601
17.	d	Sec. 602.4.4.4
18.	b	Table 601
19.	d	Table 601
20.	c	Table 601
21.	d	Sec. 603.1, #1.1
22.	c	Sec. 602.4.4, 2304.11.3.1
23.	a	Sec. 603.1, #1.2
24.	a	Sec. 603.1, #9
25.	d	Sec. 603.1, #4; Table 1505.1
26.	a	Sec. 602.4.4, 2304.11.2.2
27.	a	Table 601
28.	a	Sec. 603.1, #1.3, Exc.
29.	c	Table 601
30.	d	Table 601, Note c
31.	c	Table 601
32.	a	Table 601
33.	d	Table 601
34.	d	Table 2304.11
35.	a	Sec. 603.1, #2
36.	c	Sec. 603.1, #1.4
37.	c	Sec. 602.4.1.3
38.	d	Sec. 602.4.2.2.2, Exc. 1.2
39.	c	Sec. 602.4.3.6
40.	b	Sec. 603.1, #26

Study Session 4

2021 *International Building Code*

1.	b	Sec. 502.1
2.	a	Sec. 202
3.	c	Tables 504.4, 504.3
4.	c	Table 504.3
5.	b	Sec. 506.1.3
6.	d	Sec. 202
7.	b	Sec. 506.2.3, Eq. 5-2
8.	d	Table 504.3
9.	a	Table 504.4
10.	b	Sec. 504.3, Exc.
11.	b	Sec. 505.2
12.	b	Sec. 505.2
13.	c	Sec. 505.2.1
14.	a	Sec. 505.2.3, Exc. 3
15.	a	Sec. 505.2.3, Exc. 1
16.	b	Table 506.3.3
17.	b	Sec. 506.3.2
18.	b	Table 504.4
19.	a	Table 506.2
20.	b	Sec. 505.2.1, Exc. 2
21.	c	Table 504.4
22.	d	Sec. 507.11
23.	d	Sec. 507.2.1, #2
24.	d	Sec. 507.10
25.	c	Sec. 510.2, #1
26.	d	Sec. 504.3, Exc.
27.	b	Sec. 507.5
28.	a	Sec. 507.7, #3
29.	b	Sec. 507.8.1.1, Table 506.2
30.	c	Sec. 510.6

31.	d	Sec. 505.2.1, Exc. 1
32.	d	Sec. 505.3.1
33.	b	Sec. 507.13
34.	c	Sec. 507.11, #3
35.	a	Table 504.3
36.	b	Table 504.4
37.	b	Sec. 506.3.2, Table 506.3.3
38.	d	Sec. 506.3.3.1, Table 506.3.3.1
39.	c	Table 506.2
40.	b	Sec. 505.2.3, Exc. 4

Study Session 5

2021 *International Building Code*

1.	a	Sec. 202	31.	b	Sec. 703.3.1
2.	b	Sec. 202	32.	b	Table 705.8, Note g
3.	b	Sec. 202	33.	d	Sec. 705.11, Exc. 3
4.	b	Sec. 202	34.	c	Table 705.2
5.	a	Sec. 202	35.	c	Sec. 705.8.1, Exc. 1.1
6.	a	Sec. 202, 706.2	36.	c	Table 705.5
7.	b	Sec. 202	37.	c	Table 705.5
8.	b	Sec. 202	38.	c	Table 705.5
9.	c	Sec. 703.2	39.	a	Table 705.5, Note c
10.	c	Sec. 703.5	40.	d	Sec. 704.11
11.	d	Sec. 703.3.1, Exc.			
12.	c	Table 705.2			
13.	b	Table 705.2			
14.	d	Sec. 705.2.2			
15.	c	Sec. 705.3			
16.	c	Sec. 705.5			
17.	a	Table 705.8			
18.	d	Table 705.8			
19.	c	Table 705.8			
20.	c	Sec. 705.8.1, Exc. 1.2			
21.	c	Sec. 705.8.5			
22.	c	Sec. 705.8.5			
23.	b	Sec. 705.11, Exc. 2			
24.	a	Sec. 705.11.1			
25.	b	Sec. 705.11.1			
26.	d	Sec. 703.2.1.1			
27.	d	Sec. 705.2.3			
28.	c	Table 705.8			
29.	c	Sec. 705.11, #6; Table 705.8			
30.	a	Table 705.8, Note e			

Study Session 6

2021 *International Building Code*

1.	d	Sec. 706.3, Exc.
2.	c	Table 706.4
3.	b	Table 706.4, Note a
4.	a	Sec. 706.5
5.	b	Sec. 706.6
6.	b	Sec. 706.6.1, Exc.
7.	c	Sec. 706.7
8.	b	Sec. 706.8
9.	d	Sec. 707.3; 708.1, #3
10.	c	Sec. 707.5.1, Exc. 2
11.	d	Sec. 707.6
12.	a	Sec. 707.6, Exc. 2
13.	c	Sec. 712.1.3.1
14.	c	Sec. 712.1.9
15.	b	Sec. 706.2
16.	c	Sec. 707.3.5, 1026.2
17.	c	Sec. 708.1
18.	c	Sec. 708.3
19.	b	Sec. 708.4, Exc. 3
20.	d	Sec. 709.3
21.	b	Sec. 709.4
22.	c	Sec. 712.1.3.2
23.	a	Sec. 711.2.5
24.	d	Sec. 711.2.6
25.	c	Sec. 712.1.15
26.	b	Table 707.3.10
27.	b	Sec. 707.9
28.	a	Sec. 710.3
29.	a	Sec. 710.5.1
30.	b	Sec. 708.3, Exc. 2; 711.2.4.3, Exc.
31.	a	Sec. 706.5.2
32.	a	Sec. 709.5.1
33.	b	Sec. 712.1.7, Exc. 1
34.	a	Sec. 710.8
35.	d	Sec. 709.5, Exc. 1
36.	c	Sec. 706.1.1
37.	d	Sec. 706.2, Exc.
38.	a	Sec. 708.4.2, Exc. 3
39.	c	Sec. 710.5.3, #4
40.	c	Sec. 712.1.2

Study Session 7

2021 *International Building Code*

1.	c	Sec. 713.4
2.	d	Sec. 714.6.1
3.	b	Sec. 715.3, Exc.
4.	d	Sec. 715.1, Exc. #9
5.	b	Sec. 716.2.2.3
6.	b	Sec. 713.13.3
7.	d	Table 716.1(2)
8.	d	Table 716.1(2)
9.	b	Sec. 714.5.4
10.	c	Sec. 713.14, 3006.3, #1
11.	b	Sec. 716.2.6.1
12.	d	Table 716.1(2)
13.	a	Sec. 716.2.6.6
14.	a	Sec. 713.13.3
15.	d	Table 716.1(3)
16.	c	Sec. 716.3.2.1.2
17.	d	Table 717.3.2.1
18.	d	Sec. 717.3.3.2, #3
19.	c	Sec. 717.5.1, 717.5.1.1
20.	c	Sec. 717.5.3
21.	c	Table 716.1(3)
22.	b	Sec. 718.2.6
23.	a	Sec. 718.3.1
24.	b	Sec. 718.4
25.	a	Sec. 720.2
26.	a	Sec. 714.4.1.2
27.	a	Sec. 714.4.2, Exc. 1
28.	b	Table 716.1(3)
29.	c	Sec. 718.2.7
30.	d	Sec. 719.4
31.	b	Sec. 717.3.3.4
32.	c	Sec. 718.3
33.	d	Sec. 717.3.2.2
34.	a	Sec. 718.2.6
35.	d	Sec. 719.2
36.	b	Sec. 713.2
37.	a	Sec. 714.6.2
38.	c	Table 716.1(1)
39.	b	Sec. 717.4.1
40.	a	Sec. 717.4.2

Study Session 8

2021 *International Building Code*

1.	d	Sec. 901.6
2.	b	Sec. 202
3.	c	Sec. 202
4.	c	Sec. 903.2.1.2, #2
5.	b	Sec. 903.2.1.5
6.	c	Sec. 903.2.3, #1
7.	b	Sec. 903.2.4.1
8.	a	Sec. 903.2.2, #1
9.	c	Sec. 903.2.7, #2
10.	d	Sec. 903.2.8
11.	d	Sec. 903.2.9, #3
12.	c	Sec. 903.2.9.1, #2
13.	b	Sec. 903.2.10.1
14.	b	Sec. 903.2.11.1.3
15.	d	Sec. 903.3.1.3
16.	d	Sec. 903.3.2
17.	c	Sec. 903.3.3
18.	b	Sec. 903.3.8.2
19.	d	Sec. 904.13.1
20.	b	Sec. 905.5
21.	a	Sec. 907.2.2, #2
22.	b	Sec. 907.2.3, Exc. 1
23.	a	Sec. 907.4.2.1
24.	c	Table 907.5.2.3.2
25.	d	Sec. 907.5.2.1.2
26.	d	Sec. 904.13.1
27.	d	Sec. 905.3.4
28.	b	Sec. 909.20.3.3
29.	d	Sec. 910.2.1
30.	c	Sec. 915.1.1
31.	d	Sec. 903.3.1.2.1, #1
32.	d	Sec. 907.2.4, #2
33.	b	Sec. 909.20.1
34.	a	Sec. 913.3
35.	d	Sec. 911.1.3
36.	d	Sec. 903.2.4.2
37.	d	Sec. 903.2.10, #3
38.	c	Sec. 907.5.2.1.3.1
39.	c	Sec. 910.3.5
40.	b	Sec. 911.1

Study Session 9

2021 *International Building Code*

1.	b	Sec. 202		31.	d	Sec. 1004.6
2.	d	Sec. 202		32.	a	Sec. 1005.7.1
3.	c	Sec. 202		33.	b	Sec. 1008.2.1
4.	b	Sec. 202		34.	b	Sec. 1015.4, Exc. 1
5.	c	Sec. 202		35.	b	Sec. 1015.4, Exc. 6
6.	d	Table 1004.5		36.	d	Table 1004.5
7.	b	Table 1004.5		37.	a	Sec. 1004.8
8.	b	Sec. 1004.6		38.	d	Sec. 1008.2.1
9.	c	Sec. 1005.3.2, Exc. 1		39.	b	Sec. 1013.2
10.	c	Sec. 1005.3.1		40.	a	Sec. 1015.5
11.	d	Sec. 1005.5				
12.	d	Sec. 1005.7.1				
13.	b	Sec. 1003.3.1				
14.	b	Sec. 1003.3.1, Exc.				
15.	c	Sec. 1003.3.3				
16.	c	Sec. 1003.5, Exc. 1; 1010.1.4, Exc. 2				
17.	c	Sec. 1013.1				
18.	b	Sec. 1013.6.2				
19.	b	Sec. 1008.3.5				
20.	b	Sec. 1015.2				
21.	c	Sec. 1015.3				
22.	d	Sec. 1015.4, Exc. 4				
23.	a	Sec. 1015.6				
24.	c	Sec. 1009.3.2				
25.	c	Sec. 1009.6.3				
26.	a	Sec. 1003.3.1				
27.	d	Sec. 1004.5.1				
28.	c	Sec. 1008.3.3, #5				
29.	b	Sec. 1009.7.2				
30.	c	Sec. 1013.4				

Study Session 10

2021 *International Building Code*

1.	b	Sec. 1010.1.1	31.	a	Sec. 1010.2.9
2.	c	Sec. 1010.1.1	32.	c	Sec. 1011.2
3.	a	Sec. 1010.1.1, Exc. 3	33.	b	Sec. 1012.6.3, Exc. 2
4.	d	Sec. 1010.1.1.1	34.	c	Sec. 1014.6
5.	d	Sec. 1010.1.2, Exc. 1, 9	35.	a	Sec. 1014.9
6.	c	Sec. 1010.1.2.1	36.	b	Sec. 1010.1.1.1, Exc.
7.	b	Sec. 1010.1.3	37.	c	Sec. 1010.1.3, #2
8.	b	Sec. 1010.3.1, #6	38.	c	Sec. 1012.10.2
9.	c	Sec. 1010.1.5	39.	b	Sec. 1014.3.2
10.	b	Sec. 1010.1.4	40.	d	Sec. 1011.7.1, Exc. 1
11.	c	Sec. 1010.1.6			
12.	a	Sec. 1010.2.13			
13.	c	Sec. 1010.2.3			
14.	d	Sec. 1011.14			
15.	c	Sec. 1011.3			
16.	b	Sec. 1011.5.2, Exc. 3			
17.	c	Sec. 1011.6			
18.	b	Sec. 1014.7			
19.	b	Sec. 1011.10			
20.	d	Sec. 1014.2			
21.	a	Sec. 1014.6			
22.	d	Sec. 1014.8			
23.	a	Sec. 1012.4			
24.	a	Sec. 1012.8			
25.	d	Sec. 1010.5.3			
26.	d	Sec. 1010.3.2			
27.	c	Sec. 1010.1.7			
28.	b	Sec. 1011.2, Exc. 1			
29.	a	Sec. 1014.3.1			
30.	a	Sec. 1012.10.1			

Study Session 11
2021 *International Building Code*

1.	d	Table 1006.2.1
2.	d	Table 1006.2.1
3.	c	Sec. 1006.2.1.1
4.	b	Sec. 1007.1.1, Exc. 2
5.	c	Sec. 1016.2, #2
6.	a	Sec. 1016.2, #5
7.	a	Sec. 1016.2.1, Exc.
8.	b	Sec. 1006.2.2.4
9.	d	Sec. 1006.2.1.1
10.	b	Table 1017.2
11.	c	Sec. 1017.2.1
12.	a	Table 1006.2.1
13.	c	Table 1006.2.1
14.	b	Sec. 1017.2.2, #2
15.	b	Sec. 1018.3, Exc.
16.	a	Sec. 1016.2, #5, Exc. 2.4
17.	d	Table 1020.3
18.	a	Table 1020.3
19.	c	Table 1020.2
20.	d	Table 1020.2
21.	c	Sec. 1020.5, Exc. 4
22.	b	Sec. 1020.5, Exc. 2
23.	b	Sec. 1020.6, Exc. 3
24.	c	Sec. 1021.1, Table 1020.3
25.	c	Sec. 1021.3
26.	b	Table 1006.2.1
27.	d	Sec. 1006.2.2.2
28.	d	Sec. 1006.2.2.2
29.	b	Table 1017.2
30.	d	Sec. 1020.5, Exc. 3

31.	d	Sec. 1016.2, #5, Exc. 2.2
32.	a	Sec. 1018.4
33.	c	Sec. 1006.2.2.1
34.	d	Sec. 1018.4, Exc.
35.	d	Table 1020.3
36.	d	Sec. 1006.2.1, Exc.3
37.	b	Sec. 1017.3.2.3
38.	a	Sec. 1018.5, Exc.
39.	c	Sec. 1019.3, Exc. 2
40.	c	Sec. 1020.5, Exc. 4

Study Session 12

2021 *International Building Code*

1.	c	Sec. 1023.9.1, #1	31.	b	Sec. 1026.2
2.	d	Sec. 1025.1	32.	a	Sec. 1030.13.2
3.	d	Sec. 1025.5	33.	c	Sec. 1030.16.1
4.	b	Sec. 1023.2	34.	b	Sec. 1031.2, Exc. 3
5.	b	Sec. 1027.5	35.	a	Sec. 1031.3.2
6.	c	Sec. 1023.12.1	36.	d	Sec. 1023.4
7.	c	Sec. 1023.9	37.	a	Sec. 1024.2
8.	a	Sec. 1023.12	38.	d	Sec. 1025.2.3
9.	b	Sec. 1024.3	39.	d	Sec. 1027.6, Exc. 3.5
10.	a	Sec. 1026.4.1	40.	c	Sec. 1030.8, Exc. 2
11.	d	Sec. 1027.2			
12.	d	Sec. 1027.3			
13.	b	Sec. 1028.5, Exc., #1			
14.	b	Sec. 1029.2			
15.	b	Sec. 1030.13.1			
16.	b	Sec. 1030.2			
17.	c	Sec. 1030.5			
18.	d	Sec. 1030.6.1, #1, #2			
19.	d	Table 1030.6.2			
20.	a	Sec. 1030.6.2.1			
21.	d	Sec. 1030.7, Exc. 3			
22.	b	Sec. 1030.9.1, #2			
23.	b	Sec. 1030.14.2.1, Exc.			
24.	c	Sec. 1030.17.4			
25.	c	Sec. 1031.3.1, Exc.			
26.	d	Sec. 1026.1, Exc. 1			
27.	c	Sec. 1028.2, Exc. 2.2			
28.	b	Sec. 1028.5, Exc., #2			
29.	c	Sec. 1031.3.3			
30.	c	Sec. 1031.5.1			

Study Session 13

2021 *International Building Code*

1.	a	Sec. 202
2.	a	Sec. 202
3.	c	Sec. 1103.2.8
4.	a	Sec. 1103.2.11
5.	b	Sec. 1104.5
6.	c	Sec. 1105.1
7.	b	Table 1106.2
8.	b	Sec. 1106.3, #1
9.	c	Sec. 1106.6
10.	d	Sec. 1109.2.7.3
11.	a	Sec. 1110.12.2.1
12.	b	Sec. 1110.2.4
13.	a	Sec. 1108.6.2.3.2
14.	c	Table 1109.2.7.1
15.	b	Sec. 1108.5.1.2
16.	d	Table 1108.6.1.1
17.	b	Table 1108.6.1.1
18.	a	Sec. 1108.6.2.2.1
19.	d	Table 1109.3
20.	b	Sec. 1110.2.1
21.	c	Sec. 1110.2.1.4
22.	c	Sec. 1110.5.2
23.	a	Sec. 1110.12
24.	a	Sec. 1110.13.1, Exc.
25.	c	Sec. 1112.1, #1, Exc.
26.	c	Sec. 1104.3.1, Exc. 1
27.	a	Sec. 1104.3.2, Exc. 1
28.	d	Sec. 1106.5
29.	b	Sec. 1109.2.9.1
30.	c	Sec. 1112.3

31.	a	Sec. 1106.9.1
32.	c	Sec. 1109.2.4, Exc. 1
33.	d	Sec. 1110.2, Exc. 3
34.	c	Sec. 1110.5.2
35.	b	Sec. 1111.4.3
36.	c	Table 1105.1.1
37.	a	Sec. 1107.2.1
38.	d	Sec. 1108.5.2.1, Exc. 2
39.	c	Sec. 1110.2.3.1
40.	c	Sec. 1111.4.12.1

Study Session 14

2021 *International Building Code*

1.	b	Sec. 402.8.5	31.	d	Table 412.6
2.	c	Sec. 402.6.2, #3	32.	b	Sec. 202
3.	b	Sec. 202	33.	b	Sec. 412.3.1
4.	d	Sec. 403.4.8.1	34.	a	Sec. 420.2
5.	b	Sec. 404.8	35.	d	Sec. 423.4, 423.5
6.	d	Sec. 404.9.2, 1017.3.2.3	36.	b	Sec. 407.4.4.3
7.	b	Sec. 405.4.1	37.	a	Sec. 410.5.3.5
8.	a	Sec. 406.4.2	38.	b	Sec. 423.3.1
9.	b	Sec. 406.7.2	39.	c	Sec. 424.5
10.	b	Table 406.5.4	40.	d	Table 428.3
11.	d	Sec. 407.5.1			
12.	d	Sec. 407.5.3, #1			
13.	c	Sec. 408.3.1			
14.	d	Sec. 408.6.1			
15.	b	Sec. 409.2			
16.	b	Sec. 410.2.4, 410.2.5			
17.	d	Sec. 410.2.7			
18.	a	Sec. 411.7			
19.	b	Table 412.3.6			
20.	c	Table 414.2.2			
21.	c	Sec. 415.6.1			
22.	a	Sec. 422.2			
23.	a	Sec. 415.11.3.3			
24.	b	Sec. 417.2			
25.	b	Sec. 418.5			
26.	c	Sec. 410.4.1			
27.	d	Sec. 413.2			
28.	c	Sec. 414.2.4			
29.	b	Sec. 414.6.1.3			
30.	c	Sec. 416.2			

Study Session 15

2021 *International Building Code*

1.	b	Sec. 202		31.	b	Sec. 1404.3.3
2.	a	Sec. 202		32.	c	Sec. 1404.16.2
3.	b	Sec. 1403.12.2		33.	d	Sec. 1511.6.1
4.	d	Table 1404.2		34.	a	Table 1504.9
5.	c	Sec. 1404.12		35.	b	Sec. 1810.3.10.2
6.	c	Sec. 1402.5		36.	d	Table 1404.2
7.	d	Sec. 1405.1.1, #2		37.	c	Sec. 1503.5
8.	b	Sec. 202		38.	b	Sec. 1507.12.1
9.	b	Table 1505.1		39.	b	Table 1809.7, Note f
10.	a	Sec. 1505.2, Exc. 2		40.	c	Sec. 1810.2.1
11.	c	Table 1507.1.1(2)				
12.	b	Table 1507.1.1(2)				
13.	c	Sec. 1507.3.6				
14.	b	Sec. 1507.5.2				
15.	d	Sec. 1507.9.8				
16.	d	Table 1507.8.7				
17.	b	Sec. 1507.14.1				
18.	c	Sec. 1511.2.1				
19.	c	Sec. 1809.3				
20.	b	Sec. 1809.4				
21.	c	Table 1806.2				
22.	b	Sec. 1808.7.3				
23.	d	Sec. 1808.8.4				
24.	b	Table 1808.8.2				
25.	b	Sec. 1807.1.6.3, #9				
26.	a	Sec. 1404.12.4				
27.	c	Sec. 1505.7				
28.	d	Sec. 1507.7.2				
29.	b	Sec. 1511.5.1				
30.	b	Sec. 1804.4				

Study Session 16

2021 *International Building Code*

1.	b	Sec. 1603.1.3	31.	c	Sec. 1607.5
2.	b	Table 1607.1, #4	32.	c	Sec. 1607.9.2
3.	d	Table 1604.5	33.	c	Sec. 202
4.	a	Table 1607.1, #27	34.	c	Sec. 1705.2.4
5.	c	Sec. 1609.4.2	35.	d	Sec. 2304.5
6.	a	Sec. 1610.1	36.	b	Table 1610.1
7.	b	Sec. 1705.15.4.5	37.	d	Sec. 1705.5.3
8.	b	Sec. 1704.6.1, #3	38.	c	Sec. 1705.18
9.	b	Sec. 1906.1	39.	c	Table 2304.11
10.	d	Table 1604.3	40.	b	Sec. 2304.12.2.5
11.	a	Sec. 1604.3.7, #2			
12.	a	Sec. 1907.1			
13.	b	Sec. 202			
14.	a	Sec. 1607.16.2			
15.	b	Sec. 1907.1, Exc., #2			
16.	c	Sec. 2111.11			
17.	d	Sec. 2111.12, Exc. 4			
18.	c	Sec. 2113.9			
19.	a	Sec. 2304.12.2.1			
20.	d	Sec. 202			
21.	b	Table 2304.10.1, #7			
22.	d	Sec. 2308.6.8.1, Exc.			
23.	a	Sec. 2308.4.4			
24.	a	Sec. 2308.5.10			
25.	b	Sec. 2308.7.7			
26.	d	Table 1607.1, #31; Sec. 1607.21			
27.	b	Table 1609.3.1			
28.	a	Sec. 2109.2.4.5.2			
29.	b	Sec. 2304.13, Exc.			
30.	d	Sec. 2308.5.6			

Study Session 17

2021 *International Building Code*

1.	b	Sec. 803.1.2		31.	b	Sec. 806.2
2.	c	Sec. 803.15.4		32.	a	Sec. 1202.2.1
3.	c	Table 803.13		33.	b	Sec. 1210.2.2
4.	a	Table 803.13		34.	a	Sec. 2508.6.4
5.	d	Table 803.13, Note i		35.	c	Sec. 2512.4
6.	a	Sec. 803.5.2		36.	a	Sec. 803.3
7.	b	Sec. 804.4.2, Exc.		37.	c	Sec. 1207.2
8.	b	Sec. 806.7		38.	c	Sec. 1208.4, #1
9.	d	Sec. 806.2, Exc. 1		39.	a	Sec. 1202.5.1.2
10.	c	Sec. 806.7		40.	b	Sec. 2512.1.2
11.	b	Sec. 1203.1				
12.	c	Sec. 1204.2				
13.	a	Sec. 1204.4				
14.	b	Sec. 1206.3				
15.	c	Sec. 1208.2				
16.	b	Sec. 1208.3				
17.	a	Sec. 1209.1				
18.	c	Sec. 1209.2				
19.	b	Sec. 1210.3.2				
20.	d	Sec. 202				
21.	a	Sec. 2509.2, 2509.3				
22.	c	Sec. 2512.5				
23.	d	Sec. 3002.2				
24.	c	Sec. 3007.6.4				
25.	b	Sec. 3002.4				
26.	a	Sec. 804.4.2, Exc.				
27.	c	Sec. 1202.4.1.1				
28.	c	Sec. 1205.3				
29.	a	Sec. 2508.5				
30.	d	Sec. 3003.1.2				

Study Session 18
2021 *International Building Code*

1.	c	Sec. 2403.5	31.	d	Sec. 2405.3, Exc. 3
2.	c	Sec. 2405.3	32.	d	Table 2406.2(1)
3.	b	Sec. 2405.3	33.	a	Sec. 2407.1
4.	d	Sec. 2405.4	34.	c	Sec. 2606.7.3
5.	d	Table 2406.2(1)	35.	d	Sec. 2610.4
6.	a	Sec. 2406.3, Exc. 1	36.	c	Sec. 2403.3
7.	a	Sec. 2406.4.5	37.	b	Sec. 2406.4.2, Exc. 3
8.	c	Sec. 2406.4.2	38.	d	Sec. 2407.1.1
9.	d	Sec. 2406.4.3, Exc. 2	39.	d	Sec. 2603.8
10.	a	Sec. 2406.4.5, Exc.	40.	a	Sec. 2604.2.3
11.	d	Sec. 2406.4.6, Exc. 2			
12.	a	Sec. 2406.4.1, Exc. 1			
13.	a	Sec. 2409.3			
14.	b	Sec. 2407.1.2			
15.	d	Sec. 202			
16.	d	Sec. 202			
17.	d	Sec. 2603.3			
18.	a	Sec. 2603.4			
19.	b	Sec. 2603.4.1.1			
20.	d	Sec. 2604.2.2			
21.	c	Sec. 2605.2, #2			
22.	b	Table 2607.4			
23.	d	Sec. 2608.2, #3, Exc.			
24.	a	Sec. 2609.1			
25.	b	Sec. 2611.2			
26.	a	Sec. 2404.1			
27.	b	Sec. 2406.3, Exc. 2			
28.	c	Sec. 2406.3.1			
29.	c	Sec. 2408.3			
30.	d	Sec. 2603.4.1.13, #1			

INTERNATIONAL CODE COUNCIL®

Valuable Guides to Changes in the 2021 I-Codes®

SIGNIFICANT CHANGES TO THE 2021 INTERNATIONAL CODES®

Practical resources that offer a comprehensive analysis of the critical changes made between the 2018 and 2021 editions of the codes. Authored by ICC code experts, these useful tools are "must-have" guides to the many important changes in the 2021 International Codes.

Key changes are identified then followed by in-depth, expert discussion of how the change affects real world application. A full-color photo, table or illustration is included for each change to further clarify application.

SIGNIFICANT CHANGES TO THE IBC®, 2021 EDITION
#7024S21

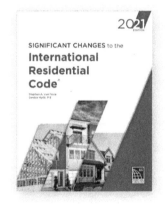

SIGNIFICANT CHANGES TO THE IRC®, 2021 EDITION
#7101S21

SIGNIFICANT CHANGES TO THE IFC®, 2021 EDITION
#7404S21

SIGNIFICANT CHANGES TO THE IPC®/IMC®/IFGC®, 2021 EDITION
#7202S21

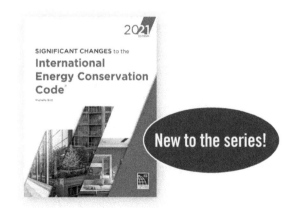

New to the series!

SIGNIFICANT CHANGES TO THE IECC®, 2021 EDITION
#7808S21

20-19101

ICC EVALUATION SERVICE®

☑ **Specify** and
☑ **Approve** *with* **Confidence**

When facing new or unfamiliar materials, look for an ICC-ES Evaluation Report or Listing before approving for installation.

ICC-ES® **Evaluation Reports** are the most widely accepted and trusted technical reports for code compliance.

ICC-ES **Building Product Listings** and **PMG Listings** show product compliance with applicable standard(s) referenced in the building and plumbing codes as well as other applicable codes.

When you specify or approve products or materials with an ICC-ES report, building product listing or PMG listing, you avoid delays on projects and improve your bottom line.

ICC-ES is a subsidiary of ICC®, the publisher of the codes used throughout the U.S. and many global markets, so you can be confident in their code expertise.

www.icc-es.org | 800-423-6587

Proctored Remote Online Testing Option (PRONTO™)

Convenient, Reliable, and Secure Certification Exams

Take the Test at Your Location

Take advantage of ICC PRONTO, an industry leading, secure online exam delivery service. PRONTO allows you to take ICC Certification exams at your convenience in the privacy of your own home, office or other secure location. Plus, you'll know your pass/fail status immediately upon completion.

 With PRONTO, ICC's Proctored Remote Online Testing Option, take your ICC Certification exam from any location with high-speed internet access.

 With online proctoring and exam security features you can be confident in the integrity of the testing process and exam results.

 Plan your exam for the day and time most convenient for you. PRONTO is available 24/7.

 Eliminate the waiting period and get your results in private immediately upon exam completion.

#1 ICC was the first model code organization to offer secured online proctored exams—part of our commitment to offering the latest technology-based solutions to help building and code professionals succeed and advance. We continue to expand our catalog of PRONTO exam offerings.

Discover ICC PRONTO and the wealth of certification opportunities available to advance your career: www.iccsafe.org/MeetPRONTO

20-18842

ISO/IEC 17065
Product Certification Body
#1000